Between Tradition and Modernity

Monographs in German History

BETWEEN TRADITION AND MODERNITY

Aby Warburg and the Public Purposes of Art
in Hamburg, 1896-1918

Mark A. Russell

Berghahn Books
New York • Oxford

Published in 2007 by

Berghahn Books

www.berghahnbooks.com

©2007 Mark A. Russell

Library of Congress Cataloging-in-Publication Data

Russell, Mark A.
  Beyond tradition and modernity : Aby Warburg and art in Hamburg's public
realm, 1896-1918 / Mark A. Russell.
    p. cm. -- (Monographs in German history ; v. 19)
  Includes bibliographical references and index.
  ISBN 1-84545-369-7
  1. Warburg, Aby, 1866-1929--Criticism and interpretation. 2. Art historians--
Germany. 3. Art, German--Germany--Hamburg--20th century. 4. Germany--
Intellectual life--20th century. I. Title.

  N7483.W36R88 2007
  709.2--dc22

                                                                    2006035607

British Library Cataloguing in Publication Data

A catalogue record for this book is available from the British Library

Printed in the United States on acid-free paper

ISBN 978-1-84545-369-5 hardback

CONTENTS

LIST OF ILLUSTRATIONS

PREFACE

One the most enjoyable aspects of undertaking research on Aby Warburg has been the experience of exploring an incredibly rich archive. Coming to the topic from an interest in modern German history, I realized that much of what was said about Warburg in the literature on Imperial and Weimar Germany was stimulating, but the product of the type of generalization of which Warburg himself was suspicious. In the field of Warburg scholarship, most research followed in the footsteps of Ernst Gombrich's "intellectual biography" in as much as it focused – quite rightly – on Warburg's achievements as a theorist and historian. Although interpretations of his legacy now vary considerably, much of this work – but certainly not all – relied principally on archival material already published by Gombrich. While my work has benefited enormously from previous research in both fields, the opportunities for opening new perspectives were exciting. The richness and complexity of Warburg's life and work invited detailed exploration as a case study in Germany's confrontation with social, political, and cultural modernism. What did Warburg's experiences and ideas have to say about the nature of Imperial Germany and its place in the sequence of events that resulted in the tragedies of twentieth-century German history? This question required a return to the rough ground of empirical evidence; it necessitated working through corners of the Warburg Institute Archive that had been left mostly untouched by previous scholarship. It also meant time spent in Hamburg – at the Staatsarchiv, Warburg Haus, and the Hochschule für bildende Künste – reconstructing the history of monuments which had either been largely neglected or whose complexity was not fully appreciated when this project was begun.

The result of this work is, I trust, a modest contribution to the rich and varied literature on Imperial Germany. It has been undertaken with a realist view of historical knowledge, explanation, and understanding and with the conviction that the past can be interrogated and reconstructed in cogent and philosophically-assured ways. I make this perspective explicit because reconstructing Warburg's life and work has challenged me to think about ideas and issues that I count as the greater lessons of this study. While philosophers of history have long engaged with these notions – and historians are fully cognizant of them – they only resonated deeply with me in the process of compiling a historical narrative from the vestiges of Warburg's life. Firstly, I have come to appreciate something which Warburg fully understood: that the position of the scholar is always changing and, consequently, the nature of the object studied is always being reconstructed. Historical narrative involves decisions of selection and the relation of individuals and events of different kinds and from different points of view; it is the product of hindsight and a host of implicit assumptions and evaluative standards. One might even say – and some scholars have construed Warburg's scholarship in this manner – that it is a writing of the self. Consequently, I have become aware of the extent to which claims to objectivity and transparency in historical writing must always be qualified.

Secondly, I have become sensitive to the inability of representing an individual in all their complexity with the means available to the historian or, for that matter, to anyone else. What originally attracted me to Warburg was an interest in his complex personality and how this might mirror the society in which he lived. But in the course of my research, I have developed a particular fascination with the extent to which a single life and identity can be complex, varied, multidimensional, and even self-contradictory. The difficulties of capturing such complexity are compounded by the various temporal and conceptual constraints within which the historian works, and the fact that there can be no God's-eye viewpoint from which to understand a historical event or personality. In the words of Marcel Proust, "none of us can be said to constitute a material whole, which is identical for everyone, and need only be turned up like a page in an account-book or the record of a will."

With this in mind, I return to the rough ground. Unless otherwise indicated, all translations from the German are my own. Where first names are used, it is with the intention of improving readability and is not the result of an undue sense of familiarity with the persons portrayed.

ACKNOWLEDGMENTS

I have accumulated many debts in the course of writing this book. The greatest is to Professor Jonathan Steinberg for his encouragement and support from the very beginning of the project. Jonathan read and commented upon early drafts of the chapters, freely shared his prodigious knowledge of German and European history and proffered many helpful insights and suggestions. His enthusiasm for the subject was a constant source of inspiration. In its early stages, Professor Richard Evans and Professor Timothy Blanning also offered important advice on the preparation of the manuscript, while Dr. Christopher Clark, Dr. Robin Lenman and Professor Peter Paret read the work at different stages of development. Their suggestions have greatly improved the finished product.

At the Warburg Institute, I am grateful to Professors Nicholas Mann and Charles Hope for permission to use the Archive and publish material contained therein. Very special thanks are due the Institute's recently-retired archivist, Dr. Dorothea McEwan, whose enthusiasm, generosity, and unfailing good humor made my many hours in the Archive pleasurable ones. Dr. McEwan shared her extensive knowledge of Warburg's life and work, provided invaluable assistance in negotiating the Institute's Archive and offered untiring aid in the transcription of Warburg's notoriously difficult handwriting. Furthermore, she has very kindly continued to provide a home for me in London during my annual visits to the Warburg Institute. During these, the newly-appointed Dr. Claudia Wedepohl, has also provided much-appreciated assistance archivist, while the Institute's photographer, Mr. Ian Jones, has prepared photographs for illustration in this volume with professionalism and characteristic good humor.

An equal expression of thanks is extended to Professor Martin Warnke and the staff of the Warburg Haus who provided a scholarly home for me in Hamburg during the project's early stages. I am obliged to the many faculty and students of Hamburg University's Art History Seminar who took an interest in my project and gave generously of their time and knowledge, especially Dr. Michael

Diers, Mr. Rainer Donandt, Dr. Karen Michels, Dr. Hans-Michael Schäfer, Dr. Charlotte Schoell-Glass, and Dr. Jörg Schilling. In the Staatsarchiv der Freien- und Hansestadt Hamburg, Dr. Rainer Hering and Mr. Ulf Bollmann helped locate pertinent material among its vast holdings. Thanks are also extended to Dr. Maike Bruhns for kindly putting a significant amount of material regarding Willy von Beckerath at my disposal. Similarly, Ms. Elisabeth Wilker, head librar- ian at the Hochschule für bildende Künste in Hamburg has aided my research on Beckerath with great enthusiasm. In the Archive of Hapag-Lloyd AG, Mr. Peter Maaß very generously supplied material relating to the S.S. *Imperator.*

None of this research could have been undertaken without the very generous financial support of the Social Sciences and Humanities Research Council of Canada, Le Fonds Québécois de la Recherche sur la Société et la Culture, the Overseas Research Students Awards Scheme of Great Britain, the Cambridge Commonwealth Trust, Sidney Sussex College, Cambridge, the German Acade- mic Exchange Service, and the Faculty of Arts and Science at Concordia Univer- sity. Nor would it have taken its current form without the interest and enthusiasm of Dr. Marion Berghahn. I am very grateful to her, Melissa Spinelli, Nora Liddell and Kristine Hunt for the care taken in transforming my manu- script into a book.

While this book is the product of numerous hours spent in archives, libraries, and at my writing desk, it is equally the result of a long period of training in the historical profession. My interest in German history, the history of art, and Aby Warburg's life and work began at the University of Toronto where I was fortunate to be encouraged and intellectually stimulated by Professor Ethan Matt Kavaler, Professor Jacques Kornberg, Professor James Retallack, and Professor Philip Sohm. A special debt of gratitude is owed to Mr. Barrie Walker of the Academic Bridging Program at Woodsworth College. It was Barrie's enthusiasm for the study of history and his excellence as a teacher that inspired me to embark upon my journey from student to professional historian. In the latter capacity, I have had the privilege of ruminating on this book's content in the stimulating intel- lectual environment nurtured by the faculty and students of my current acade- mic home – the Liberal Arts College of Concordia University, Montreal.

And yet this project has been much more than an academic exercise; it has been part of a way of life enormously enriched by friends who – directly and indi- rectly, in large and small ways – have provided encouragement, inspiration, and support along the way. Dr. Eleanora Babejova, Dr. Ronald Bachmann, Dr. Andrew Bell, Dr. Andreas Fahrmeir, Mr. Gary Friedman, Dr. Niall Johnson, Ms. Silke Mentchen and Mr. Robert "Guitar" Pain, Dr. Roopa Nair, Mr. Günther Rathje, Dr. Mark Reiff, Dr. Martin Rew and Dr. Geetanjali Gangoli, Mr. Stephen Richardson, Dr. Mark Supekar, and Dr. Pierre Wiart have all influenced the spirit in which this work has been undertaken. Thanks for the memories and here's to many more!

Finally, my most heartfelt expression of thanks is extended to my parents, Ross and Elizabeth Russell. Although my turn to academia was a departure from previous pursuits, they have unfailingly supported my decisions and encouraged me to achieve in my chosen field of endeavor. Without their unqualified love and support, none of this would have been possible.

For my parents,
Ross and Elizabeth Russell.

———————————

INTRODUCTION

I

When the architect and city planner Fritz Schumacher settled in Hamburg in 1909, his first taste of the city's social life was received in the house of Aby Warburg (1866–1929).[1] The occasion was the meeting of a discussion group, founded by twelve couples, to which Schumacher and his wife were elected. Its members included some of the leading figures of Hamburg's political and cultural life: Senator Justus Strandes; the painter Carl Wilhelm Hugo Schnars-Alquist; the industrialist Ferdinand Carl Theodor Heye; the medical professor Hermann Georg Sieveking; the founder of the Hamburg People's Library, Eduard Hallier; the architect Hugo Groothoff; and the director of the city's art gallery, Alfred Lichtwark. Meetings circulated among the participants' homes where a lecture was heard, sometimes given by the host, and a cold buffet provided.

On the occasion of Schumacher's debut, the lecture was given by Dr. Wilhelm Waetzoldt, Warburg's academic assistant. Waetzoldt spoke about the painter Moritz von Schwind, exuding "the complete charm of the sensitive art scholar." But for Schumacher, the chief impression of the evening was made by the "brilliantly witty figure" of his host. He described Warburg as follows: "He could become glowingly excited, could tell stories full of humor and, above all, could criticize with great wit what appeared improper to him in his beloved hometown. Woe unto him upon whom he drew a bead!" On this evening his target was Hugo Vogel, the Berlin painter who decorated Hamburg's city hall with giant frescos between 1901 and 1909. Schumacher tells us that Warburg gave "the most amusing descriptions" of Vogel's work. To his surprise, Lichtwark, one of the most influential exponents of contemporary art in the German Empire, sat in silence.

Schumacher's portrait may be an unusual introduction to a scholar who is now seen as an innovator in several fields of twentieth-century scholarship. But it is more than a sentimental reminiscence. Indeed, it points directly to an aspect

---

of Warburg's biography that scholars have mostly overlooked: his lively participation in Hamburg's civic affairs. Especially since the publication of Ernst Gombrich's intellectual biography in 1970, Aby Warburg has been celebrated as many
things: as a pioneering art historian and theorist, a historian of mentalities, a historical anthropologist, a cultural semiotician, a pioneer in the theory and study
of collective memory, and as the founder of the Warburg Institute.[2] And yet,
despite his current international reputation, it has often been suggested that Warburg was a hermetic scholar, a bibliophile cloistered within the private library
that became the Kulturwissenschaftliche Bibliothek Warburg in 1926. Those
scholars of German history who have turned their attention to Warburg, like
Peter Gay and George Mosse, have treated him as an intellectual working in relative isolation, especially during the Weimar Republic: Gay wrote that Warburg's
library did its work in "peaceful obscurity."[3] In contrast, the private and public
profile of the eminent German Jewish family into which he was born has been
the subject of much interest.[4] The same can be said of the family bank, M.M.
Warburg & Co., which entered the elite of international finance houses after
1900 under the direction of Aby Warburg's younger brother, Max (1867–1946).[5]
Max Warburg's career has been of special interest to scholars. He played an
important role in the political and economic life of Wilhelmine and Weimar
Germany as financial adviser to the Kaiser, financier of colonial expansion, representative of the German Treasury at the Versailles peace conference, and member of the general council of the Reichsbank.[6]

It is true that Aby Warburg remained, first and foremost, an independent
scholar deeply committed to historical problems of art, culture, and psychology.
Especially from 1910, he was also seriously engaged in fostering the growth of his
enormous library. However, it is surprising that historians have mostly ignored
Gombrich's assertion that Warburg became "a Hamburg institution, taking a
lively part in local problems."[7] Little attention has been afforded Warburg as a
perspicacious observer of Wilhelmine society and culture; even less attention has
focused on his active role in Hamburg's civic affairs. In fact, by seeing him as
immersed only in the study of recondite symbols and allegories, or claiming he
tried to distance himself from "the onrushing life around him" and was little
known outside a small group of scholars at the time of his death, some scholarship has misrepresented Aby Warburg.[8]

In a letter of 1907, Warburg exclaimed that "only the vulgar believe that
scholarship and practice have nothing to do with one another."[9] Although the
practical application of his thought was often of limited duration and experimental in nature, "practice" meant many things for Warburg. The following
short summary provides an indication of just how varied and active a role he
played in Hamburg's civic affairs. In 1905, he organized Hamburg's Folklore
Congress, participated in the city's third Art Education Day, and became a member of the Ethnology Museum's commission. He joined in the creation of Hamburg's Academic Foundation, a forerunner of the university, and was appointed
as an expert consultant to the city's commission for archaeology in 1909. In

1912, he took a role in the founding of the Cassel Foundation, which promoted academic contacts and interchange between England and Germany. In the same year, he was hired by the Hamburg-America Line as an advisor on the pictorial decoration of the steamship *Imperator,* at that time, the largest passenger ship in the world. His advice was sought by private citizens on the purchase of artworks and he was often instrumental in establishing contacts between artists and prospective buyers. His commitment to popular education began in 1899 with a lecture series on the Italian Renaissance for Hamburg's Ministry of Education. Other series given by Warburg in following years attracted wide interest, drawing audiences of up to 400 people.[10] In 1908, Professor Erich Marcks—a historian and biographer of Bismarck—wrote of Warburg's lectures in these terms: "For these things Warburg is of absolutely the first rank, more competent than any of us, and it is a service to encourage him to public engagement."[11] Warburg was also one of the many voices calling for the foundation of the University of Hamburg in 1919 and would lecture there in the later 1920s. However, despite the wealth of unpublished material in Warburg's archive, most of these aspects of his life have received only passing mention in the scholarly literature.[12]

This book is intended as a response to this deficiency. Based largely on previously unpublished documentation, it sets Warburg's life and work into its political, social, and cultural context.[13] Its purview extends from the period immediately following the publication of his doctoral dissertation in 1893 to the onset of his extended illness in 1918. Warburg was a sensitive and extremely well-informed observer of the upheavals and transformations of these years and this book explores his public response to a time of dramatic change. In particular, it examines instances in which he sought to exercise direct influence on Hamburg's civic affairs through an involvement with the construction of monumental artworks. On the one hand, Warburg saw these as a way of asserting Hamburg's unique political and cultural identity in the German Empire. In this respect, his views were in keeping with those of a group of political and cultural notables in the Free and Hanseatic City of Hamburg. On the other hand, he valued public artworks as a means of ameliorating the political, social, and psychological tensions that afflicted the city before and during the First World War; he believed in the power of images to shape the way in which the citizens of Hamburg responded to political and social turmoil and the rapid transformations of their era. Consequently, what emerges in the course of this study is the portrait of an insightful and critical observer of society and culture during the Wilhelmine age (1888–1918).

But through its focus on monuments built in Hamburg, the book concentrates on understanding how Warburg responded to art produced during his own lifetime, a period which witnessed an artistic revolution in Europe as momentous as that of the Italian Renaissance. His wife Mary, herself a painter and sculptor, facilitated contact with many contemporary artists. Warburg was of the same generation as several well-known German promoters of Impressionist and Post-Impressionist art: the art dealer, journalist, and publisher Paul Cassirer

(1871–1926); the art historian Julius Meier-Graefe (1867–1935); the collector, art critic, and sometime director of the Weimar museums, Count Harry Kessler (1868–1951); the editor of *Kunst und Künstler*, Karl Scheffler (1869–1951); and the art historian and director of the National Gallery in Berlin, Hugo von Tschudi (1851–1911). But Warburg's tastes were more ecumenical and wide-ranging than those of many of his contemporaries; his preferences extended from Symbolism and Impressionism to Italian Futurism and German Expressionism. What was it that motivated his often positive response to artistic innovation, and how was this related to his reaction to the political, social, and cultural transformations that shaped his world?

Answering this question is complicated by the fact that Warburg's biography is incredibly complex: there is much about his life and work that speaks of disunity and fragmentation. His thinking on many of the central questions that informed his scholarship and gave shape to his library was often ambivalent and subject to continual change and transformation. The intellectual influences that motivated his lifelong concerns form a varied and complex weave and scholars disagree as to its principal threads and their import. His corpus of published work is relatively small and he did not author a major book; instead, as a testament to his wide-ranging interests, the Warburg Institute Archive is filled with the wreckage of several projects. Furthermore, while loyal to his *Vaterstadt* and proud of its unique political and cultural traditions, Warburg was also a patriotic German. In this respect, his sense of identity was typical of that expressed by many citizens of the German Empire. But if a patriotic German, he was also a Jew who, no matter his attempts to emphasize his acculturated German self, could not simply abandon his Jewish ancestry and identity, nor would he be allowed to do so by non-Jewish Germans. The background to this complex individual portrait is the increasingly complicated picture of the German Empire that is emerging in the historical literature. Instead of adopting a deterministic perspective that draws a straight line from the Empire to the Third Reich, much Anglo-American scholarship insists on seeing the political, social, economic, and cultural upheavals of Wilhelmine Germany on their own terms. In Germany, as elsewhere, modernism is increasingly understood as "a dynamic that pushed in many directions at once."[14]

Warburg's response to this dynamic and the multiple and varied phenomena of modernization was complex. As Kevin Repp has written, "Capitalism, industry, urbanization, socialism all spelled uncertainty, and while some greeted the prospects of an uncharted future, others drew back in fear."[15] Warburg's attitude combined elements of both responses. A bifurcated perspective on social and cultural phenomena is found throughout his scholarship; it is at the heart of his thinking on the nature and meaning of the Renaissance. With an approach to European culture that balanced an evolutionary with a nonchronological, nonteleological perspective, Warburg's research did not chart the triumphal progress of reason and modernity. While he believed the Renaissance marked the threshold of the modern world, he concentrated on the way in which its artistic achievements sustained and reactivated primitive modes of thinking. The Florentine merchant-bankers of the fifteenth century were described in Warburg's essays as men able to reconcile the apparent opposites of rational and irrational tendencies in their psychological constitutions. Warburg described this ability to balance modern humanist learning with traditional medieval religiosity as a "psychology of compromise."[16]

The Renaissance banker's response to a time of transformation parallels Warburg's complex personality and his ambivalent adjustment to the changes and displacements of his own age. On the one hand, Warburg was an upper-class urbanite, with a liberal and cosmopolitan world view. He lived in Florence for several years and maintained an international correspondence with scholars and academic institutions. He traveled throughout Western Europe and his brothers served their banking apprenticeships in Amsterdam, Frankfurt, London, and Paris. Connected by marriage to the powerful New York banking house of Kuhn, Loeb & Co., two of Warburg's younger brothers, Paul and Felix, settled in the United States. The family had other marital links to England, Russia, and Sweden.[17] Warburg traveled across the Atlantic in the mid 1890s visiting New York, Boston, Washington, Colorado Springs, Santa Fe, and San Francisco, amongst several other destinations. In San Francisco, he spoke of sailing to Japan. He also took a keen interest in the international business of the family bank and its participation in the globalization of the world economy; besides international bond issues and foreign loans, this included the financing, in Hamburg, of the Colonial Institute, the Institute for Tropical Medicine, and the Hamburg-Morocco Society.[18]

Like his brother, Max Warburg, who "preferred to call himself a Free Conservative rather than a National Liberal," his political orientation was fundamentally liberal.[19] He hoped for a greater role for the nation's middle classes in the social and political leadership of the nation and believed the *Junkers* were unsuitable leaders for Germany. Echoing the ideas of the sociologist Max Weber (1864–1920), he lamented in 1918 that "Germany has had, even until now, no sturdy middle classes standing on their own legs and with their own critique. The aristocrat is, by nature, unsuitable as a leader."[20] In addition, Warburg's cultural criticism was future-oriented; he embraced modern art as a more accurate means of depicting the changing social and cultural environment in which he lived, directed caustic criticism at the conventional artistic tastes of the German bourgeoisie, and harbored an aversion to the cultural agenda promoted by the Imperial government in Berlin. Like many citizens of Hamburg, Warburg "supported national cohesion without necessarily showing any enthusiasm for its symbols or for its agents, Prussia and the national government."[21] Furthermore, Warburg was optimistic about many of the changes wrought by science and technology and welcomed the economic and industrial modernization of Germany fostered by institutions like his family's bank. When the Kulturwissenschaftliche Bibliothek Warburg opened its doors in 1926, it was outfitted with the latest technology including telephones, elevators, and a pneumatic mail system.[22] In December of that year, Warburg commissioned a design for an airmail stamp from the German graphic artist Otto Heinrich Strohmeyer. Executed as a linocut and never as a stamp, the abstracted image represented an airplane ascending into the sky with the motto *Idea Vincit* emblazoned on the underside of its wings. For Warburg, this icon of technological progress represented the triumph of ideas over unreason and conflict; he valued the image so much that he presented it to dozens of friends, family members, and politicians including the German foreign minister, Gustav Stresemann, when he visited Warburg's library on 20 December 1926.[23]

But Warburg's liberalism and cosmopolitanism were matched by a respect for the Kaiser and *Weltpolitik*; while no chauvinist, he strongly supported German national interests, believed firmly in an active German foreign policy, and displayed a fiery patriotism during the First World War. While he advocated political liberalization and modernization, and even made his own foray into the realm of working-class education, Warburg was no democrat. He disliked Social Democratic politics and saw the prospect of social chaos in the political mobilization of the masses. He would never be entirely reconciled to the sociopolitical transformations of his age, especially those wrought by the First World War and the revolution of 1918–19. Furthermore, his interest in contemporary art and his criticism of bourgeois materialism and artistic taste was paralleled by a life shaped by traditional values; Warburg was proud of his membership of Germany's economic elite, was suspicious of bohemian lifestyles, and disapproved of his son's ambitions to become an artist. If he adopted and benefited from many of the technological advances of the time, Warburg also perceived dangers for a world that was becoming evermore rationalized and materialistic; he criticized the destruction of symbolic and mythical thinking by technological advances that jeopardized humanity's self-conscious, contemplative bond with the world.

Along with his complex response to the transformations of the Wilhelmine age, Warburg harbored a genuine interest in contemporary art that was not guided by a positive appraisal of all that was innovative and modern over all that was academic and traditional. As a proud citizen of Hamburg, he championed public artworks which, if not avant-garde, broke with historicism and what he called "Berlin's sentimental neo-Baroque style."[24] He also approved of artists who creatively reworked their cultural tradition and reembraced mythical and symbolic thinking as a corrective response to the rationalization and mechanization of the world in which they lived. But what this book emphasizes is that Warburg's perspective on contemporary art—as with the art of any age— was never simply informed by aesthetic considerations, the exigencies of contemporary cultural politics, or phenomena that were particular to the modern world. Instead, his artistic predilections were shaped by the profundity of his thinking on the very nature of art and culture. With an approach to the study of European culture that was nonchronological, an obsession with the psychology of artistic expression, and a belief that the human mind transcended historical categorization and existed in a synchronous psychic time, Warburg assessed contemporary artworks from a perspective that surpassed a concern for the extent to which they were embedded in tradition or the degree to which they participated in a modern spirit.

II

Analysis of Aby Warburg's life and work also offers the opportunity for a study of his *Vaterstadt*, Hamburg. It provides an occasion to view the cultural, social, and political transformations of the Wilhelmine age through local contours and complexities. Following the publication of Celia Applegate's groundbreaking work in 1990, the interpretation of regional and local identities in Imperial Germany has received increased attention from historians.[25] Much of this has focused on the ways in which local customs, beliefs, idioms, and symbolism continued to shape German nationalism. As Geoff Eley has written, "One of the insights that a non-Prussian stress on locality produces is, of course, the richer and more complex materials from which German national identity had to be constructed."[26] Richness and complexity characterize Hamburg's employment of public art as public policy; they are embodied in the city's attempt, by means of monumental artworks, to express its unique identity within the German Empire. Richness and complexity also characterize Warburg's response to these undertakings and his thinking about the forms and functions of public artworks. All of these instances and events defy interpretation that tends toward employing general notions of tradition and modernity as mutually exclusive phenomena. Furthermore, they prompt a reconsideration of the way in which historians conceive of artistic innovation in Wilhelmine Germany. Consequently, the following chapters replace a perspective shaped by the canon of artistic modernism with one informed by what contemporaries thought and wrote about the art of their time.[27]

As the second-largest city in the German Empire—with a port that was the fourth-largest in the world after those of London, Liverpool and New York—Hamburg has become known as an important commercial center. German scholarship has also acknowledged the cultural role the city played within the Empire, especially in terms of the work and influence of Alfred Lichtwark (1852–1914), director of Hamburg's Kunsthalle from 1886–1914. Lichtwark was one of the most respected and influential educators in the German Empire and played a leading role in shaping Hamburg's cultural life. He wrote voluminously on matters of art and education, sought to improve instruction in Hamburg's schools, and turned the Kunsthalle into an educational institution with the intention of inspiring and developing the aesthetic sensibilities of the middle classes and the artistic energies of the recently unified nation.[28] But Anglo-American scholarship has afforded these cultural achievements much less attention; instead, Hamburg has become infamous for its philistinism and materialism during the Imperial period. The city has been described as one that subordinated aesthetic to material values and the demands of large-scale, overseas trade; it has been pictured as a city that was devoid of significant artists and cultural institutions, where the value of people and things was fixed by the merchant.[29] For many years, this image was due simply to neglect by English-language scholars; research into the art and culture of Imperial Germany has been dominated by work on Berlin and Munich.[30]

Nevertheless, there are important facts that cannot be ignored. Unlike the cities of Berlin, Munich, and Dresden, the Free and Hanseatic City of Hamburg had no resident prince or aristocracy to patronize the arts. Furthermore, the role of the state was limited and the government functioned primarily to secure conditions for profitable trade; it took a limited view regarding its duties to the population. With feeble civic cultural institutions and, most notably, the absence of a cultural ministry until after the First World War, the government failed to take the initiative in founding and supporting museums, academies, and schools. For their part, much of the city's mercantile elite rejected the notion that it was the state's responsibility to finance cultural institutions. With cultural initiatives left to private groups and the market, major artistic and intellectual projects were often neglected. Savings clubs were the most numerous clubs in Hamburg; economic independence rather than a classical education largely determined the social standing of the city's merchants.[31] The Warburgs, the Ballins, the Woermanns, and the Blohms "personified a highly dynamic entrepreneurial culture, which regarded increasing turnover, high profits, and (particularly in the shipping industry) high investment as the norm."[32] The close link of culture to the market could have devastating effects. In the nineteenth century, Hamburg demolished its Gothic cathedral and five medieval churches not only to rid the city of an extraterritorial institution, but to develop the land. It is the city from which Heinrich Heine and Johannes Brahms departed and which ordered the abolition of church music in 1788 on the grounds that it was too expensive. It is the city that sold its art collection in 1789 to raise money for its treasury and which had no art gallery until 1868.[33] There was no arts academy and no city orchestra until 1908 and no university until 1919. The much smaller city of Munich completely eclipsed Hamburg during the Imperial period as a center of artistic and musical life. It is no wonder that some historians continue to insist that all values in Hamburg rested on money values.[34]

The most recent English-language scholarship, however, offers a challenge to the persistence of this reductive assessment.[35] It reminds us that even in Hamburg, being a member of the middle classes meant the cultivation of academic, literary, and artistic interests and an active engagement with painting, theater, and music. A variety of institutions, associations, scholars, and bourgeois dilettantes devoted themselves to the arts. Indeed, it has been argued that reliance on the personal initiatives and money of Hamburg's merchants and bankers extended the "plurality and vitality of cultural life."[36] The middle classes provided considerable financial and organizational support for the city's museums.[37] Hamburg's concert hall was paid for by the ship-owner Carl Laiesz, and the Kunsthalle would have had no collection with which to fill its galleries were it not for the patronage of the Art Association, which drew its members mainly from Hamburg's elite and was one of the oldest associations of its kind in Germany.[38] Many of the Impressionist paintings that found their way into the city's art gallery were collected by the Behrens banking family.[39] With ever-growing collections in public galleries, Hamburg was a city where art was seen and appreciated.

Furthermore, it is now clear that if the two decades before the First World War were a time of great social, political, and economic change in Hamburg, they were also a time of creative tension between tradition and innovation in many fields of artistic endeavor. There are different opinions, however, as to the extent to which an atmosphere of cultural liberalism and experimentation shaped the city of Hamburg. One picture has emerged of the city's social and political elite as a group which demonstrated an "unwillingness to look forward"; it suggests that the limited creativity which existed in Hamburg was restricted to a select group of rich patrons.[40] Compared to this focus on the city's patricians, another perspective argues for a democratization of Hamburg's public culture and suggests broad public interest in modernist experimentation.[41] Despite their differences, both arguments confirm an image of the city as more culturally vibrant and open to innovation than has previously been acknowledged in English-language scholarship. As with German scholarship, the common denominator in much of the recent Anglo-American research is the life and work of Alfred Lichtwark.

As any study of Hamburg in this period must, this book acknowledges Lichtwark's influence on the city; his ideas and undertakings are referred to and commented upon throughout. However, by seeing the period through the eyes of Aby Warburg, the following discussion sheds light from an unusual source onto significant issues and events that have been largely neglected in historical scholarship. Most of the succeeding chapters detail the planning, construction, and public reception of three of the largest and most important monuments completed in Hamburg: the Bismarck memorial by Hugo Lederer and Emil Schaudt (1901–1906); the fresco decoration of Hamburg's city hall by Hugo Vogel (1901–1909); and the decoration of Hamburg's School of Art and Industry with a cycle of murals entitled *The Eternal Wave* by Willy von Beckerath (1913–1918). Two of these monuments—the Bismarck memorial and Vogel's city hall murals—rank among the largest projects undertaken in the entire Empire; as such, they warrant close study in their own right. As elsewhere in Germany, art was employed by the city's patricians to elaborate the public presentation of their authority, appeal to local patriotism, and help stem the growing support of Hamburg's working classes for Social Democracy. But for the once independent city, these public artworks were also a means of giving expression to its unique political and cultural identity within the German Empire and of combating its reputation for philistinism.

To be sure, the monuments discussed in the following chapters were not viewed as avant-garde artworks when unveiled, nor do they feature in the canon of artistic modernism. This book is not an attempt to reclaim them for that canon. What it wishes to emphasize, however, is that artworks now forgotten or ignored by scholarship were often seen as progressive by observers in the two decades before the First World War; indeed, the scholarly canon of artistic modernism is often accompanied by an incomplete understanding of how contemporaries understood new art forms.[42] In the 1890s, for example, it was a lack of historical perspective that frequently resulted in confusion about what constituted progressive innovation and what was to be rejected as philistinism.[43] Thus historians need to guard against anachronistic readings of the way in which tradition and modernity were understood. In the case of the artworks that attracted Warburg's attention, there is no doubt that their patrons and creators intended to break with the academic aesthetic conventions of the nineteenth century and incorporate innovation by transforming conventional iconography or employing nontraditional visual strategies. Of course, other artists, such as the German Expressionists, did so in a much more radical fashion. But it does well to recall the political and cultural circumstances in which all artistic innovation took place during the Wilhelmine period. It is well known that Wilhelm II disliked stylistic and thematic experimentation in art. For the Kaiser, the reinterpretation of reality and the denial of tradition implied the possibility of political and social change; through its choice of theme or its denial of aesthetic conventions, modern art questioned the stability of Imperial society and the Imperial system of government. But unlike Paris or London, Berlin did not dominate the nation's cultural life. The constitution of 1871 delegated authority for art, culture, and education to the individual states which established their own cultural ministries and bureaucracies. The poly-central nature of the German Empire meant that the large volume of cultural production simply could not be controlled by the Imperial authorities.[44] In the eyes of twenty-first-century viewers, the monuments considered in this book are not the most dramatic evidence of this truth. Yet they are literally giant demonstrations of the way in which the federal structure of the German Empire had a liberalizing effect on culture and was beneficial for the evolution of art.

With a focus on these monumental artworks, and Warburg's involvement with their histories, comes a concentration on the relatively small social formation to which Warburg belonged—Hamburg's economic, social, and political elite—creating and conflicting within a field of cultural production shaped largely by itself. This patrician elite, or *Großbürgertum*, was a collection of long-established merchant families and those who made their wealth during the industrial boom and the expansion of overseas trade during the late nineteenth century. Certain features of life in Hamburg gave the *Großbürgertum* a greater degree of cohesiveness than it possessed in other German cities: the senate was composed of an elite of interrelated patrician families and the city's administration was run by bodies of prominent citizens on a voluntary basis, instead of by a powerful body of civil servants; the educated middle class was weakened by the absence of a university; there was no royal or princely court to set the social tone; and the population was almost exclusively Protestant and thus less divided by religious rivalries.[45] As Andreas Schulz describes it, tradition and self- perception, the exercise of power, and the economic superiority of the *Großbürgertum* encouraged the creation of a stratum-specific elite culture.[46]

Of course, it is impossible, and inaccurate, to rigidly define social and cultural groups. Jennifer Jenkins has recently emphasized that there were two competing elites in Hamburg: the established merchant families and an expanding group of middle-class professionals including doctors, scientists, architects, and administrators. Although the latter were more responsive to Lichtwark's plans for cultural reform, the two groups inevitably shared many of the same interests.[47] Even Warburg was involved, in a limited way, with the propagation of bourgeois culture to a working-class audience; he was one of those members of Hamburg's elite who saw it as the duty of the privileged classes to care for the ills of society. But it is also true that many of the associations to which Warburg belonged, like the Society of Bibliophiles (which he helped to found in 1908), shut out wide circles of the city's middle-class population. In his later years, the lectures Warburg presented in his library attracted some of the most important figures in Hamburg's economic and social life, so much so that "they took on the air of a soirée."[48] The city's museums became representational forums for the upper-middle class, serving to legitimize the claims of Hamburg's patricians to social and political leadership. The large-scale art patronage that fell within the purview of princes in other German cities rested exclusively with the *Großbürgertum* in Hamburg; they provided a discriminating public for leading painters and undertook the cultural projects which required large investments of money and time.

Ultimately, with its focus on Hamburg's patricians and the monuments mentioned above, this book hopes to contribute to an understanding of Hamburg's cultural life as a multidimensional phenomenon, animated by private initiative and public discourse and charged with debate. But more to the point, it hopes to demonstrate the inadequacy of making judgments about this cultural life from a perspective that wishes to see it as either predominantly traditional or predominantly receptive to modern developments as they are often conceived by historians. Instead, the following discussion sees Hamburg as shaped by processes of political, social, and cultural modernization that did not simply consist of "the substitution of one set of attributes for another … but rather in their mutual interpenetration and transformation."[49]

III

If this book is focused on the life and work of a single individual and the history of a particular city, it is also written with an interest in the complexity and transformations of the sociopolitical and cultural life of the German Empire at large. There is now a significant body of scholarship that has rethought the nature of the *Kaiserreich* and its position in the continuum of German history. The impact of the *Bürgertum* on German society, economics, and politics has been central to this reassessment.[50] This book makes a modest contribution to the ongoing project of reforming earlier conceptions of the German Empire. Aspects of this rethinking have been inspired by challenges to the usefulness of the binary model of tradition and modernity for analyzing historical change. This book frames the history of the monuments previously mentioned, and Warburg's involvement with them, within the national context. It claims that Warburg, and many of Hamburg's political and social elite, shared the perspective of a wider middle-class constituency that saw itself as the cultural arbiter of a modern German state and hoped for a greater role for the *Bürgertum* in the social and political leadership of the nation. In so doing, it contributes to a profile of the Empire that is appearing increasingly bourgeois and, at the same time, to the image of a political, social, and cultural environment that is complicated by the interpenetration of tradition and modernity.

With the emergence of a predominantly left-wing generation of German historians in the 1960s and 1970s, the nature of the German Empire was construed as one of political backwardness, authoritarianism, and repressive, preindustrial elites. A predominantly statist approach posited the key to understanding Wilhelmine Germany as the supposed paradox that it embodied: the anomaly of a modern economy dominated by an authoritarian state, a country that stood in the front rank of industrialized nations without undergoing a bourgeois revolution. Hans-Ulrich Wehler's influential study, *Das Deutsche Kaiserreich*, emphasized the exclusion of the bourgeoisie from positions of power. Reflecting the thinking of many West German historians in the 1960s and 70s, Wehler argued that when faced with the internal political tensions and class antagonisms arising from the process of industrialization, Imperial Germany's political elite resorted to the manipulative use of demagoguery and social imperialism to deflect revolution and perpetuate their hold on power.[51] Concurrently, intellectual historians emphasized the way in which preindustrial, antimodern mentalities prevented the modernization of the political and social system. Studies such as Fritz Stern's *The Politics of Cultural Despair* and George Mosse's *The Crisis of German Ideology* argued that the problems and crises of modernity drove broad segments of the German populace to turn from liberalism, urbanism, rationality, and science to embrace an antipolitical stance marked by radical nationalism and anti-Semitism.[52] Germany, it was suggested, did not take the western world's route to modernity, but embarked on a *Sonderweg*, or special path, which resulted in the weakness of the Weimar Republic and the rise of Nazism. This teleological approach to the origins of the Third Reich laid a large portion of the blame at the feet of the German bourgeoisie and the failure of liberal politics. In an authoritarian state dominated by traditional elites, German liberals betrayed their heritage and were condemned to powerlessness.

While important dissenting voices existed in the West German academic community, a particularly powerful critique of these arguments emerged in the work of English-language historians at the end of the 1970s.[53] Richard Evans,

David Blackbourn, and Geoff Eley departed from the tendency to measure the history of the German Empire against the western European norm of liberal-democratic evolution; they abandoned the idea that modern social, economic, and cultural development requires a liberal constitution and parliamentary democracy. Instead, they sought to understand German history on its own terms.[54] Sustained by a wide array of monographic research, this initiative has transformed the image of Imperial Germany from that of a static, authoritarian social and political system to that of a dynamic society in which political, social, and cultural change emerged spontaneously from below and was not simply imposed by the political elite from above.[55] Indeed, the German Empire has come to appear increasingly modern in terms of its socioeconomic development, its cultural achievements, and even its political culture.[56] Emphasizing that "checks on popular participation, the relative weakness of parliamentary controls, and the privileges of the titular nobility" were not unusual in Europe before 1914, Eley has written that contemporaries frequently pictured the *Kaiserreich* as "an exemplary 'modern' state." The reasons for this assessment were to be found "in the technocratic efficiency of its bureaucratic and military machines, in its more interventionist relationship to the economy and society, in the vaunted excellence of its municipal governments, in its system of social administration, and … in the existence of universal male suffrage and the extent of popular political mobilization."[57]

A counterpoint to this picture is provided by scholars who, if they concur with an emphasis on the German Empire's modernity, correctly point to its dark side. This manifested itself in phenomena such as radical nationalism, social imperialism, and a belief in the efficacy of eugenics.[58] It is argued that the foundations of Nazism and the Holocaust were prepared in racist social policy that goes back to the period before 1914.[59] Detlev Peukert has posited "the genesis of the 'Final Solution' from the spirit of science."[60] Yet the predominant trend in scholarship on the German Empire has been away from a teleology that draws bold lines between Bismarck and Hitler, towards a perspective which emphasizes the discontinuities, the competing visions, and the potential that constituted Germany's encounter with political, socioeconomic, and cultural modernism.

In the case of the *Bürgertum*, there is now a large body of literature which demonstrates that, far from submitting to reactionary authority, this diverse social group embraced the Wilhelmine period with enthusiasm and self-confidence. In fact, a recent assessment has stated that "the *Kaiserreich*'s dominant culture is now widely acknowledged to have been explicitly and self-confidently 'bourgeois.'"[61] Of course, no matter the extent to which revisionist historians emphasize its modernity, they are still faced with the backwardness of the Empire's monarchy, its military, and its bureaucracy. Yet in a highly perceptive reframing of this bifurcated image, Geoff Eley has challenged the binary model of tradition and modernity and suggested that historians need to free themselves from the distinction between liberalism understood as modernizing and authoritarianism understood as backward. In particular, he has argued that an authoritarian state was not incompatible with the interests and values of the German bourgeoisie. A state with authoritarian features, he writes, "should not be assumed automatically to express the political dominance of a landowning aristocracy and other preindustrial elites. On the contrary, it might also articulate the interests of the bourgeoisie and might even provide a framework for the latter's social and political hegemony."[62] Authoritarian forms "might be quite functional and modern relative to the conditions and requirements of capitalist production, societal cohesion, and state effectiveness of that time."[63]

Thus if the *Bürgertum* failed to control political power on the national level, a broad scholarly consensus now believes that there was a middle-class revolution that made Germany's bourgeoisie as influential as those of France and Britain. Bourgeois values permeated the Empire "in everything from taste, fashion, and the everyday conduct of affairs to the main lines of the German Empire's public culture, including the ethos of local administration; the prevailing views of law, morality, and the social order; the notions of private property and social obligation; and the general principles of public life."[64] Indeed, the German Empire can now be seen as "a classic embodiment of bourgeois values" in terms of "the constitutionalizing of public authority via parliamentary institutions; in the recodifications of commercial and civil law; in the models of administrative efficiency, particularly at the level of the city; and in the growth and elaboration of public opinion."[65] Although its history and position was unique within the Empire, Hamburg bears witness to the accuracy of this assessment.

The purview of this book is art and culture that, as has often been emphasized, was not a peripheral affair for nineteenth-century Germans. On the contrary, it was an important component of middle-class identity, and cultural innovation was not relegated to the fringes of society.[66] Scholars of Wilhelmine Germany continue to investigate the ways in which art was shaped by, and gave expression to, social and political concerns. For the *Bürgertum*, art and culture became an important medium to articulate their vision of national identity; it was also a means of shoring up the idea of a united Germany at a time of social strife and political divisions. Having disappeared from official political symbolism, a markedly nationalist bourgeois culture sought an art that would proclaim the democratic-republican heritage of the German Empire. More than simply harboring the conviction that they deserved to be the bearers of a national culture, sections of the *Bürgertum* saw culture as a way of modernizing and reforming Imperial society.

In conjunction with his deeply intellectual response to the monuments constructed at the behest of Hamburg's government and patrician elite, Aby Warburg sympathized with the constituency within the *Bürgertum* that sought to stamp the German Empire with their values. Although the monuments examined in the following chapters were not the products of a particular middle-class association with pretensions to social and cultural reform, the most important impetus behind their construction was similar to those harbored by such associations: that is, the desire to proclaim the political, social, and cultural traditions of a merchant republic, governed by its burghers, within an Empire presided over by a *Hohenzollern* king and aristocracy.

IV

Chapter one offers a brief biography focusing on key themes in Warburg's life and work. It establishes the personal and intellectual background for the following study by exploring Warburg's complex identity as scholar, citizen of Hamburg, and German Jew. It also begins to define the contours of the political, social, and cultural context in which he lived and worked, and establishes the nature and tone of his public persona and his ideas with respect to art in Hamburg's public realm. It does this, in part, through a comparison with the ideas and goals of Alfred Lichtwark. The second chapter analyzes Warburg's first substantial musings on contemporary art: an unpublished play written in 1896 entitled "Hamburg Conversations on Art." This document opens perspectives onto his opinions regarding contemporary cultural debates in Hamburg, his attitude to artists such as Arnold Böcklin and Max Klinger, and his personal investment in the artistic innovation of his day. The chapter argues that, as with many of his generation, Warburg claimed social and cultural progress under the banner of artistic innovation. It also provides a point of departure from which to examine the intellectual and scholarly foundations for his interest in contemporary art and to explore his ambivalent response to the various processes of modernization.

The following three chapters reconstruct the history of three of Hamburg's most important works of public art. They do this by analyzing the detailed statements of purpose prepared by the artists, as well as the voluminous body of official minutes, memoranda, and letters produced by the patrons who commissioned them and the committees who oversaw their construction. The speeches, musical accompaniment, guest lists, and even seating arrangements of the ceremonies that marked their dedications reveal the way in which the city fathers rehearsed the political and even the moral order of the city of Hamburg. In addition, it has been possible to reconstruct how the monuments were seen and understood by different sectors of Hamburg's public. Establishing interpretative communities for the artworks has involved the use of several sources: the many minutes, letters, and notes on Hamburg's cultural and political affairs that Warburg collected in his archive; contemporary art and cultural journals, in particular, *Der Lotse*, Hamburg's short-lived "weekly for German culture"; numerous newspaper articles; and, most importantly, the large body of commentary provided by correspondents to the Hamburg press. Along with the history of each monument, chapters three to five explore Warburg's increasing involvement in Hamburg's civic affairs. They also elucidate various facets of his thinking about the forms and functions of public artworks.

Chapter three is a detailed account of the history of Hamburg's Bismarck memorial, the most important monument of its kind. Beginning with an overview of the city's political history, it describes the monument's construction as an attempt by the city's patrician elite to counteract the politicization of the city's working classes. The chapter also demonstrates that it was a monumental expression of the city's autonomous cultural identity vis-à-vis the Imperial court in Berlin. Warburg's enthusiastic response to the monument's formal and iconographic innovation, and his reaction to public opinion, is analyzed in the context of his concurrent research on Renaissance Florence. His opinions provide insight into his thinking about the role of public art as a means of ameliorating social tensions and as a way of opposing the cultural agenda fostered by the Kaiser's court. The chapter emphasizes the ways in which Warburg's political and cultural opinions were shaped by Hamburg's unique historical identity and were representative of the attitudes of the city's patrician elite.

The fourth chapter details the history of the mural decoration of the great hall in Hamburg's city hall. The paintings are discussed in terms of the government's desire to monumentalize a collective memory of the city's unique history and identity within the German Empire. Close attention is paid to the search for an artistic style and compositional format that would break with the traditions of academic history painting. The chapter focuses on Warburg's negative response to the project—and to the artist, Hugo Vogel—in his working papers, correspondence, and an article that he wrote for the journal *Kunst und Künstler* in 1910. These previously neglected documents constitute an important exposition of the reasons why he opposed the art of the German academies and the aesthetic and cultural policies fostered by the Kaiser. They also afford an understanding of Warburg's ideas regarding the role of public artworks as the bearers of collective memory. Importantly, this episode demonstrates the way in which Warburg's opinions influenced how critics, cultural commentators, and politicians viewed the murals.

The final chapter outlines Warburg's most active involvement with the production of monumental artworks: the painting of Willy von Beckerath's mural cycle in the School of Art and Industry. Not only was Warburg a friend and financial supporter of the artist, but his intervention on Beckerath's behalf was of the utmost importance in the execution of this large-scale commission. The paintings are analyzed in the context of local hopes that Hamburg would become a leading center for the production of art and design in the German Empire. The chapter details Warburg's close relationship with Beckerath, particularly through the use of his correspondence. It focuses, however, on the unpublished address given by Warburg at the murals' dedication. Here he enumerated a brief but substantial synopsis of the role he felt public art must fulfill as a means of public enlightenment, especially in a time of war. These events not only reveal the constancy of Warburg's thinking about the role of art in Hamburg's public realm; they also open perspectives onto his positive attitude to cultural innovation, especially German Expressionism, as well as his reaction to the First World War. The narrative ends in 1918 with Warburg's mental collapse, an event that coincided with the demise of the German Empire.

Notes

1. Fritz Schumacher, *Selbstgespräche: Erinnerungen und Betrachtungen* (Hamburg, 1949), p. 299f.
2. The impetus to renewed scholarly interest in Warburg was provided by Ernst Gombrich, *Aby Warburg: An Intellectual Biography*, 2nd ed. (Chicago, 1986); since then, the literature on Warburg has grown dramatically and more recent contributions include Philippe-Alain Michaud, *Aby Warburg and the Image in Motion* (New York, 2004); Georges Didi-Huberman, *L'image survivante: Histoire de l'art et temps des fantômes selon Aby Warburg* (Paris, 2002); Bernd Villhauer, *Aby Warburg's Theorie der Kultur: Detail und Sinnhorizont* (Berlin, 2002); *Art History as Cultural History: Warburg's Projects*, ed. Richard Woodfield (Amsterdam, 2001); Matthew Rampley, *The Remembrance of Things Past: On Aby Warburg and Walter Benjamin* (Wiesbaden, 2000).
3. Peter Gay, *Weimar Culture: The Outsider as Insider* (New York, 1968), p. 30; George Mosse, *German Jews Beyond Judaism* (Bloomington and Cincinnati, 1985), p. 50ff.
4. Although both accounts are journalistic and unreliable in many instances see Ron Chernow, *The Warburgs: The Twentieth-Century Odyssey of a Remarkable Jewish Family* (New York, 1993); David Farrer, *The Warburgs: The Story of a Family* (New York, 1974).
5. Eduard Rosenbaum and Ari J. Sherman, *M.M. Warburg & Co., 1798–1938: Merchant Bankers of Hamburg* (London, 1979); Alfred Vagts, "M.M. Warburg & Co. Ein Bankhaus in der deutschen Weltpolitik, 1905–1933," *Vierteljahreshefte für Sozial- und Wirtschaftsgeschichte* 45 (1958), pp. 289–398.
6. Niall Ferguson, "Max Warburg and German Politics: The Limits of Financial Power in Wilhelmine Germany," in *Wilhelminism and Its Legacies: German Modernities, Imperialism, and the Meanings of Reform, 1890–1930*, eds. Geoff Eley and James Retallack, (New York and Oxford, 2003), pp. 185–201; Niall Ferguson, *Paper and Iron: Hamburg Business and German Politics in the Era of Inflation, 1897–1927* (Cambridge, 1995); Werner E. Mosse, *The German-Jewish Economic Elite 1820– 1935: A Socio-Cultural Profile* (Oxford, 1989), p. 197ff.
7. Gombrich, *Aby Warburg*, p. 191.
8. Kurt W. Forster, "Aby Warburg's History of Art: Collective Memory and the Social Mediation of Images," *Daedalus* 105 (1976), p. 170; Heinrich Dilly, "Sokrates in Hamburg: Aby Warburg und seine kulturwissenschaftliche Bibliothek," in *Aby Warburg: Akten des internationalen Symposions, Hamburg, 1990*, eds. Horst Bredekamp, Michael Diers, and Charlotte Schoell-Glass (Weinheim, 1991), p. 137.
9. Warburg Institute Archive, London (hereafter WIA) III.2.1: Zettelkasten 57 (Hamburg), 057 031993.
10. Warburg's involvement in Hamburg's Vorlesungswesen is briefly recounted in Werner von Melle, *Dreißig Jahre hamburger Wissenschaft, 1891–1921*, 2 vols. (Hamburg, 1923), vol. 1, p. 197ff; see also Carl H. Landauer, "The Survival of Antiquity: The German Years of the Warburg Institute" (Ph.D. diss., Yale University, 1984), p. 39.
11. Hamburg, Staatsarchiv (hereafter St.A.H.) 361–6: Hochschulwesen—Dozenten—und Personalakten, II, 474, Aby Warburg: Erich Marcks to Max Förster, 27 April 1908.
12. Certain aspects of Warburg's involvement in Hamburg's public affairs are dealt with in Michael Diers, *Warburg aus Briefen: Kommentare zu den Kopierbüchern der Jahre 1905–1918* (Hamburg, 1991); Christiane Brosius, *Kunst als Denkraum: zum Bildungsbegriff von Aby Warburg* (Pfaffenweiler, 1997).
13. For research that takes Warburg's biography beyond a preoccupation with his scholarship see Bernd Roeck, *Florenz 1900: Die Suche nach Arkadien* (Munich, 2001); idem, *Der junge Aby Warburg* (Munich, 1997); Anne Marie Meyer, "Aby Warburg in His Early Correspondence," *The American Scholar* 57 (1988), pp. 445–452.
14. Kevin Repp, *Reformers, Critics and the Paths of German Modernity: Anti-Politics and the Search for Alternatives, 1890–1914* (Cambridge, Mass., 2000), p. 11.
15. Ibid., p. 27.

16. WIA. III.43.3; TS of 43.1–2: Grundlegende Bruchstücke zu einer pragmatischen Ausdruckskunde Bd. 2, 1896–1903, no. 420, p. 168.
17. This point is emphasized in Ferguson, "Max Warburg and German Politics," p. 187.
18. Ibid., p. 188.
19. Ibid., p. 187.
20. WIA. General Correspondence (GC): Warburg to Gustav Pauli, 10 October 1918.
21. Celia Applegate, *A Nation of Provincials: The German Idea of Heimat* (Berkeley, 1990), p. 13.
22. Tilmann von Stockhausen, *Die Kulturwissenschaftliche Bibliothek Warburg: Architektur, Einrichtung und Organisation* (Hamburg, 1992).
23. Dorothea McEwan, "'Die siegende, fliegende Idea.' Ein Künstlerischer Auftrag von Aby Warburg," in *Der Bilderatlas im Wechsel der Künste und Medien*, eds. Sabine Flach, Inge Münz-Koene, and Marianne Streisand (Munich, 2005), pp. 121–151.
24. WIA. III.27.2.2: Bismarck Denkmal, fol. 6.
25. Applegate, *A Nation of Provincials*.
26. Geoff Eley, "Introduction 1: Is There A History of the Kaiserreich?" in *Society, Culture, and the State in Germany, 1870–1930*, ed. idem (Ann Arbor, 1996), p. 9.
27. Beth Irwin Lewis has stressed the need for such a perspective in idem, *Art for All? The Collision of Modern Art and the Public in Nineteenth-Century Germany* (Princeton and Oxford, 2003).
28. A comprehensive treatment of Lichtwark's life and ideas is Hans Präffcke, *Der Kunstbegriff Alfred Lichtwarks* (Hildesheim, Zurich, and New York, 1986); see also Jennifer Jenkins, *Provincial Modernity: Local Culture and Liberal Politics in Fin-De-Siècle Hamburg* (Ithaca and London, 2003); Carolyn Kay, *Art and the German Bourgeoisie: Alfred Lichtwark and Modern Painting in Hamburg, 1886–1914* (Toronto, 2002); *Kunst ins Leben: Alfred Lichtwarks Wirken für die Kunsthalle und Hamburg von 1886 bis 1914*, exh. cat. (Hamburger Kunsthalle, 9 December 1986—1 February 1987); for an excellent bibliography of Lichtwark's writings see Werner Kayser, *Alfred Lichtwark* (Hamburg, 1977); for the perspective of a contemporary see Gustav Schiefler, *Eine hamburgische Kulturgeschichte, 1890–1920: Beobachtungen eines Zeitgenossen*, eds. Gerhard Ahrens, Hans Wilhelm Eckardt, and Renate Hauschild-Thiessen (Hamburg, 1985), pp. 61–67.
29. See especially Richard J. Evans, *Death in Hamburg: Society and Politics in the Cholera Years, 1830–1910* (Oxford, 1987), p. 36f; Ferguson, *Paper and Iron*, p. 63ff.
30. See amongst others, Peter Paret, *The Berlin Secession: Modernism and its Enemies in Imperial Germany* (Cambridge, Mass. and London, 1980); Peter Jelavich, *Munich and Theatrical Modernism: Politics, Playwriting, and Performance, 1890–1914* (Cambridge, Mass., 1985); Maria Makela, *The Munich Secession: Art and Artists in Turn-of-the-Century Munich* (Princeton, 1990).
31. Ferguson, *Paper and Iron*, p. 63.
32. Ibid., p. 47.
33. Evans, *Death in Hamburg*, p. 36f.
34. Ferguson, *Paper and Iron*, p. 65.
35. Peter Hohendahl, ed., *Patriotism, Cosmopolitanism, and National Culture: Public Culture in Hamburg, 1700–1933* (Amsterdam and New York, 2003).
36. Jenkins, *Provincial Modernity*, p. 42.
37. Birgit-Katharine Seemann, *Stadt, Bürgertum und Kultur: Kulturelle Entwicklung und Kulturpolitik in Hamburg von 1839 bis 1933 am Beispiel des Museumswesens* (Husum, 1998).
38. Werner Jochmann, "Handelsmetropole des Deutschen Reiches," in *Hamburg: Geschichte der Stadt Hamburg und ihrer Bewohner*, eds. idem and Hans-Dieter Loose, 2 vols. (Hamburg, 1982–88), vol. 1, p. 104; Eckart Klessmann, *Geschichte der Stadt Hamburg* (Hamburg, 1988), p. 423.
39. Evans, *Death in Hamburg*, p. 65.
40. Kay, *Art and the German Bourgeoisie*, p. 69.
41. Jenkins, *Provincial Modernity*.
42. This point is emphasized in Lewis, *Art for All?*.

43. Maria Rennhofer, *Kunstzeitschriften der Jahrhundertwende in Deutschland und Österreich, 1895–1914* (Vienna and Munich, 1987), p. 173.
44. Robin Lenman, *Die Kunst, die Macht und das Geld: zur kulturgeschichte des kaiserlichen Deutschland, 1871–1918* (Frankfurt and New York, 1994), p. 19f; idem, *Artists and Society in Germany, 1850-1914* (Manchester and New York, 1997), p. 102ff.; Peter Paret, "Literary Censorship as a Source of Historical Understanding: A Comment," *Central European History*, 18 (1985), pp. 360–364.
45. Richard J. Evans, "Family and Class in the Hamburg Grand Bourgeoisie, 1815–1914," in *The German Bourgeoisie: Essays on the Social History of the German Middle Class from the Late Eighteenth to the Early Twentieth Century*, eds. idem and David Blackbourn (London and New York, 1991), p. 133f.
46. Andreas Schulz, "Weltbürger und Geldaristokraten: hanseatisches Bürgertum im 19. Jahrhundert," *Historische Zeitschrift* 259 (1994), pp. 637–670.
47. Jenkins, *Provincial Modernity*, p. 86f.
48. Landauer, "The Survival of Antiquity," p. 36.
49. Dean Tipps quoted in Matthew Jefferies, *Politics and Culture in Wilhelmine Germany: The Case of Industrial Architecture* (Oxford and Washington, 1995), p. 4.
50. Major studies of the German bourgeoisie include Jürgen Kocka, ed., *Bürgertum im 19. Jahrhundert: Deutschland im europäischen Vergleich*, 2 vols. (Munich, 1988); Lothar Gall, *Stadt und Bürgertum im 19. Jahrhundert* (Munich, 1990).
51. Hans Ulrich Wehler, *Das Deutsche Kaiserreich, 1871–1918* (Göttingen, 1973); for a summary of the historiographical context see Hans-Ulrich Wehler, "Historiography in Germany Today," in *Observations on the Spiritual Situation of the Age*, ed. Jürgen Habermas (Cambridge, Mass., 1984), pp. 221–259.
52. Fritz Stern, *The Politics of Cultural Despair: A Study of the Rise of the Germanic Ideology* (Berkeley, 1961); George L. Mosse, *The Crisis of German Ideology* (London, 1966).
53. Perhaps the most important challenge to Wehler's image of the Kaiserreich from within the West German academic community was mounted by Thomas Nipperdey; see idem, "Wehlers 'Kaiserreich.' Eine kritische Auseinandersetzung," in idem, *Gesellschaft, Kultur, Theorie. Gesammelte Aufsätze zur neueren Geschichte* (Göttingen, 1976), pp. 360–389.
54. See, for example, Richard Evans, ed., *Society and Politics in Wilhelmine Germany* (London, 1978); David Blackbourn and Geoff Eley, *The Peculiarities of German History* (Oxford and New York, 1984); Geoff Eley, *From Unification to Nazism: Reinterpreting the German Past* (Boston, 1986); Richard Evans, *Rethinking German History: Nineteenth-Century Germany and the Origins of the Third Reich* (Boston, 1987).
55. For a summary of much revisionist thinking see Eley, "Introduction 1."
56. For an overview of Wilhelmine culture see Matthew Jeffries, *Imperial Culture in Germany, 1871–1918* (Houndmills, 2003).
57. Geoff Eley, "German History and the Contradictions of Modernity: The Bourgeoisie, the State, and the Mastery of Reform," in *Society, Culture and the State in Germany, 1870–1930*, ed. idem (Ann Arbor, 1996), p. 93.
58. Ibid., p. 96ff.
59. Michael Burleigh and Wolfgang Wippermann, *The Racial State: Germany, 1933– 1945* (Cambridge, 1991).
60. Detlev Peukert, "The Genesis of the 'Final Solution' from the Spirit of Science," in *Nazism and German Society, 1933–1945*, ed. David F. Crew (London and New York, 1994), pp. 274–299.
61. Eley and Retallack, *Wilhelminism and Its Legacies*, p. 3.
62. Eley, "German History and the Contradictions of Modernity," p. 90.
63. Eley, "Introduction 1," p. 7.
64. Ibid., p. 5.
65. Ibid., p. 6.
66. Jeffries, *Imperial Culture in Germany*, p. 2.

Chapter One

THE LIFE AND WORK OF ABY WARBURG
IN ITS HAMBURG CONTEXT

"I should have been a roaring lion in the Judean desert; instead, I've become a lap-dog in Harvestehude."—Aby Warburg

I

The self-characterization that gives this chapter its epigraph is taken from a written collection of sayings, or "Warburgisms" recorded by Aby Warburg's son, Max Adolf.[1] In most cases, we do not know when Warburg spoke these pithy expressions, to whom, or on what occasions. Some may have been uttered only once, capturing the imagination of listeners with their peculiar poignancy or humor. Others may have formed part of Warburg's repertoire of repartee. He may or may not have taken them seriously.

A few sharp phrases cannot catch the full complexity of a man who also described himself as a "Hebrew by blood, a Hamburger at heart, and a Florentine in spirit."[2] But the quote above provides more than an affecting epigraph; to my mind, Warburg was committed to introspection and took trouble to define, as precisely as he could, who he was. Any serious examination of Warburg's work rests on an assessment of his self. Therefore, this chapter begins with a short biography, a discussion of the major themes of Warburg's scholarship, and an examination of the self-acknowledged components of his identity. While the principal ideas will be discussed in greater depth in the succeeding chapters, this overview provides an introduction to the personal and intellectual context of his engagement with art in Hamburg's public realm. The chapter then turns to a comparison of Warburg's ideas concerning the public consumption of art with those of Alfred Lichtwark. Besides establishing the local and cultural context, this comparison will emphasize the distinctive nature of Warburg's methods and goals. Finally, the chapter examines an exhibition of Albrecht Dürer's drawings which Warburg mounted in Hamburg's Volksheim, or People's Home, in 1905. This foray into working-class education reveals the specific individual and collective benefits which Warburg believed were to be derived from the serious contemplation of art by the general public.

II

Although some scholars have posited connections between his personal life and his scholarship, relatively little of substance has been written about the particular familial, social, and cultural milieu that was home to Aby Warburg.[3] Born in June 1866 into Hamburg's German-Jewish economic elite, he was the eldest son of Moritz (1838–1910) and Charlotte Warburg (1842–1921). The family had established itself in Altona, adjacent to Hamburg, in the late seventeenth century, but "remained little more than minor moneychangers" until after the Napoleonic Wars.[4] They became the Rothschild's principal Hamburg agents in 1865 and the family bank rose to national and international prominence after 1900 under the direction of Max Warburg. At the time of Aby Warburg's death in 1929, M.M. Warburg & Co. was the largest and most prestigious private bank in Germany.[5] It was assumed that the eldest son would train as a banker and exercise his birthright to the leadership of the family enterprise. But at the age of thirteen, Aby Warburg sold this birthright to Max for the promise that his younger brother would financially support his book-buying habit for the duration of his life. His choice of career was a controversial one and he faced considerable pressure from his family to become a doctor, research chemist, or rabbi instead.[6] Moritz Warburg could only envision success and fulfillment for his son within a Jewish context.

When Warburg entered the University of Bonn in 1886, studying art history meant studying the art of the Renaissance. Much of his early research focused on the meaning and historical importance of the Italian Renaissance. His doctoral dissertation was completed at the University of Straßburg under the direction of the art historian Hubert Janitschek. This was published in 1893 as *Sandro Botticelli's "Birth of Venus" and "Spring": An Examination of Concepts of Antiquity in the Early Italian Renaissance.*[7] In this attempt to elucidate how Botticelli (c. 1445–1510) and his patrons imagined the classical past, Warburg established the problems and working methods that informed his lifelong research and the content of his library. Fundamental to his approach was the correlation of textual sources and pictorial expression. In his dissertation, Warburg related Botticelli's paintings to texts from classical antiquity that had been adapted by philosophers and poets such as Agnolo Poliziano and others in the circle around Lorenzo de' Medici. This resulted in an understanding of the Renaissance that abandoned the concept of rebirth. Instead, Warburg's thinking was dominated by the idea of *Nachleben*, which might be translated as survival. While preserving a perspective on the Renaissance as the threshold of the modern world, he emphasized that it was not simply about the recovery of the lost traditions of antiquity; more fundamentally, it embodied a process of cultural memory that sublimated human anxieties and passions that had been given formulaic expression in classical antiquity and were long stored in the collective unconscious.[8]

Warburg construed the legacy of pagan antiquity to fifteenth-century Italy as twofold: the Apollonian, calm grandeur of much classical statuary and the Dionysian passion of frenzied maenads found, for example, on antique sarcophagi. What attracted him to Botticelli was not the artist's imitation of classical poise, but his depiction of movement and agitation. When he found what he called the "animated accessories" of billowing hair and fluttering drapery in his painting, and in the work of Domenico Ghirlandaio (1449–94), Warburg read them as psychic gestures and expressions of antiquity's psychological legacy. He believed that Poliziano had instructed Botticelli to include these expressions of the classical imagination in his work. This focus on the otherwise unconsidered aspects of artworks was central to his method; as he famously described it, "God dwells in minutiae" (*Der liebe Gott steckt im Detail*).[9] Warburg understood these "pathos formulae" (*Pathosformeln*) as pictorial records of nervous excitation, which gave graphic expression to abstract psychological processes; this emotive gestural language demonstrated to him the irrational impulses that still played upon the mind of Renaissance man. Thus Warburg abandoned the Enlightenment view of antiquity as an idealizing influence leading to calm beauty—the view of Johann Winckelmann (1717–68) and Gotthold Lessing (1729–81). Artists like Botticelli reactivated antiquity's primitive content; their work amounted to "a fragile cultural superstructure placed over a more primitive layer of human emotive behavior manifest in the dynamism of incidental details."[10] For Warburg, the recovery of classical antiquity was not simply the cause and result of cultural progress: if the concept of survival signified temporal continuity, it also signified chronological disruption. Thus Warburg's model of history was not a linear one. Instead, he proposed a dialectical model of European culture that fluctuated between humanist learning and Dionysian pathos.

Most broadly stated, the goal of Warburg's research was an attempted synthesis of art and cultural history with the purpose of delineating the changing nature of humanity's intellectual orientation. In particular, Warburg sought to understand the influence of pagan antiquity on the European intellectual makeup in all its forms—from art and literature, to science and jurisprudence. Over a period of many years of "arduous wandering through the world of the symbol," he pursued the ideas and psychological mechanisms that accounted for the existence of art, literature, myth, religion, and science.[11] Warburg insisted that he was an "image or picture historian," not an art historian; his goal was to trace the transmission of thought, "the highways of culture, the pathways of the mind or intellect," as they were embodied in pictorial expression.[12] Writing in 1923, he gave expression to the way in which his approach to images differed from much of the art-historical scholarship of his day: "I had developed a downright disgust with aestheticizing art history. The formal contemplation of images—not conceived as a biologically necessary product situated between the practices of religion and art … seemed to me to give rise to such a sterile trafficking in words."[13] This was the perspective from which he judged the art of his own age.

Warburg's relation of pictorial imagery to biological urges demonstrates that he understood visual symbols as the product of "the depths of human experience."[14] In exploring the manifestations of this experience, he dissolved the boundary between high art and craft and adopted an approach that was multi-disciplinary; in 1925, he explained to his brother Max that "the novelty of my method consists in the fact that, in studying the psychology of artistic creation, I bring together documents from the domain of language as well as from the plastic arts or from the world of religious and secular drama."[15] But although he drew on a wide range of sources and scholarship, and was insistent on the need to breach the borders that had traditionally divided academic disciplines, his published work paid close attention to individual images and texts and was rigorously informed by theory. Theory, however, was not given explicit expression in Warburg's published works; instead, it was elaborated in a collection of philosophical notes and aphorisms that he continually reworked and which were never published. In fact, because they are scattered across many unpublished sources, scholars must be cautious about making Warburg's ideas appear more unified and systematic then they actually were. Nonetheless, there are some major themes that can be drawn from both published and unpublished sources as we proceed.

Warburg's particular concern was symbolism and the psychology of pictorial expression; his scholarship might be described as an anthropology of the visual. Whether they took the form of monumental fresco paintings, personal devices and mottos, postage stamps, press photographs, wax votive figures, or the pageantry of the theater, images embodied the thought processes that Warburg hoped to excavate; they were documents of the manner in which humanity orientated itself, intellectually, within the cosmos. Pictorial expression had primitive origins as "the visual inscription of an empathetic bodily experience"; the symbolic impulse was the product of pagan passions and a collective experience of fear and trauma.[16] Warburg's research followed the chronological and geographical transmission and metamorphosis of these images and "pathos formulae." He understood them as an archive of collective memory construed as a matter of inherited anxieties; "the engrams of the experience of suffering," Warburg wrote, "live on as an inheritance preserved in the memory."[17] As inheritors of this memory, artists—such as Albrecht Dürer, Max Liebermann, or Emil Nolde—could sublimate the primitive passions of antiquity; pathos could become superior formal poise in the service of enlightenment and humanization through a process of symbolic idealization. Thus in one respect, Warburg's image research was tracing human cognitive development from irrational to rational modes of intellectual orientation; he was exploring the history of "how numerology turned into mathematics, how alchemy gave birth to chemistry, how invocations and incantations evolved into a corpus of religious texts and songs, stories and literature; how astrology, through scientific observations of the celestial sphere became astronomy." [18] But at any stage of this cultural transformation, humanity could regress from abstract, conceptual formulations into a mimetic-empathic urge, a primitive mode of orientation that was the product of an "inability to disengage from immersion in immediate sense experience." This was a "perpetual psychological disposition" that played "a constant role in determining the form of cultural activities."[19] Thus this dialectical model of intellectual and cultural development has been described as "the tension between Apollo and Dionysus as expressed, historically, in aesthetic forms."[20]

Before proceeding, it would do well to remember that Warburg's research was less original and pioneering than it is sometimes made out to be. In addition to the influences listed above, many of Warburg's interests were shared by scholars like Julius Meyer, Eugène Müntz, Anton Springer, and August Schmarsow.[21] This is not to diminish the fact, however, that Warburg made important contributions to twentieth-century scholarship. These include his insistence on a multidisciplinary approach to the study of artworks; an analysis of visual documents that—instead of seeing them with fixed meanings and simple connections to literary texts—explored the changing nature of their representational meaning; and a philosophical and cultural perspective that employed images in pursuit of an archaeology of modern cultural sensibility.

What was it that guided the young scholar's interest in symbolism to an interpretation of art in the light of psychology and hence to a psychology of culture? Apportioning intellectual influence on Warburg's theories, as well as precisely defining the essence of his thinking, has proved difficult and has divided scholars. The interpretation that dominated scholarship for over 25 years was that of Ernst Gombrich. Gombrich emphasized the influence of Enlightenment thought on Warburg, as well as the work of Charles Darwin and nineteenth-century evolutionism.[22] But a younger generation of scholars has downplayed these influences and pointed to links with twentieth-century thinkers including Walter Benjamin and Sigmund Freud.[23] What can be said with certainty is that the conceptual and methodological impetuses to Warburg's scholarship were derived from a wide array of sources.

A profound impact on the focus and nature of Warburg's exploration of fifteenth-century Florence was exercised by Jacob Burckhardt in his book *The Civilization of the Renaissance in Italy*, first published in 1860. Although he challenged the image of the Renaissance created by the celebrated Swiss historian, Burckhardt's work stimulated Warburg's interest in the cultural contexts of art. At the University of Bonn, Warburg studied cultural history with Karl Lamprecht, art history with Carl Justi and Henry Thode, and ancient religions with Hermann Usener. Gombrich ascribes such importance to Lamprecht's influence on the young student that he describes him as "Warburg's real teacher."[24] Lamprecht (1856–1915) abandoned the Rankean vision of history with its emphasis on individuals and its belief that political events and institutions alone were worthy of historical investigation. Instead, he practiced a psychology of historical phenomena and sought to understand the mentalities that underlay economics, legal contracts, political institutions, philosophic reasoning, and artistic creation. He was especially interested in the phenomena of historical change, which he conceived of as psychic transition.[25] The subjects and methods of the historian of religion, Hermann Usener (1834–1904), also have their resonance in Warburg's work. Usener was interested in the primitive origins of cultural phenomena, and employed philological methods and the formal analysis of myths in an effort to explain "myths, images, and linguistic forms in anthropological terms." He was "practicing an anthropology of religion" that sought the traces of mythical ideas in religious practice.[26] Furthermore, it must be remembered that Warburg lived during an important period for the historical study of symbols. He was captivated, for example, by the attempt of the Italian philosopher, Tito Vignoli, to describe mythology from the perspective of associationist psychology.[27] His thinking on mimesis—with its implication of empathetic, emotional engagement in pictorial representation—as a primitive form of intellectual orientation was informed by the work of the aesthetician Friedrich Theodor Vischer.[28] Furthermore, as Peter Burke explains, the period of Warburg's early life was marked by significant interchange between the disciplines of history and anthropology and it is clear that he familiarized himself with contemporary anthropological theory.[29]

Warburg was also a member of that generation of scholars to whom Friedrich Nietzsche spoke so powerfully in *The Birth of Tragedy*, published in 1872. For this generation, the idealized image of the ancient world began to break down in the light of historical and anthropological evidence. As noted above, Warburg took a special interest in the violent aspect of classical culture, and his teacher, Usener, explored the origins of Greek myth in primitive thought.[30] Warburg's lifelong fascination with the irrational aspect of humanity's psychological make-up has led Georges Didi-Huberman to picture him as a Dionysian figure dancing with the maenads.[31] It is true that Warburg once described Nietzsche as "our greatest prose-poet, a dancing prophet."[32] As we will see in chapter two, there were some general affinities between Warburg and many of those who fell under the influence of Nietzsche's writings: Warburg challenged the social and religious conventions of the German-Jewish economic elite into which he was born, sided with the avant-garde artists of his day, and lamented the demystification of the world and the instrumental attitude to nature that came with the rationalization of modernism. Notes drafted for the final seminar in a series on Jacob Burckhardt which he offered at Hamburg University in 1926–27 suggest that Warburg may have felt a kinship to Nietzsche in terms of the latter's mental breakdown; Warburg construed this as the result of Nietzsche's desire to make common cause with history's "demon of destruction" and his inability to withstand "the traumas of his vocation."[33] In his last years he hung Hans Olde's drawing of the sick Nietzsche in his home.[34] Philippe-Alain Michaud contends that while Warburg saw Burckhardt as representing the Apollonian pole of his own thinking, he saw Nietzsche as representing the Dionysian pole.[35]

Yet it would be incorrect to describe Warburg as a Dionysian figure or an unreserved Nietzschean. If he profited from Nietzsche's scholarship on pagan antiquity, he also had serious reservations about his methods and conclusions. In 1905, he wrote "if Nietzsche had only been familiar with the data of anthropology and folklore! Even in his case their specific gravity would have served as a regulating force for his dream-bird flight."[36] More importantly, Warburg never unconditionally embraced the Dionysian legacy of pagan antiquity. That said, it will become clear in the course of the following discussion that it is too simple to see Warburg as a latter-day Enlightenment figure whose scholarship attempted to exorcise history's demons. The point to be made, however, is that much of his work was aimed at ameliorating the influence of these forces. Furthermore, Warburg's lifestyle cannot be described as Dionysian; it was strictly bourgeois and governed by a belief "in hard work, competition, achievement ... rationality and the rule of law."[37] It should be remembered that he opposed his son's ambitions to become an artist and mocked those who looked to the Renaissance "in search of a licence and a pattern for unrestrained individualism and sensuality," and those who traveled to Italy with a copy of *Thus Spoke Zarathustra* in their pockets, "intoxicated by the idea of the 'superman.'"[38]

When Warburg left the University of Straßburg he had no concrete career plans or employment prospects and suffered frequent bouts of depression. In 1892, he began to study medicine in Berlin. The following year he undertook twelve months' service as a gunner in an artillery regiment in Karlsruhe.[39] He sailed to the United States for the marriage of his brother Paul in the autumn of 1895. While in America, Warburg visited the Smithsonian Institution in Washington, the University of California, Berkeley and Stanford University. He discovered the work of the eminent anthropologist, Franz Boas, as well as the research conducted on Native Americans by Frank Cushing and James Mooney. He also traveled to the Pueblo Indian communities of New Mexico and Arizona, enticed by the prospect of studying "primitive" peoples at a stage of cultural development suspended between magic and logic and caught between immersion in the natural world and sublimation in symbolic representations. As Warburg put it, "the link between pagan religious ideas and artistic activity is nowhere better to be seen than with the Pueblo Indians, and one could find in their culture rich material for an inquiry into the origins of symbolic art."[40] While claiming these studies had an important influence on his interpretation of the art of Renaissance Italy, Warburg did not assemble the data collected in America into lecture form until 1923.

In 1897, Warburg married the artist, Mary Hertz (1866–1934), and the following year visited the University of Kiel with the intention of applying for a *Privatdozentur*. Unfortunately, he was not made welcome and noted in his diary that

"I lack the power to do justice to any duties; I have decided once and for all I am not suited to be a *Privatdozent*."[41] But finding permanent, paid employment would never be a pressing consideration for Aby Warburg; as his brother Max reminded him in 1890, "the way you want to live you will always be able to live, thanks to a very wealthy father."[42] Furthermore, Warburg was a member of several societies including the Society for Hamburg's History and the Society of Bibliophiles, and it was these audiences that provided a forum for his independent research until such time as his library came to fulfill the same role.

Warburg's research remained focused on Florence in the years following the completion of his doctoral dissertation and he resided in the city until 1904.[43] "Florence," he wrote, "has answers to all the questions that the cultural historian can ask."[44] In part, his attraction to the city was probably rooted in personal experience. Both Hamburg and Florence possessed an identity as commercial republics, jealous of their independence; both were dominated by a group of powerful families, men of commerce not unlike his own father and brothers. But Florence also offered a large amount of material for a case study of how pagan antiquity shaped the European intellectual makeup at one of the most important junctures on its road to modernity. In 1902, Warburg published two major pieces of research entitled *The Art of Portraiture and the Florentine Bourgeoisie* and "Flemish Art and the Early Florentine Renaissance." In these works, he paid particular attention to the development of portraiture from an art form that represented individuals principally as religious patrons to one that gave face to self-conscious individuals. While the depiction of fifteenth-century bankers and merchants as witnesses to religious events—in frescoes and painted altarpieces— bore witness to a religious concept of existence, Warburg experienced the likenesses of these patrons as profane. As Philippe-Alain Michaud explains, "in the desire physically to appear in an image, Warburg sees an aesthetic translation of the will to power of a new class of merchants and materialist entrepreneurs."[45] This was indicative of a significant shift in images away from their ritual bases and cultic origins.

Yet in keeping with his nonevolutionary perspective on history, Warburg "stressed that the process of disengagement from a predominantly religious disposition was not as unequivocal as his contemporaries assumed."[46] Indeed, his study of religious donor portraits pointed, once again, to the persistence of primitive modes of thought in the late fifteenth century. Warburg claimed that portraits depicting real individuals as witnesses to religious events were actually attempts "to come closer to the Divine through a painted simulacrum," even in a period that Jacob Burckhardt had described as the first modern age.[47] These allegedly worldly-wise Renaissance businessmen were anything but indifferent to the religious aspects of artistic patronage; in fact, they were as dedicated to their patron saints as their medieval predecessors. This was a corrective to Burckhardt's image of Renaissance man defying superstition with worldly assurance. More accurately, the Florentine merchant-banker emerged in Warburg's essays as a man able to reconcile the apparent opposites of rational and irrational tendencies in his psychological constitution; a phenomenon which, as we have noted, Warburg labeled a "psychology of compromise."[48] This phenomenon was examined most famously in a major essay of 1907 entitled "Francesco Sassetti's Last Injunctions to His Sons." Through a study of Sassetti's will (which spoke of Fortuna as a pagan demon), his tomb in Santa Trinità, and the *impresa* of his fellow merchant, Giovanni Rucellai, Warburg revealed the interpenetration of rational and irrational thought patterns in the psychology of one of Florence's greatest bankers. Sassetti's thought combined the pagan pragmatism of an Etruscan merchant with the idealism of a medieval Christian.

Although Warburg published a limited number of essays in these years, they were informed by extensive rumination on abstract psychological processes and the psychology of artistic expression. In the 1880s and 90s, he began a collection of notes and philosophical aphorisms with the titles "Basic Fragments of a Pragmatic Science of Expression" (*Grundlegende Bruchstücke zu einer pragmatischen Ausdruckskunde*), "Basic Fragments of a Psychology of Art" (*Grundlegende Bruchstücke zur Psychologie der Kunst*), and "Symbolism as the Determination of Boundaries" (*Symbolismus als Umfangsbestimmung*).[49] As indicated above, Warburg was creating "a typological map of human cognitive and cultural evolution."[50] Through the evidence of its symbolic practices, he was tracing the progress of human consciousness from primitive magic to the abstract and conceptual thought of the modern mind. He was mapping this development in terms of "empathic identification—symbolic mediation—allegorical representation."[51] These concepts will become clearer if we expand upon the previous summary of Warburg's thinking on the psychology of pictorial expression.

In its primitive condition, humanity confused symbols with the concepts they were supposed to signify and projected subjective states of being onto the objective world; people engaged in primitive impulses of mimesis in which the depiction of intense bodily movement characterized the artist's "empathetic identification" with, and immersion in, the events to which he gave form. As Matthew Rampley has indicated, Warburg's thought emerged from "an established topos of eighteenth- and nineteenth-century philosophical and anthropological discourse," which equated the primitive and the mimetic. Warburg associated the mimetic impulse with "a lack of self-consciousness ... a lack of conceptual abstraction ... an anthropomorphised view of nature," and thus with the earliest state of human being.[52] In the modern world, humanity commanded a more rational symbolic practice that separated symbol from concept; through a process of "symbolic mediation" humanity acquired an intellectual distance between itself and the objective world, a space pervaded by discursive thought.

In the Renaissance, Warburg discovered a period of transition between primitive and modern modes of intellectual orientation and artistic expression. When he turned his attention north of the Alps, he found a milestone in the intellectual freedom of modern man in the life and art of Albrecht Dürer (1471–1528). In an essay published in 1905 and entitled "Dürer and Italian Antiquity," Warburg presented Dürer as the artist who "instinctively countered the pagan vigor of

Southern art" with "Apollonian clarity."[53] He self-consciously balanced passion with reflective calm; by assimilating both the Apollonian and Dionysian energies of antiquity's psychological legacy he helped extend humanity's mental range. Many years later, in "Heathen-Antique Prophecy in Word and Image at the Time of Luther," Warburg showed how Dürer transformed astrological symbols into self-conscious allegories; in his hands, Saturn, "most fearful of all the astrological deities," became "an allegory of the melancholic self-absorption of genius."[54] "Logic," Warburg explained, "sets a mental space between man and object by applying a conceptual label; magic destroys that space by creating a superstitious ... association between man and object."[55]

Yet, what needs to be emphasized once more—and what is of utmost importance for understanding the way in which Warburg judged the art of his own era—is that he did not see history as a linear process. Inasmuch as he adhered to an evolutionary model, it was certainly not teleological; as Margaret Iversen has argued, "it comprehends both gains and losses."[56] Humanity was not witness to the triumphal procession of Apollonian logic and beauty; rational thought did not always triumph over primitive fears or magical-associative thought patterns by a process of evolution. Nor did Warburg expect that art would increasingly eliminate or sublimate primitive pathos in the modern world. Recent scholarship has argued, quite correctly, against a narrow understanding of Warburg as simply a latter-day Enlightenment rationalist anxious to exorcise the irrational impulses that still haunted the modern mind.[57] Instead, Warburg believed the human mind transcended historical categorization; it existed not simply in historical time, but in a synchronous psychic time. The purpose of mapping the transmission and metamorphosis of images was not to delineate and order historical events, but to follow the "paths traced or taken by the mind."[58] This exercise proved that the passions to which the frenzied maenads of antiquity gave expression were both archaic and eternally present. From this perspective, the Renaissance could not be seen simply as a moment of transition between primitive and modern modes of thought. Warburg's work on Francesco Sassetti had demonstrated the persistence of magic and superstition in Renaissance Italy. The cultic images financed by the bankers of fifteenth-century Florence functioned "through the *lack* of critical distance, in other words through the predominance of the empathic-mimetic urge."[59] The taste of these men for the naturalism of Flemish art indicated "a primitive positivism—predicated on a lack of cognitive distance."[60]

Thus Warburg's historiography and theories of pictorial expression are built around dynamic contrasts of logic and magic, reason and unreason, and he conceived of these energies in terms of polarity, not contradiction. Consciousness oscillated between these opposites in an eternal process of compensation; there was never a resolution or neutralizing synthesis. As inheritors of cultural memory, artists fluctuated between rational distance and empathetic projection, between self-conscious symbolization and the free flow of imagination.[61] Artistic achievement consisted in incorporating logic and magic, reason and unreason, as a manifestation of *Denkraum*. *Denkraum* was a state of consciousness pervaded by reason, but in which intuition, imagination, and emotion could operate under its influence; because of the eternal presence of the irrational, it existed between the poles of logic and magic, reason and unreason.[62] In fact, Warburg believed that Dionysian passion was a necessary check on the potential excess of artifice; too much logic and self-conscious symbolization could result in an art of empty rhetoric and emotional vacancy. Symbolism could become disconnected from the basis of its meaning in a process of inflation—a process of "allegorical representation"—in which cultural enlightenment undermined itself. Warburg believed this was the case with Baroque art and allegory, and it was in these very terms that he criticized the murals completed by Hugo Vogel in Hamburg's city hall in 1909.[63] Nonetheless, it is important to remember that because he equated Dionysian passion with the unconscious, Warburg was acutely aware of the possibility of recidivism. There was always the danger that people would be carried away by the Dionysian side of human nature; this is partly how he understood the events of the First World War. In his own words, "all mankind is eternally and at all times schizophrenic."[64]

Warburg took up permanent residence in his native Hamburg in May 1904. He was now the father of two children, with another expected, and was looking for serenity to reflect upon his Italian research. In particular, he was hoping to publish a book based on his analysis of the inventories of Medici art holdings; this was provisionally entitled *Secular Flemish Art in Medicean Florence*.[65] Despite earlier pronouncements to the contrary, he had not given up hope, even at the age of thirty-eight, of a university career; there were indications that the University of Bonn would accept his application for *Habilitation*. Although he had published little, Warburg enjoyed a respected reputation. But his public activities distracted him from further pursuing a university lectureship. In 1905 he mounted an exhibition of Dürer's drawings in the Hamburg Volksheim, was a participant in the city's third Art Education Day, organized Hamburg's Folklore Congress, and became a member of the ethnology museum's commission.[66] When, in 1906, the University of Bonn invited him to submit his *Habilitationsschrift* and he was called to a university chair in Breslau, Warburg declined both invitations. Faced with the perennial problem of marrying historical facts to his theoretical ruminations, he was making no progress on his book on the Medici inventories; ultimately, it would never materialize.

The most important distraction from his publication plans was his commitment to a continually growing private library. Indeed, to many people, Warburg is known principally as an inveterate bibliophile and founder of the Kulturwissenschaftliche Bibliothek Warburg, now the Warburg Institute.[67] He did not regard the assemblage of his library as secondary to his research; both undertakings were equal contributions to his scholarly project. It was in 1901, with financial help from his family, that he began to collect books systematically for the creation of his library. By 1911, his collection numbered 15,000 volumes, but it was not until the spring of 1914 that he first discussed a plan for turning his library into a research institute with Fritz Saxl (1890–1948). Hired in January of 1914, Saxl became Warburg's principal assistant and succeeded him to the library's directorship upon his death.[68] For most of Warburg's life, the library was housed in his private dwelling, although it was accessible for scholarly use. Finally, in 1926, it was institutionalized as the Kulturwissenschaftliche Bibliothek Warburg, a semi-public library housed in facilities built adjacent to Warburg's private home in the Heilwigstraße. By that time, its holdings numbered 46,000 volumes.

Devoted to the multidisciplinary study of the legacy of pagan antiquity to European culture, this was the sort of reference collection which he saw as "the root of German superiority."[69] Its compilation and organization were guided by Warburg's intellectual project and methods; the collection encouraged readers to overcome the barriers established between specialized fields of research and to discover the interactions and relations between different modes of expression that revealed "the essential forces of the human mind and its history."[70] Before a process of "normalization" was undertaken by Saxl in the early 1920s, the library's organization was especially idiosyncratic and often baffled scholars upon their first visit. Saxl described his first encounter with it in 1911 as follows:

> The arrangement of the books was equally baffling and he [the student] may have found it most peculiar, perhaps, that Warburg never tired of shifting and re-shifting them. Every progress in his system of thought, every new idea about the inter-relation of facts made him re-group the corresponding books. The library changed with every change in his research method and with every variation in his interests. Small as the collection was, it was intensely alive, and Warburg never ceased shaping it so that it might best express his ideas about the history of man.[71]

The bulk of the collection was not devoted to art history. Given Warburg's interest in tracing the journey of images, both literal and metaphorical, the library was comprised of works of and on anthropology, cosmology, folklore, language, literature, magic, natural science, philosophy, politics, religion, and sociology. "Books," as Saxl put it, "were for Warburg more than instruments of research. Assembled and grouped, they expressed the thought of mankind in its constant and in its changing aspects."[72] Warburg characterized the library's role and purpose in several formulations, many of which employ the metaphor of observation post: he described it as "the revolving observation tower, from which the intellectual past of the Orient and Occident can be viewed" and as "a tower observing the trade routes of cultural exchange."[73]

It is clear that Warburg understood the value and effectiveness of private financing in the field of academic research; he studied it in fifteenth-century Florence, and witnessed its workings in the United States.[74] There is no doubt that he intended M.M. Warburg & Co. to play a similar role in academic patronage to that which had been played by the Medici fortune. In a letter to Max Warburg, he stressed that "I really am a fool for not insisting even more that we should demonstrate by our example that capitalism is also capable of intellectual achievements of a scope which would otherwise not be possible."[75] Not only did Warburg see his library and justify it to his family as a rational investment, he considered it as an aggrandizement of the family name: "Other rich families have a horse stable," he proclaimed, "you have my library—and that is more; because those who accumulate material goods must also do something for the development of the mind."[76]

But the ever-growing collection of books was not focused exclusively on the Italian and Northern European Renaissance. Especially from 1908, Warburg's attention turned to the work that made him famous in his lifetime: the study of astrological imagery. He was particularly interested in astrological motifs as pictorial forms that guided humanity in its quest to orientate itself in the cosmos. Influenced by the work of the eminent specialist in the field, Franz Boll (1867–1924), Warburg read widely in the history of mythology and astrology and pondered questions of cultural change, in particular, the continuity of star imagery from antiquity to modern times. On the one hand, Warburg's astrological research was another means of challenging the idea of the Italian Renaissance as steeped only in classical learning. In a lecture given in 1908 to the Association for Hamburg History and entitled, "The Gods of Antiquity and the Early Renaissance in Southern and Northern Europe," Warburg demonstrated how the Renaissance was indebted to the Middle Ages, which "had followed late antique traditions and had perfectly preserved the memory of the ancient gods in its literary and artistic forms."[77] The presence of the Olympian gods in the Renaissance was not the result of a departure from medieval convention; it was, more accurately, the product of a process of reform. On the other hand, the study of astrology provided Warburg with the most telling example of the bipolarity of the image in European culture and hence the human psyche. As Gombrich writes, "A figure of Venus in the *Quattrocento* may partake of both functions; it may be conceived as the planet whose picture is supposed to bring about a given effect—or as an evocation of the classical goddess of love."[78] For Warburg, astrology was "the persistent representative of a primitive consciousness, but at the same time it is the essential component of an emerging instrumental rationality—cultural enlightenment." Warburg saw "both mimeticism and its opposite, scientific objectivism, at work" in the practice of astrology.[79]

Warburg's work on astrological imagery resulted in one of his most widely read essays: "Italian Art and International Astrology in the Palazzo Schifanoia, Ferrara."[80] This was presented as a lecture at the Art Historical Congress in Rome in 1912, a gathering of art historians from across Europe that Warburg helped to organize. Dating from 1469–70, the frescoes by Francesco del Cossa, Ercole de' Roberti, and others in the Palazzo Schifanoia embodied the bifurcated manner in which the Renaissance appropriated antiquity: the images combined Olympian deities with astral demons that had passed from Hellenistic to Indian, Arabic, and medieval European astrology. In this single fresco cycle, Warburg found primitive fetishism combined with the sublimation of astrological imagery in humanistic scholarship. Magic was transformed into a means of learning and the basis was being laid for the transformation of astrology into modern astronomy. The lecture earned him widespread recognition in the academic community and is now commonly used as a means of introducing students to methods which Warburg sometimes described as "iconology."[81]

By the time the lecture was delivered in 1912, Warburg was much consulted on matters of research and his library was increasingly used by the scholarly community. In 1909, he had bought the house at 114 Heilwigstraße where he lived until the end of his life; he needed more room to house his private library. Warburg was also gaining some recognition among the general public. Upon the publication of an essay in 1911 entitled "Two Scenes from King Maximilian's Captivity in Bruges on a Sheet of Sketches by the So-Called Master of the Housebook," the *Hamburgischer Correspondent* described Warburg as the "well-known local art scholar." "This fine publication," it continued, "makes the public wish again to read and hear more from Dr. Warburg than his genteel reticence allows."[82] By 1912, Warburg was also heavily involved in various public and private initiatives. He was appointed as an expert consultant to Hamburg's government commission for archaeology in 1909 and participated in the founding of the Cassel Foundation in 1912, an institution that promoted academic contacts and interchange between England and Germany. He was also hired by Albert Ballin, General director of the Hamburg-America Line, to advise the company on the pictorial decoration of the steamship *Imperator*, at the time, the largest passenger ship in the world.[83] Describing himself as "an honest broker of artistic culture," his advice was also sought by private citizens on the purchase of artworks and he was often instrumental in establishing contacts between artists and prospective buyers.[84] In January of 1912, Warburg was called to the chair of art history in Halle, which had been previously occupied by Adolph Goldschmidt. But he again refused to relinquish his independence, in part, because of his involvement in the campaign for the founding of a university in Hamburg, a goal that was finally achieved in 1919.[85] In acknowledgment of the patriotic element of his refusal of the offer from Halle, Hamburg's senate conferred the title of professor on Warburg in 1913.

The First World War proved to Warburg that barbarism and irrationality did not belong to the past; he suffered horribly under the weight of its events. Early in the struggle, he decided to use the weapon he had at hand, his library, in a desperate effort to understand humanity's descent into unreason.[86] These years saw him engaged in the feverish collection and cataloguing of newspaper articles, pamphlets, brochures, and books—every article of printed matter that documented the war's major events, worldwide reactions to them and the effects of propaganda. In a turmoil of emotion, he sought to combat propaganda and understand the truth. But as we will see in chapter five, Warburg was also an ardent supporter of Germany's war effort. When Italy signed the Treaty of London on 26 April 1915—committing the country to war in alliance with Britain, France, and Russia—Warburg cut himself loose from his concern with Italian culture. Henceforth, he sought to apply his knowledge and experience of political propaganda to another period of crisis in German history, the Reformation.[87] The fruits of his investigations were first presented as lectures in the autumn of 1917 and published in 1920 under the title "Pagan-Antique Prophecy in Words and Images in the Age of Luther." In this essay, Warburg examined the popular astrological pamphlets and literature of the early sixteenth century. In so doing, he demonstrated how humanists like Melancthon, who aided Germany in its struggle for liberation from the Christian paganism of Rome, were themselves in the grip of superstitious fears with their talk of comets, portents, prophecies, and their belief in astrology. Once again, Warburg emphasized the persistence of irrationality in human thought. In showing up the polarity of reason and unreason in the human mind, he claimed that "the historian of civilization furnishes new grounds for a more profoundly positive critique of a historiography that rests on a purely chronological theory of development."[88]

This feverish work had a debilitating effect on Warburg's body and mind. He suffered from sleeplessness and fear, especially the fear of falling seriously ill; he became increasingly pessimistic, irritable, and bad tempered. All his life, he was prey to depressions, anxieties, and obsessions, never forgetting that the continuation of his work was threatened by psychosomatic processes over which he had only limited control.[89] Warburg knew he was fighting for his sanity. His breakdown coincided with the collapse of Imperial Germany; in October 1918 he suffered a mental collapse, a fate he long feared would befall him. He later recorded an account of the crisis which precipitated his institutionalization:

> On November 18 1918, I became very afraid for my family. So I took out a pistol and wanted to kill myself and my family. You know, it's because bolshevism was coming. Then my daughter Detta said to me, "But father, what are you doing?" Then my wife struggled with me and tried to take the weapon away from me. And then Frede, my younger daughter, called Malice (Max and Alice, my brother and his wife). They came immediately with the car and brought Senator Petersen and Dr. Franke with them. Petersen said to me: "Warburg, I have never asked anything from you. Now I am asking you please to come to the clinic with me, for you are ill."[90]

In 1921, after stays in clinics in Hamburg and Jena, Warburg was transferred to the Bellevue Sanatorium in Kreuzlingen, Switzerland, which was presided over by a student of Freud, Ludwig Binswanger. Here he was diagnosed as a manic-depressive schizophrenic and did not return to Hamburg until 1924.[91]

In response to an inquiry about Warburg's case made by Freud, Binswanger wrote a rather pessimistic report about his patient in November 1921:

> Already in his childhood Prof V. [that is, Aby Warburg] showed signs of anxiety and obsession; as a student, he had already expressed delusional ideas; he was never free from obsessional fears, etc.; and his literary productivity greatly suffered from this. On this basis, a very serious psychosis set in, probably set off by a pre-senile state, and the material, which until then had been elaborated neurotically, was expressed in a psychotic form. Combined with this was an intense psychomotor excitation, which is also persistently present,

although it is subject to extreme fluctuations. Here he has been placed in the locked ward, but in the afternoon he is usually calm enough so that he can receive visitors, have tea with us, go out on excursions, etc.

He is now still quite dominated by his fears and defensive maneuvers, which remain on the border between obsession and delusion, such that, despite his capacities for formal logic being completely intact, there is no more place for any activity in the scientific domain. He is interested in everything, possesses excellent judgment concerning people and the world, his memory is outstanding; but it is possible to focus his attention on scientific themes only for very brief moments.

"I do not believe," Binswanger concluded, "that a restoration of the situation *quo ante* of the acute psychosis or a resumption of his scientific activity will be possible."[92] Fortunately, Binswanger was mistaken and Warburg secured his release from the sanatorium by proving his self-control in the presentation of a slide lecture to fellow patients. Published first in English in 1939 as "A Lecture on Serpent Ritual," Warburg recalled his experiences during his trip to America in 1895.[93] He described how the Hopi Indians sought to avert famine through symbolic manipulation of lightning, which they believed produced rain. They did this by dancing with snakes, the tangible symbols of lightning. For Warburg, the ambiguity of the snake—which could be both healing and destructive—stood for the double-edged influence of antiquity's psychological legacy and for the ambivalence of imagery itself. In keeping with his rejection of historical linearity, he did not perceive the ritual dance as simply a transitional stage from magic to logic, but understood it as a simultaneous act of primitive magic and a quest for enlightenment. In this respect, it could be seen as the counterpart to modern man's mastery of electricity.

After a six-year absence, Warburg returned to Hamburg to find his private library transformed. From 1921, Saxl had undertaken a program of reorganization and institutionalization, which saw the collection opened to a wider academic public; lectures were also organized and published. Transferred from the confines of his private dwelling to a new structure built on the adjoining plot of land, the library opened its doors, in 1926, as the Kulturwissenschaftliche Bibliothek Warburg.[94] With Aby Warburg as its director, it was soon functioning as part of the University of Hamburg and attracted both young and established academics, scholars like the art historian Erwin Panofsky, and the philosopher Ernst Cassirer.[95]

Speaking of himself as someone who had returned from the land of the dead, these years saw Warburg immersed once more in scholarly work and research.[96] From 1925, he conducted seminars at the University of Hamburg on the Florentine Renaissance and, most famously, on Jacob Burckhardt in 1926/27. From 1927, Warburg's interest in the role of cultural and social memory was directed toward the production of a picture atlas which he entitled *Mnemosyne*, or *Memory*. Presented as a stock of images suspended in collective memory, the atlas was meant to show how antiquity provided the material for the European language of pictorial representation; it was to chart the journey of images and ideas over time and across space.[97] Unfortunately, the atlas was incomplete when Warburg died suddenly of a heart attack on 26 October 1929. A memorial service was held at the Ohlsdorf crematorium with several Hamburg senators in attendance. Many wreaths were laid including one on behalf of the senate.[98] Aby Warburg was celebrated as a significant figure in Hamburg's social, cultural, and civic life.

After the death of its founder, the Warburg family asked Fritz Saxl to become director of the Kulturwissenschaftliche Bibliothek Warburg. In the months following the Wall Street crash of 1929, the Library continued to function mainly through the munificence of Warburg's brother Felix, who had been living in the United States since 1894. Plans were laid to publish Warburg's collected writings and these appeared in 1932. But soon after the Nazi seizure of power in the following year, it became clear to Saxl that "our work in Germany had come to an end."[99] Concerned to preserve the tradition of German humanism and the library's holdings, the members of the library's staff and the Warburg family planned for its emigration to London.[100] Fears that the German authorities would protest did not materialize; they expressed their willingness to tolerate the transfer as long as the Warburg family did not publish a statement hostile to the Nazi regime. When the freighter *Hermia* left Hamburg on 12 December 1933 with approximately 60,000 books on board, it was with the official understanding that the library would be on loan to London for only three years. The tragic events of German history, however, prevented its return to Hamburg and it was incorporated into the University of London in 1944 as the Warburg Institute.

III

Warburg's words, quoted in the epigraph to this chapter, speak of a sense of mission frustrated and unfulfilled, the "roaring lion" become "lap-dog." Warburg certainly gave leonine proportions to his scholarly research and was moved by a tremendous sense of purpose, even to the extent that he expected his family to subordinate themselves to his work.[101] But his unpublished papers are strewn with the wreckage of many projects. In April 1907, he noted in his diary that "it looks as if, up to my fortieth year, there had been a blockage in the association fibers between those carrying my general ideas and those concerned with the visual impressions that underlie these ideas, and as if this had prevented them from interweaving naturally and crossing the threshold of consciousness in this form."[102] But the blockage did not clear in later life; by the time of his death, Warburg had published scarcely 350 pages. The quotation also suggests that Warburg struggled with the fact that he never held an academic post. This problem, however, was largely of his own making; as noted earlier, he was offered university positions but did not accept them.

More particularly, the words, "I should have been a roaring lion in the Judean desert," remind us that Warburg was a self-conscious German Jew. The reference to the "Judean desert" speaks of isolation, and the entire phrase suggests that

Warburg aspired to this. It seems more likely, however, that he is commenting on the inevitability of his intellectual isolation, rather than its desirability; Warburg's scholarly work was both idiosyncratic and pursued outside of the official academic community. But his words are not simply an expression of any isolation he felt as a Jew in Imperial Germany; as his assistant Gertrude Bing wrote, "he never forgot that Imperial Germany treated the Jews well ... and he didn't like to hear people criticize the fact."[103]

Some authors have argued for the formative, hermeneutic influences of Warburg's Jewish identity on his scholarly preoccupations.[104] Matthew Rampley has suggested, quite reasonably, that Warburg's interest in anti-Semitism was aroused, in part, because it "presented a parallel example of the resurgence of the primitive."[105] Charlotte Schoell-Glass has gone further to contend that the sum of Warburg's scholarship was a response to anti-Semitism.[106] Understandably, his longed-for assimilation of German Jews as full members of German society left him sensitive to the presence of anti-Semitism and there is no doubt that it offended his deeply-felt patriotism. As a young man, Warburg was outraged by his first serious encounter with anti-Semites in the weeks immediately following his arrival at the University of Straßburg in 1889.[107] In November of that year, he wrote his mother that someday he would "devote himself to solving the Jewish question so their descendants wouldn't suffer professional discrimination."[108] He encountered similar anti-Semitic prejudice during his military service in 1892–93. Over the years, he collected numerous press cuttings documenting anti-Semitic outrages and, in his youthful zeal, he continued to think of turning his efforts against the problem.[109] He was horrified by the Dreyfus Affair, and in 1900 he planned to write an essay for the Hamburg journal *Der Lotse* that never materialized.[110] In 1916, at the height of the First World War, Warburg helped his brother Max pen a memorandum entitled "The Jewish Question in the Framework of German Politics," which criticized the government's unequal treatment of German-Jewish soldiers.[111] Examined at greater length in chapter five, this was distributed by Max Warburg in the official circles of Berlin. It argued that equal treatment of German Jews was of critical importance for Germany in terms of its international reputation and the legitimization of its war effort. In December 1917, Max Warburg was proposed by Hamburg's senate as its preferred candidate in a senatorial election. To his surprise, his candidacy was rejected by the citizens' assembly, an act which the press interpreted as anti-Semitic.[112] In sum, there is no doubting that the specter of anti-Semitism cast a shadow over Warburg's life.

Nevertheless, it is an oversimplification to view his sensitivity to anti-Semitism as the principal impetus behind his scholarship. Apart from the memorandum penned in 1916, there is little material on the subject in Warburg's own hand. Furthermore, it is important to remember that the current of anti-Semitism in Hamburg was much less substantial than that in other German cities.[113] That is not to say it did not exist: many examples could be cited. Percy Ernst Schramm's grandmother, a Protestant matron of Hamburg's *Großbürgertum*, listed four categories of unacceptable marriage partners for her younger sister: officers, nobles, actors, and Jews.[114] Julius von Eckardt wrote that "despite a decided friendliness toward the Jews, the Old Hamburg elite [*Althambürgertum*] closed themselves off socially against the 'Jewish element.' With very few exceptions, Hamburg's wealthy and respected Jews stood outside of 'Society.'"[115] But the fact remains that, as a commercial republic, the social tone was not set by officers and aristocrats. Thus, on the subject of anti-Semitism, Moritz Warburg once remarked that "we are lucky here in Hamburg that it provides no soil for such nasty acts."[116] Along with legal emancipation came acceptance of Jews "not only as commercial and professional partners, but also as officials in associational life and public administration, and friends in social life."[117] As a young student, Warburg attended the Johanneum along with the sons of the Hamburg elite, and along with other Jews he played a prominent role in Hamburg's cultural life.[118] If he failed to gain election as a senator, Max Warburg sat for many years as a conservative member of Hamburg's citizens' assembly; he was also one of the few German Jews who had access to the Kaiser. To look beyond the Hamburg context, the fact that Warburg never took up a university post was not because he had fewer opportunities as a German Jew. On the contrary, he maintained friendly contacts with Wilhelm Bode and others among the upper echelons of the German academic administration.[119] Ultimately, his scholarly preoccupations were the product of a complex web of intellectual and cultural influences.[120]

At the same time, there is no doubting that he remained conflicted about his Jewish identity; he once described himself as a "futurist" sitting none too comfortably on the fence between "Zionists" and "those who assimilate."[121] Yet Warburg considered himself to be every bit a citizen of Hamburg and a German as he was a Jew, and there would be no adherence to Jewish practice in his lifestyle. Identifying specifically Jewish characteristics in Warburg's thought remains a speculative affair, not least because he tried consciously to eradicate them.[122] Of course, he could not simply jettison his Jewish ancestry, nor would the society in which he lived allow him to do so; his sometime student, Carl Georg Heise, reports that a sense of having betrayed his community and family plagued Warburg during his mental breakdown in 1918.[123] But in 1887, he wrote to his mother that "I am not at all ashamed to be a Jew, on the contrary I am trying to show others that representatives of my kind are well suited, in accordance with their talents, to insert themselves as useful links in the chain of present-day cultural and political developments."[124] This pronouncement could be read as evidence that Warburg was, as his mother suspected, given to self-shame and self-hatred. It may be taken as indicative of a refusal to face the fact that many Germans did not accept Jews as full Germans. But the fact remains that in spite of, or because of, painful moments when he was made to feel an outsider, Warburg insisted on subjugating his Jewish self and emphasizing his acculturated German self. As a student, his refusal to conform to Jewish religious and cultural observance was a source of grief for his parents; his unwillingness to comply with dietary laws, for example, led to bitter debate with his father. In a letter to

Moritz Warburg, he wrote that "since I do not arrange my course of study according to the quality of ritual restaurants but according to the quality of my teachers, I do not eat ritually."[125] At the University of Bonn, he mixed well with Germany's social elite and took up fencing. An ardent patriot, he undertook his military service in 1892/93 with enthusiasm; many years later his brother Max would say that Aby Warburg believed in Germany's victory in the First World War because he believed in the superiority of German culture.[126] If it was difficult for many German Jews to see past Martin Luther's anti-Semitism, Warburg viewed him as "one of the great liberators of mankind, a heroic figure fighting for enlightenment and the emancipation of faith from the shackles of a narrow dogma."[127] He even wrote that Luther "had helped to free him from a Jewish orthodoxy that had tried to enslave him."[128] Furthermore, he was critical of Zionism and, in 1929, referred to Zionists as "desperados of this life."[129]

A major source of tension between Warburg, his parents, grandparents, and siblings arose with his courtship of Mary Hertz and the question of his children's upbringing. Mary Hertz's family was only recently converted to Protestantism from Judaism and this probably served to sharpen the conflict engendered by the couple's betrothal. There was no precedent in the Warburg family of marrying outside their religious faith and Moritz Warburg pleaded with his son to reconsider his choice of bride.[130] But all appeals fell on deaf ears and, when the couple married on 8 October 1897 in Wiesbaden, Warburg's parents were not present. They met the newlyweds the following day, however, and it seems that Mary Hertz was soon accepted by the Warburg family.

One of the most important reasons behind Warburg's obstinate separation from his Jewish upbringing was his opposition to religious practice as primitive and irrational. When he made notes for an autobiography in the early 1920s, Warburg commented on how he had left school as a convinced evolutionist and found it unbearable that man should bow under the yoke of God.[131] Writing his mother in 1887, he told her that he wanted "to shake off that which could never ever organically adapt itself to my being."[132] When, in 1908, he was sent a questionnaire by the Hamburg Jewish community, he returned it blank and with a note which read "I am in no way subject to the Jewish community, neither as member, nor as object, rather I quite explicitly resigned from it and am to be regarded by it as a Dissident."[133] Upon the death of his father in 1910, Warburg refused to attend the funeral and to recite the mourner's *kaddish*. In a letter to his brother Max, he explained that the memorial in his father's synagogue, which was presided over by Rabbi Nobel and officials of the Talmud Torah School:

> acquires, in a natural and subjectively absolutely justified manner, the character of a demonstration for the faithful Jews. I do not wish to disturb this. I am after all in the eyes of others an unreliable customer, but in my own eyes a political opponent of elementary schools such as the Talmud Torah School, and above all I am "Cherem" [banned] through my mixed marriage and as the father of non-denominational children whom I shall never lead to Judaism.

The mourner's *kaddish*, he emphasized, signified acceptance of a moral inheritance and he would not make himself "guilty of such public hypocrisy."[134]

Ultimately, scholars must guard against reductive understandings of the effect of Warburg's Jewish heritage on his scholarship and be open to the complex nature of his identity. George Mosse, however, made Warburg into a symbol of German Jewry in the Weimar Republic: politically left-wing, committed to the ideals of *Bildung* and the Enlightenment, and hypersensitive to anti-Semitism. Invoking the specter of the Third Reich, he pictured him as an anti-fascist hero.[135] Of course, it goes without saying that if he had lived to see it achieve political power, Warburg would have been appalled by Nazism and become its victim. The point to be made, however, is that scholars must avoid an anachronistic interpretation of what it meant for Warburg, and others, to be a German Jew. Warburg's work was an important contribution to scholarship by an acculturated German who considered his Jewish origins to be but one of the building blocks of his identity. While committed to the ideals of *Bildung* and the Enlightenment, he was, like many other German Jews, politically and socially conservative, a monarchist, and an ardent nationalist. As such, he was not always the preserver of what Mosse has called "Germany's better self" and was not forced by anti-Semitism to be so.[136]

Furthermore, Warburg's interest in the work of the German Expressionists or the Italian Futurists cannot be touted as representative of the cultural stance of the German-Jewish economic elite, nor can it be understood as indicative of a special affinity between German Jews and modernity. As Werner Mosse has argued, the German-Jewish economic elite played little part in German modernism, whether in painting, literature, or music; theirs was a liberal-bourgeois, not a radical or revolutionary, culture.[137] Of course, while amounting to less than one percent of the population in 1910, German Jews were overrepresented in "modern" professions such as finance, large-scale commerce, journalism, publishing, medicine, and scientific research.[138] Given their prominence in pursuits that enjoyed high visibility, German reactionaries and conservatives routinely defined German Jews as "modern" and explained the destructive aspects of modernity by its association with Jewish depravity.[139] Several outstanding German-Jewish figures, like Max Liebermann and Paul and Bruno Cassirer, were indeed influential agents of cultural modernism.[140] But most German Jews shared the traditional aesthetic tastes of their countrymen, although they were perhaps less ready to condemn modern art as an assault on the purity of German culture.[141]

While taking "roaring lion" to be a proclamation of his work's importance, it leads us to a phenomenon that is often posited as the source of Warburg's idiosyncratic ideas: his mental illness. On one of his visits to the Swiss sanatorium where Warburg was confined in the early 1920s, Heise heard terrible screams coming from the building. When they met, Warburg said to Heise, "Did you just hear a lion roar? Imagine, that was me!"[142] Considering his interest in historical psychology, many scholars point to the highly personal aspects of Warburg's reading of the past; there can be no doubt that he had a considerable personal investment in his scholarship.[143] It is plausible that Warburg's interest in the oscillation of consciousness between superstitious fear and rational, conceptual thought—as a permanent element of humanity's existence—was the result of very personal experiences. Gombrich may be correct when he writes that his constant struggle against his own demons "merged in his mind with the struggle of mankind against irrationality and primitive impulses."[144] Bernd Roeck has suggested that Warburg's understanding of cultural history was born of his own mental illness and that one of Warburg's great representatives of humanity's struggle against unreason, the Florentine merchant Francesco Sassetti, "is at the same time Warburg himself."[145] His interest in demonic forces and the irrational and their role as a characteristic feature in mythological and astrological traditions may well have grown from a consciousness of his own mental state. He may not have been detached from his own body and unconscious when he wrote passages such as "all mankind is eternally and at all times schizophrenic."[146] But attempting to draw a definitive causal link between Warburg's illness and his theories of art and culture involves much speculation. The evidence to support such a link is either lacking or, in the case of the diaries kept by Warburg while in the sanatorium at Kreuzlingen, uninformative to the nonpsychiatrist, as Gombrich has already suggested.[147] Moreover, such speculation hinders an appreciation of the extent to which Warburg's ideas were a product of intellectual currents extending from the Enlightenment to the Fin-de-Siècle.

Finally, if Warburg envisioned himself as a "lap-dog," he ensured that his listeners knew his proper home was the quarter of Hamburg where one could find such an "adornment": Harvestehude, home of Hamburg's *Großbürgertum*. As with many of those involved in Hamburg's cultural life, Warburg would have agreed with Lichtwark when he wrote, "I can do nothing else, I must see and feel everything as a Hamburger."[148] Historians now recognize the extent to which national unification failed to unite Germans; until the First World War and thereafter, German society continued to be divided along class, ethnic, religious, gender, and geographical lines. Compounding these divisions was the persistence of strong local and regional identities. In many parts of the new nation, calling oneself a German did not preclude holding onto any one of a number of other self-interpretations.[149] In Warburg's case, he was not only a proud citizen of Hamburg, but was proud of his status as a member of the city's elite.[150] It would even seem that his academic interests were colored by that elite's pragmatic, mercantile attitude. He took an active interest in the family business and often described his academic work in terms derived form mercantile life: "I'm an academic private banker," he wrote to Max Warburg in 1906, "whose credit is as good as that of the Reichsbank."[151] Furthermore, while his thought was, in many respects, unconventional and pioneering, his lifestyle was strictly bourgeois. As Felix Gilbert has written, Warburg's "own life showed him to set a disciplined, rational decision above patterns formed on the basis of traditions or emotions."[152]

IV

Warburg was but one of several individuals who concerned themselves with art in Hamburg's public realm, be it in the form of exhibitions, education, or the construction of public monuments. Certainly the most prominent, and the most studied, was Alfred Lichtwark. Apart from playing a leading role in shaping Hamburg's cultural life in the two decades before the First World War, the director of the Kunsthalle was one of the most respected and influential educators in the German Empire. Like Warburg, he was motivated by social and political concerns and his audience was principally Hamburg's middle classes. A comparison of their ideas will demonstrate the distinctive nature of Warburg's interests and aims with respect to art in Hamburg's public realm.

Both men shared certain political and cultural perspectives. They anticipated the political maturity of Germany's middle classes, but questioned its present fitness to lead the German Empire. In this respect, they echoed the concerns of the sociologist Max Weber (1864–1920). As previously mentioned, Warburg did not believe the aristocracy formed a suitable leadership for the nation. According to Lichtwark, the *Bürgertum* had already succeeded the aristocracy in the political, social, and economic leadership of the German Empire. Nonetheless, it was still much too uncultured to properly direct the Empire's future development.[153] Consequently, both men directed their pedagogical endeavors principally at Germany's middle classes in the hope of producing a cultured and intelligent *Bürgertum* capable of leading the German nation.

Lichtwark's ideal of a cultured middle class was to be achieved by creating cultivated consumers and educators. His cultural criticism was future-oriented and focused on the development of Germany as an industrial nation. As Peter Gay explains, "Lichtwark contended that an elevated German taste would give his country a better chance in a race among the nations in which it had been scoring badly."[154] "While the Germans slept," Lichtwark exclaimed, "its neighbors were awake and working."[155] With this in mind, he wrote voluminously on matters of art and education, sought to improve instruction in Hamburg's schools, and turned the Kunsthalle into an educational institution with the intention of inspiring and developing the aesthetic sensibilities of the *Bürgertum* and the artistic energies of the recently unified nation. As we will see in chapter two, it was Lichtwark's dynamism which Warburg once captured rather disparagingly with the epithet "Director Fireworks."[156]

The model of artistic achievement which Lichtwark presented to the *Bürgertum* was the work of contemporary German and French artists, and the Kunsthalle soon came to own one of the finest collections of modern art in Germany.[157] The following chapter explores this issue in greater depth and demonstrates that Warburg was also an enthusiastic supporter of artistic modernism. Nevertheless, Warburg and Lichtwark expressed differing views on matters of art and education. In 1898, Lichtwark published a historical study of Hamburg portraiture entitled *The Portrait in Hamburg*.[158] This was part of his attempt to revitalize neglected local talents and set a foundation for future artistic growth. But in a letter of 1905, Warburg expressed the damning indictment that, when it came to contemporary portraiture, Lichtwark was guilty of misunderstanding the characteristics of Hamburg's *Bürgertum* and of fostering their misrepresentation.[159] Warburg certainly did not align himself with those in Hamburg who opposed modern portraiture, especially the portrait of Mayor Carl Petersen commissioned by Lichtwark from Max Liebermann in 1891.[160] Yet seeming to forget Lichtwark's promotion of local artists, Warburg accused him of ignoring the artistic sobriety he saw as native to Hamburg. Lichtwark, he claimed, would do better to reconsider the virtues of earlier Hamburg artists like Julius Oldach (1804–30), than to encourage Hamburgers to patronize outsiders like the "theatrical poster painter" Franz von Stuck (1863–1928), a member of the Munich Academy and founding member of the Munich Secession.

In the same letter, Warburg states that concerning Lichtwark's "administrative technique and means of stimulating ideas, I long entertained factually grounded doubts."[161] It is well known that Lichtwark formulated specific plans for expanding and organizing the collection of paintings in the Kunsthalle. Yet Carl Georg Heise tells us that Warburg viewed Lichtwark's "unsystematic manner of collecting which did not clearly distinguish between personal taste and objective purpose" as "detestable." Equally disturbing for Warburg was what he saw as Lichtwark's "criminal neglect ... of the antique."[162] In an essay of 1909, Warburg emphasized the didactic importance of classical art and lamented how "crammed together in semi-darkness in Hamburg's art gallery, gods and heroes, who should greet the admirer on high and in clear light, exist as immigrants between decks."[163]

But perhaps the most significant charge leveled against Lichtwark was that his methods promoted "the all too pleasurable interaction with artworks."[164] It is certainly not the case that Lichtwark was adverse to the academic study of art. Yet this did not assuage Warburg's fears that his efforts to improve the cultural character of the *Bürgertum* encouraged a superficial approach to artworks. After all, Lichtwark had stated that one should see "art as an expression of feeling, not as knowledge," and explained that art education taught "the ability to enjoy art, or, as used to be said, understand art."[165] Thus he promoted a type of education in which the work of art affected the viewer unconsciously and indirectly. As Christiane Brosius explains, "With Lichtwark, and many other art educators around 1900, it was not so much critical judgment but 'pure feeling' that was the measure and ideal: only with its help could the quality of art be judged."[166] Germans had "for too long lived for intelligence," Lichtwark wrote. "It is time now for ethical, religious, and artistic energies to develop fully."[167] Yet for Warburg, it was a proper distance from emotion that was necessary for the serious engagement with art and that self-reflective calm from which enlightenment sprang. In his eyes, Lichtwark promoted an approach to art that lacked the intellectual depth and critical faculty essential to the task of producing responsible, enlightened individuals. Furthermore, Lichtwark's attempted reform of German taste was tied to an agenda of nationalism. Gay writes that "collective good taste in the arts was, to him, almost literally a matter of national health."[168] While there is no denying that Warburg was an ardent nationalist, he did not envision art education as tied to an expressly patriotic or economic agenda.

Also disturbing for Warburg was Lichtwark's belief that the best means of reforming German taste was through "serious dilettantism."[169] The artistic dilettantism of the middle classes was to act as an agent between artist and consumer and "form an important lever for the development of art and craft."[170] But for Warburg, artists had the infinitely important task of assimilating the psychological legacy of antiquity; an artist was "binding himself to operate as an organ of social memory" and from his perspective, dilettantes were not sufficiently educated to fulfill this function.[171] He wrote that "Hamburgers' lack of education—in relation to that of other states—is such that the patriotic dilettante lacks the critical standard, the enlightenment which antique culture brings to all historical contemplation."[172] Unreflective impressions and sensations could not be equated with the knowledge and self-conscious reflection critical for the cultivation of *Denkraum*. "Dilettantes!" Warburg wrote in 1908; "There is the danger that they will also be a threat as teachers and authors."[173] In his mind, there could be no surrogate for academically trained art educators directing the public to contemplation of art by professional artists.

Gombrich has emphasized the fact that Warburg was no John Ruskin; he did not preach to the nation, but to an academic and social elite.[174] His audience was that small portion of society that was capable of self-education, an elite cultural club that constituted itself as the public to be addressed. We have seen that he was connected to a circle of private scholars in Hamburg institutionalized in the Society of Bibliophiles. As Hans Wilhelm Eckardt has argued, this society stood in conscious confrontation with Lichtwark and his programs.[175] The purpose of this exclusive club was not the dissemination of literature for the betterment of society, but the collection of high quality editions; their audience was not the working-class public, but the society's members. While Hamburg's city library was criticized for its distance from the public and its allegiance to a small group of educated elite, Warburg remained a friend of its director, Robert Münzel, a man he believed well suited to be a "faithful custodian of the spiritual and intellectual treasures of the entire world."[176] If, as previously indicated, the lectures that Warburg gave in his library during his later years took on the air of a soirée, he once told Heise that "when I speak, I speak, of course, not for the many, but for my fellows."[177]

But there was at least one important occasion when Warburg deviated from this rule.[178] This was in 1905 and in response to the exigencies of Hamburg's social and political development. In the two decades before the First World War, working-class political organization brought industrial strife and demands for political reform to the city. By 1904, thirteen Social Democrats sat in the citizens' assembly, enough to entitle them to representation on the assembly's various committees and commissions.[179] As a response to the politicization of the working classes and the popularity of the Socialists, Hamburg witnessed concerted attempts at cultural reform. After 1890, as Jennifer Jenkins has indicated, elite societies were challenged by new associations with large memberships.[180] These promoted the democratization of middle-class culture as a cure to modern social and economic dislocation. A people's theater was founded in 1893, educational evenings were arranged by the Literary Society from 1898, concerts of classical music for the general public were organized by the Hamburg Friends of Music, and inexpensive reproductions of artworks were marketed by the Society of Hamburg Friends of Art. With Lichtwark as their guiding spirit, many of these groups drew their members from Hamburg's elite, people who saw it as the duty of the privileged classes to care for the ills of society.

Warburg was a sensitive observer of Hamburg's politics and his attitude regarding the political aspirations of the working classes was a complex one. On the one hand, he feared the prospect of social chaos. In a letter of 1909 he writes, "To me, the masses are tolerable only in a well-ordered state; a mediocre human animal in a controlled situation is bearable, but as 'an individual that runs free' a completely intolerable product of imaginary liberation."[181] On the other hand, Warburg recognized the benefits of educating the large mass of Hamburg's working poor and of stimulating "the popular appreciation for art."[182] He was a financial supporter of the Volksheim from 1903 and his brother-in-law, Wilhelm Hertz, was a member of the board of directors. Financed by the donations of wealthy patrons, the Volksheim was modeled on the English social reform project of Toynbee Hall. The patrician elite who directed the institution saw its mission as the eradication of class conflict. This was to be achieved by fostering contacts between the middle and working classes that would engender mutual respect.[183] Rejecting the role of Germany's Social Democratic Party as destructive, the Volksheim established an educational program of lectures and exhibitions designed to transform the working classes by instilling a process of self-cultivation. Aesthetic education figured prominently as an object lesson in the values, morals, and history symbolized in artworks. It was also thought that lifestyles could be altered if aesthetic taste was refined by training the eye to appreciate art. This would result in a civilizing of the working classes; it would create an educated, cultured, moral, and patriotic public. At the time that it founded its first facility in Rothenburgsort, in 1905, many among Hamburg's patrician and middle classes saw the goals of the Volksheim as particularly urgent and desirable.[184]

Hamburg's political and social problems were very much on Warburg's mind in 1905, the year he mounted his exhibition in the Volksheim. Entitled "Dürer As Mirror of Himself and His Time—100 Drawings," the exhibition opened on 14 May, with an illustrated lecture by Warburg. The artworks displayed were reproductions of Dürer's drawings and were exhibited by themes such as "Still life," "Apostles," and "Dürer's family." Warburg had no reservations about employing reproductions; in this instance, the artworks' authenticity was not as important as the viewer and how he or she perceived the work of art. However, it was his hope that visitors to the exhibition would be inspired to seek out the originals in the Kunsthalle.

Among Warburg's papers are two drafts for the introductory lecture he delivered under the title "Dürer as Human Being and Artist." This was accompanied by forty-nine slides. Even when directed at a working-class audience, Warburg would not dilute his intellectually rigorous approach to art-historical research. Indeed, he told his audience to view the artworks as if they were confronting "a book that one wanted to read."[185] The aim was not simply a formal analysis of Dürer's art, nor an explanation of its iconography. In keeping with the intentions of his scholarship, Warburg sought "to supply a historical corrective to the narrowly aesthetic view so often taken" of the Renaissance.[186] He wanted to lay bare the deeper levels of the artwork and set the creative power of the artist into the context of his times; his goal was to demonstrate how Dürer, in his life and art, reacted to an age of intellectual, religious, and cultural change. The exhibition was intended to "help the visitors to look beyond the tough and unfamiliar historical shell of the work to its universal humanity."[187]

In his lecture, Warburg established the historical context for Dürer's art through a discussion of Martin Luther and the Reformation. He also treated the artist's personality and his family life. The exhibition placed its emphasis on Dürer's self-portraits as documents of a self-conscious individual progressing to artistic maturity. Warburg chose reproductions of drawings as opposed to paintings because he felt drawings related Dürer's personal impressions in a particularly strong and fresh manner.[188] They were a storehouse of the artist's energy as a "membrane of psychological expression."[189]

Thus the Dürer exhibition was more than a demonstration of "a chapter in the self-education of humanity toward enlightenment about itself and the world."[190] At a time of heightened social tension in Hamburg, it was an attempt to mitigate the potential dangers of humanity's schizophrenic condition through a serious engagement with Dürer's art. In this respect, Warburg, and the Volksheim itself, demonstrate a debt to German Enlightenment thinkers and the concept of *Bildung*.[191] A program for individual education, cultivation, and self improvement, *Bildung* described the personal cultivation of reason and aesthetic taste with the purpose of raising the individual from superstition to enlightenment; it emphasized "that self-control which the bourgeois prized so highly."[192] The goal of *Bildung* was "the enlightened, responsible human being who possessed the ability to form his own judgment in a calm conceptual space."[193] Instead of simply attempting to cultivate aesthetic taste, Warburg was presenting his audience with a historical figure who was master of the mental space that he referred to as *Denkraum*. The concept of *Bildung* also formed the foundation of Lichtwark's ideas, and as Jenkins emphasizes, cultural reformers considered aesthetic questions to be "about more than painting and literature; they also addressed liberal views of social order, particularly the continuing importance of *Bildung* for ordering society."[194] As noted earlier, Warburg found the masses tolerable "only in a well-ordered state." But he feared that the democratization of culture, and the education of the masses by reform pedagogues in particular, would lead to the devaluation of *Bildung* and the dissolution of humanism.

Clearly, Warburg's ambitions extended beyond any practical attempt to ameliorate the political condition of Hamburg's working classes and the social conflict this brought to the city. By promoting the serious contemplation of Dürer's art, he was hoping not only to create an appetite for enlightenment, but to prompt the cultivation of *Denkraum* among the working-class viewers. Furthermore, he hoped to turn this intellectual space of calm reflection and rational orientation into a permanent social function. For Warburg it was "the critical self-reflection—*sophrosyne*—of the individual that resists the call of mass intoxication."[195] "Art is not a field of luxury," he told his audience; the merely formal appreciation of art was overly concerned with enjoyment and sensation and left too little room for enlightenment.[196] Adapting his language to suit the audience, Warburg said that "Dürer was a foreman of this enlightenment and a real worker."[197] Yet in the case of his Volksheim exhibition, Warburg's own efforts as teacher met with failure. This is not surprising given the ambitious intellectual demands that he made on his working-class audience. Seventy people attended his lecture, but few visited the exhibition. Most of those who did, the Volksheim reported, found it unintelligible.[198] In June 1905, the third of three lectures by Friedrich von Borstel—a member of the board of directors—to accompany the exhibition was canceled due to continued low attendance.[199] The exhibition was closed in July. The Volksheim subsequently reported the inability of visitors to project their thoughts into a distant historical period and noted the "insensitivity of the unschooled eye for the intimate appeal of the drawings." It even decided that the designation "exhibition" was best avoided in the future, as it fostered the image of the Volksheim as a museum, an image the board did not want to project.[200]

Warburg ascribed the exhibition's failure to the fact that "no interpreter was constantly present" to help the visitors interpret the drawings correctly.[201] With this remark, he seems to question the efficacy of his own efforts by acknowledging their intellectually elitist nature. In any case, despite his attempts, and those of the Volksheim, to lessen social tension, it was as the result of continued confrontation that Hamburg's working classes made their political gains before 1914. Nonetheless, Warburg believed that "all patrons of the Volksheim are not really naïve," and suggested that progress could be made with "greater guns and a more refined and persistent cannonade."[202] Immersion in his scholarship would keep him from undertaking this himself and most of his later efforts on behalf of the public good would be directed, not at Hamburg's working classes, but at its middle classes and patrician elite. Yet the Volksheim exhibition highlights essential aspects of Warburg's involvement in Hamburg's civic affairs, which are pursued in the following chapters: his sensitivity to the political and social transformation of Hamburg; his belief that the public consumption of art could help ameliorate the social and psychological tensions that came with this transformation; and the degree to which his ideas were shaped by his scholarship and pursued, even in the public realm, with an uncompromising intellectual rigor. Writing of Warburg after he was discharged from the sanatorium in Kreuzlingen, Fritz Saxl said that "he lived and worked convinced that the scholar does not choose his vocation but that in all he does he is obeying a higher command."[203] This was the conviction that Warburg brought to his involvement with art in Hamburg's public realm.

Notes

1. Warburg Institute Archive, London (hereafter WIA) III.17.2: "Warburgismen" gesammelt von Max Warburg, p. 1.
2. WIA. III.10.3: Diary 1903–14, p. 95.
3. For work that emphasizes this aspect of his life see Bernd Roeck, *Der junge Aby Warburg* (Munich, 1997); Georg Syamken, "'Amburghese di cuore,'" in *Aby M. Warburg. "Ekstatische Nymphe ... trauernder Flußgott": Portrait eines Gelehrten*, eds. Robert Galitz and Brita Reimers (Hamburg, 1995), pp. 24–31; Anne Marie Meyer, "Aby Warburg in his Early Correspondence," *The American Scholar* 57 (1988), pp. 445–452.
4. Niall Ferguson, "Max Warburg and German Politics: The Limits of Financial Power in Wilhelmine Germany," in *Wilhelminism and Its Legacies: German Modernities, Imperialism, and the Meanings of Reform, 1890–1930*, eds. Geoff Eley and James Retallack (New York and Oxford, 2003), p. 186.
5. See David Farrer, *The Warburgs: The Story of a Family* (New York, 1974); Eduard Rosenbaum and Ari Sherman, *M.M. Warburg & Co., 1798–1938: Merchant Bankers of Hamburg* (London, 1979).
6. Ron Chernow, *The Warburgs: The Twentieth-Century Odyssey of a Remarkable Jewish Family* (New York, 1993), p. 60.
7. See Aby Warburg, "Sandro Botticelli's *Birth of Venus and Spring*," in idem, *The Renewal of Pagan Antiquity: Contributions to the Cultural History of the European Renaissance*, trans. David Britt (Los Angeles, 1999), pp. 89–156.
8. See Matthew Rampley, *The Remembrance of Things Past: On Aby M. Warburg and Walter Benjamin* (Wiesbaden, 2000).
9. Warburg used this expression on several occasions; see for example WIA. GC: Warburg to Johannes Geffcken, 16 January 1926; WIA. GC: Warburg to Max Friedländer, 10 March 1926.
10. Rampley, *Remembrance of Things Past*, p. 52.
11. WIA. III.45.2; TS of 45.1: Symbolismus als Umfangsbestimmung, 1896–1901, p. 26.
12. Warburg quoted and translated in Dorothea McEwan, "Aby Warburg's (1866–1929) Dots and Lines. Mapping the Diffusion of Astrological Motifs in Art History," *German Studies Review* 29, no. 2 (May 2006), p. 243.
13. Warburg quoted and translated in Philippe-Alain Michaud, *Aby Warburg and the Image in Motion* (New York, 2004), p. 301.
14. Richard Woodfield, "Warburg's 'Method,'" in *Art History as Cultural History: Warburg's Projects*, ed. idem (Amsterdam, 2001), p. 267.
15. Warburg quoted and translated in Michaud, *Aby Warburg and the Image in Motion*, p. 233.
16. Rampley, *The Remembrance of Things Past*, p. 88.
17. Warburg quoted and translated in ibid., p. 126, nte. 240.
18. McEwan, "Aby Warburg's (1866–1929) Dots and Lines," p. 244.

19. Matthew Rampley, "Mimes and Allegory. On Aby Warburg and Walter Benjamin," in *Art History As Cultural History*, p. 125.
20. Michaud, *Aby Warburg and the Image in Motion*, p. 238.
21. Roland Kany, "Schon die Mitwelt versetzte Aby Warburg unter die Wandelsterne," *Frankfurter Allgemeine Zeitung*, 11 March 1999.
22. Ernst Gombrich, *Aby Warburg: An Intellectual Biography*, 2nd ed. (Chicago, 1986); idem, "Aby Warburg und der Evolutionismus des 19. Jahrhunderts," in *Aby M. Warburg: "Ekstatische Nymphe,"* pp. 52–73.
23. For instance, Rampley, *The Remembrance of Things Past*; Georges Didi-Huberman, "Foreword," in Michaud, *Aby Warburg and the Image in Motion*, pp. 7–19.
24. Gombrich, *Aby Warburg*, p. 37.
25. See Roger Chickering, *Karl Lamprecht: A German Academic Life (1856–1915)* (Atlantic Highlands, NJ, 1993); Luise Schorn-Schütte, *Karl Lamprecht: Kulturgeschichtsschreibung zwischen Wissenschaft und Politik* (Göttingen, 1984); for Lamprecht's influence on Warburg see Kathryn Brush "Aby Warburg and the Cultural Historian Karl Lamprecht," in *Art History as Cultural History*, pp. 65–92; Gombrich, *Aby Warburg*, pp. 30–37; less useful is Christiane Brosius, *Kunst als Denkraum: zum Bildungsbegriff von Aby Warburg* (Pfaffenweiler, 1997), p. 122ff.
26. Kurt W. Forster, "Introduction," in Warburg, *The Renewal of Pagan Antiquity*, p. 7.
27. See Gombrich, *Aby Warburg*, p. 68ff.
28. Matthew Rampley, "From Symbol to Allegory: Aby Warburg's Theory of Art," *Art Bulletin* 79, no. 1 (March 1997), pp. 41–55.
29. Peter Burke, "History and Anthropology in 1900," in *Photographs at the Frontier: Warburg in America, 1895–1896*, eds. Benedetta Cestelli Guidi and Nicholas Mann (London, 1998), pp. 20–27.
30. Gombrich, *Aby Warburg*, p. 12.
31. Georges Didi-Huberman, *L'image survivante. Histoire de l'art et temps des fantômes selon Aby Warburg* (Paris, 2002).
32. WIA. GC: Warburg to Jacques Dwelshauers, 27 July 1909.
33. Warburg quoted and translated in Gombrich, *Aby Warburg*, p. 257.
34. Carl Georg Heise, *Persönliche Erinnerungen an Aby Warburg*, eds. Björn Biester and Hans-Michael Schäfer (Wiesbaden, 2005), p. 69.
35. Michaud, *Aby Warburg and the Image in Motion*, p. 260.
36. Warburg quoted and translated in Gombrich, *Aby Warburg*, p. 185.
37. David Blackbourn, "The German Bourgeoisie: An Introduction," in *The German Bourgeoisie: Essays on the Social History of the German Middle Class from the Late Eighteenth to the Early Twentieth Century*, eds. idem and Richard Evans (London and New York, 1991), p. 9.
38. Gombrich, *Aby Warburg*, p. 111.
39. See Roeck, *Der junge Aby Warburg*, pp. 81-91.
40. Warburg quoted and translated in Ulrich Raulff, "The Seven Skins of the Snake: Oraibi, Kreuzlingen and Back: Stations on a Journey into Light," in *Photographs at the Frontier*, p. 64f.
41. Warburg quoted and translated in Gombrich, *Aby Warburg*, p. 95.
42. Max Warburg quoted in Meyer, "Aby Warburg in His Early Correspondence," p. 447.
43. See Bernd Roeck, *Florenz 1900. Die Suche Nach Arkadien* (Munich, 2001).
44. Aby Warburg, "The Art of Portraiture and the Florentine Bourgeoisie," in idem, *The Renewal of Pagan Antiquity*, p. 187.
45. Michaud, *Aby Warburg and the Image in Motion*, p. 106.
46. Rampley, *The Remembrance of Things Past*, p. 81.
47. Warburg, "The Art of Portraiture and the Florentine Bourgeoisie," p. 190; Jacob Burckhardt, *The Civilization of the Renaissance in Italy*, trans. S.G.C. Middlemore (New York, 1954).
48. WIA. III.43.1.2; TS of 43.2, pp. 122–175: Grundlegende Bruchstücke zu einer pragmatischen Ausdruckskunde, Bd. 2, 1896-1903, no. 420, p. 168.

49. WIA. III.43, 44 and 45: Grundlegende Bruchstücke zu einer pragmatischen Ausdruckskunde also bore the title Grundlegende Bruchstücke zu einer (monistischen) Kunstpsychologie [Basic Fragments of a (monistic) Psychology of Art].

50. Rampley, *The Remembrance of Things Past*, p. 42.

51. Ibid.

52. Ibid., p. 16f.

53. Warburg, "Dürer and Italian Antiquity," in idem, *The Renewal of Pagan Antiquity*, p. 556.

54. Rampley, "From Symbol to Allegory," p. 50.

55. Warburg, "Pagan-Antique Prophecy in Words and Images in the Age of Luther," in idem, *The Renewal of Pagan Antiquity*, p. 599.

56. Margaret Iversen, "Aby Warburg and the New Art History," in *Aby Warburg: Akten des internationalen Symposions, Hamburg, 1990*, eds. Horst Bredekamp, Michael Diers, and Charlotte Schoell-Glass (Weinheim, 1991), p. 286.

57. See amongst others Margaret Iversen, "Retrieving Warburg's Tradition," *Art History* 16 (1993), pp. 541–553; Rampley, "From Symbol to Allegory."

58. McEwan, "Aby Warburg's (1866–1929) Dots and Lines," p. 244.

59. Rampley, *The Remembrance of Things Past*, p. 75.

60. Ibid., p. 78.

61. For a study that emphasizes Warburg's supposed Dionysian proclivities see Didi-Huberman, *L'Image Survivante.*

62. Warburg also spoke of the "Denkraum der Besonnenheit," the realm of reflective reason; see for example idem "Heidnisch-antike Weissagung in Wort und Bild zu Luthers Zeiten," in idem *Gesammelte Schriften. Die Erneuerung der heidnischen Antike: Kulturwissenschaftliche Beiträge zur Geschichte der europäischen Renaissance*, eds. Horst Bredekamp and Michael Diers, 2 vols. (Berlin, 1998), vol. 2, p. 534.

63. Warburg, "The Mural Paintings in Hamburg City Hall," in idem, *The Renewal of Pagan Antiquity*, pp. 711–716.

64. Warburg quoted and translated in Gombrich, *Aby Warburg*, p. 223.

65. Drafts of this essay, along with notes and documentation, are found in WIA. III.58 and 64–67.

66. He also encouraged his brother Max to patronize the ethnology museum; WIA. Kopierbuch I: Warburg to Georg Thilenius, 28 August 1905.

67. This aspect of Warburg's intellectual legacy has attracted much scholarly attention; see Gertrude Bing, "The Warburg Institute," *The Library Association Record* 1 (1934), pp. 262–266; Fritz Saxl, "The History of Warburg's Library, 1886–1944," in Gombrich, *Aby Warburg*, pp. 325–338; Martin Jesinghausen-Lauster, *Die Suche nach der Symbolischen Form. Der Kreis um die kulturwissenschaftliche Bibliothek Warburg* (Baden-Baden, 1985); Ulrich Raulff, "Von der Privatbibliothek des Gelehrten zum Forschungsinstitut: Aby Warburg, Ernst Cassirer und die neue Kulturwissenschaft," *Geschichte und Gesellschaft* 23 (1997), pp. 28–43; Hans-Michael Schäfer, *Die Kulturwissenschaftliche Bibliothek Warburg: Geschichte und Persönlichkeiten der Bibliothek Warburg mit Berücksichtigung der Bibliothekslandschaft und der Stadtsituation der Freien und Hansestadt Hamburg zu Beginn des 20. Jahrhunderts* (Berlin, 2003).

68. Saxl held this position until his death in 1948.

69. Warburg to Max Warburg, 21 May 1911, quoted in Raulff, "Von der Privatbibliothek des Gelehrten zum Forschungsinstitut," p. 33.

70. Saxl, "The History of Warburg's Library," p. 327.

71. Ibid., p. 327.

72. Ibid.

73. McEwan, "Aby Warburg's (1866–1929) Dots and Lines," p. 251.

74. See Raulff, "Von der Privatbibliothek des Gelehrten zum Forschungsinstitut."

75. Warburg quoted and translated in Gombrich, *Aby Warburg*, p. 130.

76. Warburg quoted in Heise, *Persönliche Erinnerungen an Aby Warburg*, p. 30.

77. Warburg quoted and translated in Gombrich, *Aby Warburg*, p. 188.
78. Ibid., p. 198f.
79. Rampley, *The Remembrance of Things Past*, p. 59.
80. Aby Warburg, "Italian Art and International Astrology in the Palazzo Schifanoia, Ferrara," in idem, *The Renewal of Pagan Antiquity*, pp. 563–592.
81. See Peter Schmidt, *Aby M. Warburg und die Ikonologie* (Bamberg, 1989); William S. Heckscher, "The Genesis of Iconology," in idem, *Art and Literature: Studies in Relationship* (Baden-Baden, 1985), pp. 253–280.
82. "Kleines feuilleton," *Hamburgischer Correspondent*, 16 August 1911; found in WIA. III.2.1: Zettelkasten 53 (Geschichte), after 053 030171.
83. See Michael Diers, *Warburg aus Briefen: Kommentare zu den Kopierbüchern der Jahre 1905–1918* (Weinheim, 1991), pp. 85–91.
84. Aby Warburg, "Art Exhibitions at the Volksheim," in idem, *The Renewal of Pagan Antiquity*, p. 718.
85. Michael Diers has argued that Warburg's voice carried little weight in the debate over the building of a university in Hamburg; see idem, "Der Gelehrte, der unter die Kaufleute fiel: ein Streiflicht auf Warburg und Hamburg," in *Aby Warburg*, pp. 45– 53.
86. For a concise account of Warburg's activities during the war see Karl Königsreder, "Aby Warburg im 'Bellevue,'" in *Aby M. Warburg. "Ekstatische Nymphe,"* pp. 74–98.
87. Martin Warnke has also pointed to Warburg's "passionate interest in politics" in idem, "Vier Stichworte: Ikonologie—Pathosformel—Polarität und Ausgleich— Schlagbilder und Bilderfahrzeuge," in Werner Hofmann, Georg Syamken, and Martin Warnke, *Die Menschenrechte des Auges: über Aby Warburg* (Frankfurt a.M., 1980), p. 75.
88. Aby Warburg, "Pagan-Antique Prophecy in Words and Images in the Age of Luther," in idem, *The Renewal of Pagan Antiquity*, p. 599.
89. Hans Liebeschütz, "Aby Warburg (1866–1929) as Interpreter of Civilization," *Leo Baeck Institute Yearbook* 16 (1971), p. 232.
90. Warburg quoted and translated in Michaud, *Aby Warburg and the Image in Motion*, p. 173.
91. Königsreder, "Aby Warburg im 'Bellevue,'" p 82.
92. Binswanger quoted and translated in Michaud, *Aby Warburg and the Image in Motion*, p. 174.
93. Aby Warburg, "A Lecture on Serpent Ritual," *Journal of the Warburg Institute* 2 (1938–39), pp. 277–292; see amongst others Ulrich Raulff, "The Seven Skins of the Snake"; Michael Steinberg, "Aby Warburg's Kreuzlingen Lecture: A Reading," in Aby Warburg, *Images from the Region of the Pueblo Indians of North America*, trans. idem (Ithaca and London, 1995), pp. 59–114; Sigried Weigel, "Aby Warburg's Schlangenritual: Reading Culture and Reading Written Texts," *New German Critique* 65 (1995), pp. 135–153; Salvatore Settis, "Kunstgeschichte als vergleichende Kulturwissenschaft: Aby Warburg, die Pueblo-Indianer und das Nachleben der Antike," in *Künstlerischer Austausch / Artistic Exchange: Akten des XXVIII. Internationalen Kongresses für Kunstgeschichte, Berlin, 15. –20. Juli 1992*, ed. Thomas W. Gaethgens, 2 vols. (Berlin, 1994), vol. 1, pp. 139–158; Kurt W. Forster, "Die Hamburg-Amerika-Linie, oder: Warburgs Kulturwissenschaft zwischen den Kontinenten," in *Aby Warburg*, pp. 11–37; Claudia Naber, "Pompeij in Neu-Mexiko: Aby Warburg's amerikanische Reise," *Freibeuter* 38 (1988), pp. 88–97; Gombrich, *Aby Warburg*, pp. 216–238.
94. See Tilmann von Stockhausen, *Die Kulturwissenschaftliche Bibliothek Warburg: Architektur, Einrichtung und Organisation* (Hamburg, 1992); see also Karen Michels, "Ein Versuch über die K.B.W. als Bau der Moderne," in *Porträt aus Buchern: Bibliothek Warburg und Warburg Institute: Hamburg—1933—London*, ed. Michael Diers (Hamburg, 1993), pp. 71–81.
95. A personal account of the functioning of the library in these years is given by a student of Warburg's in René Drommert, "Aby Warburg und die Kulturwissenschaftliche Bibliothek in der Heilwigstraße," in *Aby M. Warburg. "Ekstatische Nymphe,"* pp. 14–18.
96. This period of Warburg's life is well summarized in Claudia Naber, "'Heuernte bei Gewitter': Aby Warburg, 1924–29," in *Aby M. Warburg. "Ekstatische Nymphe,"* pp. 104–129.

97. See amongst others Gombrich, *Aby Warburg*, pp. 283–306; Peter van Huisstede, "Der Mnemosyne-Atlas: ein Laboratorium der Bildgeschichte," in *Aby M. Warburg. "Ekstatische Nymphe,"* pp. 130–167; Werner Hofmann, "Der Mnemosyne-Atlas: zu Warburgs Konstellationen," in ibid., pp. 172–183; Dorothee Bauerle, *Gespenstergeschichten für Ganz Erwachsene: ein Kommentar zu Aby Warburgs Bilderatlas, Mnemosyne* (Münster, 1988); Roland Kany, *Mnemosyne als Programm: Geschichte, Erinnerung und die Andacht zum Unbedeutenden im Werk von Usener, Warburg und Benjamin* (Tübingen, 1987).

98. *Hamburger Nachrichten*, 30 October 1929.

99. Saxl, "The History of Warburg's Library," p. 336; see, however, Peter Gay, *Weimar Culture: The Outsider as Insider* (New York, 1968), p. 34 where he argues that in their efforts to root out so-called Bolshevik culture, the Nazis would find no suspicious materials in Warburg's essays.

100. For the story of the library's migration see Michael Diers, "Porträt aus Büchern: Stichworte zur Einführung," in *Porträt aus Buchern*, pp. 9–27; Nicholas Mann, "Kulturwissenschaft in London: englisches Fortleben einer europäischen Tradition," in *Aby M. Warburg. "Ekstatische Nymphe,"* pp. 210–227; Dieter Wuttke, "Die Emigration der Kulturwissenschaftlichen Bibliothek Warburg und die Anfänge des Universitätsfaches Kunstgeschichte in Grossbritannien," *Artibus et Historiae* 10 (1984), pp. 133–146.

101. Max Warburg, "Rede gehalten bei der Gedächtnis—Feier für Professor Warburg am 5. Dezember 1929 von Max Warburg," typescript (Hamburg, 1929).

102. Warburg quoted and translated in Gombrich, *Aby Warburg*, p. 140.

103. Gertrude Bing quoted and translated in Chernow, *The Warburgs*, p. 204.

104. See for example Michael P. Steinberg, "Aby Warburg's Kreuzlingen Lecture"; Christa-Maria Lerm, "Das jüdische Erbe bei Aby Warburg," *Menora: Jahrbuch für deutsch-jüdische Geschichte* (1994), pp. 143–171; Georg Syamken, "Warburgs Umwege als Hermeneutik More Majorum," *Jahrbuch der Hamburger Kunstsammlungen* 25 (1980), pp. 15–26; Liebeschütz, "Aby Warburg."

105. Rampley, *The Remembrance of Things Past*, p. 36.

106. Charlotte Schoell-Glass, *Aby Warburg und der Antisemitismus: Kulturwissenschaft als Geistespolitik* (Frankfurt a.M., 1998).

107. See Roeck, *Der junge Aby Warburg*, pp. 71–75.

108. Chernow, *The Warburgs*, p. 61.

109. See Schoell-Glass, *Aby Warburg und der Antisemitismus*, pp. 53–75.

110. WIA. GC: Warburg to Max Warburg, 14 July 1900.

111. Schoell-Glass, *Aby Warburg und der Antisemitismus*, pp. 121–153.

112. See, for example, *Hamburger Echo*, 8 December 1917.

113. For the low incidence of anti-Semitic prejudice in Hamburg see Helga Krohn, *Die Juden in Hamburg: die politische, soziale und kulturelle Entwicklung einer jüdischen Grossstadtgemeinde nach der Emanzipation, 1848–1918* (Hamburg, 1974); Richard J. Evans, "Family and Class in the Hamburg Grand Bourgeoisie, 1815–1914," in *The German Bourgeoisie*, eds. idem and David Blackbourn (London and New York, 1991), p. 133f; Erika Hirsch, *Jüdisches Vereinsleben in Hamburg bis zum Ersten Weltkrieg: jüdisches Selbstverständnis zwischen Antisemitismus und Assimilation* (Frankfurt a.M., Berlin, Bern, New York, Paris, and Vienna, 1996).

114. Percy Ernst Schramm, *Neun Generationen: dreihundert Jahre deutscher "Kulturgeschichte" im Lichte der Schicksale einer Hamburger Bürgerfamilie (1648 - 1948)*, 2 vols. (Göttingen, 1964), vol. 2, p. 414.

115. Julius von Eckhardt quoted and translated in Jennifer Jenkins, *Provincial Modernity: Local Culture and Liberal Politics in Fin-de-Siècle Hamburg* (Ithaca and London, 2003), p. 86f.

116. Moritz Warburg quoted and translated in Chernow, *The Warburgs*, p. 61.

117. Niall Ferguson, *Paper and Iron: Hamburg Business and German Politics in the Era of Inflation, 1897–1927* (Cambridge, 1995), p. 61.

118. See Helga Krohn, *Die Juden in Hamburg*, pp. 115–122.

119. Raulff, "Von der Privatbibliothek des Gelehrten zum Forschungsinstitut," p. 32.

120. This point has been emphasized by Lerm, "Das jüdische Erbe bei Aby Warburg."
121. WIA. Kopierbuch IV, 249: Warburg to an anonymous correspondent, 28 February 1912.
122. On this point see Steinberg, "Aby Warburg's Kreuzlingen Lecture," pp. 79–81 and 87; Meyer, "Aby Warburg in His Early Correspondence."
123. Heise, *Persönliche Erinnerungen an Aby Warburg*, p. 60.
124. Warburg quoted and translated in Meyer, "Aby Warburg in His Early Correspondence," p. 447.
125. Warburg quoted and translated in ibid.
126. Max Warburg, "Rede gehalten bei der Gedächtnis-Feier für Professor Warburg," p. 6.
127. Gombrich, *Aby Warburg*, p. 207.
128. Chernow, *The Warburgs*, p. 195.
129. Warburg quoted and translated in Dorothea McEwan, "Gegen die 'Pionere der Diesseitigkeit,'" *Zeitschrift des Zentrums für Literaturforschung Berlin* 4, no. 8 (April 2004), p. 11.
130. See ibid., p. 11.
131. Ibid.
132. Warburg quoted in Roeck, *Der junge Aby Warburg*, p. 74.
133. Warburg quoted and translated in Chernow, *The Warburgs*, p. 122.
134. Warburg quoted and translated in Meyer, "Aby Warburg in His Early Correspondence," p. 451.
135. George Mosse, *German Jews Beyond Judaism* (Bloomington, Ind. and Cincinnati, 1985), p. 50ff.
136. Ibid., p. 82.
137. Werner E. Mosse, *The German-Jewish Economic Elite, 1820–1935: A Socio-Cultural Profile* (Oxford, 1989), p. 327; see also Peter Gay, "Encounter with Modernism: German Jews in Wilhelminian Culture," in idem, *Freud, Jews and Other Germans* (Oxford, 1978), pp. 93–168 where he argues that there was little in the Jewish cultural heritage and in their particular social situation that would turn German Jews into principled modernists; Walter Laqueur, *Weimar: A Cultural History, 1918–1933* (New York, 1974), pp. 72–77.
138. Peter Pulzer, *Jews and the German State: The Political History of a Minority, 1848–1933* (Oxford, 1992), p. 23; on p. 22, however, Pulzer makes the point that most German Jews were in "fairly humdrum occupations."
139. See Shulamit Volkov, *The Rise of Popular Antimodernism in Germany: The Urban Master Artisans, 1873–1896* (Princeton, 1978), esp. pp. 313–319.
140. For such figures see Peter Paret, "Bemerkungen zu dem Thema: Jüdische Kunstsammler, Stifter und Kunsthändler," in *Sammler, Stifter und Museen: Kunstförderung in Deutschland im 19. und 20. Jahrhundert*, eds. Ekkehard Mai and Peter Paret (Cologne, Weimar, and Vienna, 1993); Shulamit Volkov has written of the "unique capacity of German Jews to respond to the challenge of modernity" in idem, "The Dynamics of Dissimulation: Ostjuden and German Jews," in *The Jewish Response to German Culture*, eds. Jehuda Reinharz and Walter Schatzberg (Hanover, N.H. and London, 1985), p. 199; Reinhard Rürup argues that that German Jews were "as a social group, undoubtedly representatives ... of middle-class modernity" in idem, "Kontinuität und Diskontinuität der 'Judenfrage' im 19. Jahrhundert," in idem, *Emanzipation und Antisemitismus* (Göttingen, 1975), pp. 74–94.
141. Paret, "Bemerkungen zu dem Thema," p. 184.
142. Heise, *Persönliche Erinnerungen an Aby Warburg*, p. 62.
143. See Bernd Roeck, "Psychohistorie im Zeichen Saturns: Aby Warburgs Denksystem und die moderne Kulturgeschichte," in *Kulturgeschichte Heute*, eds. Wolfgang Hardtwig and Hans-Ulrich Wehler (Göttingen, 1996), pp. 231–254; Didi-Huberman, *L'image survivante*.
144. Gombrich, *Aby Warburg*, p. 11f.
145. Roeck "Psychohistorie im Zeichen Saturns," p. 240.
146. Aby Warburg quoted and translated in Gombrich, *Aby Warburg*, p. 223.
147. Gombrich, *Aby Warburg*, p. 9.

148. Lichtwark quoted in Schramm, *Neun Generationen*, p. 301.
149. For a groundbreaking study on this topic see Celia Applegate, *A Nation of Provincials: The German Idea of Heimat* (Berkeley, Los Angeles, and Oxford, 1990).
150. Felix Gilbert has even argued that Warburg's study of Florentine merchant-bankers "helped to strengthen his conviction that he had a right to belong to the ruling group of the empire," in idem, "From Art History to the History of Civilization: Gombrich's Biography of Aby Warburg," *Journal of Modern History* 44 (1972), p. 390.
151. Warburg quoted and translated in Raulff, "Von der Privatbibliothek des Gelehrten zum Forschungsinstitut," p. 30, nte. 8; on this point see also Horst Günther, "Aby Warburg und seine Brüder," in Ferdinand Seibt, et. al., *Deutsche Brüder: zwölf Doppelporträts* (Berlin, 1994), pp. 254–286.
152. Gilbert, "From Art History to the History of Civilization," p. 390.
153. See Alfred Lichtwark, *Der Deutsche der Zukunft* (Berlin, 1905).
154. Peter Gay, *Pleasure Wars* (New York and London, 1998), p. 186f.
155. Alfred Lichtwark, "Dilettantismus und Volkskunst," in idem. *Erziehung des Auges: Ausgewählte Schriften*, ed. Eckhard Schaar (Frankfurt a. M., 1991), p. 89.
156. WIA. III.26.3: Hamburgische Kunstgespräche, fol. 7.
157. See Carolyn Kay, *Art and the German Bourgeoisie: Alfred Lichtwark and Modern Painting in Hamburg, 1886–1914* (Toronto, 2002), pp. 41–69.
158. Alfred Lichtwark, *Das Bildnis in Hamburg*, 2 vols. (Hamburg, 1898).
159. WIA. GC: Warburg to Mayer Seligmann Goldschmidt, 17 March 1905.
160. For an account of this incident see Kay, *Art and the German Bourgeoisie*, pp. 41–69.
161. WIA. GC: Warburg to Mayer Seligmann Goldschmidt, 17 March 1905.
162. Heise, *Personliche Erinnerungen an Aby Warburg*, p. 16.
163. Aby Warburg, "Kommunale Pflichten und allgemeine Geistespolitik," in idem, *Ausgewählte Schriften und Würdigungen*, ed. Dieter Wuttke (Baden-Baden, 1979), p. 305.
164. Heise, *Persönliche Erinnerungen an Aby Warburg*, p. 16.
165. Lichtwark quoted in Brosius, *Kunst als Denkraum*, p. 107; Alfred Lichtwark, "Selbsterziehung," in idem, *Erziehung des Auges*, p. 84.
166. Brosius, *Kunst als Denkraum*, p. 110.
167. Lichtwark quoted and translated in Gay, *Pleasure Wars*, p. 186.
168. Gay, *Pleasure Wars*, p. 186.
169. Lichtwark, "Selbsterziehung," p. 84.
170. Lichtwark, "Dilettantismus und Volkskunst," p. 88.
171. Warburg, "The Mural Paintings in Hamburg City Hall," p. 715.
172. Warburg quoted in Brosius, *Kunst als Denkraum*, p. 93, nte. 107.
173. Warburg quoted in ibid., p. 92.
174. Gombrich, *Aby Warburg*, p. ix.
175. Hans Wilhelm Eckardt, "Bücher und Geschichte: zur Entwicklung der Gesellschaft der Bücherfreunde zu Hamburg," *Zeitschrift des Vereins für Hamburgische Geschichte* 74/75 (1989), pp. 177–188.
176. Aby Warburg, "In Memory of Robert Münzel," in idem, *The Renewal of Pagan Antiquity*, p. 726; for a discussion of Warburg's relationship with Münzel see Horst Gronemeyer, "Aby Warburg und Robert Münzel—eine Freundschaft von Bibliothek zu Bibliothek," in *Porträt aus Büchern*, pp. 35–42.
177. Warburg quoted in Heise, *Persönliche Erinnerungen an Aby Warburg*, p. 42.
178. Warburg also planned an exhibition on the history of astrology and astronomy that was posthumously mounted in the Hamburg planetarium in 1930.
179. Hans Wilhelm Eckardt, *Privilegien und Parlament: die Auseinandersetzung um das allgemeine und gleiche Wahlrecht in Hamburg* (Hamburg, 1980), p. 38.
180. Jenkins, *Provincial Modernity*, p. 119.
181. WIA. Kopierbuch III, 136: Warburg to Dwelshauers, 27 July 1909.

182. Warburg, "Art Exhibitions at the Volksheim," in idem, *The Renewal of Pagan Antiquity*, p. 711.
183. See Jenkins, *Provincial Modernity*, pp. 90–101 and passim; Gustav Schiefler, *Eine Hamburgische Kulturgeschichte, 1890–1920: Beobachtungen eines Zeitgenossen,* eds. Gerhard Ahrens, Hans Wilhelm Eckardt, and Renate Hauschild-Thiessen (Hamburg, 1985), pp. 332–337; St.A.H.731–1, 1175: Hans-Joachim Rackow, "Das Hamburger Volksheim: Entstehung, Organisation und Zielsetzung: ein Beitrag zur Volksbildungsarbeit des liberalen Protestantismus im Wilhelminischen Reich," (Examensarbeit f.d. Lehramt an Volks-und Realschulen, Hamburg, 1980); St.A.H. 731–1, 1585: Susanne Hager, Joachim Mottel, and Renate Sander, "Entstehung und Entwicklung der Hamburger Volksheim unter Berücksichtigung sozialpädagogischer Aspekte," (Diplomarbeit, Hamburg, 1986).
184. Two other facilities were founded in Barmbek and Hammerbrook in 1908.
185. WIA. III.60.1: 100 Handzeichnungen: Dürer als Spiegel seiner selbst und seiner Zeit, fol. 7.
186. Aby Warburg, "Francesco Sassetti's Last Injunctions to His Sons," in idem, *The Renewal of Pagan Antiquity*, p. 249.
187. Warburg, "Art Exhibitions at the Volksheim," p. 717.
188. WIA. III.60.1, fol. 3.
189. Brosius, *Kunst als Denkraum*, p. 145.
190. WIA. III.60.1, fol. 26.
191. This debt is discussed in Brosius, *Kunst als Denkraum*, pp. 44–71.
192. Mosse, *German Jews Beyond Judaism*, p. 6.
193. Brosius, *Kunst als Denkraum*, p. 104.
194. Jenkins, *Provincial Modernity*, p. 6.
195. Rampley, *The Remembrance of Things Past*, p. 90.
196. WIA. III.60.1, fol. 25.
197. WIA. III.60.1, fol. 26.
198. St.A.H. Bibliothek Z760/1: "Maibericht," *Monatliche Mitteilungen des Volksheims* 3 (June 1905).
199. Ibid., "Junibericht," *Monatliche Mitteilungen des Volksheims* 4 (July 1905).
200. Ibid., "Julibericht," *Monatliche Mitteilungen des Volksheims* 5 (August 1905).
201. Warburg, "Art Exhibitions at the Volksheim," p. 717.
202. Warburg quoted in Brosius, *Kunst als Denkraum*, p. 148.
203. Saxl, "The History of Warburg's Library," p. 335.

Chapter Two

ABY WARBURG'S "HAMBURG COMEDY"
The Personal Concerns and Professional Ambitions
of a Young Scholar

I

"Justice, air, and light also for the moderns; progress in abbreviation." This was the epigram that Aby Warburg appended to a short play entitled "Hamburg Conversations on Art: Hamburg Comedy, 1896."[1] Preserved in the Warburg Institute Archive, it was penned by Warburg for his family's new-year celebrations of that year and was dedicated to his fiancée, Mary Hertz. The action of the three-act comedy centers on an argument over the worth of contemporary art; the protagonists are a young impressionist painter and the art-loving uncle of his fiancée. Historians may be surprised to find the founder of the Warburg Institute expressing himself in histrionic mode; renewed interest in Warburg has focused on the scholarship of an innovative art historian and pioneer in the field of cultural memory. As a result, this short work of fiction has received little attention from Warburg scholars.[2]

Drama, however, was not an unfamiliar form of expression for Aby Warburg. In fact, he once wrote that he felt "kinship to Shaw as a latent dramatist."[3] Amateur theatrics were a favorite pastime of the Warburg family and Aby Warburg claimed that if he had been two centimeters taller, he would have become an actor.[4] According to many who knew him, his gift for impersonation and his talent with accents would have ensured his success.[5] At Kösterberg, the family's summer home in Blankenese, everyone took part in staging plays in the outdoor theater. When Max and Alice Warburg celebrated their fifth wedding anniversary in 1903, Aby Warburg performed a skit in which he portrayed his brother, twenty-five years later, speaking from Hamburg to Paul Warburg in New York via an apparatus that transmitted their voices and images. At the same time, Max Warburg portrayed his brother seated at a desk and writing an essay on the Medici habit of wearing white socks with blue dots, a peculiarity he attributed to Flemish influence. Mocking his brother's pedantry, Max Warburg proclaimed that the essay would be so dense that no one would be able to understand it.[6] What makes the unpublished draft of "Hamburg Conversations on Art" so interesting, however, is that it is one of the few instances in which Warburg expressed his views—albeit indirectly—on contemporary art.

The play reveals Warburg as a perspicacious observer of, and commentator upon Wilhelmine society and culture. In particular, it demonstrates that, like many of his generation, Warburg understood that he was "living through a 'turning point in the times.'"[7] Kenneth Barkin has enumerated several factors that accounted for this phenomenon: Bismarck's dismissal in 1890 and the sense of losing the Empire's helmsman; the Reichstag elections of the same year which saw an unprecedented rise in the number of socialist deputies and inflamed the fears of those who believed the Empire was especially vulnerable to centrifugal political and social forces; the Social Democrats' adoption of a Marxist program at their Erfurt conference in 1891; Chancellor Caprivi's trade treaties of the early 1890s, which meant greater involvement in the world economy; increased urbanization along with a revolution in consumption and marketing; and the diminished role of the *Bildungsbürgertum*.[8] The advent of a modern, industrialized, and capitalist society found its champions in several influential voices, like that of the sociologist Max Weber. In the field of culture, secession movements opposed to the policies of official art academies and salons—which arose in Berlin, Dresden, Karlsruhe, Munich, Düsseldorf, and Weimar—could not have survived without a positive reaction among a minority of progressive critics and museum officials, as well as patrons from the field of commerce and industry.[9] Nonetheless, fears about the disorienting effects of rapid social change, the artificiality of modern society, and modernism's threat to German culture were raised by many influential critics such as the sociologists Ferdinand Tönnies (1855–1936) and Werner Sombart (1863–1941) and the author Julius Langbehn (1851–1907). Thus, as Kevin Repp has argued, "the generation of 1890 grew up in an atmosphere of tense uncertainty, where every aspect of life seemed open to flux and change." This was "an inescapable fact of life for the children of 'Bismarck's Empire.'"[10]

Warburg was a member of the generation for whom modernity remained a central question. The political, social, economic, and cultural transformations of the 1890s all found expression in Hamburg, and Warburg's thinking was formed by and responded to the exigencies of his times. Thus this chapter begins by examining the topical allusions of the play and establishes the context of its creation. In particular, Warburg imitates and parodies public debates over developments in the visual arts that marked Hamburg's cultural life in the last decade of the nineteenth century. For the city's artists, art patrons, and cultural administrators, art was never thrust into the center of public life as it was during that tumultuous decade in the city's history. In an atmosphere of political and social tension, it was common for art, even with no identifiable political theme, to be politicized by its conservative opponents; artistic innovation was often equated with questionable or dangerous social and political views. Political, social, and cultural tensions grew concurrently in Hamburg: while the threat to authority posed by increased labor organization and politicization boiled over in the dockers' strike of November 1896, cultural tensions reached their zenith in the general meeting of the Art Association in March of that year.[11] While the former crisis culminated in two days of rioting in the inner city, the latter was a riotous assembly in which committee incumbents were shouted down and those who supported modern art were forced from office. This chapter argues that Warburg's comedy was directly inspired by this tumultuous transformation of Hamburg's Art Association.

The chapter also examines the play as an expression of very personal concerns. In his brief discussion of the work, Ernst Gombrich suggests its tone of generational conflict was the product of Warburg's strained relationship with his parents and grandparents. Familial tension was the result of his stubborn separation from Jewish religious orthodoxy, and his courtship of the daughter of one of Hamburg's senatorial families that had recently converted from Judaism to Protestantism.[12] This chapter expands upon this idea by exploring the ways in which Warburg's enthusiasm for innovative art forms emerged, in part, as an expression of his rebellion against the religious, social, and professional conventions of the German-Jewish economic elite into which he was born.[13] The play was a humorous, but nonetheless serious, expression of his determination to break with the world of his parents. It reveals that, as with many of his generation, Warburg claimed social and cultural progress under the banner of artistic innovation.

Warburg lived through an artistic revolution in Europe as momentous as that of the Italian Renaissance. In Germany, artistic innovation became a topic of heated public debate; art was politicized and functioned as a locus for competing visions of German national identity. For some influential critics—most famously Julius Meier-Graefe—a denationalized Impressionism came to signify modernism itself; the work of artists like Max Liebermann was to replace the link with the Greco-Italian tradition that had animated German national identity since the days of the Prussian antiquarian and aesthete Johann Winckelmann. Other cultural commentators, like Julius Langbehn, decried the influence of foreign artistic currents and saw the symbolism of an artist like Arnold Böcklin as representative of a true German spirit in the arts. In his play, Warburg embraces both of these artistic currents as significant facets of a modern German art. Thus this chapter will also look beyond personal concerns to the intellectual and scholarly foundations for Warburg's attraction to the wide range of artistic experimentation that colored his own era.

It is important to note that, on one level, Warburg's catholic taste in contemporary art was not unusual for his generation. During the 1890s, many observers embraced as progressive what now seem divergent and even antithetical artistic trends. As indicated in the book's introduction, the scholarly canon of artistic modernism is often accompanied by an incomplete understanding of how contemporaries understood new art forms. In the 1890s, it was a lack of historical perspective which often resulted in confusion about what constituted important innovation. As Maria Rennhofer has shown, it was not uncommon for the editors, critics, and publishers of any one of a number of contemporary art journals to disagree on what should be praised as progressive and what rejected as philistinism.[14] But it is also true that influential art journals, like *Pan* (founded in 1895), deliberately presented themselves as non-partisan and gave voice to many different movements in German art.[15] Furthermore, the secession movements that appeared in several major German cities during the 1890s were complex organizations full of diversity and even contradictions.[16] They advocated artistic freedom, but did not produce stylistic programs or manifestoes; they were composed mostly of established artists with academic training, but embraced a variety of nonacademic trends in contemporary art, both Impressionist and anti-Impressionist. Ultimately, they even failed to provide a sense of unity among their participants and succumbed to internal divisions.

On another level, however, Warburg was not simply one among many educated, lay observers of the arts in Germany. His interest in modern art is closely allied with his research into the role of symbolism and art in European culture. We have noted that, during the 1880s and 1890s, Warburg thought seriously about the psychology of artistic expression and developed ideas that guided his research and shaped the content and organization of his library. As this endeavor coincided with a period of dramatic experimentation in the arts, it seems important to examine the nature of any relationship which may have existed between changes in artistic practice and Warburg's scholarship. His long-time colleague, Fritz Saxl, suggested that it was the ideas of the English Pre-Raphaelites that encouraged Warburg to study the Florentine Renaissance in the first place.[17] The aim of this chapter, however, is not to argue for a direct causal relationship between artistic practice and Warburg's scholarship. Instead, it suggests there was a symbiotic relationship between his interpretation of the art and culture of fifteenth-century Florence and his emotional and intellectual investment in the social and cultural development of modern Europe. This investment reveals the ambiguous nature of Warburg's attitude toward the complex and various processes of modernization. While championing new art forms that more accurately represented the changing social and cultural milieu to which he belonged, Warburg feared a world that was becoming evermore rationalized and materialistic; he was concerned about the prospect of a culture in which symbolic and mythical thinking was replaced by a technology that destroyed humanity's self-reflective orientation within the cosmos. But although Warburg attributed particular dangers to the technological and cultural developments of the 1890s, the perspective he brought to bear on its art was informed by his nonteleological approach to history and culture and his interest in tracing the paths taken by the mind, not in historical time, but in synchronous psychic time. This was a perspective that was not governed or circumscribed by consensual understandings of what was traditional and what was modern in German culture.

II

Warburg set his play on a Sunday afternoon in June 1896, clearly marking it as a contemporary drama and emphasizing its genesis in personal experience and concerns. As the product of an amateur dramatist, the plot is simplistic, the characterization overstated, and the dialogue unsubtle. The strong language of the protagonists' confrontation is employed for comic effect, but also as a measure of the seriousness of the debates being parodied. The scene, set in the parlor of a country house on Hamburg's Alster Lake, reveals the influence of naturalistic, middle-class family dramas in the style of Henrik Ibsen, with whose work Warburg was familiar.[18] The note of social criticism that the play strikes would not have been unfamiliar to Hamburg's *Großbürgertum*. Ibsen was probably the first modern playwright to have his work presented on the Hamburg stage, while Gerhard Hauptmann's early works, such as *The Weavers,* were first brought to Hamburg's public in 1895 by the Free Stage Association. One had to be a member to see these plays, as public performances were prohibited.[19] These productions were mostly frowned upon by Hamburg's *Großbürgertum* because of their political connotations.

Warburg enumerates the cast of characters on the first page following the titles. These are types compounded from individuals who composed his social, and perhaps even his familial, milieu and are humorously sketched as follows: F.C.M. Merckendorff, a full-bearded, quiet, "simple" merchant of fifty years who likes nothing better than a little peace; his wife, Mrs. Merckendorff, née Martens, a fussy, "well-preserved" woman who is "still good-looking"; their twenty-year-old daughter Eva who is "very nice," but "like all Evas"; her fiancé, Alfred Runge, an Impressionist painter who "does not look his twenty-nine years," "is not overly didactic, is jolly and yet serious"; Eduard G.H. Martens, Mrs. Merckendorff's "elegant, well-preserved" brother, a man of fifty-two years who was once a coffee merchant and is now a man of private means and member of the Hamburg Society for Art Preservation. Warburg cast his brother Max as Mr. Merckendorff, his sister Olga as Mrs. Merckendorff, his sister Louise as Eva, his brother Fritz as Alfred, and himself as Uncle Eduard. Every detail reveals that the characters are members of Hamburg's *Großbürgertum*: the presence of a maid; the taking of a second breakfast; the use of English phrases; the cigars, pale sherry, and ginger cakes; the fondly-remembered visits to Florentine art galleries, and the plans to travel to the sea where father will enjoy the lobster, porter, and ale.

In the first scene, Warburg briefly sketches a context for the drama that follows. Eva's plan for a boating party is promptly revealed as a ploy to escape Uncle

Eduard's impending visit. This, she is convinced, will only bring another rancorous encounter between her art-collecting uncle and Alfred. Last Sunday, we learn, both wanted to "rip each other's head off on account of modern art." The particular object of contention was an award-winning picture by Alfred. Father tries to allay Eva's fears by announcing that the two men have since settled their differences; Uncle Eduard has withdrawn his allegation that modern trends had resulted in the "ruin of the solid Hamburg taste in art," while Alfred has denied any intention to wound Eduard by calling him an "old philistine." Yet Eva quips that if Uncle Eduard is not a philistine, there are no philistines. Chiding her for disrespect, mother reminds Eva that Eduard's aesthetic taste concurs with that of Karl Hinrich Schneider, the great art collector. Schneider, Eva replies, may be an authority in his canning business, but pictures are not "bottled fruit."

In the second scene, Alfred arrives bearing a picture which he describes as "hideous," but explains that it is a gift for Uncle Eduard in the hope of preserving familial peace. Eduard enters in scene three and immediately complains that yesterday's visit to the Kunsthalle was not a pleasant one. Under the gallery's new head, "Director Fireworks" (Alfred Lichtwark), the collection of old-master prints and drawings has been closed to the public due to lack of space and money. Alfred agrees, regretting that the "one-sided, modern direction of our revered Fireworks" has resulted in the neglect of Italian art. But unanimity is abruptly shattered when Uncle Eduard complains that the Kunsthalle seems to value the work of Anders Zorn more than that of the old masters. He denounces Zorn's etchings as "streaked rubbish" and says his very name smacks of "poison and bile." In Eduard's opinion, there is no trace of "orderly execution" in Zorn's work; his sketchiness and neglect of clear outline amounts to nothing but "unclear, conceited trash."

Alfred responds angrily, exclaiming that what Uncle Eduard takes for clumsiness and lack of technique is actually technical innovation in the work of "one of the most significant living artists." Accurately or mechanically recorded detail is "boring"; the artist can only learn from sense impression. Indeed, it is the German Impressionists who, in their attempt to capture the winter mists on Hamburg's canals, produce work with "much more real atmosphere than a carefully illustrated broadsheet." The public simply must be educated to appreciate this type of art.

Taking Uncle Eduard's side, Mr. Merckendorff complains that life has enough unpleasantness to offer; one does not need to hang more on the wall. Furthermore, if popular taste admires the work of Moritz von Schwind or Valentin Ruths, this can only amount to "a very justifiable and beneficial opposition ... against the impressionistic excesses of modern art." But what harm would it do, Alfred protests, to hang a landscape by Arnold Böcklin or an etching by Max Klinger on the wall. Uncle Eduard, however, has no time for Böcklin; his "indecorous sea creatures are repulsive, monstrous inventions of an unhealthy imagination." As for Klinger, his work "is simply crazy and occasionally even indecent." Referring to the series of etchings that Klinger entitled *A Love*, Eduard exclaims that no good Hamburg family with young children would have it in their home. He goes on to denounce a poster designed by the Hamburg painter Ernst Eitner as "dreadful." Here Warburg is making direct reference to recent events in Hamburg's Art Association. To this, Alfred retorts that "art is for mature, lively people who want to grasp life and not for old dodderers or teenage girls!"

Finally, in a huff, Uncle Eduard announces his departure: "new and old don't go together. The old yields to the superior new." But Alfred stays his exit and, retrieving the picture with which he arrived, presents it to him as a gift. Much to his own surprise, Uncle Eduard is delighted with this image of "a respectable picnic," describing it as a "small concession to Hamburg taste." Eva, however, is shocked; she recognizes the work as an impressionist landscape that Alfred has ruined by the addition of a group of figures. Quietly, however, Alfred assures her that the original is preserved unaltered at home; his gift to Uncle Eduard is only a copy.

<h1 style="text-align:center">III</h1>

The author of the play was an intelligent, ambitious and idealistic thirty-year-old who, although he played the role of Uncle Eduard, identified with the young painter, Alfred. The character's family name, Runge, may be a reference to the painter Philipp Otto Runge (1777–1810). Now considered a major exponent of German Romantic painting, Runge's work was rediscovered by Alfred Lichtwark in the late 1880s and exhibited in Hamburg's Kunsthalle from 1892. The artist was a pioneer in the study of light and color who broke with the traditions of the old masters and was conscious of his role as a renewer of art. As such, he was celebrated by members of Warburg's generation as a progenitor of modern art.[20] Warburg's epigram, "justice, air, and light also for the moderns," may be recalling Runge's phrase—known to contemporaries like the Hamburg judge, art enthusiast and author Gustav Schiefler (1857–1935)—about "air and light and animated life" finding form in painting.[21]

The renewal of art was very much a subject of debate in Hamburg in the 1890s. The play reflects this debate as it was expressed in newspapers, art journals, exhibition reviews, and the transformation of the collections and educational mission of the Kunsthalle under Litchwark's directorship. In particular, Warburg took his inspiration from the event at which these debates erupted into a raucous confrontation between the exponents of conventional and reforming trends in the visual arts: the general meeting of Hamburg's Art Association in March 1896. Although he was traveling in the United States until May of that year, Warburg was informed about what had transpired through correspondence with family members.[22] Before elaborating upon the nature and substance of events in the Art Association, we need to examine the cultural context in which Warburg's play was written. This has recently become the topic of significant scholarly attention.[23]

As we have seen, there is much evidence that points to Hamburg's philistin-ism in matters of art. This perspective is reinforced by another dramatic sketch from the period. In 1909, Warburg hired Wilhelm Waetzoldt (1880–1945) as his academic assistant.[24] While in Hamburg, Waetzoldt wrote numerous pieces of art criticism for the *Hamburgischer Correspondent* and was admired for his ability to arouse the public's interest in art. In December 1910, fourteen years after War-burg composed his comedy, Waetzoldt wrote a play of his own. Entitled "Con-versation on Art at Christmas," it appeared in the *Hamburgischer Correspondent*.[25] This took the form of a discussion between an art dealer and connoisseur, but the debate was no longer over the propriety of Impressionist or Symbolist art. Ham-burg's public was now confronted with the work of Expressionist artists like Emil Nolde. Waetzoldt had only praise for the latter when his work was exhibited at the Commeter Art Galleries early in 1910.[26] He applauded Nolde's success in placing the "emotive power of color" in the forefront of his work, admiring his floral still lives and landscapes for their range of rich and strong tones. He also praised the religious pictures—*The Last Supper* and *Pentecost*—for their ability to portray the "passionate ardor" of the disciples and their "fanatic emotions." Waet-zoldt valued the powerful expression wrought by the "contraction" and "abbrevi-ation of reality" in Nolde's graphic work.

In the play, a connoisseur enters an art dealer's gallery, which is hung with a Christmas exhibition. The works are mostly "tasteless," overpriced landscapes and still life paintings. Claiming to know what good art is, the dealer is also antic-ipating sales. Thus he immediately explains that "one cannot always exhibit pic-tures that are good, there must also be those that will sell." When the connoisseur implies that it is fraudulent to deliberately neglect quality works of art for the sake of good business, he is labeled an idealist. "Young artists do not paint what the public likes," he is curtly informed. Echoing the idealism of Warburg's Alfred character, the connoisseur suggests a solution: educate the public, enable them to recognize kitsch, tell them that quality is fashionable. Many people, he explains, simply don't trust themselves enough to admit that they have taste. But the deal-er is alarmed: "Who will then buy my kitsch?" he asks. The taste for kitsch will disappear, he is assured, and so will those artists who create it; only the talented will survive. But the dealer protests that he must cater to all tastes; the connois-seur will find that which is good art and the rest of the public that which satis-fies them. "That would be all well and good," exclaims the connoisseur, "if the power of inferiority was not so great. One bad picture does more damage than the good done by ten fine ones. There is no moderation in the face of kitsch, only complete abstinence."

Waetzoldt's play suggests the persistence of traditional taste among Ham-burg's *Bürgertum*. This is seemingly corroborated by a government report on the city's art market for 1910, which reads: "As before, public taste is directed almost exclusively to older, traditional works. As a result, the modern school goes unconsidered in trade and exhibitions."[27] But recent research has proved that this was not the case and has challenged Waetzoldt's impressions. It is now known that many major collectors in Hamburg purchased the work of artists ranging from Max Liebermann to Edvard Munch and the Expressionist painters of *Die Brücke*. Furthermore, it is clear that Hamburg was a city where art was seen and appreciated in ever-growing public collections. This was due, in large measure, to the efforts of Lichtwark. In his play, Warburg refers to him as "Director Fireworks," an epithet that was probably born of Lichtwark's energetic transformation of the organization and mission of the Kunsthalle. The quip may also have been inspired by Lichtwark's approach to art education that, as explained in chapter one, Warburg thought promoted hedonism instead of the serious contemplation of artworks. Nonetheless, Warburg shared Lichtwark's taste for artistic modernism and his belief that transforming Hamburg into an important cultural center meant setting it upon a footing independent of cultural currents fostered by the Imperial Court in Berlin. In fact, by naming his protagonist Alfred, Warburg may have intended to give voice to Lichtwark's arguments.[28] Lichtwark was determined to confront the old with the new, to expose Hamburg's public to the art of Wilhelm Trübner, Max Slevogt, Lovis Corinth, Fritz von Uhde, Heinrich Zügel, Leopold von Kalckreuth, Max Klinger, and especially Max Liebermann.[29] His association with contemporary artists meant that, from 1895, exhibitions in the Kunsthalle brought important works of modern German, French, Dutch, Danish, and English art to public attention. Lichtwark also invited foreign artists to paint Hamburg with their progressive techniques and methods. The first of these was Anders Zorn of Sweden followed by Laurits Tuxen of Denmark, Frits Thaulow of Norway, and the French artists Albert Marquet, Pierre Bonnard, and Eduard Vuillard.[30] As Carolyn Kay has demonstrated, "a considerable number of citizens, interested in the contemporary arts and literature, applauded Lichtwark's initiative."[31]

Warburg's play reflects these significant changes at the Kunsthalle, especially the transformation of the print collection.[32] The graphics department, visited by Uncle Eduard, was opened in 1890 and comprised an exhibition hall and reading room. One of Lichtwark's many convictions was that "our art scholarship has ... focused too long and with overly strong predilections on Italian art."[33] Thus in 1891, a collection of graphic art was founded comprising works by Zorn, Klinger, James Whistler, and Adolph von Menzel. By 1900, this was the most significant collection of modern graphic art in Germany.[34] Like the fictional Alfred, Warburg defended the quality and importance of this collection and it is hardly surprising to find him doing so. In 1888, he had been greatly impressed by an exhibition of contemporary painting in Munich, especially with the bold realism and disregard for aesthetic convention expressed by Fritz von Uhde and Max Liebermann.[35] But in keeping with the fictional Alfred, Warburg also lamented the corresponding decrease in attention paid to Italian art.

The play also highlights the fact that not everyone shared the enthusiasm of Warburg and Lichtwark for progressive developments in the visual arts. In 1911, Lichtwark wrote that in Hamburg, "I don't have to deal with one emperor; a whole pack of emperors reigns here and they see only the red kerchief of modernism which hangs from my pocket."[36] Opposition to Lichtwark's initiatives grew especially after Max Liebermann's portrait of Hamburg's mayor, Carl Petersen, was unveiled to the public in Berlin in April 1892. When he awarded the commission to Liebermann, Lichtwark hoped that the portrait would inaugurate a new tradition of German portraiture. But the impressionist brushwork, lack of detail, and unsentimental treatment of the sitter was rejected by Petersen as slanderous; instead of a dignified appearance, Petersen claimed Liebermann made him look old and common. He prevented the picture from being publicly displayed in Hamburg until 1905.[37] Warburg, however, jumped to the defense of Liebermann and the German Impressionists. It behooves any public institution all the more, he wrote, "to support that movement in art which tries to learn from nature."[38] For Warburg, Impressionist artists regarded the real appearance of the world with sharpened vision; their work was very different from "petty *bourgeois* sentimentality" and its desire to hang one's "friendly uncle" or a "blossoming maiden in muslin" in a tasteful frame over the sofa.[39]

Lichtwark also took local artists under his tutelage, giving them instruction and teaching them to appreciate Hamburg's artistic traditions. He acted as manager and dealer for a group whose presence became significant enough for critics to speak of a "Hamburg School." This was institutionalized in 1897 with the foundation of an exhibiting society called the Hamburg Artists' Club. Regarding itself as the opponent of the ruling cultural establishment, the group stood at the center of debates about the value of modern art. The work of Ernst Eitner (1867–1955), Julius von Ehren (1869–1944), Thomas Herbst (1848–1915), Arthur Illies (1870–1952), Jean Paul Kayser (1869–1942), Alfred Friedrich Schaper (1869–1956), and Arthur Sieblist (1870–1945) ranged between a dark-toned Realism to an Impressionism and Post-Impressionism that attempted to recreate the effects of light and atmosphere on the eye.[40] The Impressionists of the group favored a light palette, abandoned illusionistic detail for the use of loose, visible brushwork, and largely rejected narrative content to focus on aesthetic experience, yet often emphasized social reality. Lichtwark believed their modern depictions of Hamburg and the landscape of Lower Saxony were an ideal form of popular art education; viewers would be encouraged, through familiarity with the appearances of their surroundings, to closely observe the transformation of these appearances in art.[41] Impressionist painting found many patrons in Hamburg, especially among the city's elite. But when fifty-seven of the Club's paintings were exhibited in the Kunsthalle in 1896, the exhibition met with public ridicule. To many viewers, the unsentimental *plein air* painting of the Artists' Club appeared all the more revolutionary, as they transformed the otherwise familiar environs of the city. Their work was foreign to the pathos and sentimentality favored by the *Bürgertum* and Lichtwark claimed with dismay that every child in Hamburg knew the permanent gallery devoted to contemporary pictures of the city as the "chamber of horrors."[42]

Many of the "emperors" with whom Lichtwark had to contend were members of the Art Association. Emerging first as a discussion group for art enthusiasts in

1817, it was the first middle-class art union in Germany. For many years it was the point of departure for Hamburg's undertakings in the field of the visual arts; it dominated the organization of exhibitions in the city.[43] By the 1890s, older, conservative members held a majority on the Association's steering committee. Not surprisingly, the young artists nurtured by Lichtwark were criticized by the Association's group of older, established artists and collectors who rejected stylistic innovation and also objected to Lichtwark's art-buying policies, didactic ambitions, and his preference for innovative artists. Events heated up dramatically in 1896 when a press campaign was launched against Lichtwark and Impressionist painting. Robert Wichmann, owner of the well-known Hamburg confectionery Reese and Wichmann, publicly attacked Lichtwark in the *Hamburger Nachrichten* in February of that year. His article appeared as a brochure at the end of the month, while another article by the painter Joseph Michael, in the *Hamburger Fremdenblatt* in March, supported Wichmann's campaign against "diseased growths" in contemporary art.[44]

But the spark that ignited the powder keg of opposition to Lichtwark was struck when a poster designed by Ernst Eitner was adopted as an advertisement for the Art Association's exhibition for 1896. The artist was influenced by French Impressionism, and from 1895 he turned to the use of strong, unnatural coloring. Although the Art Association purchased some of his works in 1893/94 for a members' auction, he was not popular with the public.[45] Eitner's poster depicted a violet-colored, abstracted, half-length portrait of a fully-clothed woman with languorous facial expression and palm leaf in hand. This was set against an orange background with text also printed in violet. It immediately encountered opposition in the Art Association, its detractors complaining about the unnatural representation and the lurid orange and violet colours of Eitner's abstract image. Further debate followed in the city's newspapers on the place and desirability of modern art as furthered by Lichtwark and prominently displayed in the Kunsthalle.[46] As Kay explains, Lichtwark's critics rejected modern art as "pagan, degenerate, akin to French poster art and thus un-German."[47]

With Uncle Eduard's mention of Eitner's poster, Warburg makes direct reference to these events. He held a high opinion of the artist; Eitner, he wrote, "plays too fine an instrument to use it as a bugle in the fun fair of life. Friends of art, who know how to value the real, essential qualities of Lower Saxony's artistic community, therefore have all the more moral duty to lighten the struggle of such a distinguished and modest artist for his artistic, moral, and economic existence."[48] "A sunny meadow landscape with water," by Eitner, costing 800 marks, was among eight paintings by young artists that Warburg purchased for his brothers Paul and Felix.[49]

When writing his play, Warburg must have been thinking of the most dramatic effect of Eitner's poster: the turbulent general meeting of the Art Association at the end of March 1896. This event has recently been the object of detailed analyses by two scholars who reach opposing conclusions as to its significance for the support of modern art in Hamburg.[50] Before examining these, we need to understand the nature and immediate consequences of the meeting. This was attended by more than the Association's 1,478 members and many who were otherwise indifferent to its activities.[51] In his diary, Arthur Illies provides an account of what transpired. It is easy to forget that the following passage records the meeting of an association devoted to the dissemination and appreciation of art and not the proceedings of a political rally:

> I entered the general meeting and the hall was already almost completely full of people and still more were pouring in. On a raised dais sat the Association's executive and the senate syndic, von Melle. Von Melle gave a richly theatrical welcome address followed by a Mr. Arthur Lutteroth [a Hamburg merchant] who introduced the real theme of the meeting, namely the protest against the so-called new direction in art. Since the brochures of Wichmann, Feddersen, etc. had already set the scene, the protest against Eitner's poster, which had been chosen for the Art Association's spring exhibition in the art gallery, got the ball rolling. After it had hung for a short time on the advertising pillars, it had to be withdrawn as it aroused so much opposition ... Mr. Lutteroth now held forth about the poster, about Lichtwark's hypermodern attitude to art, and about the painting of the "Young Hamburgers" who he described simply as "scribblers." It was a fairly long speech. Schiefler then stood up with the intention of responding. But then a caterwauling was raised in the hall, chairs were knocked about and the entire assembly broke into an uproar. Nonetheless, Schiefler tried to speak, but in vain. Obviously, the chairman could no longer control the situation, or perhaps wanted it to continue. But, be that as it may, Schiefler was shouted down. Other speakers tried to speak, but the hubbub would not allow it. Then Brinckmann [director of Hamburg's Museum of Art and Industry] stood and pounded with both fists upon the table. Rising above the rumpus with a thundering voice, he was able to speak for a moment. He refused to tolerate, in a circle of educated men who supposedly wanted to strive for the sake of culture, such an undignified and uncultured manner of engagement. But after the first shock of his interruption had disappeared, he was again shouted down ... the meeting finally ended with a general resolution on the part of the entire Art Association to reject all modern cultural endeavors in Hamburg.[52]

The Art Association was instantly transformed: a quarter of the committee was voted out of office and Wichmann and his supporters installed their candidates in a more conservative steering committee. Ernst Juhl lost his position as secretary and business manager to the painter Eduard Sack, while von Melle resigned his office and was replaced by the district court judge Dr. Paul Crasemann. The revolt marked the end of the Art Association's spring exhibitions in the Kunsthalle until their resumption in 1903; Lichtwark had no desire to accommodate those who tried to bind his hands. In an essay published in 1897 entitled "The Campaign Against the New Direction in Art," Schiefler wrote of the negative effect of such events on Hamburg's artistic life, events that "contain a great threatening danger for seeds, upon whose blossoming the standing of Hamburg in the field of intellectual culture in part depends."[53] He hoped the antimodern campaign would not destroy young talents or, through its influence on patrons, force them to emigrate.

In her discussion of these events, Carolyn Kay argues that they clearly demonstrate "the popular rejection of modernism in Hamburg at this time." The scandal, she contends, "brought out into the open Hamburg's resistance to new visions and perspectives in German art." Setting "bourgeois against bourgeois," Kay emphasizes that by losing the support of the Art Association, Lichtwark lost an important ally in his efforts to expose Hamburg's public to modern art. Ultimately, only a select group of rich patrons supported his exhibition and educational efforts.[54] In an opposing assessment, Jennifer Jenkins argues that "the debacle of 1896 had more to do with personality conflicts and personal jealousies than with a grand rejection of modernism."[55] Not only, she contends, did things continue much as before, but "Lichtwark continued to collect both international and local modernist art, if anything at a more rapid pace and with more daring choices."[56] Indeed, Hamburg continued to be animated by a "growing public interest in modernist experimentation."[57] With reference to the events of March 1896, Schiefler explained that the persistence of an aged and conservative steering committee emasculated the Art Association as a promoter of art and resulted in its degeneration into an organization for the "raffling off" of pictures. As late as 1915, the managing director, Theodor Brodersen, regarded the Realist painter, Leopold von Kalckreuth, as suspiciously modern.[58] Nonetheless, Jenkins is right to argue that public and private support for modern art among Hamburg's middle classes remained substantial in the wake of the events of 1896. However, while Kay's conception of the constituency that supported artistic modernism in Hamburg seems too narrow, Jenkins's seems too broad. And yet both perspectives confirm an image of the city as more artistically vibrant and open to reform than has previously been acknowledged in English-language scholarship.

What is important here, however, is Warburg's attitude to the events of March 1896. Although he did not address the issue other than in the form of his play, there can be no doubt that he would have regarded the rejection of Eitner and Lichtwark by the Art Association as another expression of the local philistinism that so often provoked his caustic criticism. Indeed, one can only imagine that the affair was especially disturbing to someone so keenly interested in artistic innovation and its place in Hamburg's public realm. But the point to be made is that, no matter the findings of recent scholarship; no matter the obvious successes of Lichtwark in building a collection of modern art in Hamburg; and no matter that he acknowledged many other positive aspects of the city's encounter with cultural modernism, Warburg continually returned to criticism of Hamburg's philistinism, at least in the Imperial period. With his scholarly sophistication, and cosmopolitan interests and orientation, Hamburg never met Warburg's expectations as a city in which art, especially the most modern, was given its due of serious consideration.

IV

What was it that inspired Warburg to reanimate these events, to bring the conflict into his own home in the form of a play and to side with the progressive artists of his day? Gombrich suggested a compelling personal reason in the form of his courtship of the artist Mary Hertz whom he married in 1897.[59] Mary exhibited with the Association of Hamburg Friends of Art, designed ornamental borders and drew vignettes for the art journal *Pan*, and was commissioned by Lichtwark to paint "private artistic scenes."[60] But Gombrich neglects the fact that Mary Warburg's work reflects little of the progressive aspects of her artistic milieu; she remained heavily influenced by traditional trends. As Sabina Ghandchi has shown, her work displays a "conventional and practiced repertoire of motifs and themes." She avoided "all that was aggressive and 'too modern': the radical social and artistic transformations of the twentieth century do not find expression in her work."[61] It was never her intention to become a public success and, although Warburg had been struck by Mary's intelligent response to art when they met in Florence in 1888, there is no evidence to prove that he took her seriously as an artist. Instead, Max Adolph Warburg records how his father referred to his mother's pastels as painted with "a small dirty finger." According to Warburg, his wife was happiest in her artistic pursuits, "with a hat made of newspaper and a medium-sized rhubarb leaf."[62]

It is more plausible that Warburg saw his personal and professional situation as analogous to that of contemporary painters struggling to separate themselves from the social, moral, and artistic conventions of their forebears. In the play, Uncle Eduard taunts Alfred with the notion that public taste will force art to remain grounded in traditional aesthetic forms. In real life, Warburg knew that pursuit of his personal and professional goals implied a break with the past, a revolt against his elders, an escape from parental certainties seen as more complacent than his own. He mocks Uncle Eduard's manner and dress describing it as "entirely in Sunday parade order, black coat, top hat," a description that Warburg insisted was not a caricature. During the Fin-de-Siècle, it was not unusual for artists and art critics to associate artistic innovation with generational conflict and change.[63] Of course, the supporters of progressive art forms were not only the very young; Lichtwark, for instance, was forty-four in 1896. In his comedy, however, Warburg portrays the social conventions that stood in the way of the development of art as those which also hindered his personal ambitions as a young man. The "light and air" that he demanded for "the moderns" was needed not only to refresh parlors overstuffed with bourgeois furnishings and hung with conventional artworks; it was required to sweep out social conventions, both German-Jewish and bourgeois, which stood in the way of his personal development. The personal discontent harbored by the young Warburg is reflected in the brief philosophy of history that he noted in 1889: "Antiquity: Attempt to find satisfaction in life, pleasure, or self-destruction. Middle Ages: Self-destruction for the sake of a future personal life … Modern Times: Restriction of enjoyment; self-destruction for the sake of an impersonal life."[64] Thus, Warburg may have chosen to express himself in comic mode, but the personal circumstances that inspired the play were less than humorous. As explained in chapter one, Warburg's break with Jewish religious orthodoxy had already engendered considerable conflict within his own family. In 1896, it was his courtship of Mary Hertz, whose family had recently converted to Protestantism, which generated much consternation and debate in the Warburg family. The play was intended to sound a strong note in the ears of his parents.

In addition to the obstacles placed in the path of his personal development were those that hampered his professional ambitions. Wolfgang Mommsen has written that the aesthetic revolution of the Fin-de-Siècle "found its social equivalent in the decomposition of the *Bürgertum* as a unified class with its own ethos and specific lifestyle."[65] Mommsen's claim for the original social unity of the *Bürgertum* is contentious, and it is more accurate to speak of significant changes in bourgeois life at the end of the nineteenth century than of decomposition.[66] But the concurrence of aesthetic innovation with a change in bourgeois lifestyle rings true in the case of Aby Warburg; while championing artistic innovators, Warburg's life took a different course, in terms of vocation, from that of his parents' generation. The increasing demands of business on the *Bürgertum* made the retention of an active interest in culture more difficult at the turn of the century. This led to the decision by many members of this class to make their academic or artistic interests into their profession, and there was a clear diminution in the control that parents were able to wield over their sons' vocational choices: Max Warburg had to be dissuaded from pursuing a military career, his brother Paul from studying science, while their father Moritz failed to redirect Aby Warburg from his career as an art historian.[67] Just as the artists of his generation broke from official academies and salons, Warburg broke with the conventions that had governed his ancestors' choice of profession.

The generational conflict that characterized Warburg's early adult life is highlighted in the play by reference to the debate over the art of Max Klinger (1857–1920). Damned by Uncle Eduard, Klinger was a figure often used by contemporary critics as a metaphor for the artist suffering at the hands of an uncomprehending public.[68] Klinger entered the leading ranks of modern German artists in the 1890s and was appointed as a professor at the Royal Academy of Graphic Art in Leipzig in 1897. He was one of many artists who turned to the erotic as a source of inspiration. In so doing, he broke with the iconographical traditions of the nineteenth century and aimed to disrupt the comfortable social and moral assumptions of Germany's middle classes; he sought to visualize contemporary social and gender conflicts and to expose hypocritical sexual conventions. Klinger was praised by many critics as a genius in the Renaissance tradition and as a savior of German art; Karl Scheffler, editor of *Kunst und Künstler*, described his art as "sumptuous in all parts, princely in every expression, great and heroic, rich and honorable, sweeping and intimate."[69] Lichtwark collected Klinger's work for the Kunsthalle and commissioned him to produce a Brahms memorial for Hamburg's concert hall.[70] In addition to the character of Alfred, Aby Warburg's sister Olga was an admirer of Klinger's art, as was his fiancée Mary Hertz who had read the treatise entitled *Painting and Drawing* that the artist published in 1891.[71] But amongst the general public, only a minority of exhibition-goers appreciated the liberating effect of Klinger's work; most found it offensive and he was widely damned.[72] The languid, eroticized mood of paintings like *The Blue Hour* (1890), in which three adolescent nudes lounge by a body of water at dusk, provoked criticism that Klinger was responsible for the decline of contemporary morals.[73]

Most of Warburg's elders found their aesthetic tastes satisfied by natural or ethereal beauty, dramatic historical episodes, and morally elevating or humorous allegories. Popular art journals, like *Die Kunst für Alle* (founded 1885), discussed art mainly from a moral, idealistic, and patriotic point of view, reflecting the concerns of their middle-class readers.[74] In his play, Warburg parodies the middle-class belief that art should be beautiful and morally uplifting, but the object of his mockery was probably not principally his immediate family. The Warburgs were not the Jewish equivalent of the north German merchant family portrayed in Thomas Mann's *Buddenbrooks* (1901). They were fond of music and art; when Warburg's mother moved to Hamburg from Frankfurt after her marriage to Moritz Warburg, she was appalled to find the city had no art gallery and was bewildered by its Englishness.[75] The family collected the work of the Dutch Realist, Jozef Israëls, and the German Impressionist, Max Liebermann, and Charlotte Warburg took a special interest in the art of Edvard Munch.[76] Thus, instead of looking to his family, Warburg seems to have modeled Uncle Eduard and Mr. Merckendorff on Robert Wichmann and those who had publicly opposed Lichtwark and Eitner and had forced the Art Association to adopt a more conservative steering committee. It was these conservative voices who would have praised the Austrian painter and illustrator Moritz Ludwig von Schwind (1804–71) as a "justifiable and beneficial opposition" to modern art. A product of Biedermeier Vienna, Schwind's sentimental portrayals of bourgeois life were executed in a lyrical style, while his romantic rendering of the German past earned him a reputation as a painter of national sagas, myths, and legends.[77] For Schwind, as for the Merckendorffs, art was "the balm of life, a charmed circle of wish-fulfillment."[78]

An artist less well-known to art historians, but considered by the Merckendorffs and Uncle Alfred as one of the pillars of "solid Hamburg taste" is the landscape and maritime painter Johann Georg Valentin Ruths (1825–1905). In the 1890s, Ruths "stood like a Nestor at the head of Hamburg's artistic community."[79] Critical of German Impressionism, his mature work bridges the gulf between the naturalistic representations of the north German landscape by the "Hamburg Realists"—Hermann Kauffmann (1808–1889), Otto Speckter (1807–1871) and Jacob Gensler (1808–1845)—and the Impressionist renderings of the "Young Hamburgers."[80] His landscapes are sober and academic; as Lichtwark explained, Ruths painted Hamburg's harbor before the time in which "smoke and soot from factory chimneys and steamer funnels impressed the atmosphere with a heavy, melancholy character."[81] As a result, his work was widely admired by the public and a successful exhibition was mounted by the Art Association in 1898.[82] Official recognition of his academic style in Hamburg came when, in conjunction with the Bremen artist, Arthur Fitger (1840–1909), he painted the main staircase of the Kunsthalle with allegorical landscapes. It is the idea of making concessions to this sort of popular taste which rouses Alfred's anger.

Alfred's tastes tend towards the art of Klinger, and in his play Warburg makes reference to the artist's infamous series of etchings entitled *A Love* (1887). Critics heralded Klinger for revitalizing the graphic medium in Germany.[83] His print-making reflected an interest in French Naturalist literature with its psychological, social, and political concerns. In the graphic cycle to which Warburg refers, and which Uncle Eduard denounces as improper for well-brought-up people, Klinger criticized the double standard of bourgeois morality.[84] The prints relate the events of a middle-class woman's illicit love affair that ends in abandonment by her lover, an attempted abortion, and death. Perhaps the most disturbing image is the last in which the figure of death holds the aborted fetus over the woman's corpse. It is hardly surprising that the work meets with Uncle Eduard's indignation; when *A Love* was exhibited at the Berlin Academy Exhibition in 1888, it met with a "censorious fate"; one of the images was rejected on the grounds of indecency, prompting Klinger to withdraw the entire series.[85]

This is not to suggest that Warburg's appreciation for Klinger's art marks him as a Bohemian. As previously discussed, he was suspicious of Bohemian lifestyles and opposed his son's ambitions to become an artist. The point being made, however, is that as a young man Warburg found his desire to escape some of the constraining religious, social, and professional conventions of the German-Jewish economic elite reflected in concurrent transformations in the form and content of art. While stating his enthusiasm for artistic reform, Warburg was asserting his right to freely establish his life's course.

Warburg was not the only young man among the city's *Großbürgertum* who challenged the values and assumptions of his class. Another of these was a friend and associate of Warburg's: the author, lawyer, and eventual syndic of Hamburg's citizens' assembly, Carl Mönckeberg (1873–1939). Son of Hamburg's eminent mayor, Johann Georg Mönckeberg, he was critical of the "military patriotism" of the *Bürgertum* and complained to his father of the "sober, dull, and unimaginative realism" that prevailed in Germany.[86] As an author who joined Lichtwark's circle of writers and artists, he sought to break free of the strictures of his father's social class and attacked its philistinism. In his diary, Arthur Illies tells us that Mönckeberg "explained to me that we stand at a cultural and social turning point—completely new social relationships must be created in order to do justice to the problems that have emerged with time."[87] His plays were purposefully provocative and meant to shock the members of his social class. One of these was the drama *Illusions*, which he wrote in 1895; it attracted an audience of

1,200 when performed by the People's Theater Association.[88] Schiefler writes that the play "aroused horror" among Hamburg's *Großbürgertum*.[89] But as was the case with Warburg's play, Mönckeberg's lenient father allowed it, amongst others, to be performed by the family in their own home. When Mönckeberg became editor of a journal devoted to Hamburg culture and entitled *Der Lotse*, Warburg supported his efforts with enthusiasm.[90] As Alfred remarks in the play, "the public must be educated."

Warburg was also enthusiastic about young American artists whose work he encountered while visiting the U.S. in 1895 and 1896. In April 1897, at Lichtwark's suggestion, an entire issue of *Pan* was devoted to Hamburg's art scene. The issue included poems by Gustav Falke and Klaus Groth and illustrations by Eitner, Illies, Kayser, Olde, Siebelist, von Ehren, and Julius Wohlers. Among essays on Hamburg's private art collections, popular art education, and dilettantism was an article by Warburg on American "chap books."[91] "Chap book" was a generic title for several American literary and artistic reviews that appeared in the 1890s. Published by young writers and artists and dubbed "periodicals of protest," these journals sought to familiarize their readership with the modern movement in literature and art. Through poems, essays, short stories, and art, they strove to "combat the thoughtless, vulgar lust for sensation." Warburg had a high opinion of their content, describing it as "gourmet food"; in his mind, they published "sensitive analyses" of several English and French writers, like Anatole France, who critically "probe the whole fin-de-siècle Pantheon" including Aubrey Beardsley, Oscar Wilde, Robert L. Stevenson, and Henrik Ibsen. He praised their sense of critical distance from fin-de-siècle decadence and applauded the European-educated artist Bruce Porter for his "idealistic nature, with its deep ironic aversion to the general vulgar and insincere philistinism."

Looking beyond the context of Hamburg's *Großbürgertum*, it is well known that the progressive aspects of Warburg's cultural and social vision were shared by many of his generation. Perhaps the most apparent indication of Warburg's affiliation with a wider climate of critical and reformist social opinion is his membership in the *Deutsche Werkbund*.[92] This was just one of a wide variety of middle-class leagues and associations attracting younger men and women and espousing various ideas of cultural and social renewal.[93] As Thomas Nipperdey described it, "Wilhelmine society was a society of reform movements and of reforms."[94] Composed mostly of urban, middle-class Germans, these groups directed their energies to a great diversity of goals ranging from clothing reform to the reform of town planning. Many propounded an economic and political vision of a stable and prosperous society. Founded on 5 October 1907, the *Werkbund* was an alliance of industrialists, civil servants, academics, artists, designers, and architects that addressed the educated urban elite. It sought not only to restore artistry to architecture, interior design, the applied arts, and commercial products through the employ of modern technology; it also sought to raise the wages and self-esteem of the working classes and harbored the hope "of social unity through improved quality of life for all."[95] This commitment to social change linked it to the world of public institutions and reforming public authorities.

But this reform movement was diffuse; "no single set of social, economic, or cultural criteria alone determined the overall pattern." Nor was it "free from the dark potential scholars have uncovered in the radical nationalism, rationalizing utopias, illiberalism, and cultural despair of the fin de siècle."[96] Furthermore, the marginal impact of these associations on the political sphere and their search for aesthetic or cultural answers to economic and political questions has often led to negative assessments by historians. It is becoming more common, however, to stress the extent to which reformers were socially engaged and to see them as an important "force for change" in Imperial Germany.[97] In these movements and the art they produced, it was no longer the monarchically-constituted nation that sought its symbolic expression. According to Wolfgang Hardtwig, it was rather "the middle-class nation, which communicated with itself regarding its orientation in norms and values independent from and indeed even against the conservative state and imperial leadership."[98] The belief of the Wilhelmine reformers was that "the modern age needed cultural legitimation, that a society based on industry and commerce could no longer rely on means of expression developed by the aristocracy."[99] It is important to note that, beyond membership, Warburg's practical involvement with the *Werkbund* was minimal. But the point to be made is that, as a young man coming to maturity in Wilhelmine Germany, he sympathized with the ambitions of those who sought a form of aesthetic expression that would more accurately reflect the rapidly changing social, economic, and cultural dimensions of their world.

In addition to personal concerns, Warburg's perspective on contemporary art was inflected by his professional endeavors. "Light and air" were also required to free art from bourgeois hedonism and to establish its study on a serious, scientific foundation. The subject of Warburg's scholarship, Italian Renaissance art, was extremely popular among Germany's middle classes and the advance of reproductive techniques meant that images by Raphael, Titian, and Leonardo were hung in many middle-class homes.[100] But Warburg was a caustic critic of the neo-Renaissance trend in art and design that marked the late nineteenth-century. Deploring the fashionable aestheticism of his day, there is a recurring tone of aversion towards middle-class taste in his writings. Bourgeois hedonism was an obstacle to the true understanding of art, just as the ownership of art was "an obstacle to a proper analytical grasp of artifacts."[101] Warburg had a strong aversion to "the modern languid art-lover" of the 1890s and what he called "hero-worshipping dilettantism."[102] He scorned those readers of John Ruskin who traveled to Italy in search of an idyllic world of art, and, as previously mentioned, mocked the followers of Arthur de Gobineau and Friedrich Nietzsche who looked to the Renaissance for a model of unrestrained individualism and sensuality.[103] His professional goal was the consolidation of art history as a serious academic discipline. "We of the younger generation," he wrote, "want to attempt to advance the science of art so far that anyone who talks in public about art without having specially and profoundly studied this science should be considered just as ridiculous as people who dare to talk about medicine without being doctors."[104] Warburg wanted to save artists like Botticelli from the decadents, "to save the *Quattrocento* from sentimental gush," just as the progressive artists of his generation sought to save art from the academies and salons.[105]

In his play, Warburg seems to privilege art as a means for his generation to express and understand the rapid transformations of the world in which they lived. At the climax, Alfred proclaims that "art is for mature, lively people who want to grasp life and not for old dodderers or teenage girls!" In his scholarship, we have noted that Warburg turned to an interpretation of art in the light of psychology and hence to a psychology of culture. Around the turn of the century, he attempted to understand why sophisticated, humanist-educated Florentine bankers and merchants of the fifteenth century demonstrated a fascination for the naturalism of Flemish art and for the Gothic aesthetic fashionable with the French court. Why did Florentine patrons and the artists they employed—artists who were exposed to the many surviving examples of ancient art to be found in Italy—continue to depict the gods and personages of antiquity in French Gothic fashions? From Warburg's perspective of historical psychology, these questions held symptomatic value for the development of European culture; they revealed the tension between self-conscious symbolization and empathetic identification with the world that characterized humanity's mental makeup. His response was many-sided and never expressed in a single formulation. On the one hand, the Gothic aesthetic was an impetus to the emergence of the classicizing, idealized style of the Renaissance, a style that supplanted the illustrative reality of much medieval art and reawakened mankind to the beauty of humanity.[106] This was in keeping with his notion of the dialectical nature of the Italian Renaissance and the historical process as the result of conflicting energies. But Warburg also understood the Gothic style as an ally of classical idealism; in its own right it was a symptom of Renaissance man's zest for life and joy in the sensuous beauty of the world.[107]

However, what seems to have dominated Warburg's thinking during the 1890s was the role of the Gothic aesthetic as a negative influence on the development of style. When he published a book review entitled "The Picture Chronicle of a Florentine Goldsmith" in 1899, he considered the adoption of Flemish naturalism to be an impediment to the emergence of classical form and ideal beauty in fifteenth-century Italian art.[108] The art of Leonardo, Raphael, and Michelangelo could only flower once the vestiges of Gothic civilization had been thrust aside and Florentines derived from ancient art the energy they needed to expel the forces of medieval naturalism. With this perspective, Warburg was projecting his own cultural environment onto the world of the wealthy Italian art patrons who preceded his family by 400 years.[109] His declared opposition towards the "wealth and Frenchifying elegance" that characterized Germany's economic elite was directed at the merchants and bankers of fifteenth-century Florence who, as Warburg was keenly aware, played an economic and cultural role similar to that of his own family.[110] As Philippe-Alain Michaud has written, Warburg's "library was set up as a counterpoint to the values on which its material existence depended, as a haven of thought in the midst of a world devoted to the pragmatism of the marketplace."[111] Just as he criticized his contemporaries, Warburg scorned the bourgeoisie of Renaissance Florence for its vanity, materialism, and its taste for the fashionable style of the French court. This regressive taste was the product of a middle-class investment in the materialities of life.[112] Warburg found this, for example, in the frescoes of the Tornabuoni Chapel in Santa Maria Novella in Florence, completed in 1490. These were painted by Domenico Ghirlandaio and depicted scenes from the life of the Virgin and Saint John the Baptist. But Warburg found them to be a domestic art, devoid of Christian devotion: "one would rather think that this is an official family party; an old butler stands in a Renaissance loggia and busies himself at a genuine antique buffet to get the punch ready. A young servant hurriedly brings the lemon he has been waiting for so long." He described the patron—the banker Giovanni Tornabuoni—as a "saturated sponge of prosperity ... well-fed and well-padded ... with his imposing bulk and his large tired eyes, whose broad back had been so comfortably warmed by the sun of good fortune."[113] In the play, Uncle Eduard and Mr. Merckendorff defend the public's conventional artistic tastes by claiming that people have a right to appreciate whatever they have paid for. In the Renaissance, Warburg understood attempts to visualize the heroic past through fifteenth-century dress and custom as hostile to the emergence of beauty and an ideal style. The taste for the illustrative mode of medieval art was a regressive cultural influence, as was the taste of modern Germans for the products of Germany's official salons and Uncle Eduard's fondness for an artist's ability to accurately reproduce every detail of a landscape.

Furthermore, as Gombrich reminds us, Warburg's ruminations on the liberation of Hellenic goddesses and nymphs from the heavy, stiff costume of the French court occurred at the same time as the campaign for the "new woman." A lively issue during the 1890s, it often focused on the question of dress and a woman's right to unrestricted movement.[114] A clothing reform movement demanded dresses without stays and the abolition of the corset. In addition to the desire for freer movement and easier breathing, some authors claimed that restrictive French fashions were threatening the fertility of the German race.[115] Just as Warburg realized that conventional art forms were no longer appropriate for Germany's changing social and cultural milieu in the 1890s, he looked for evidence of a similar attitude emerging among Florentine artists of the late fifteenth century. "Naive and innocuous though it might seem," he explained, "this realistic costume style *alla franzese* was in fact the most powerful enemy of that elevated style of emotive rhetoric *all'antica* which was to shake off the sumptuous burden of fashionable dress, once and for all, only in the heroic manner of Antonio Pollaiuolo."[116] As previously indicated, this turn to Greek and Roman artistic models in the work of Pollaiuolo (c. 1432–98), Botticelli, and Ghirlandaio, amongst others, was not simply a move towards self-reflective calm and an idealized depiction of life. Warburg believed that these artists looked to those aspects of ancient art that represented the human form in animation, not in calm repose. In depicting the body in motion and giving expression to a joie de vivre, the progressives among fifteenth-century Italian artists had much in common with the progressives of the 1890s who gave expression to the dynamism of modern life through the abbreviated style of Impressionism.

In his play, Warburg writes of the technical innovation born of sense impression which characterizes the work of the Impressionists. In opposition to Uncle Eduard's damning assessment, Alfred praises the work of Anders Zorn (1860–1920), the Swedish artist whose name sparks the altercation. Represented in the exhibitions of the German Secessionists during the 1890s, Zorn was the first foreign artist invited by Lichtwark to work in Hamburg.[117] He was by no means an avant-garde painter. Along with Giovanni Boldini, John Singer Sargent, and James Whistler, Zorn painted the aristocracy and nouveau riche of Europe and America.[118] Broadly speaking, he was an Impressionist who remained true to the appearance of his models.[119] The lively brushwork and candid nature of his compositions lend his paintings a feeling of improvisation. He was influenced by *Japonisme* and salon art, and his bravura brushwork provoked comparisons with Titian, Velázquez, and Rembrandt.[120] In addition to his fame as a portrait painter, Zorn was one of the most sought-after graphic artists of his day and extended his impressionistic style to his etchings. One of his best known graphic works is his portrait of the Paris dancer Rosita Mauri of 1889. With broken lines that do not seek to hide their artifice, Zorn created sketchy, yet boldly defined representations of form, literal interpretations of Warburg's notion of "progress in abbreviation."

Material and scientific progress, however, was not an unambiguous blessing in Warburg's mind. This emerges in his attitude toward the Swiss painter Arnold Böcklin (1827–1901), another prominent artist praised by Alfred and damned by Uncle Eduard in the play. Böcklin was one of the most important exponents of European Symbolist painting. Broadly defined, the Symbolist movement was a reaction to the materialism of modern society and stressed the subjective, the irrational, the spiritual, and the existence of deeper levels of consciousness; much of it rejected traditional iconography in its efforts to give expression to an ideal world beyond the world of appearances. Although he was Swiss and lived most of his life in Italy, Böcklin was adopted by the German public and championed by German critics. The artist drew his subject matter from the tales of classical antiquity, but did not paint the world of the gods. Instead, he produced fantasy landscapes and seascapes, often gigantic and garishly-colored, and populated by satyrs, nymphs, tritons, and naiads. In certain respects, Böcklin remained within the academic tradition: he deplored Impressionism and favoured a naturalistic rendering of detail; he employed traditional symbols and allegories, attempting to evoke spirituality through myth and religion; his themes were romantic and were praised by critics for their challenge to Realism. But his interpretation of classical themes was idiosyncratic in its combination of literalness and allegory.[121]

Given the lack of identifiable literary reference, the vagueness of Böcklin's imagery left his work open to numerous interpretations. In the 1890s, when cultural criticism was infiltrated by nationalist rhetoric, patriotic critics proclaimed Böcklin as a prophet of a new Germany; his art was described as representing what was essential in the German national character and as giving visual form to national consciousness. The art historian, Carl Neumann, said that "Böcklin's roots go far into the heart of our soil, where the deepest racial characteristics lie."[122] After his death in 1901, Böcklin's art came under attack by the critic and art historian Julius Meier-Graefe and his reputation quickly declined. In 1905, Meier-Graefe published *The Case of Böcklin*, in which he criticized the artist's work as a symptom of German degeneracy and philistinism. This was part of Meier-Graefe's larger assault on German culture that condemned its militarism, materialism, and imperialism.[123] But during the 1880s and 1890s, Böcklin received extensive patronage from Germany's middle classes and attained a degree of celebrity matched by few living artists; his Florence studio was visited by the future Wilhelm II. Uncle Eduard's familiarity with Böcklin's work is indicative of the extent of his fame. Hamburg's Art Association mounted a successful public exhibition of his work in 1898 and Warburg's mother and sister Olga were both attracted to his art.[124]

On a visit to Basel in 1898, Warburg noted in his diary: "wonderful Böcklins, like a refreshing bath in wind and waves."[125] While Warburg did not comment on the artist as an embodiment of German racial characteristics, he would not have been offended by the nationalist rhetoric which accompanied the reception of Böcklin's art. We have noted that Warburg was an ardent nationalist whose service with an artillery regiment in Karlsruhe in 1892/93 prompted him to criticize the *Bürgertum* as "soft" and "lazy."[126] But the reasons for his interest in Böcklin are rooted elsewhere. On one level, Warburg must have felt some affinity with Böcklin as "the voluntary exile, the seeker."[127] In the 1890s, both men lived in self-imposed exile in Florence where they pursued original projects in their respective fields of endeavor.

On a more profound level, Warburg experienced Böcklin's painting from the perspective of the topics that fill his notebooks in the 1890s: the practice of symbolism and the psychology of pictorial expression. When he traveled to the American southwest in 1895/96 in order to observe the rituals and symbols of the supposedly primitive Hopi Indians, Warburg described the landscape as of a Böcklinesque nature seemingly created for secret pagan rituals.[128] He saw Böcklin as a modern pagan who gave expression to primitive impulses; for Warburg, "pagan" meant the opposite of the restraint associated with reason and Judeo-Christian ethics. He even once lamented that his contemporaries had lost "the practice of the orgiastic ecstasies of antiquity."[129] Böcklin's art was the embodiment of what the editor of *Der Kunstwart*, Ferdinand Avenarius, called for in the journal's pages: an art of fantasy and imagination necessary to promote an ethical and human vision in the face of bourgeois materialism.[130]

Warburg gave expression to these views on the occasion of Böcklin's death in Florence in 1901. Along with Heinrich Brockhaus and the sculptor Adolph von

Hildebrand, he arranged for a memorial service to be held in the Palazzo Medici-Riccardi.[131] He also composed a report on the funeral, entitled "Bocklin's Passing" and dated 18 January 1901.[132] The many surviving drafts of this report, and the language in which it is written, demonstrate the literary ambitions that Warburg continued to harbor as a young man. Beginning with the words "the great Pan is dead," Warburg eulogizes Böcklin in romantic language that pays tribute to the artist's "pagan" imagination. He writes, "Will no mysterious pirates suddenly appear on the hills of Fiesole, pale, black-bearded, wrapped in ragged fluttering red cloaks, to carry him off on their shoulders at lightning speed to their ghost-ship and on to the dark-blue raging sea?" Such statements challenge any image of Warburg standing at the end of an intellectual tradition that saw Greek classicism as a mark of rationality.[133] As discussed in chapter one, Warburg believed that artistic creation oscillated between two poles. One pole consisted of self-conscious symbolization and was indicative of humanity's ability to create a self-reflective distance between itself and the world; the other was marked by primitive impulses of mimesis in which the depiction of intense bodily movement characterized the artist's empathetic immersion in the events to which he gave form.[134] Warburg believed that a measure of emotion and passion was a necessary check on the potential excess of artifice in artistic creation; an excess of logic and self-conscious symbolization could result in an art of empty rhetoric and emotional vacancy. Böcklin's art emphasized the Dionysian aspect of antiquity; his animated figures gave voice to a joie de vivre and a spirit that rejected modern materialism. Warburg writes that "in our age of traffic, of distance-destroying chaos, he could still be found to stand against the current and forcefully to assert the pirate's right of a romantic idealism; to evoke through the mythopoeic power of the image." This was something that many of the fifteenth-century Florentines whom Warburg studied would have appreciated. On this point, Warburg writes of the "enigmatic type of personality whose explosive and yet harmonious vital energies show themselves in the way in which the Medicean Florentine joyously welcomes any stirring of the soul as an extension of his mental scope."[135] This was not the case with Hamburg's philistines, like the fictional Merckendorffs and their love of contemporary costume pictures.

But with his mention of "distance-destroying chaos," Warburg suggests that the romantic idealism of Böcklin, and the satyrs and nymphs that he painted, were threatened by the hyperrationality and materialism of the modern age. Indeed, in addition to its celebration of Böcklin's art, Warburg's report seems a melancholy reflection on a world that was passing away; the scene of Böcklin's funeral is taken as an allegorical representation of machinery mercilessly destroying the power of myth. Warburg was particularly irritated by the presence of a press photographer at the funeral. He writes that "arrogantly planted before the open grave stands … the impertinent, one-eyed staring Cyclops of the technical age, the photographic camera; dancing in the vicinity is its shutter-snapping contemporary with black goatee, a plundering hyena's smile on his lips." Despite the fact that Warburg's research benefited enormously from developments in photography, in this instance he saw the camera as a technical intrusion on the imaginative world of the artist that destroyed any mental space for calm reflection.

Warburg ruminated on this subject during his American sojourn and gave expression to his thoughts in "A Lecture on Serpent Ritual," published in 1938.[136] Here Warburg writes that "telegram and telephone destroy the cosmos. Mythical and symbolic thinking strive to form spiritual bonds between humanity and the world, shaping distance into the space required for devotion and reflection: the distance undone by the instantaneous electric connection." Modern technology released humanity from the symbolic relationships it used to have with nature, "bringing with it a series of rational substitutions for the ritual behavior" with which people "once confronted the impenetrability of phenomena."[137] In the Renaissance, "the mediation of scientific and philosophical inquiry by the continuing belief in marvels and wonders prevented the establishment of what Max Weber referred to as the 'iron cage' of modernity."[138] But Warburg writes that "the culture of the machine age destroys what the natural sciences, born of myth, so arduously achieved: the space for devotion, which evolved in turn into the space required for reflection." Thus, far from an optimistic belief in progress, Warburg was ambivalent about the achievements of the modern world. While the "the process of rationalization represented a progressive creation of the '*Denkraum*' necessary to the establishment of civilization *per se*," Warburg was deeply concerned with the retrogression caused by the demystification of the world and an instrumental approach to nature.[139] On this point he seems at one with the Symbolist painters of his generation, just as he would be with the Expressionists who followed them. *Denkraum*, the zone of reasoning in which distance and detachment allowed for contemplation and reflection on the world and natural phenomena, was being threatened by the speed of electrotechnical information; the symbols that permitted humanity to meditate upon the universe in tranquility were being destroyed. "The modern Prometheus and the modern Icarus, Franklin and the Wright brothers," he continues, "who invented the dirigible and the airplane, are precisely those ominous destroyers of the sense of distance, who threaten to lead the planet back into chaos."[140] Upheld by the young protagonist of Warburg's play, Bocklin's art was a counterpoint to technological, social, and cultural developments that reached a new intensity in Warburg's lifetime.

Yet, in one important respect, we need to qualify the notion that Warburg's remarks on the occasion of Böcklin's death were a lament for a world that was passing away. As noted in the previous chapter, it would be wrong to see Warburg's thinking as completely divorced from an evolutionary understanding of historical processes. But from the predominantly nonchronological perspective of his scholarly enterprise, the dangerous developments of his age were not unique historical phenomena; they were but another move in the dialectic of psychology and culture, a swing back towards the loss of an interval between the self and the world, the loss of that self-reflective space of rational thought which Warburg called *Denkraum*. What was passing away had done so before and, presumably, would do so again. Warburg had already seen this in the Renaissance, which if it embodied a crucial stage of human enlightenment, was also "a lost moment." As Matthew Rampley explains, "it was also eventually eclipsed by the processes central to its emergence: allegorisation, rationalization, mathematization." The Renaissance gave way to the Baroque age.[141] Thus, from the perspective of psychic time—and quite apart from its response to phenomena particular to Warburg's lifetime—Böcklin's art was a transformative engagement with the past; similar to the Renaissance itself, "it offered a model for what an enlightened culture might be—sublimating primitive mimetic impulses while still preserving their memory."[142] In the case of Hamburg's Bismarck memorial, Warburg would again display enthusiasm for an artist's response to contemporary and topical developments in German society and culture. But as he did with Böcklin, he would engage the issues surrounding its construction from a nonchronological perspective on European culture that pursued the paths taken by the human mind in a synchronous psychic time.

Notes

1. Warburg Institute Archive, London (hereafter WIA). III.26.3; the file contains notes, character sketches, and drafts in several hands, including that of Warburg's secretary; the play is dated 31 December 1896.
2. See Ernst Gombrich, *Aby Warburg: An Intellectual Biography*, 2nd ed. (Chicago, 1986), p.93ff; Bernd Roeck, *Florenz, 1900: Die Suche Nach Arkadien* (Munich, 2001), p. 216f; Cecilia Lengefeld, "Ich kann leichter Kunstfreunde gewinnen als du Was?" *Frankfurter Allgemeine Zeitung*, 31 December 2002; Cecilia Lengefeld, *Anders Zorn: Eine Künstlerkarriere in Deutschland* (Berlin, 2004), pp. 89–92.
3. Warburg quoted and translated in Gombrich, *Aby Warburg*, p. 148, nte. 1.
4. Max Warburg, "Rede gehalten an der Gedächtnis-Feier für Professor Warburg am 5. Dezember 1929," typescript (Hamburg, 1929); Horst Günther, "Aby Warburg und seine Brüder," in Ferdinand Seibt et. al., *Deutsche Brüder: zwölf Doppelporträts* (Berlin, 1994), p. 266.
5. See for example René Drommert, "Aby Warburg und die kulturwissenschaftliche Bibliothek in der Heilwigstraße," in *Aby M. Warburg. "Ekstatische Nymphe … trauernder Flußgott": Portrait eines Gelehrten*, eds. Robert Galitz and Brita Reimers (Hamburg, 1995), p. 17.
6. Ron Chernow, *The Warburgs: The Twentieth-Century Odyssey of a Remarkable Jewish Family* (New York, 1993), p. 114.
7. Kevin Repp, *Reformers, Critics and the Paths of German Modernity: Anti-Politics and the Search for Alternatives, 1890–1914* (Cambridge, Mass., 2000), p. 230.
8. Kenneth D. Barkin, "The Crisis of Modernity, 1887–1902," in *Imagining Modern German Culture: 1889–1910*, ed. Françoise Forster-Hahn (Washington, 1996), p. 30.
9. See Robin Lenman, *Die Kunst, die Macht und das Geld: zur Kulturgeschichte des kaiserlichen Deutschland, 1871–1918* (Frankfurt a. M. and New York, 1994); idem, *Artists and Society in Germany, 1850–1914* (Manchester and New York, 1997), pp. 142–184.

10. Repp, *Reformers*, p. 20f.
11. For the dockers' strike see Michael Grüttner, *Arbeitswelt an der Wasserkante: Sozialgeschichte der Hamburger Hafenarbeiter, 1886-1914* (Göttingen, 1984), pp. 165-183.
12. Gombrich, *Aby Warburg*, p. 93.
13. See Anne Marie Meyer, "Aby Warburg in his Early Correspondence," *The American Scholar* 55 (1988), pp. 445–452; Bernd Roeck, *Der junge Aby Warburg* (Munich, 1997), pp. 71–75.
14. Maria Rennhofer, *Kunstzeitschriften der Jahrhundertwende in Deutschland und Österreich, 1895–1914* (Vienna and Munich, 1987), p. 173.
15. Beth Irwin Lewis, *Art for All? The Collision of Modern Art and the Public in Late-Nineteenth-Century Germany* (Princeton and Oxford, 2003), pp. 268–275.
16. On this point see ibid.; Maria Makela, *The Munich Secession: Art and Artists in Turn-of-the-Century Munich* (Princeton, 1990); Nicolaus Teeuwisse, *Vom Salon zur Secession: Berliner Kunstleben zwischen Tradition und Aufbruch der Moderne, 1871–1900* (Berlin, 1986); Peter Paret, *The Berlin Secession: Modernism and Its Enemies in Imperial Germany* (Cambridge, Mass., 1980).
17. Fritz Saxl, "Das Warburg-Institut," in *Porträt aus Büchern: Bibliothek Warburg und Warburg Institute, Hamburg, 1993, London*, ed. Michael Diers (Hamburg, 1993), p. 130.
18. WIA. Family Correspondence (hereafter FC): Warburg to Mary Warburg, 14 Sept. 1902.
19. Gustav Schiefler, *Eine Hamburgische Kulturgeschichte, 1890–1920: Beobachtungen eines Zeitgenossen*, eds. Gerhard Ahrens, Hans Wilhelm Eckardt, and Renate Hauschild-Thiessen (Hamburg, 1985), p. 172.
20. Helmut R. Leppien, "Lichtwarks Wirken für die Kunsthalle," in *Kunst ins Leben: Alfred Lichtwarks Wirken für die Kunsthalle und Hamburg von 1886–1914*, exh. cat. (Hamburger Kunsthalle, 9 December 1986—1 February 1987), p. 11.
21. Schiefler, *Eine Hamburgische Kulturgeschichte*, p. 105.
22. WIA. FC: Olga Warburg to Warburg, 19 March 1896; WIA. FC: Mary Hertz to Warburg, 1 April 1896.
23. Jennifer Jenkins, *Provincial Modernity: Liberal Culture and Liberal Politics in Fin-de-Siècle Hamburg* (Ithaca and London, 2003); Carolyn Kay, *Art and the German Bourgeoisie: Alfred Lichtwark and Modern Painting in Hamburg, 1886–1914* (Toronto, 2002).
24. For a synopsis of Waetzoldt's career, see Hans-Michael Schäfer, *Die Kulturwissenschaftliche Bibliothek Warburg: Geschichte und Persönlichkeiten der Bibliothek Warburg mit Berücksichtigung der Bibliothekslandschaft und der Stadtsituation der Freien und Hansestadt Hamburg zu Beginn des 20. Jahrhunderts* (Berlin, 2003), pp. 114–122.
25. Wilhelm Waetzoldt, "Kunstgespräch zu Weihnachten," *Hamburgischer Correspondent*, 6 December 1910.
26. Wilhelm Waetzoldt, "Nolde-Ausstellung bei Commeter," *Hamburgischer Correspondent*, 17 February 1910.
27. Hamburgisches Welt-Wirtschafts-Archiv, Hamburg (HWWA), Abteilung Bibiliothek, A9n2/2: *Jahresbericht der Detaillistenkammer zu Hamburg für 1910*, p. 241.
28. This suggestion is made in Lengefeld, *Anders Zorn*, p. 90.
29. See Helmut R. Leppien, "Das Neue gegen das Überkommene," in *Kunst ins Leben*, pp. 18–46.
30. Henrike Junge, "Alfred Lichtwark und die 'Gymnastik der Sammeltätigkeit,'" in *Sammler, Stifter und Museen: Kunstforderung in Deutschland im 19. und 20. Jahrhundert*, eds. Ekkehard Mai and Peter Paret (Cologne, 1993), p. 207.
31. Kay, *Art and the German Bourgeoisie*, p. 18.
32. Leppien, "Lichtwarks Wirken für die Kunsthalle," pp. 9–17.
33. Alfred Lichtwark, *Das Bildnis in Hamburg*, 2 vols. (Hamburg, 1898), vol. 1, p. 1.
34. Indina Woesthoff, *"Der glückliche Mensch": Gustav Schiefler (1857–1935): Sammler, Dilettant und Kunstfreund* (Hamburg, 1996) p. 69.
35. See Gombrich, *Aby Warburg*, p. 39.

36. Lichtwark quoted in Carsten Meyer-Tönnesmann, *Der Hamburgische Künstlerclub von 1897* (Frankfurt a.M., 1985), p. 106.
37. See Kay, *Art and the German Bourgeoisie*, pp. 41–69.
38. Warburg quoted and translated in Gombrich, *Aby Warburg*, p. 155.
39. WIA. III.27.1.2: Critical Notes on Contemporary Art, 1900–1901, fol. 2.
40. A comprehensive treatment of this period of Hamburg's art history is found in Meyer-Tönnesmann, *Der Hamburgische Künstlerclub von 1897.*
41. Woesthoff, *"Der glückliche Mensch,"* p. 75.
42. Lichtwark to Max Liebermann, 2 April 1911 in Alfred Lichtwark, *Briefe an Max Liebermann* (Hamburg, 1947), p. 267.
43. See Marina and Uwe M. Schneede, "Der Zweck des Kunstvereins ist mehrseitige Mittheilung über bildende Kunst," in *Industriekultur in Hamburg: des Deutschen Reiches Tor zur Welt*, ed. Volker Plagemann (Munich, 1984), pp. 336–340; Hans Platte, *150 Jahre Kunstverein in Hamburg* (Hamburg, 1967).
44. For these articles see Meyer-Tönnesmann, *Der Hamburgische Künstlerclub*, p. 106f.
45. Schiefler, *Hamburgische Kulturgeschichte*, p. 113; for a short biography of Eitner see Meyer-Tönnesmann, *Der Hamburgische Künstlerclub*, pp. 49–53; see also Anne-Gabriele Ther, "Ernst Eitner: Leben und Werk" (Ph.D. diss., University of Hamburg, 1985).
46. Staatsarchiv, Hamburg (St.A.H.) Zeitungsausschnittsammlung 517, Kunstverein.
47. Kay, *Art and the German Bourgeoisie*, p. 120.
48. WIA. Kopierbuch III, 341: Warburg to Paul Wohlwill, 22 April 1910.
49. WIA. Kopierbuch IV, 487: Warburg to Paul and Felix Warburg, 17 November 1913; the other artists mentioned in the letter are Schimmelpfeng, Rathgen, Papes, Bertha Derflein, Schmauser, Pistenmayer, and Köhler.
50. See Jenkins, *Provincial Modernity*; Kay, *Art and the German Bourgeoisie.*
51. See Meyer-Tönnesmann, *Der Hamburgische Künstlerclub*, pp. 105–109; Schiefler, *Hamburgische Kulturgeschichte*, p. 104ff.
52. Arthur Illies, *Aus Tagebuch und Werk, 1870 bis 1952*, ed. Kurt Illies (Hamburg, 1981), p. 96f; for a discussion of these events see Kay, *Art and the German Bourgeoisie*, p. 90ff.
53. Schiefler quoted in Meyer-Tönnesmann, *Der Hamburgische Künstlerclub*, p. 108.
54. Kay, *Art and the German Bourgeoisie*, pp. 120 and 99.
55. Jenkins, *Provincial Modernity*, p. 210.
56. Ibid., p. 211.
57. Ibid., p. 295.
58. Schiefler, *Hamburgische Kulturgeschichte*, p. 106.
59. Gombrich, *Aby Warburg*, p. 93.
60. See Sabina Ghandchi, "Die Hamburger Künstlerin Mary Warburg, geb. Hertz: Werkliste," (M.A. diss., University of Hamburg, 1986), pp.12f and 42.
61. Ibid., p. 42.
62. WIA. III.17.2: "Warburgismen" gesammelt von Max Warburg, p. 4.
63. On this point see Carl E. Schorske, "Generational Tension and Cultural Change: Reflections on the Case of Vienna," in *The Turn of the Century: German Literature and Art, 1890–1915*, eds. Gerald Chapple and Hans H. Schulte (Bonn, 1981), pp. 415–431.
64. Warburg quoted and translated in Philippe Alain-Michaud, *Aby Warburg and the Image in Motion* (New York, 2004), p. 239.
65. Wolfgang Mommsen, *Bürgerliche Kultur und Künstlerische Avantgarde: Kultur und Politik im deutschen Kaiserreich 1870 bis 1918* (Frankfurt a.M. and Berlin, 1994), p. 109.
66. Jürgen Kocka has been instrumental in challenging the notion of the Bürgertum as a class in a Marxian or Weberian sense; see idem, "Bürgertum und Bürgerlichkeit als Probleme der deutschen Geschichte vom späten 18. zum frühen 20. Jahrhundert," in *Bürger und Bürgerlichkeit im 19. Jahrhundert*, ed. idem (Göttingen, 1987), pp. 21–63; idem, "The European

Pattern and the German Case," in *Bourgeois Society in Nineteenth-Century Europe*, eds. idem and Allen Mitchell (Oxford and Providence, 1993), pp. 3–39.

67. On Max Warburg's plans for a military career see idem, *Aus meinen Aufzeichnungen* (New York, 1952), p. 10.

68. Lewis, *Art for All?*, p. 91.

69. Karl Scheffler, "Max Klinger," *Der Lotse* 2, no. 38 (21 June 1902), p. 330.

70. See Volker Plagemann, *"Vaterstadt, Vaterland, schütz Dich Gott mit starker Hand": Denkmäler in Hamburg* (Hamburg, 1986), pp. 124–128.

71. WIA. FC: Olga Warburg to Warburg, 2 April 1895; WIA. FC: Mary Hertz to Warburg, 2 April 1894 and 16 December 1894.

72. Lewis, *Art for All?*, p. 84.

73. Warburg's sister, Olga, claimed to have been greatly impressed by this painting; see WIA. FC: Olga Warburg to Warburg, 2 April 1894.

74. Paret, *The Berlin Secession*, p. 110f; for an overview of the most important German art journals see Lewis, *Art for All?*; Rennhofer, *Kunstzeitschriften der Jahrhundertwende in Deutschland und Österreich*, pp. 36–104.

75. Meyer, "Aby Warburg in His Early Correspondence," p. 446.

76. Roeck, *Der junge Aby Warburg*, p. 21; WIA. FC: Charlotte Warburg to Warburg, 5 April, 1894.

77. See Gerhard Pommeranz-Liedtke, *Moritz von Schwind: Maler und Poet* (Dresden, 1984).

78. William Vaughan, *German Romantic Painting* (New Haven and London, 1994), p. 213.

79. Schiefler, *Hamburgische Kulturgeschichte*, p. 89.

80. See Volker Plagemann, *Kunstgeschichte der Stadt Hamburg* (Hamburg, 1995), p. 286ff.

81. Alfred Lichtwark quoted in "Alfred Lichtwark über Kauffmann and Ruths," in *Kunst ins Leben*, p. 68.

82. Platte, *150 Jahre Kunstverein*, p. 21.

83. For Klinger's graphic work see Frances Carey and Anthony Griffiths, *The Print in Germany, 1880–1933: The Age of Expressionism* (London, 1984), pp. 43–59; *Max Klinger: Zeichnungen, Zustandsdrucke, Zyklen*, exh. cat. (Munich, Museum Villa Stuck, 24 October 1996–12 January 1997); Elizabeth Pendleton Streicher, "Max Klinger's *Malerei und Zeichnung*: The Critical Reception of the Prints and their Texts," in *Imagining Modern German Culture*, pp. 229–249.

84. For illustrations see *Max Klinger*, pp. 124–133.

85. Streicher, "Max Klinger's *Malerei und Zeichnung*," p. 241.

86. Renate Hauschild-Thiessen, *Bürgermeister Johann Georg Mönckeberg* (Hamburg, 1989), p. 29f.

87. Illies, *Aus Tagebuch und Werk*, p. 91.

88. Jenkins, *Provincial Modernity*, p. 139.

89. Schiefler, *Hamburgische Kulturgeschichte*, p. 81.

90. WIA. General Correspondence (hereafter GC): Aby Warburg to Max Warburg, 13 November 1900.

91. Aby Warburg, "American Chapbooks," in idem, *The Renewal of Pagan Antiquity: Contributions to the Cultural History of the European Renaissance*, trans. David Britt (Los Angeles, 1999), pp. 703–710.

92. For the Deutsche Werkbund see amongst others Joan Campbell, *The German Werkbund: The Politics of Reform in the Applied Arts* (Princeton, 1978); Lucius Burckhardt, ed., *The Werkbund: History and Ideology* (Woodbury, N.Y., 1980); Elisabeth Domansky, "Der Deutsche Werkbund," in Lutz Niethammer et. al., *Bürgerliche Gesellschaft in Deutschland: historische Einblicke, Fragen, Perspektiven* (Frankfurt a. M., 1990), pp. 268–274; Wolfgang Hardtwig, *Nationalismus und Bürgerkultur in Deutschland, 1500–1914* (Göttingen, 1994), pp. 246–273; Matthew Jeffries, *Politics and Culture in Wilhelmine Germany: The Case of Industrial Architecture* (Oxford and Washington, 1995); Mark Jarzombek, "The Discources of a Bourgeois Utopia, 1904–1908, and the Founding of the Werkbund," in *Imagining Modern German Cul-*

ture, pp. 126–145; F. Schwartz, *The Werkbund: Design Theory and Mass Culture Before the First World War* (New Haven and London, 1996).

93. For a survey of the phenomenon see Diethart Kerbs and Jürgen Reulecke, eds., *Handbuch der deutschen Reformbewegungen, 1880–1933* (Wuppertal, 1998).

94. Nipperdey quoted in Matthew Jeffries, *Imperial Culture in Germany, 1871–1918* (Houndmills, 2003), p. 192.

95. Repp, *Reformers*, p. 284.

96. Ibid., pp. 229 and 227.

97. Jeffries, *Imperial Culture in Germany*, p. 221; see also Repp, *Reformers*.

98. Hardtwig, *Nationalismus und Bürgerkultur in Deutschland*, p. 272.

99. Jeffries, *Politics and Culture*, p. 289.

100. See Percy Ernst Schramm, *Neun Generationen: dreihundert Jahre deutscher "Kulturgeschichte" im Lichte der Schicksale einer Hamburger Bürgerfamilie (1648–1948)*, 2 vols. (Göttingen, 1964), vol 1, p. 461.

101. Kurt W. Forster, "Aby Warburg's History of Art: Collective Memory and the Social Mediation of Images," *Daedalus*, 105 (1976), p. 171.

102. Warburg quoted and translated in Gombrich, *Aby Warburg*, p. 111.

103. Ibid.

104. Aby Warburg quoted and translated in ibid., p. 39f.

105. Ibid., p. 97.

106. See Aby Warburg, "On *Imprese Amorose* in the Earliest Florentine Engravings," in idem, *The Renewal of Pagan Antiquity*, pp. 169–183.

107. See Aby Warburg, "Peasants at Work in Burgundian Tapestries," and "Airship and Submarine in the Medieval Imagination," in idem, *The Renewal of Pagan Antiquity*, pp. 315–323 and 333–337.

108. The book reviewed for the *Allgemeine Zeitung* was Maso Finiguerra, *A Florentine Picture Chronicle* (London, 1898); see Aby Warburg, "The Picture Chronicle of a Florentine Goldsmith," in idem, *The Renewal of Pagan Antiquity*, p. 165ff.

109. This point is stressed in Richard Woodfield, "Warburg's 'Method,'" in *Art History as Cultural History: Warburg's Projects*, ed. idem (Amsterdam, 2001), pp. 259–293.

110. Warburg quoted and translated in Gombrich, *Aby Warburg*, p. 152.

111. Michaud, *Aby Warburg and the Image in Motion*, p. 176.

112. Woodfield, "Warburg's 'Method,'" p. 273.

113. Warburg quoted and translated in Michaud, *Aby Warburg and the Image in Motion*, p. 115.

114. Gombrich, *Aby Warburg*, p. 109.

115. Jeffries, *Imperial Culture in Germany*, p. 198.

116. Warburg, "On *Imprese Amorose*," p. 171.

117. For Zorn's career in Hamburg and Germany see Lengefeld, *Anders Zorn*.

118. Lenman, *Artists and Society in Germany*, p. 170.

119. Richard Hamann and Jost Hermand, *Impressionismus* (Munich, 1973), p. 275.

120. For a comparison to Rembrandt see Axel Romdahl, *Anders Zorn als Radierer* (Dresden, 1924), p. ii.

121. For a catalogue raisonné of Böcklin's work see Rolf Andree, *Arnold Böcklin: die Gemälde* (Basel and Munich, 1977).

122. Neumann quoted in Shearer West, *The Visual Arts in Germany, 1890–1937: Utopia and Despair* (New Brunswick, NJ, 2001) p. 38.

123. See Robert Jensen, *Marketing Modernism in Fin-de-Siècle Europe* (Princeton, 1994), pp. 257–263; Elizabeth Tumasonis, "Böcklin's Reputation: Its Rise and Fall," *Art Criticism* 6, no. 2 (1990), pp. 48–71; Paret, *The Berlin Secession*, pp. 170–182.

124. Platte, *150 Jahre Kunstverein*, p. 21; see WIA. FC: Charlotte Warburg to Warburg, 20 December 1897; WIA. FC: Olga Warburg to Warburg, 18 December 1897.

125. Warburg quoted and translated in Gombrich, *Aby Warburg*, p. 152.

126. Warburg quoted in Roeck, *Der junge Aby Warburg*, p. 86.
127. WIA. III.27.3.1: Funeral A. Böcklin, 1901; the report is dated 18 January 1901.
128. WIA. FC: Warburg to Moritz and Charlotte Warburg, 29 November 1895.
129. WIA. GC: Warburg to Jacques Dwelshauers, 27 July 1909.
130. Lewis, *Art For All?*, p. 77.
131. WIA. GC: Invitation to Böcklin's memorial service, 24 January 1901.
132. WIA. III.27.3.1.
133. See Margaret Iversen, "Retrieving Warburg's Tradition," *Art History* 16 (1993), pp. 541–553; Matthew Rampley, "From Symbol to Allegory: Aby Warburg's Theory of Art," *Art Bulletin* 79 (1997), pp. 41–55.
134. See Matthew Rampley, "Mimesis and Allegory. On Aby Warburg and Walter Benjamin," in *Art History As Cultural History*, pp. 121–149.
135. Warburg quoted and translated in Woodfield, "Warburg's 'Method,'" p. 274f.
136. Published as Aby Warburg, "A Lecture on Serpent Ritual," *Journal of the Warburg Institute* 2 (1938–39), pp. 277–292.
137. Michaud, *Aby Warburg and the Image in Motion*, p. 226.
138. Matthew Rampley, *The Remembrance of Things Past: On Aby M. Warburg and Walter Benjamin* (Wiesbaden, 2000), p. 71.
139. Ibid.
140. Warburg, *Images from the Region of the Pueblo Indians of North America*, trans Michael Steinberg (Ithaca and London, 1995), p. 54.
141. Rampley, *The Remembrance of Things Past*, p. 66.
142. Ibid.

Chapter Three

POLITICAL SYMBOLISM
AND CULTURAL MONUMENTALISM
Hamburg's Bismarck Memorial, 1898–1906

I

"Simply sublime, sculptural and yet of a transcending visionary quality."[1] These were the words with which Aby Warburg greeted the unveiling of the Bismarck memorial in Hamburg on 2 June 1906. (Figure 3.1) Four years had passed since Hamburg's mayor, Johann Georg Mönckeberg, expressed the desire of the Committee for the Erection of a Bismarck Memorial in Hamburg (hereafter referred to simply as the committee) to build a monument unlike any other.[2] The result was a dramatic expression of Imperial pride in a city that cherished its republican traditions. The monument was intended as one of many pilgrimage sites in the new Empire. Speeches by senior politicians and cultural administrators associated with the project—Mayor Mönckeberg, Mayor Heinrich Burchard, and Professor Dr. Georg Treu—are filled with nationalist and imperialist rhetoric.[3] As Mönckeberg explained at the memorial's unveiling, it was a symbol of the nation, a shrine of national identity:

> From a proud height the Bismarck Memorial looks down upon the Elbe. To those brothers drawn far away across the sea it calls in parting: preserve your German character in foreign lands. And to those returning from afar, the Bismarck Memorial—the first greeting of the old homeland upon entry into the harbor—should evince the memory of the power and greatness of the united German Empire. [4]

Karl Scheffler described the memorial as "a lighthouse of national thought."[5] Newspapers across the Empire reported on the unveiling in similar terms. They referred to the construction of Hamburg's Bismarck memorial as a national deed. "Here, in one place," reported the *Deutsche Welt*, "what is great, powerful, and invincible in the German soul has gathered itself together."[6]

Figure 3.1. Hugo Lederer and Emil Schaudt, Bismarck Memorial, Hamburg, 1906.
Source: Photo by author.

Hamburg's Bismarck memorial was born of a genuine appreciation for Bismarck's accomplishments and was to be "a sign of the inextinguishable thankfulness that fills our hearts for the departed."[7] Scholarly interest in the Bismarck memorial is often born of the fact that it is perhaps the greatest expression of the Bismarck cult that flourished in Germany at the turn of the century. The monument's place and importance in the development of German memorial art has also been discussed.[8] What this chapter argues, however, is that the committee sought to fulfill two other goals in the guise of a monument to Bismarck. Behind the eulogies that accompanied the memorial's construction lie two other impulses and it is within this context that the chapter examines Warburg's response to it.

The first of these was a pressing desire on the part of Hamburg's patrician classes to defend their political privileges in the face of dramatic social change and attendant demands for political reform. The building of the Bismarck memorial was a political act; it was an outstanding instance in which public art was employed as public policy. Felix Gilbert claims that Warburg had no interest in social questions, while Christiane Brosius has argued that his response to the memorial "appears in this case to be untouched by the predominant political and nationalistic debates."[9] But while his unpublished papers make no explicit mention of politics in relation to the memorial, it is certain that Warburg was neither uninformed nor uninterested. What traces of political opinion he has left behind indicate general political sympathy with the ambitions of those responsible for the memorial's construction. In a manner similar to his exhibition of Dürer's drawings in the Volksheim in 1905, Warburg turned to art as a way of confronting social and political change in Hamburg.

The second impulse was a determination shared by the artists, politicians, and scholars who presided over and supported the memorial's construction to assert Hamburg's cultural aspirations and independence. It was a way of insisting on Hamburg's distance from the *Hohenzollern* aesthetic that dominated state and official organizations for supporting art. As a reaction to the banality of the Siegesallee and the highly emotional, allegorical, and naturalistic neo-Baroque aesthetic favored by the Kaiser, it was also a means of dissenting from the political and social vision of the Empire broadcast by Imperial political imagery. As such it is an example of the markedly nationalist bourgeois culture, which saw art as a way of modernizing and reforming Imperial society, sought to stamp the German Empire with its values, and wanted to give expression to the democratic–republican aspect of the Empire's heritage.

More particularly, it was a way of shrugging off a reputation as a city hostile to the arts, a city that subordinated aesthetic to material values. It meant looking to new trends in German art. In this respect, the monument is proof of the fact that artworks excluded from the canon of artistic modernity were often seen as progressive by contemporary observers. There is no doubt that the memorial's patrons and creators intended to break with academic aesthetic conventions and incorporate innovation by transforming conventional iconography. Nonetheless, the function of the monument as a memorial, its symbolism, and even its semi-abstracted forms were governed by a tradition of commemorative artworks and monumental sculpture; the Bismarck memorial was clearly not an avant-garde work of art. Instead, it might be seen as an example of the interpenetration of traditional and modern characteristics and functions and thus reflective of the complex nature of Hamburg's political, social, and cultural life.

If the building of the Bismarck memorial reveals a cultural sphere in Hamburg animated by debate, the same can be said of Warburg's unpublished papers. He concurred with the committee's efforts to boldly mark Hamburg's spot on Germany's cultural map. For Warburg, building the Bismarck memorial meant that "for the first time in the history of art, Hamburg would take a lively and supportive interest in the resolute application of independent taste in the development of German memorial art."[10] Although living principally in Italy until 1904, he followed the building of the Bismarck memorial with interest; he collected his thoughts in fragmentary notes and accumulated a large number of newspaper clippings on the subject as well as photographs.

Warburg published nothing on the memorial nor did he lecture on the subject. It is hard to imagine, however, that his views remained unknown to friends and associates. He took up his interests with passion and possessed a gift of oratory that could glow with enthusiasm and wit or bite with a criticism that bordered on callousness.[11] The latter was the case when he addressed criticisms that were directed at the committee's plans for the Bismarck memorial. His unpublished papers provide an insight into the public debate that accompanied the monument's construction. They also reveal the portrait of a patriotic citizen of Hamburg who championed the memorial and detested what he called "Berlin's sentimental neo-Baroque style."[12] Of course, his interest in the monument was not born of an attraction to art for art's sake; it is a simplification to say that the Bismarck memorial won his praise because it was "a new and modern form of idealism."[13] His delight in the highly stylized monument built in Hamburg is grounded in his interest in the psychology of artistic expression; what he believed the Bismarck memorial achieved was not particularly "new" or "modern." Instead, he assessed the artwork from a perspective that transcended a concern with the extent to which it was embedded in tradition or the degree to which it participated in a modern spirit. Furthermore, when Warburg "took up the cudgels" to defend the Bismarck memorial "against the Philistines," it was not simply because the artist rejected "the tasteless realism displayed even in the symbolic personages of traditional monuments."[14] Warburg's attitude to the memorial's rejection of naturalistic detail must be understood differently than it previously has; it must be seen as more ambivalent than purely positive. This can be done if his unpublished remarks on the monument are read in the context of the historical research that preoccupied him at this time.

Edgar Wind criticized Ernst Gombrich's biography of Warburg for losing "the incisive style of the man ... in the polluting swarm of ephemeral notations." Gombrich's focus on Warburg's fragmentary notations, he claimed, resulted in the image of a scholar dominated by "a disproportionate sense of tentative gropings."[15] When we come to study Warburg's response to Hamburg's Bismarck memorial, all that remain are fragmentary thoughts and "tentative gropings." Nonetheless, a fascinating picture emerges of the scholar at work. Most importantly, when unpublished remarks and published essays are read in conjunction it is not only disjunctions of thought that emerge; often it is unity and continuity.

II

"Hamburg and Bismarck—the city's self-conscious *bourgeoisie* and the Pomeranian *Junker* … an opposition that must have seemed unbridgeable."[16] This is the way in which Percy Ernst Schramm introduced the story of a relationship that concluded with the building of Hamburg's Bismarck memorial. In the 1860s and 1870s, Bismarck had been the principal threat to Hamburg's jealously guarded political and economic independence. Until 1871, Hamburg had existed as a republic for several centuries and thought of itself as having a unique political and cultural identity: its citizens were proud of their independence from aristocratic traditions. This tradition of independence in the past resulted in claims to autonomy in the present. In the person of Gustav Heinrich Kirchenpauer, seven times Mayor of Hamburg between 1869 and 1886, the city possessed a long-standing representative who had little sympathy for Bismarck.[17] He objected to Prussia's dominant position in the Empire and regretted the ever-shrinking sovereignty of the small states. With the Empire's turn to economic protectionism in 1878/79, Bismarck insisted upon the end of Hamburg's anomaly status by which the city remained outside the Customs Union.[18] Kirchenpauer, a majority in Hamburg's government as well as most of the commercial interests represented on Hamburg's board of trade, regarded entry into the Union as harmful for the city's foreign commerce.[19] Even during the cholera epidemic of 1892, Hamburg revealed its fear of Prussian intervention in its politics by its failure to adopt Prussian models for dealing with the disease.[20]

Nonetheless, Hamburg's history in the last quarter of the century is one of ineluctable political, bureaucratic, and economic harmonization with the Empire.[21] Negotiation by Senator Johannes Versmann in the Bundesrat and a campaign by Hamburg businessmen led to the Reich-subsidized building of a free port, which Hamburg retained upon entry to the Customs Union in 1888. The free port ensured that German tariffs did not disrupt Hamburg's trade and, in sum, economic integration into the Empire did nothing to hinder the city's prosperity. On the contrary, rapid growth in trade, shipping, and industry turned a commercial port into a modern world city.[22] As Niall Ferguson points out, Bismarck's acceptance of German colonial expansion in the 1880s and the construction of a German battleship fleet did much to reconcile Hamburg's commercial community to the Empire's economic policy.[23]

By the 1880s, a pro-Prussian party had emerged in the senate led by Johannes Versmann and supported by Carl Friedrich Petersen, Johann Georg Mönckeberg, and Heinrich Burchard. When the latter assumed his position on the Bundesrat, his role was not to defend Hamburg's particularism. Instead, it was "to give to the Reich on Hamburg's part what was due to it, and above all in questions of internal policy not to interfere too much with the Reich Chancellor and the leading federal state."[24] In the wake of the war against France in 1870/71, Hamburg's government awarded Bismarck honorary citizenship "in thankful recognition of his service in the re-establishment of the German empire."[25] When dismissed by Wilhelm II in 1890, Bismarck settled close to Hamburg, in Friedrichsruh, where he spent the last years of his life. Henceforth, he moved within the official and private circles of the city whose overseas merchants he counted as the most reliable and skilled representatives of the German Empire.[26] A local newspaper, the *Hamburger Nachrichten*, became Bismarck's voice and the means by which he attacked old enemies. Three days after Bismarck's death, on 2 August 1898, Mayor Versmann and 855 of Hamburg's citizens signed an appeal for a Bismarck memorial that appeared in local newspapers.[27]

This was a time of increasing social and political tensions in the port city exacerbated by dramatic population growth. From 300,000 in 1871, the city's population grew to 750,000 by 1901 and overshot the 1 million mark shortly before the First World War.[28] Around 58 percent of this growth was the result of immigration driven by the economic attraction of the city, especially the prospect of work that, for men, was to be found mostly as fitters, builders, and seamen in the shipyards.[29] As a result, tens of thousands of workers' families were crowded into the squalid and miserable alley quarters near the harbor, where they were the victims of archaic sanitation, polluted air, and overcrowding, and were prey to epidemics, the most infamous being the cholera epidemic of 1892.[30] It was these conditions that prompted Walther Classen, founder of the Volksheim, to write in 1900 that "we have a chaos underneath us."[31]

Tremendous contrasts existed between Hamburg's rich and poor that the city's government did much to maintain. Hamburg was ruled by *Honoratiorenpolitik*, the politics of notables. Businessmen and lawyers dominated Hamburg's two government bodies: the senate and the citizens' assembly. The senate was the city's highest administrative authority and was dominated by an elite of interrelated patrician families like the Amsincks, Burchards, Sievekings, and Westphals. Composed of eighteen members elected for life, it controlled all branches of government administration, appointed high officials, called for elections to the citizens' assembly, promulgated laws, and acted as Hamburg's foreign representative. "At the moment an intensified power rests with Hamburg's Senate as with no crowned head in the empire," wrote the district judge Geert Seelig in 1901. This was salutary, he believed, because it "secured the leadership of the state in a concentrated will."[32] In law-making, the senate cooperated with the citizens' assembly. In 1906, this body was comprised of 160 members elected for six years and drawn from notables, property owners, and citizens with yearly incomes exceeding 1,200 marks.[33] Its responsibilities included taxation, the state budget, and state treaties.[34] The political groups that composed the assembly corresponded to the differing economic interests of Hamburg's middle-classes, not to national political parties. Balancing the interests of property-owners, merchants, ship-builders, and industrialists was the purpose of their deliberations. A "relaxed, gentlemanly mode of discussion, compromise and a general willingness to deal with the other party were the order of the day."[35] Political business was often executed outside the chamber around the dinner tables of Hamburg's senators and city officials. Percy Ernst Schramm equated the importance of these *Herrendiners* to the function of lubricating oil in the operation of a machine.[36]

The importance of these informal gatherings for the creation of a climate of political opinion points to the most striking feature of Hamburg's government: its exclusivity. Even after the suffrage reform of 1896, most Hamburgers could not qualify to become citizens and hence to vote; they could not sustain an annual income of 1,200 marks for a minimum of five years. In 1893/94, citizens amounted to only 3.5 percent of Hamburg's population. By 1903/04, this figure had risen to just 5.3 percent.[37] Yet many of these new citizens came from skilled and well-paid sections of the working class: 12,000 of the new citizens registered between 1901 and 1903 were wage or salary earners instead of property owners.[38] Besides increased numbers of workers with the rights of citizens, the 1890s saw increased labor organization and a growing number of industrial disputes. By 1890 there were over eighty trade unions in Hamburg with 40,000 members.[39] These were pitted chiefly against the Hamburg-Altona Employers' Association founded by the ship builder Hermann Blohm and dedicated to the destruction of Social Democracy. Matters came to a head during the dockers' strike of November 1896 to February 1897, which involved 16,000 workers, paralyzed the city's commerce, and ended in two days of rioting in the inner city. It shocked Hamburg's middle-classes and caused a sensation throughout Germany.[40] The 1890s also saw ever more political organization among the working classes; by the middle of the decade the Social Democrats counted almost 15,000 men and women amongst their numbers out of an industrial work force that amounted to only 30,106 workers in 1890 and 45,000 in 1900.[41] In the Spring of 1901, Otto Stolten was elected to the citizens' assembly as Hamburg's first Social Democratic deputy. With 37.7 percent of the vote on 13 February 1904, the party acquired twelve more seats in the citizens' assembly.[42] The electoral success of the Social Democrats ended the "cosy atmosphere" of Hamburg's politics, introducing political polemic and social criticism into assembly debates, something which the majority of members found "profoundly distasteful and disturbing."[43]

It is no wonder that Hamburg's government was alarmed about the threat from below at the turn of the century, and that its patrician members should strive to protect their political privileges and prevent more political power falling into the hands of the working classes. Less than four months before the Bismarck memorial's unveiling, in February 1906, the senate and citizens' assembly passed legislation to split the electorate into two classes and introduce proportional representation, a measure known as the "suffrage robbery."[44] To its opponents in the senate, the suffrage reform was an anachronism, especially in light of recent political reform in Austria and Russia.[45] According to Percy Ernst Scrhamm, one had the feeling that clinging to tradition on the Elbe "must lead to ossification."[46] But as Richard Evans has shown, it was to tradition and its invention that the government, especially the senate, turned in the 1890s in order to elaborate the public presentation of its own authority.[47] It was at this time that, as the senate secretary Julius von Eckardt put it, the "state burst externally into bloom," and that a Bismarck memorial was conceived and built.[48]

Even before the opening of the neo-Renaissance city hall in 1897, the senate had adopted an increasingly grand style. As Evans relates, "receptions and formal occasions proliferated, and pomp and ceremony took the place of the old quiet way of doing things."[49] For example, Hamburg's government paid little attention to ceremonial presentations of authority for most of the nineteenth century; senators rarely appeared in their full uniform of office after 1860.[50] But by the 1890s, the senate wore their sixteenth-century costume at most ceremonial occasions and whenever they appeared collectively before the public. The costume symbolized a system of government steeped in experience, hallowed by the ages, rooted in the past, and irremovable in the future. The senate's invention of tradition was designed to serve a legitimizing function: to engender respect in the popular mind for an apparently ancient system of rule. As Evans argues "pride in Hamburg's heritage … was an essential element in the local patriotism to which the grand *bourgeoisie* appealed in its struggle to prevent the growing support of Hamburg's working class for the 'anti-Hamburg' Social Democrats."[51]

If the building of a monument to a deceased leader was a traditional undertaking, the Bismarck memorial was not an invention of tradition, nor a means of stimulating pride in Hamburg's heritage. The project was not initiated nor financed by the government. But the lack of direct contacts between state and public in Hamburg were compensated for by the many indirect connections between the working classes and Hamburg's patricians in their role as charitable and civic-minded patriots. There were numerous foundations and private welfare associations that expressed the essence of Hamburg's ruling ideology. Through these, Hamburg's merchant families exercised a decentralized form of rule over the population. Of these associations, Alfred Lichtwark wrote that "there were times in which their influence actually reached farther than any organ of the state. Of course, they existed fundamentally only in an altered form: on their executive committees sat the same men who in the senate and citizens' assembly were hindered in freer work through the rigid forms of the constitution."[52] These same men were subscribers to the Bismarck memorial project and it is their views that the monument represents. Like the senate's official costume, the Bismarck memorial was a political symbol born of a deep-seated concern for social stabilization among Hamburg's dominant classes. Similar to the senate's adoption of pomp and ceremony, it was designed to shore up and intensify the notion of community. As political and social conflict reached ever higher levels in Hamburg, those with political and economic power sought an effective symbol that would offer the disenfranchised a sense of political and social participation and identity, and would engender a sense of political and social community. They conceived and built the Bismarck memorial as an antirevolutionary device and means of social integration.

But why Bismarck? Why should Hamburg's patrician classes turn to a statue of the Iron Chancellor to fulfill this function? Warburg envisioned Hamburgers fearfully confronting Bismarck's image as if the statue would wield its sword against wrong-doers.[53] One response on the part of Hamburg's government to the working-class threat was increased policing and the development of state organizations intended to subject the population to heightened surveillance.[54] But the memorial was not simply a way of intimidating the working classes nor was repression the only means of integrating the masses into Hamburg's social structure. Both Richard Evans and Niall Ferguson have shown that the enthusiasm of large-scale industry for confrontation with labor was not shared by all employers, and that there was no unified bourgeois front against socialism.[55] As discussed in chapter one, a cultural reform movement developed in Hamburg from the late 1880s that, through popular education and public enlightenment, sought the rapprochement of the classes through the extension of bourgeois society and its values.[56] The suffrage reforms of 1906 were passed in opposition to the wishes of Mayors Mönckeberg and Burchard, two senior politicians closely associated with the memorial project who regarded the revocation or limitation of previously granted political rights as disturbing.[57] Instead, the image of Bismarck was a way of making manifest and concrete a somewhat abstract idea of community in an attempt to check the rise of socialism.

A Bismarck memorial was the objectification of a myth that offered participation and identity.[58] After his death in 1898, Bismarck quickly grew to mythic proportions in Germany's collective memory. Loosed from his individuality and from his historical personality by a score of writers and artists, the Iron Chancellor was raised as a symbol of nation, the embodiment of Germany, the German nature, and the German mentality. As the founder of the German Empire, no one figure was better suited as a symbol of national self-definition and this symbol, and the myths that it incorporated, were quickly adopted by the German middle classes. At the turn-of-the-century, commemoration of Bismarck reached the proportions of a national cult. Although this phenomenon encompassed a whole range of different groups with different purposes, its practitioners increasingly conceived of Germany as a community of Germanic people instead of a nation-state.[59] What middle-class patrons thought they were doing when building Bismarck memorials—and this is made explicit in Hamburg's case in the words of Mönckeberg and Georg Treu—was reflecting the way in which Bismarck had grown to the proportions of a hero in the consciousness and hearts of the German people.[60]

In a design competition mounted by the committee in 1901, prize-winning designs by artists like Wilhelm Kreis and Bruno Schmitz were not conceived simply as a means of invoking the memory of the Empire's founder.[61] Instead, they were designed as a functional part of a liturgy, like the altarpiece in a church, a place where cult and artistic representation were melded into a magic unity. They were conceived as an assembly point for citizens, a site of cultic ceremony including patriotic speeches and torch-lit ceremonies, and their emotional impact was calculated as part of an event. As Nietzsche wrote of German culture, "the cult of feeling was erected on the site of the cult of reason."[62] In the cultic ceremonies around the Bismarck towers, Germans were joined in a bond of national community expressed in a shared outpouring of patriotic sentiment for Bismarck and thus for Germany. What was being celebrated here was the national cult of Germanness; in the presence of such a structure, the individual should feel part of the mass.

III

Aby Warburg's name does not appear on the appeal for a Bismarck memorial. This was probably because he was living in Italy at the time. But the names of his father Moritz, his brothers Max and Paul, and his cousin Aby S. Warburg do. As a member of Hamburg's economic elite, it is not surprising that Warburg and his family supported a project to commemorate Bismarck.

"Red Wednesday" is mentioned as an important political event in Warburg's diary. The phrase was coined by the right-wing press to describe the general strike and demonstrations by workers on 17 January 1906 intended to express opposition to the government's proposals to alter the suffrage laws. That evening, Max Warburg, a member of the conservative faction of the citizens' assembly from 1903, attended the debates on the proposals with his wife Alice. In view of the riots and looting which occurred, Aby Warburg waited anxiously for his brother's return home. But like Mönckeberg, Burchard, Senator Holthusen, Senator von Melle, and Carl Peterson, chairman of the United Liberal faction in the citizens' assembly, neither Aby nor Max Warburg supported the proposed suffrage reforms. All feared a politicization of the citizens' assembly; as Max Warburg put it, politics belonged "in Berlin."[63] Equally unwelcome was the fear expressed by Mönckeberg that "an aristocracy of money would emerge in the place of an aristocracy of intellect."[64]

In a letter to his brother written on 11 January 1906, Aby Warburg explained that he considered the right to vote to be the "most sensitive instrument of the state," and criticized the one-sided, party-political effort to circumscribe it as "mindlessness" and "social quackery."[65] He prepared the outline of a speech for Max on the theme of the suffrage reform bill. This may have been written for the assembly's sitting on 28 February 1906, when the bill was passed with a vote of 120 to 35.[66] Here Warburg speaks out against the "plutocratic repression" of the patrician representatives and pens the following lines under the heading "concluding thoughts":

> Let us not make the same grave political mistakes as the Social Democrats who want to achieve through the hostile, mechanical pressure of the masses what can only be achieved

and must be achieved through communal reason in our Hanseatic merchant republic, through the firm will to mutual comprehension: an equally sensible and willing working community.

Without doubt, we find ourselves now in a critical and serious position; but in the most favorable cases, this law will mechanically reduce the symptoms of this crisis instead of grasping the reasons for the crisis by the organic roots.

What is being sought is, in my layman's opinion, a cure à la Doctor Eisenbart to whom I would not like to entrust the well-being of our body politic. Therefore, I will vote against the proposal.[67]

Max Warburg did just that, adding that proportional representation would be as suitable as a "punch in the eye."[68] As far as he was concerned, it only lent a sense of confidence to "those parties which had a blind—be it pious, be it wild, in both cases fanatic—horde permanently behind it."[69]

But Aby Warburg's solutions to Hamburg's political and social problems were idiosyncratic and idealistic; in short, they were unrealistic. He nurtured the image of an ideal Hanseatic society in which an equality of political and economic interests would be obtained not through party politics, but through "communal reason." He explains in a letter to Max:

Frankly, in my opinion, one has the duty here in Hamburg, to show the rest of the wealthy that on the historical foundation of a free, bourgeois, merchant culture, a politically successful and peaceful community can arise that will no longer let itself be hindered by the political phrases of the Reichstag parties in the fulfillment of the immediate duty of Hamburg's citizens: that everyone according to the measure of his intellectual and material abilities raises and maintains the capacity and enthusiasm for work.[70]

Warburg believed that the professional classes must be given a greater role in the running of the state. These included "the workers, the bureaucrats, and the representatives of academic education: doctors, judges, teachers, pastors."[71] To schematize these groups, he writes, "simply by tax brackets would degrade them into the representatives of their own rightful interests and remove from the state the advantage of obtaining insight and assistance from the representatives of the professional classes themselves." And so Warburg called for a suffrage based on profession in which half the citizens' assembly would be elected on the basis of the general suffrage, the other on the basis of professional education. These ideas recall those that motivated middle-class movements for cultural reform, discussed in chapter two. As Kevin Repp explains, "the impulse to build and participate in these institutions was also inseparable from the professional aspirations motivating the generation of 1890." There was the conviction among members of the middle classes "that expert knowledge was a more desirable basis for public policy than the tactical ploys of party politicians, and Wilhelmine reformers saw opportunities for themselves as well as for the nation in establishing the framework for a non-partisan decision-making process."[72] "In the face of the hate-sowing party phrases, which level out the professional classes," the representation of professional interests was for Warburg "the most natural" form of parliamentary representation. This was the solution that Max Warburg proposed in the citizens' assembly. Each profession would receive appropriate representation. But just how this representation would be guaranteed and how it would be apportioned were questions that he could not answer.[73] Not surprisingly, the political solutions espoused by Max and Aby Warburg were rejected as impractical.

What is instructive, however, is the extent to which Warburg's politics mixed liberal values with an authoritarian disposition. It is unlikely that he felt completely comfortable with any of the factions in Hamburg's government. But his vision is one of liberal governance in a parliamentary system that recognized the primacy of free trade and the importance of economic growth. It is also a socially conservative stance that does not envisage the relinquishing of privilege by the upper-middle classes. Instead, it promotes cautious reform and is far removed from recommending universal manhood suffrage. The fundamental tenets of Warburg's political vision were widely shared by Hamburg's ruling, middle-class merchants whose interests and values were not incompatible with authoritarianism. In *Death in Hamburg*, Richard Evans demonstrated that, especially after the cholera epidemic of 1892, an interventionist, repressive state apparatus emerged to police the poor and politically radical. Even with its tradition of republican self-rule, Hamburg was as authoritarian as any political entity within the German Empire.[74] Jennifer Jenkins has correctly modified this view by emphasizing that "the expansion of the public political sphere did not signal the decisive end of civic discussions on liberalism and liberal values in Hamburg."[75] But the reality of the city's politics serves to complicate any notion of liberalism understood as modernizing and authoritarianism understood as backward when applied to the German Empire.

If anything, Warburg's study of Florence's fifteenth-century merchants and bankers probably strengthened his conviction that he had a right to belong to the ruling group of the Empire. As indicated in chapter one, Warburg was uncomfortable with the development of a public sphere that was based on the need to politically address the masses. We have seen that he feared the prospect of social chaos and wrote that "to me, the masses are tolerable only in a well-ordered state."[76] While Warburg was opposed to the politics of the Social Democrats, the cholera epidemic of 1892 may have served to reinforce his fear of modern mass society. Thus, on one level, Warburg must have understood Hamburg's Bismarck memorial as a rallying point at the foot of which the masses were supposed "to order themselves with military strictness in patriotic festivals," putting aside their political grievances.[77] But on another level, as the following discussion indicates, the memorial was a means of creating an appetite for self-reflective calm in a city divided by ever more political and social tension. Just as when he mounted his Dürer exhibition in the Volksheim, Warburg believed that individual, critical self-reflection would resist "the call of mass intoxication."[78]

Clearly, it would be wrong to think of Warburg as an apolitical scholar. He shared a disdain for *Tagespolitik* with many German intellectuals. His essay

"Pagan-Antique Prophecy in Words and Images in the Age of Luther," published in 1920, illustrated the danger that day-to-day political exigencies posed to culture.[79] But Warburg was not afraid to mix politics with his work as a cultural historian. He collected political books for his library and during the Weimar years, when his sympathies lay with the German Democratic Party and the German People's Party, he allowed his library to be used for overtly political purposes: as a headquarters from which to transport supporters of both parties to the polls.[80] Warburg was also a proud German who praised Bismarck's creation of a single German nation and admired his success in holding it together.[81] He once described Bismarck as the "colossal hero."[82] The historian Percy Ernst Schramm recalls how Warburg said to him: "There exists between the Prussian nobles and us, the old Jewish families, a subterranean relationship. We do not live as we want, but as we should."[83] Warburg did just that when he served with enthusiasm as a noncommissioned officer in a field artillery regiment in Karlsruhe. In a letter home, he wrote "we drilled so much this week that I could hardly move myself in the evening. But that does no harm at all. It becomes clear now for the first time how soft and lazy a large part of our so-called good society is."[84] Hamburg's Bismarck memorial is one of the most powerful expressions of the nationalism, militarism, and imperialism that permeated the German middle classes in these years. Aby Warburg was reconciled to all of these overtones.

IV

We have seen that Hamburg has long had the reputation of a city hostile to the arts; the city's image was and often still is that of a city whose culture subordinated aesthetic to material values, a city where the value of people and things was fixed by the merchant.[85] At the beginning of this century, many erudite Hamburgers despaired at the state of Hamburg's cultural life. In 1900, Alfred Lichtwark lamented: "A million people—and is there a poet, a composer among us who makes his living from his art? A million people—and where are the painters, the sculptors, the architects who correspond to this economic flowering?"[86] Warburg noted that the interest of the educated in Hamburg was predominantly literary.[87] But Hamburg's theater life was described as "weak" and the only aspect of its cultural life that received positive comment was its music.[88] Even here Hamburg proved incapable of attracting and retaining the great composers.[89] Gustav Schiefler lamented that his generation of Hamburgers had grown up in an epoch of political and economic struggle and had focused almost exclusively on material betterment, thereby forgetting about art.[90]

Yet the preceding chapters have argued that a vibrant cultural life developed in the city, stimulated by the initiatives of Alfred Lichtwark and supported by Hamburg's merchants and bankers. Indeed, Schiefler could write in 1896 that "Germany's modern spiritual development has to take account of Hamburg as an essential factor."[91] In 1890, Julius Langbehn had already proclaimed the age of art's blossoming in northern Germany.[92] In 1899, Wilhelm Uhde wrote "There is a state in the German Empire in which great powers are latent, and from which the best can be hoped: Hamburg."[93] Looking at the influence of English culture on the city and the achievements of popular art education, Otto Graut-off claimed that "the preconditions of a great culture are undoubtedly present here."[94] Clearly, contemporary erudite opinion was not all frustration; there was the conviction in Hamburg and elsewhere that the city had cultural potential that needed proper cultivation if it was to flower. "People in the Empire today have turned their gaze with great expectations on Hamburg," wrote Carl Mönckeberg in 1900, "and have entrusted its cultural talents with a confidence that really must first be earned in deeds."[95] The building of the Bismarck memorial was one of these deeds.

In October 1900, the memorial's proponents gained an important ally in *Der Lotse*, "Hamburg's Weekly for German Culture." This short-lived journal became an advocate of the committee's plans and a voice for criticism of the arts in Berlin.[96] It was edited by Siegfried Heckscher and Carl Mönckeberg, son of the committee's chair, and was intended to address questions of art, science, education, politics, and economy. It was to act as a mediator between the pub-lic and art, thereby fostering cultural life in Hamburg. Before its appearance, a group of artists, writers, and art enthusiasts had met regularly to discuss such a publication. These included Warburg, Mönckeberg, Schiefler, the artists Arthur Illies and Ernst Eitner, and the poet Gustav Falke.[97] But the most important ini-tiative came from Lichtwark. He believed that indifference to culture was not the fault of art and artists; culture simply lacked a presence in the public con-sciousness. "For how many political, social, academic, and artistic endeavors would there be money and energy if they were urgently and constantly held before the eyes of the public," he asked.[98] Warburg was excited by the appear-ance of *Der Lotse*; "That is Hamburg's culture!" he wrote to his brother Max.[99] He planned to write an essay about anti-Semitism in Hamburg for the journal that, however, never appeared.[100]

Among many critical and progressive essays that addressed German art and culture, *Der Lotse* published articles by Karl Scheffler, Heinrich Pudor, Otto Brandis, and Cornelius Gurlitt, all citizens of Hamburg who criticized the neo-Baroque aesthetic favored by the Kaiser and who supported new trends in sculp-ture that they saw being pursued in Hamburg. Harald Olbrich has labeled the few years around 1900 as a time of "the crisis of the memorial," a period when artists and art critics sought a way out of the historicism of prevailing aesthetic trends.[101] The Bismarck memorial was an actualization of anti-Wilhelmine ten-dencies in a city where pride in republican traditions and strong particularistic and anti-Prussian feeling existed long after its incorporation into the Empire.

Der Lotse was quick to take aim at the national Bismarck memorial begun in 1892 and completed in June 1901. It was erected on the Königsplatz before the Reichstag in Berlin. Its sculptor, Reinhold Begas (1831–1911), dominated the sculptural arts in the capital. His dynamic neo-Baroque style was a favorite of the Kaiser, whose artistic projects elevated it to "official" status. Begas's bronze figure of Bismarck dressed in his military uniform and spiked helmet was known to contemporaries as the most lifelike representation of the chancellor, especially as it captured two of his most common speaking gestures: the movement of his neck and the spreading of the fingers of his right hand, which rests on an Imperial charter.[102] But the monument is a mixture of naturalism and allegory; Bismarck is surrounded by allegorical sculpture groups that are only loosely bound to him: Atlas bearing the globe representing the awakening of German power; a Siegfried-like youth forging the German sword; a reading Sibyl reclining on a sphinx, representing the wisdom of the state; and a helmeted woman trampling a beast, symbolizing the strength of the state that crushes the threat of socialist uprising.

In his contribution to *Der Lotse*, Karl Scheffler attacked the artistic vision of Begas and the Kaiser.[103] Scheffler was a prominent art critic in Berlin and editor of the journal *Kunst und Künstler* from 1907. His book, *Berlin: The Destiny of a City* (1910) castigated the capital for its cultural banality and the influence this had on other German cities.[104] In *Der Lotse*, Scheffler claimed that such "dynastic representational art" did not engender love and trust. Instead, it promoted "subservient idolization" and incorporated "exactly the opposite of the qualities that constitute the idea of Bismarck." Begas's monument only gave immortality to the "boastful art of our time, to the unfree spirit of the present that tolerates it." More specifically, Scheffler claimed that Begas's multifigure allegorical group was a poor work of art. Seen from the front it presented "a wild, rugged" silhouette; the spaces between the figures were "indescribably disturbing." "Must one of the radical 'Secessionists,'" Scheffler asked, "speak to Professor Begas about the rules of art?" But more importantly, nothing about the allegories themselves spoke directly and uniquely of Bismarck. In Scheffler's opinion, the ambivalence of the allegory made it suitable for any number of figures including Field Marshal Helmuth Moltke, War Minister Albrecht von Roon or Kaiser Friedrich. In the end, Scheffler concluded, the Königsplatz would be better without any monument at all.

Scheffler also wrote an article in which he denounced Berlin's claim to cultural and artistic achievement.[105] Its only claim to artistic importance, he asserted, was its significance as an art market. The genuine love of art was not to be found in Berlin. Instead, "the bourgeoisie want to show off their possessions," and "the court politicizes [artistic] apotheosis." What interest in contemporary art actually existed did not amount to real love of the same. "In the sandstone palaces, a generation of parvenus is arising that knows nothing of culture and art, but that sponsors fashion as a replacement for both; it does not want the beautiful, but the new, and concerns itself only with eternal values that are still in demand. Because for them, money is the measure of value for every ideal." Also in the pages of *Der Lotse*, the author Heinrich Pudor criticized Berlin for its lack of impressive architecture.[106] He claimed that cities a tenth the size of Berlin, like Lüneberg,

Halberstadt, and Rostock, played a more significant role in the history of architecture than Germany's capital. This was because Berlin continued to build in the neo-Baroque style. This style was decadent, it was the style of Catholicism and of Rome, and it made the Reichstag and Berlin's cathedral appear like "large soap bubbles." Such structures would never find a resonance in the heart of the German people, never touch the German soul, and never satisfy the yearning of Germans. But how was this to be done? According to Pudor, Berlin must build in the Renaissance or Gothic style and build in brick. Brick architecture was the architecture of northern Germany to which Pudor claimed Berlin belonged. It was the style of the city's Marienkirche.

Another essay by the judge Otto Brandis was highly critical of the Kaiser's influence on art and the recently completed decoration of the Siegesallee.[107] Wilhelm's influence on the arts in Prussia should not be underestimated; to a great extent, the fine arts were dependent upon the favor of the government and the emperor.[108] The decoration of the Siegesallee, a gift from the Kaiser to Berlin, was completed between 1897 and 1901 by twenty-seven Berlin artists. Along the avenue running between Kemperplatz and Königsplatz, thirty-two over-life-size marble statues of the rulers of Brandenburg and Prussia were erected. The speech that the Kaiser made at the celebration of its completion is well known to historians. "But when art, as often happens today, shows us only misery, and shows it to us even uglier than misery is anyway," he exclaimed, "then art commits a sin against the German people."[109] This sentiment lay at the heart of what Warburg called "the general Imperial idea about modern art's direction of march."[110]

Brandis did not share the Kaiser's belief in narrowly defined aesthetic truths. That which is considered beautiful changes from age to age and people to people, he claimed. Misery can also be a bearer of beauty and it is art's right to find beauty in sorrow. But most importantly, the artwork must bear the character of the artist, must bear the stamp of his individuality; if not, it ceases to be art. It was this individuality that the Kaiser suppressed with his aesthetic dictums and his demand that artists "give unto the Kaiser what belongs to the Kaiser." The numerous monuments to Kaiser Wilhelm, Bismarck, and Moltke "must, because of the uniformity of the purpose, degenerate into characterless types, into mass-produced items." The effect of the statues lining the Siegesallee "is at best decorative within the frame of the tree-filled surroundings; one may never compare them to great sculpture." A citizen of the Free and Hanseatic City of Hamburg, Brandis proudly claimed that art had always been threatened by princely courts and only blossomed in the Free City of Athens, the Republics of Florence and Venice, and the Netherlandish states freed from Spanish rule.

According to the art historian, Cornelius Gurlitt, Berlin's sculptors were too deeply mired in "petty realism" to produce genuine monuments.[111] Gurlitt had no doubt that their art would quickly fall into decline. They would soon learn that all sculpture must be as simple as possible in order to achieve perfection; it must become architectonic. Gurlitt claimed that naturalism had reached the limits of its effectiveness in sculpture. Rejuvenation of the art, he believed, must now be sought in the simplification of form. The focus in modern sculpture must be on achieving a strong unified impression, on the decisive emphasis of size as opposed to the richness of style derived from imitation of the Baroque. Simple enlargement of mass was, however, inartistic. It must be accompanied by the refinement or simplification of form to replace a naturalism that was inappropriate for large-scale statuary. "According to my estimation, our Bismarck memorials should appear this way instead of those realistic statues standing on all sorts of plinths," Gurlitt concluded.[112] "Things are going forward," he wrote, "and he who wants to hold fast to one standpoint will soon be astonished that he is alone and is no longer understood." In the exhibition of Bismarck memorial designs in Hamburg, he noted, there were "very competent" works to be seen.

Warburg's musings evince a similar distaste for what he referred to as Berlin's theatrical and sentimental Baroque style. He regarded the Italian Renaissance as a high point of European art. This is clear in the public lectures on Leonardo da Vinci that he gave in the Kunsthalle beginning in the autumn of 1899.[113] If his scholarly interest was focused on the expressions of pagan frenzy that Italian artists borrowed from the ancients, he also valued the recovery of the classical world's serene, contemplative beauty. Warburg continued to be influenced by the Enlightenment notion that if painting and sculpture cast off static restraint, it abandoned moral perfection; he believed the geniuses of the High Renaissance were able to use antique artistic forms to invoke pathos and represent psychological states without succumbing to mannerism and the Dionysian energies of antiquity's psychological legacy. They balanced passion with reflective calm. But the triumph of classical beauty in Western culture was short-lived; the dramatic art of the Italian Baroque, an art of "excessive movement" resulting in "an ornamental mannerism of ragged outlines," was an art of empty rhetoric and cliché.[114] It was an art of outward show emptied of expressive content, an art of decorative flourishes designed to impress the viewer rather than move him or her. For Warburg, the nineteenth-century reappearance of this aesthetic was a cause for concern.

Warburg complained about the "pernicious influence of the theater, realistic expression, and theatrical decoration" on contemporary German sculpture.[115] The sense of what was fundamental and essential had been lost in sculpture and architecture as a result of the theater's influence. Sculpture became "cheap showmanship," which through "arbitrarily transposed affectations of lively communication deceived the public about its inner emptiness."[116] The sculptural products of "Berlin's sentimental neo-Baroque style" amounted to a "wax museum of patriotic spectacle."[117] The allegorical groupings into which this sculpture was often formed were a jarring mixture of naturalism and idealism. Warburg characterized these allegories as

an obtrusively teeming mass of real animals and winged genii, which, in the clash of their incompatible natures, arouse discordant reactions in the beholder: much Hagenbeck and a little *Willehalm*. This conflict becomes especially intolerable when the principal figure is realistically treated while the paraphernalia are in an idealistic style; when, for instance, an earth sprite suddenly hands the Imperial Crown to a glee club.[118]

Warburg was as keen as Scheffler and the committee to see the demise of the Begas school in Berlin and believed that "only fortunate fusion of architectural and plastic elements can give rise to a monument possessed of inner persuasive power."[119] He once referred to the Bismarck memorial's designer, Hugo Lederer, as a "tamed Baroque artist."[120]

Warburg's thoughts on the art promoted by the Kaiser and Imperial government are not as explicitly marked by the political and social overtones that characterize the critiques of other commentators. Yet one suspects they were motivated by more than aesthetic and cultural concerns. Matthew Rampley has suggested that Warburg's vehement reaction to the Baroque aesthetic of early modern Europe was "partly due to his recognition of the political significance of this process."[121] In 1895, Warburg wrote an article on the pageant mounted to celebrate the arrival in Florence of Grand Duke Ferdinand's wife, Christine of Lorraine, in 1589; he understood these spectacles were "a show for the limited and illiterate understanding of the underlings. Master and Slave."[122] Rampley points to the fact that "evident in the pageant of 1589 was the emerging use of spectacle in the sixteenth and seventeenth centuries as a means of underpinning the absolute monarchies of Europe, in which there was a supervenience of visibility and power." He goes on to suggest that "this stood in opposition to his [Warburg's] own communal politics, in which he saw the mercantile republic of Hamburg as the ideal form of polity."[123] We have seen that Warburg's "communal politics" were not democratic and have noted their authoritarian tenor. But we have also noted that he sided with those who defended Hamburg's political, social, and cultural traditions within the Empire. Therefore it is not unreasonable to suggest that the comments about Berlin's "wax museum of patriotic spectacle" were motivated, if not by a concern for the authoritarian disposition of national governance, than at least by a concern for the extent to which policies established in Berlin encroached upon Hamburg's political and cultural autonomy.

What is clear in so much of the commentary surrounding Hamburg's plan for a Bismarck memorial is the intention to break with traditional modes of representation and embrace innovation. The idea was shared by Scheffler and others that the spirit of Bismarck demanded a special artistry to give it voice: instead of naturalism, stylized and architectonic forms best imparted Bismarck's essence to the viewer. Massive, monolithic stone forms were the most effective vehicle to steer the thoughts of the viewer toward Bismarck's deeds and his importance for the German people. In practical terms, what the committee wanted was a monument that looked and functioned more like a placard than a work of fine art. It must be a monument of "enormous size, powerful mass, and clear outlines" that would command a wide visual field and proclaim the glory of Bismarck better than any other.[124] Simple symbols and powerful structures would replace allegories that were often difficult to decipher; simplicity of design was intended to appeal to the simplest of people. The committee's thinking on the matter dovetailed with developments in the commemoration of Bismarck, as practitioners of the cult demanded the use of supposed Germanic art forms to give expression to their vision.[125] In 1898, the *Burschenschaftliche Blätter* called for a Bismarck memorial that would be "a symbol of unity, of towering dimensions, but simple and unostentatious, simple in form and on a massive foundation decorated only with the arms or motto of the Iron Chancellor."[126] The challenge led, in 1899, to a design competition for a Bismarck column. Wilhelm Kreis, who also submitted a design to the Hamburg competition, was awarded the top three prizes. His designs for Bismarck columns—stone, altar-like braziers on massive, squat towers devoid of any figural representation of Bismarck—exerted a strong influence on German memorial art; fifty such columns were built according to his designs.[127] The purpose of the architectonic monuments produced by Kreis and others was twofold: to promote an artistic style conceived of as distinctly German and to elevate Bismarck to a symbol, to a mythical figure representing German unity. As Thomas Nipperdey explains, the German nation was to be both "represented and addressed in a sturdy, simple and serious form, in the form of composure and concentration."[128]

And so, in 1902, Mönckeberg announced that Bismarck would not be honored in Hamburg as he was in other cities, as "the great statesman, the first Chancellor of the Reich, the powerful speaker." He would be portrayed as he lived in German hearts: "a powerful personality, free from battles … free from the stains with which the parties, out of hate and jealousy, sought to darken his fame, free from faults and errors." "The national hero of modern times, the man through whom the German people saw the fulfillment of their centuries-old longing" could only be portrayed in Hamburg as "the ideal figure, the embodiment of all that we think of, wonder at, and honor at the sound of his name."[129] The committee stressed the need for a new artistic idiom in opposition to the Emperor's taste. Its members clearly intended to leave Berlin's smaller and conventional national Bismarck memorial in the shadow of their gigantic project. As Nipperdey argues, "behind Bismarck monuments stands not an artistic, but also a political protest against *Wilhelminismus*, against pathos and prestige, trivialization and boasting."[130]

V

The committee for the erection of a Bismarck memorial was elected at a meeting in the chamber of commerce on 2 August 1898 with Mayor Versmann as its chair. Its members included some of Hamburg's most eminent cultural figures: Lichtwark; Justus Brinckmann; the architect Martin Haller, builder of Hamburg's city hall; the painter, Valentin Ruths. Initiated by the citizens of the city, the Bismarck memorial would also be funded by them. In barely eight weeks, the committee had collected 400,000 marks in public donations.[131]

In the committee's first meeting on 1 October 1898, the discussion centered on the monument's location. Bismarck "belonged in the most distinguished part of the city," it was decided, not in the harbor quarter.[132] But Lichtwark and Ruths briefly turned the discussion to artistic form. Pertinent to the question of location was a decision as to whether Hamburgers wanted to erect "a more decorative, widely visible, towering monument" or one of "high artistic achievement." Did citizens want a monument that looked and functioned like a placard, or one that looked and functioned like a work of fine art? They pointed out that many monuments to Kaiser Wilhelm I, although often set in impressive architectural frames, were poor-quality works of art. The Kaiser Wilhelm memorial in Koblenz, built by the Berlin sculptor Emil Hundrieser and the architect Bruno Schmitz, was mentioned as an example.[133] Simple statues, stripped of all details, could be effective monuments and there was danger in insisting that decorative aspects should be sacrificed to purely artistic ones. "But it is highly desirable," Lichtwark and Ruths concluded, "that one strives to avoid the unsatisfactory artistic execution of details that is the fault of most new monuments."

Nonetheless, the committee was divided when it met again in January 1899.[134] Some members insisted on the construction of "an impressive monument of uncommon magnificence," a monument of colossal form that would command a wide visual field. Only an "uncommon and exceptional" artwork could properly commemorate an "uncommon and exceptional" man. Others argued for a monument of moderate proportions and of "perfect beauty." Yet despite debate as to its form, one important conviction united the factions: "The conventional, universally recognized form of the Bismarck memorial, as it is raised in numerous cities, is to be avoided if possible."

In order to achieve this goal, it was decided to solicit monument designs for a competition. This would allow the committee, now headed by Mayor Mönckeberg, to choose from a wide range of possibilities. But the committee clearly had a predilection for new trends in German art; the competition was to "offer younger forces the opportunity to show their creative formal abilities."[135] This was the topic of conversation on 7 March 1899 and it is clear that Berlin was regarded as a model and a rival.[136] The circular published to announce the artistic competition for Berlin's Bismarck memorial in 1894 was deemed indispensable as a model for Hamburg's competition; when the location for reception and storage of the models was discussed, it was noted that the committee responsible for Berlin's Bismarck memorial had received ninety-four submissions; the question of the number and value of prizes to be awarded was accompanied by the assertion that thirty prizes had been awarded in Berlin with a total value of 80,000 marks; when the number of artistic judges was discussed, it was noted that Berlin had boasted sixteen. The announcement of the design competition for Hamburg's Bismarck memorial appeared in the *Berliner National-Zeitung*, among many other newspapers, on 17 June 1901. It appeared directly below a report on the unveiling ceremony of the national Bismarck memorial in Berlin on the previous day.[137]

Two hundred and nineteen artists participated in Hamburg's design competition, more than twice the number that participated in Berlin.[138] Scarcely ever before, according to Georg Fuchs, had such a competition occupied the representatives of German cultural life so intensely.[139] To Albert Hofmann, this show of numbers was a statement of discontent with Berlin's art policies on the part of German artists. It was also a sign of the artists' trust in the composition of the prize jury which was composed partly of artists.[140] As Ilonka Jochum-Bohrmann maintains, artists knew that their designs would be judged more from an artistic standpoint in Hamburg than in Berlin, where the imperial government's art policies would exercise important influence. The committee imposed no restrictions on the form the designs should take. It invited artists to submit sculptural or architectural designs or a combination of the two; it invited them to exercise their powers freely.

Despite Hamburg's invitation to artistic freedom, most artists contributed either designs for structures that often resembled the popular Bismarck towers or over-sized versions of common Bismarck-monument types that included a naturalistic portrayal of the Iron Chancellor. According to Fuchs, the competition amounted to "a massive excess of tastelessness, archaic shortcomings, and culturally unfavorable banality."[141] But in the opinion of Professor Georg Treu, a member of the prize jury, the competition had encapsulated all the competing tendencies in German art and was a display of its richness. The eclecticism of earlier times stood beside the ever stronger naturalism of the present; the "products of dainty confectioners" beside "the sculptural bombast and theatrical showmanship that is currently the order of the day for official memorials."[142] But the most outstanding competition entries, he believed, marked a break with "a hermaphroditic imitation of the misunderstood Antique, with the decorative, superficial sculpture of the Baroque, with the convention of the usual market and street monuments." Responsible for this unleashing of new forces was, "besides the greatness of the task and the richness of the means, before all the complete freedom granted to the artists which cannot be valued enough."[143] Hamburg had looked to the future of art, had given it voice and helped to foster it. In Hamburg, wrote Treu, "not only is the spirit that knows how to see the way to the future alive, but also the boldness to pursue it."[144]

The 219 entries were put on public display in the Velodrome in January 1902 and the prize jury awarded ten prizes in all. Designs for massive memorial temples, towers, and over-life-size, but naturalistic representations of Bismarck were all thought worthy of recognition. But first prize was awarded to the sculptor Hugo Lederer (1871–1940) and the architect Johann Emil Schaudt (1871–1957), both based in Berlin, for a design entitled "An Offering of Thanks." A commentary included in their portfolio was short and to the point. It was impossible, they explained, to interpret Bismarck as a soldier, diplomat, or as the old gentleman from Friedrichsruh. "The embodiment of the spirit of a great era with his own immortal deeds lived in the people as a German national hero, as the Iron Chancellor," they explained. "His name is a hero's name. The endeavor of the artist was the monumental realization of this idea—to erect a monument simple and solemn as the dignity of the task demands."[145]

A student of Christian Behrens, Lederer was only thirty years old at the time, but had been working independently in Berlin since 1895.[146] For the Hamburg competition, he and Schaudt designed a gigantic plinth twenty meters tall, adorned with eight allegorical male figures representing the German tribes. A relief representing Germania adorned the front of the plinth.[147] On it stood a bare-headed, armor-clad, caped Bismarck of fifteen meters without the orders or paraphernalia of office.[148] He stood stiffly erect, his hands clasped in front of him on the pommel of a huge sword which he held tip down. Two large eagles squatted at his feet. "Sculpture," Lederer once wrote, "must not be modeled, it must be built."[149] This was the dictum he applied in Hamburg: his Bismarck resembles the ancient colossi of Egyptian pharaohs in that it appears to have been built of massive blocks instead of carved from stone. It is a monolith; a static, axial form of near perfect symmetry. Details of dress and facial features are simplified and ponderous. The modeling is not naturalistic; it is heavy and indelicate with almost no attempt to capture the intricacies of bodily mass defined in space. The emphasis is on two dimensions, on powerful line and silhouette. The impression of power is heightened by the choice of granite as the building material. Bismarck never appeared like this in real life. Lederer and Schaudt's design was a symbolic representation, an easily legible allegory, a totem.

The committee announced that the decision to award first prize to "An Offering of Thanks" had been unanimous.[150] Warburg's diary, however, tells us that thirty members voted for the design while two, Voigt and Reimer, voted against.[151] Lederer's inventive remodeling of the memorial site was praised and the design considered best to meet the requirement of visibility from the furthest possible distance, especially the harbor. Against the advice of Lichtwark, the Platz des Elbpavillons, a hill of thirty meters in the west end of the city, had been chosen by the committee as the memorial's location. From here it would dominate the approach to the harbor.

Hamburg's Bismarck memorial combines the two trends of sculptural and architectonic Bismarck commemoration that grew in importance after 1890. Its innovations emerge from a tradition and form a bridge between the archaizing monumental style of memorial architecture propagated by the architect Bruno Schmitz since the 1880s and the *völkisch* monumental primitivism propagated by architects like Wilhelm Kreis since the late 1890s.[152] Lederer was one of several young sculptors, like Ernst Barlach (1870–1938), August Gaul (1869–1921), Louis Tuaillon (1862–1919), Hermann Hahn (1869–1942), Fritz Klimsch (1870–1960), and Arthur Volkmann (1851–1914) who employed simplified and abstracted forms to give more concentrated expression to their ideas.[153] Most were inspired by the Munich sculptor Adolf von Hildebrand (1847–1921). His book, *The Problem of Form in the Fine Arts* (1893) was the most widely read work of art theory before the First World War.[154] Hildebrand's neo-classical style was a reaction to the neo-Baroque style of Begas. His theory of sculptural art was founded on two principles: sculpture must capture the permanent and essential aspects of nature and it must be architectonically constructed. These ideas inspired an entire generation of German sculptors seeking to overturn the historicism that dominated German plastic art at the end of the nineteenth century. In Hamburg, the committee's catalogue of prize-winning entries spoke of the "tower-like" qualities of Lederer and Schaudt's design.[155] The author, Georg Treu, praised the "massive, permanent forms" of the monument. Only a monument of "towering proportions, powerful mass, clear outlines, and powerful internal organization" could be erected on the chosen site, he explained. In Hamburg, wrote Treu, "a new memorial art had spoken which in architecture and sculpture sought simple force and greatness and thereby preserved its German characteristics in form and mood." In its archaic, massive architecture and the mythical timelessness of its sculpture, Lederer's design gave outstanding expression to the Bismarck cult of the turn-of-the-century.

It also tapped into a much more ancient tradition. According to the committee, Lederer had designed a "gigantic Roland," the "embodiment of heroic greatness and symbol of fortified watchfulness."[156] There is no evidence, however, to suggest that Lederer conceived of his design as a modern Roland column. The ancient cult of Roland, paladin of Charlemagne, found its medieval expression in legend and song while columns depicting the knight were placed on the market squares of some northern German cities.[157] Hamburgers would have known the famous Roland column in Bremen and many would have seen what was then believed to be a Roland column in the town of Wedel northwest of the city.[158] Although their exact origin and meaning is not understood, it is believed they symbolized royal jurisdiction or a city's right to hold markets. Karen Lang has suggested that, for modern Germans, these Roland columns functioned as a popular symbol of "valiant protection."[159] The committee claimed that this archaically armed and armored figure captured, in a heroic pose, "the way the figure of Bismarck gradually grew in the awareness of the people."[160] Warburg himself once referred to the Bismarck memorial as the "border guard."[161]

VI

Large numbers of art critics and scholars were attracted to Hamburg's design competition. Many responded favorably to the winning design and praised the stimulus that Hamburg had given to new directions in the arts. Writing for the *Deutsche Bauzeitung*, Albert Hofmann described Hamburg's Bismarck memorial as the high point of a thousand-year history of monumental art. Hamburg's memorial committee "had laid the ground for confidence in the future, confidence that German memorial art in the north had not fallen into irreversible decline."[162] After all the "wretched naturalistic emperors and chancellors," wrote Scheffler in *Der Lotse*, Lederer's Bismarck was an original contribution to German art.[163] The concept of portraying Bismarck as Roland was fresher than the "entire allegorical extravagance of the Begas school." According to Georg Fuchs, there was something modern in the message of Lederer's design and the power with which it was expressed.[164] It marked a transformation in European culture from "the insubstantial art imitation of a plebeian age" to an art of "sincere, upright, sovereign, powerful mankind." Like the works of Peter Behrens, Melchior Lechter, Charles Rennie Mackintosh, and Henry van de Velde it was the art of life felt as "greater, deeper, richer, happier, holier" than before.

Lederer's monument was very different from those to which Hamburgers were accustomed. In general, the city possessed many less monuments than a royal capital like Munich. Nonetheless, a relatively large number were erected between 1890 and 1914. Not only the senate and citizens' assembly, but various middle-class groups and associations had an interest in celebrating Hamburg's significance. This was often done by public, sculptural reference to important political and cultural figures and important events in the city's history. There were military monuments, monuments commemorating the city's mayors, religious monuments, and statues celebrating Johannes Brahms, Heinrich Heine, Gotthold Lessing, and Friedrich von Schiller. The sculptural program of the city hall celebrated the city's political, economic, and cultural history; the art gallery bore allegories of art and portraits of famous artists on its facade; the Deutsche Schauspielhaus was home to the images of poets, theater directors, and actors. Bridges and fountains became bearers of monuments that elucidated the city's history. One of the city's grandest monuments was dedicated to Kaiser Wilhelm I. The city government spent 750,000 marks to have Johannes Schilling erect this monument in front of the city hall between 1900 and 1903.[165]

But almost all of these monuments were traditional in conception and execution. As Brigitte Meißner explains, founders and donors placed the highest value on a naturalistic style of art.[166] The committee responsible for the erection of a monument to Mayor Carl Friedrich Petersen accepted the design by Victor Oskar Tilgner because "the stance is natural and dignified; the verisimilitude of the portrait is surprisingly successful; the official costume is accurately reproduced, finely rendered, and skillfully fits the form of the body."[167] The memorial to Kaiser Wilhelm I, composed of an equestrian portrait accompanied by several allegorical sculpture groups and reliefs, was reminiscent of Begas's work in Berlin. Not surprisingly, it met with Warburg's criticism for its "lack of style."[168] Upon the recommendation and insistence of Lichtwark, Adolf von Hildebrand was chosen to design the monument to Mayor Heinrich Burchard that was unveiled in November 1914. But Hildebrand's attempt to objectify Burchard's personality met with criticism because the portrait's facial expression did not match personal recollections of him.[169] The documentary style of the Petersen monument was much more in keeping with the tastes of Hamburg's middle classes.

When the Velodrome exhibition opened in January 1902, a debate quickly developed among Hamburgers. This focused not on the political or social sentiments embodied in the Bismarck memorial, but on the form it should take.

According to one contemporary observer, the exhibition was the only topic of conversation in Hamburg throughout its duration. It "heated natures to passion," split old friendships, and even threatened familial peace.[170] The committee itself was fractured when Lichtwark withdrew from the prize jury. Committed to the project from the beginning, Lichtwark had a strong distaste for historicism in the arts. But he spurned colossal works of sculpture and believed "that a more refined, reflective, and artistically sensitive posterity could not countenance them."[171] He referred to the design by Lederer and Schaudt as an "embarrassing, stylized graven image."[172] Many other citizens of Hamburg objected to the design.[173] Local newspapers gave voice to these objections in the form of readers' letters, many of which found their way into Warburg's files.[174]

Not all letters to Hamburg's newspapers, especially the *Hamburgischer Correspondent*, were negative. Nor were their opinions opposed purely and simply to Lederer's artistic vocabulary. Few, if any objections to the design were born of an aversion to modern art. Criticisms of the design were most often based on opinions as to how Bismarck should be remembered and how his achievements should be communicated to future generations. Some writers concurred with the committee's artistic aspirations and praised Lederer's design as a "monument to Hamburg's artistic understanding."[175] Some admired the design for the powerful impression it made upon the viewer. "When looking at the monument," wrote one reader, "we don't think of the statesman and diplomat, nor of the parliamentary speaker or the gentleman from Friedrichsruh, nor of the man with his various weaknesses, but of the hero who performed the great national deed, the unification of Germany."[176] Clearly, some saw in the monument what Mönckeberg and the committee intended them to see. Others argued that abstract artistic form was necessary for the instruction of future generations. Contemporaries of Bismarck may find his spirit and greatness reflected in a naturalistic portrait statue, but future generations would not. They would laugh at the fact that the "pilot of the ship of state" always wanted to be portrayed in uniform. Bismarck's individuality was not embodied in his uniform but in the core of his nature and being. It was this that Lederer and Schaudt captured so well.[177] The apparently archaic costume was nothing other than a hero's costume.[178]

But many Hamburgers thought differently about portraying Bismarck in the guise of Roland. At least one observer found the symbolism simply too confused to be effective.[179] Others found it "unnatural to give our great German Bismarck the form of a legendary hero whom the French can name as their own at least with the same right as we Germans." The military defeat of France enabled Bismarck to found the German Empire. Should Bismarck be commemorated in the form of a knight whom the defeated nation could claim as their own?[180] The very idea was anathema to many Hamburgers. In any case, was not Bismarck much more powerful than Roland or any other knight of days gone by?[181] But objections to Lederer's "gigantic Roland" were not always the product of nationalist sentiment. Some worried that Lederer's stylized design gave the monument the appearance of a death mask rather than of a living human being.[182] Others, while admiring the design especially vis-à-vis its impression of power, rejected what they argued was an anachronistic manner of portraying Bismarck. One author among many claimed that Bismarck "in this form, is foreign to all of us who knew him personally."[183] More importantly, future generations would be confused to find the founder of the German Empire in the guise of a medieval knight. So, they argued, would the many foreign nationals who congregated in this center of world trade. Why not portray Bismarck "as he was, riding over the battlefields of France, in the uniform of his king, the same uniform he wore when setting the emperor's crown upon the king's head in Versailles?"[184] Only in this manner would future generations understand the significance of Bismarck. Would anyone ever think of portraying Goethe in any other manner than the well-known conventions?[185] No matter that all other German cities had portrayed Bismarck as he appeared in real life. Surely in Hamburg the portrayal of what was great and true would not diminish its effect.[186] Hans Hundrieser's naturalistic portrayal of Bismarck found widespread favor among the Hamburg public for its "incomparable beauty."[187] It was awarded a second prize in the design competition and was eventually executed for the city of Lübeck.

Mönckeberg responded angrily to the public's criticisms of the artistic leadership and judgment of the committee. He labeled their expressions of discontent as nothing but "nonsense" spouted by "raging philistines."[188] For his part, Warburg could be very critical of the efforts of Hamburg's cultural administrators. He once described them as "coachmen on a water wagon" and accused them of conducting a Punch and Judy show "to astonish the natives."[189] But in this instance his support was behind what he described as "a select group of German experts in association with the capable men of our city" and the leadership they exercised.[190] "Here in Hamburg," he wrote to Theodor Brodersen in 1913, "everything goes along the path of healthy progress, if only the experts listen calmly to their consciences and conduct themselves according to the same, unconcerned by the majority of the day. Evidence: Lederer's Bismarck memorial that, in the event of a plebiscite in 1902, would have been defeated and today finds almost only enthusiastic supporters, but in no case more opponents."[191]

Warburg "carefully collected" the "voice of the people," clipping the many dissenting letters from local newspapers.[192] But his interest did not lie with the objections to the supposed adoption of French iconography for the portrayal of Bismarck. Instead, his thoughts revolved around the issues of abstraction and naturalism in the arts and his criticisms were directed at the public's demand for the latter. As in many other instances, he took up the weapon of sarcastic wit and, as he had done in the 1890s in response to events in the Art Association, satirized the public's outrage in a short dramatization entitled "Walpurgis Night on the Stintfang."[193] A subtitle, later crossed out, read "A Vision from the Year 2500." In the drama, the "citizens' souls of 1901" are resurrected to gather with their families at the foot of the Bismarck memorial. In a chorus of "hopeless insistence" they begin again to express their opposition to the memorial. "Is that my Bismarck? Is that your Bismarck? Is that our Bismarck?" they cry with hoarse vehemence. Suddenly one, "the spirit of the simple bourgeois Grollhagen, the only one who in his outer appearance has still retained something of the respectable corpulence of a well-meaning patriot", rises to address the assembled souls. The Bismarck memorial is a "monster, a mummy, a puppet" he exclaims, because "the so-called experts" did not want to listen to the voices of the simple men and their families. Of course, Grollhagen had no understanding of the issues under discussion, but he had enough courage to voice his opposition to Lederer's design in 1901: "That is not our great, loyal Bismarck!" Hamburgers, he explains, wanted to look upon the Bismarck memorial and see what Bismarck thought and felt. They wanted to see him portrayed as Anton von Werner had portrayed him, as the founder of the German Empire, or as the painter Christian W. Allers had, within the circle of his family. "He stood humanly near to us and for our good money we could or may demand this direct radiant warmth. That has not happened and no one feels comfortable with him," laments Grollhagen. Quite the opposite: Hamburgers now confront his image with some fear as though he would wield his sword against wrong-doers. And for this, Hamburgers have spent their good money! Yet there is spiteful consolation in disappointment. "That is our revenge," exclaims Grollhagen, "the revenge of the simple man, that he now stands there with a grim expression, without life and change and virtually unworthy of love." Suddenly Grollhagen's speech is cut short as the eyes of the eagles squatting at Bismarck's feet light up sulfurous yellow and "with a single flap of their wings, they expiate the profanation of the night air."

On one level, Warburg's criticisms of public taste echo Mönckeberg's desire to eschew all that was superficial and time-bound in order to capture the essence of Bismarck. To the complaint that Hamburgers had never known Bismarck as he was depicted in Lederer's design, Warburg responded:

> Would one, therefore, know him better, because one recognized the *cuirass* or the helmet or the rider's boots or the orders that he wore in life? Must Bismarck be holding the bolting horse of a *Germania* by the bridle so that we understand his significance for the German Empire? Or is it necessary that on the plinth a grandson is taught by his upright grandfather who it is that towers above?

Warburg's answer was no; such art was only the "deceptive appearance of human lifelikeness" intended to make the viewer feel comfortable with the figure that stood on the plinth.[194] Bismarck as he was known—standing and speaking in the Reichstag, or receiving Hamburgers on his birthday as a friendly neighbor—was "only the temporary shroud to which, for contemporaries, the inaccessibility and mysteriousness of his appearance was superficially confided."[195] A monument built of "a charm more proper to the music hall and circus pantomime" could never capture the essence of Bismarck and provide "access to the man"; nor could the artistic equivalent of "egalitarian backslapping and ingratiating amiability," which Warburg parodied in his drama. An artwork could only recreate Bismarck's essence "by keeping its distance and demanding a more profound objectivity."[196] With this sudden shift to theoretical reflection at the end of his drama, Warburg begins to generalize about the role and possibilities of art. He leaves the specific subject of Bismarck portraiture behind and in the following lines bares the theoretical framework with which he evaluated Lederer's design and the public's response:

> It marks the lowest stage of aesthetic culture when a work of art is used merely to gain possession of a lost object in effigy. The higher development of taste consists in keeping one's distance and trying to understand the object by means of comparisons within the field of vision. The commercial philistine does not like to be thwarted in his desire to gain possession by a closer approach (my Bismarck, our Bismarck) and if he is disturbed in his artistic feeding time he is irritated and becomes nasty.[197]

The ideas informing this passage are scattered through unpublished notes dating from the turn-of-the-century and it is among these that Warburg's real interest in the Bismarck memorial is to be found.

VII

Fundamental to understanding Warburg's thinking on the Bismarck memorial is the difference he posited between art that attempts "to gain possession of a lost object in effigy" and his notion of "keeping one's distance." Here we return to ideas touched upon in previous chapters. In the first formulation, he expresses his belief that the mimetic impulse is indicative of a lack of artistic self-consciousness and a lack of conceptual thought. This was characteristic of primitive modes of artistic practice and empathetic absorption in an image. With the phrase "keeping one's distance", Warburg draws upon his conception of that intellectual space—defined as *Denkraum*—that was pervaded by discursive thought, separated symbol from stimulus, and was embodied in rational, self-conscious artistic practice and reception. With his criticism of those who demanded a naturalistic portrayal of Bismarck, Warburg seems to equate citizens of Hamburg with the merchants and bankers of Renaissance Florence; in his mind, their taste for the naturalism of Flemish art indicated a primitive positivism and lack of self-conscious reflection. But the criteria Warburg used to judge the Bismarck memorial were not informed by a simple model of evolutionary psychology, nor was his measure of the monument's success guided by a superficial enthusiasm for the displacement of traditional modes of representation by forms considered "modern" by contemporaries.

We have seen that, in the early years of his research, Warburg focused on the nature of artistic practice in terms of its evolution from—and in its perpetual oscillation between –magical and metaphorical thought patterns and logical, abstract, and conceptual ones. In one respect, he was charting humanity's course from paganism to rationality. The remarks and aphorisms that he compiled on this subject beginning in the 1880s are fragmentary, cryptic, and often repetitive. They are not always an accurate guide to his mature thought; he occasionally returned to his notebooks to comment that he no longer understood certain ideas or to indicate the irrelevance of others. Yet the entries collected under the titles "Basic Fragments of a Pragmatic Science of Expression" (*Grundlegende Bruch- stücke zu einer pragmatischen Ausdruckskunde*), "Basic Fragments of a Psychology of Art" (*Grundlegende Bruchstücke zur Psychologie der Kunst*), and "Symbolism as the Determination of Boundaries" (*Symbolismus als Umfangsbestimmung*) are a guide to his thoughts at the time of the building of the Bismarck memorial.[198]

It would be incorrect to see Warburg's thinking as completely divorced from an evolutionary understanding of historical processes. More rational artistic practices were, he believed, indicative of more advanced psychological develop- ment. The *Greifmensch* (the person who grasps) stood at the beginning of War- burg's evolutionary trajectory. In his primitive condition, the *Greifmensch* lacked the degree of self-consciousness necessary to make a clear distinction between his own being and the objects that inhabited his environment. Filled with fear of the world, the *Greifmensch* confused symbols and the concepts they were used to signify; he projected subjective states of being onto the world around him. An important word for Warburg in his attempts to explain this state of being is *Aneignung*, or appropriation. The *Greifmensch* appropriates the objective world by "grasping" it through primitive impulses of mimesis, in which the depiction of intense bodily movement characterized the artist's empa- thetic immersion in the events to which he gave form. As Matthew Rampley explains, "for Warburg 'realism' is not simply a matter of representational verisimilitude. Rather, it is a central manifestation of mimetic experience, based on an immersion in minutiae—a primitive positivism—predicated on a lack of cognitive distance."[199] This was the pagan realm, a realm of magic, supersti- tious practices, and anthropomorphism, what Warburg described as "conver- gence, connection through subjective mimetic turmoil," or "the overpowering compulsion, in the lower cultural levels, to the maintenance of magic (pagan) forms of causality of bodily connection."[200]

The *Denkmensch* (the thinking person) stood at the other end of Warburg's evolutionary trajectory. The *Denkmensch* lived in the lucid sphere of rational convention where objectification was expressed in language and science. He was the "thinking man" who used his powers of speech and writing for comparison and description.[201] He commanded a rational symbolic practice that separated signifier from signified, and had acquired a feeling of distance between himself and his environment, a space pervaded by discursive thought. Warburg consid- ered this rational detachment from the unconscious, emotion, and myth as "the task of so-called *Bildung* and the criterion of progress of the human race."[202]

These ideas were tested and reinforced during Warburg's visit to the United States in 1895 and 1896 for the wedding of his brother Paul. Motivated by a desire to understand the relationship between cultural production and artistic practice—"to revitalize art history by opening it up to anthropology"—he was drawn to the Pueblo Indian communities of the American Southwest.[203] As we saw in chapter one, he found amongst the Hopi Indians an opportunity to study the link between pagan religious ideas and artistic activity in a "primitive" society, one suspended between magic and logic. It was an occasion for Warburg to examine psychological and cultural transitions that mirrored those that had occurred in ancient Greece at the dawn of rationalism. Native American thought also became "the experimental model of a historical formation," which would influence his interpretation of artistic practice in Renaissance Italy.[204] The findings that were eventually published in 1939 are multi-faceted.[205] Warburg's interest in the psychology of symbolism resulted in an interesting experiment that corroborated his thinking on the development of artistic practice. While visiting Keams Canyon, Arizona, he conducted an experiment on fourteen Hopi children: he told them the story of a boy who fell into a pond during a thunderstorm and asked them to draw an image of the storm, including the lightning. What interested him was whether the children would draw a naturalistic representation of lightning in the form of a zigzag line or the Hopi lightning symbol, the serpent with a forked tongue. Twelve of the children drew zigzags while only two drew serpents. Clearly, Hopi culture was developing from a magical to a rational mode of understanding the world.

Many of the notes that Warburg compiled upon his return to Germany were concerned with the processes by which humanity evolved from *Greifmensch* to *Denkmensch*. How does humanity break the bond of primal unity with the world? How does it liberate itself from magic fears? How does it attain the conceptual space necessary to produce a zone of reasoning—or *Denkraum*—between stimulus and reaction? In part, he concluded, through decoration, clothing, and the possession of property.[206] This marked the self-conscious use of symbolic forms and the intervention of human artifice, which led to enhanced self-consciousness and hence to the feeling of differentiation between the self and the objective world.[207] For Warburg believed that "the consciousness of substitution exists in the symbolic act."[208] But his thinking on the nature of art escaped the confines of any particular historical formation. As we have already seen, Warburg questioned linear, triumphalist accounts of historical progress and was skeptical of the effects of rationalization and the achievements of modern technology. Thus eschewing historical time for a synchronous psychic time, he placed art between complete emancipation from the world in the objectification of language and science and recession into empathetic absorption in the object. Art was "the gravitational relationship in the plane between subject and object."[209] The artist engaged in "successful appropriation" of the world around him in as much as he "scanned" and "paraphrased" it, but possessed no will to "converge" with it in a way that amounted a loss of his self-consciousness and to a "subordination" or "dedication" of the subject to the object.[210] "In the case of art," Warburg writes, "the process is such that the latent tendency is to grant to invention the power of subject subordination."[211] But art created "a new nervous differentiation, which in its ('scientific') expression signifies an increasing measure of distance between subject and object."[212] The artist stood between the *Greifmensch* and *Denkmensch* and his art was "a product of the *repeated* attempt on the part of the subject, to create a distance between himself and the object."[213]

It was predominantly from the perspective of psychic time that the Bismarck memorial appeared to Warburg as an exemplary expression of artistic energy. The stylized form of the memorial was clearly not an attempt to gain possession of Bismarck in effigy; it was a deliberately constructed symbol that referred to concepts in no way intrinsic to it. In his research on Renaissance Florence, Warburg had noted that the Italian penchant for the realism of Flemish art was a symptom of a particular lack of cognitive or critical distance. As Rampley explains, "with Flemish realism, the fact that classical myth was narrated in contemporary guise again signified a lack of distance, manifest this time in a lack of historical reflection."[214] In *The Art of Portraiture and the Florentine Bourgeoisie* (1902), Warburg examined the way in which patrons of art were portrayed as participants in the sacred stories depicted by artists; their images occupied the same physical and temporal space as religious figures. This realism stemmed from "an older pagan mimetic urge, in which image and physical actuality occupy the same continuum."[215] Earlier, it was suggested that the Bismarck cult loosed the Iron Chancellor from his historical personality and raised him to a timeless symbol of the German nation. But for Warburg, Hamburg's Bismarck memorial was about restoring cognitive distance and proper historical understanding. Far from being simply a reminder for the passerby, the monument was a challenge to the viewer to reflect seriously upon Bismarck and contemplate his deeds.

As a cognitive challenge to the viewer, Warburg understood the monument's eschewal of naturalism as a necessary counterpoint to a trend that, since the sixteenth century, had made art subject to the demands of the "individual interests of the private man."[216] This had led to a "democratically coordinated attitude to men in pictures," but at the same time to the demand for "consideration of the tired viewer," the public that wants to protect itself from the unpleasant aspects of life and wants only to be conducted through a "familiar milieu."[217] This consideration is expressed through artistic "politeness," through "theatrical, anecdotal, patriotic damping" of the artwork.[218] It resulted in the "exaggeration of that which was worth seeing," in "historical theater pathos" that facilitated "collegial empathy or open-mouthed astonishment."[219] This was in part the fault of the "petty bourgeois proprietor who wants to have everything pleasantly and clearly narrated." But it was also the fault of the artist, "the deliveryman who comes to his house in order to wait upon his relaxation in which he recalls that which is pleasant."[220] The Bismarck memorial broke with the sentimental naturalism that Warburg saw as a common denominator in bourgeois taste and that he criticized in his drama "Hamburg Conversations on Art."

But if its form was considered progressive or even modern by several who supported its construction, Warburg did not see the memorial as embodying a new form of idealism. Instead, it tapped into a long established canon of representation. To the twenty-first-century eye, Lederer's statue looks decidedly un-classical in inspiration. But it is certain that Warburg related it to antique art, although with some hesitation. In a note of 1901, he writes "It is exceedingly interesting to me to observe, and of virtually epoch-making significance, that one can see so sharply in the winning design of Lederer and Schaudt the successful decision in favor of a concentrated, simplified formal language in which architecture and sculpture reflect upon their very own means."[221] It is significant that Warburg originally wrote the word "classicizing" instead of "concentrated," but crossed it out in favor of the latter. And yet in a diary entry dated 25 January 1902, Warburg seems to have reconsidered the use of the word "classical" in relation to the Bismarck memorial. "From here," he writes, "one can reckon the beginning of the classical reaction."[222] Lederer's monument was part of a classically-inspired aesthetic trend, a trend that Warburg contemplated with the belief that "every age has the renaissance of antiquity it deserves."[223]

Although Warburg's work rarely considered the plastic arts, fragments dating from 1900 to 1903 contain undeveloped ideas that suggest he viewed sculpture as the ideal form of artistic objectification, as the highest form of symbolism. He speaks, for example, of the attainment of rational detachment from the object "through objective architectonic crystallization" and differentiates between "mimetic intensification as subjective action" and "tectonic moderation as objective deposition."[224] He also establishes an opposition between "painterly *Nahkunst*" (art of subjective proximity) and "architectonic *Fernkunst*" (art of objective detachment) and speaks of "architectonic storage, harmonic storage."[225] Warburg sided with the neo-classicists of his generation. In addition to Böcklin, he also praised the sculptor Adolph von Hildebrand (1847–1921). "In Böcklin and Hildebrand antiquity lives on in the two accents of movement: Dionysiac, enhancing, Böcklin outline in color; Apollonian, restraining, Hildebrand, façade."[226] In fact, Warburg championed one of Hildebrand's architectural projects for Hamburg, but in vain.[227]

But for Warburg, the Bismarck memorial was much more than a didactic instrument or simply a powerful reminder to Hamburg's working classes of the political and social order of the city and the German Empire. In fact, it was as much an inducement to psychological balance and the cultivation of *Denkraum* as it was the expression of a desired social order. Lederer had counteracted emotion with self-conscious deliberation and abstract thought. Just as when he promoted the serious contemplation of Albrecht Dürer's art to the working-class public in 1905, Warburg was hoping to turn the intellectual space of calm reflection and rational orientation into a permanent social function at a time of growing social and political unrest. His enthusiastic response to Lederer's work was informed by a realization that rational mastery of unreason and emotion was in no way a presumable privilege of his age. As discussed in chapter two, he often despaired about the state of the modern world, writing that "there is no distance anymore" and speaking of "our age of ... distance destroying chaos."[228] Rational detachment from the world, he believed, was destroyed through an act that was an "enemy of art," the act of "actual, psychological, imaginary, visible, intellectual appropriation" of the symbol.[229] But at the time of the Bismarck memorial's unveiling, Warburg's concern was to promote critical self-reflection as an antidote to mass intoxication in the realm of politics.

In his unpublished papers, Warburg made no comment on the Bismarck cult itself. Yet it is certain that he would have regarded the cultic ceremonies that surrounded Bismarck monuments as psychological regression and the manifestation of a new German paganism. He would have observed this phenomenon with great interest, just as he observed a similar phenomenon while in Rome on 11 February 1929. This was the day on which Mussolini and the Pope signed a concordat proclaiming reconciliation between Italy and the Catholic Church. In the busy streets, Warburg was separated from his companions who waited anxiously for him at the Hotel Eden. When he did not return for dinner, they telephoned the police. At last, he returned late in the evening and when reproached replied soberly: "You know that throughout my life I have been interested in the revival of paganism and pagan festivals. Today I had the chance of my life to be present at the re-paganization of Rome, and you complain that I remained to watch it."[230]

At the time of the Bismarck memorial's construction, Warburg was busy "watching" developments in fifteenth-century Florence. In a lecture summary from 1901 entitled "Flemish and Florentine Art in Lorenzo de' Medici's Circle Around 1480," he enumerated problems that would occupy him for several years. An inventory of works of art in the Medici Villa di Careggi presented him with a puzzling picture: among Italian artworks were sixteen Flemish tapestries and many paintings of northern European origin depicting popular religious and secular themes. Here was a jarring picture of Burckhardt's or Gobineau's first modern men decorating their palaces with the manifestations of the devout Gothic world they were supposed to have left behind. Warburg was certain that this was no mere oddity and set about investigating the phenomenon; as we have seen, he wanted to understand the attraction of artistic naturalism for Florence's bankers and merchants. What he concluded was that it was favored, in part, as a mode of symbolizing empathic identification in pictures, and was an expression of "the inveterate impulse to associate oneself, or one's own effigy, with the Divine."[231] When Florentines like Jacopo Tani had themselves painted in the company of their patron saints in self-effacing prayer and as witnesses to holy visions, what was happening was a type of "picture magic." The level of likeness carried with it a magical force linking the person portrayed to the protective divinity; it was at least representative of the desire to be close to the divine. The fact that the figures in the foreground of Ghirlandaio's fresco depicting the confirmation of the rule of the Order of St. Francis by Pope Honorius III—located in the Sassetti Chapel of Santa Trinità in Florence—could be identified as various members of the Sassetti and Medici families indicated the loss of historical and symbolic distance between viewer and representation. Clearly, the worldly-wise merchants of fifteenth-century Florence were in no way indifferent to religion and Warburg's findings challenged Burckhardt's view of Renaissance man as defying superstition with worldly assurance. "We are reluctant to acknowledge," Warburg wrote, "how medieval the man of the Renaissance really was, the man whom we salute as a superman, the liberator of the individual from the dark prisons of the Church."[232]

However, this "oscillating condition of consciousness" did not result in chaos. Instead, the great representative figures of the Renaissance demonstrated what Warburg labeled "a psychology of compromise."[233] In *The Art of Portraiture and the Florentine Bourgeoisie*, he argued that this balance was struck in the figure of Lorenzo de' Medici. Machiavelli had seen the side of Lorenzo that was "childish-popular and romantic-artistic" as a weakness. With a personality split between serious and light-hearted pursuits, Lorenzo seemed to combine two people within himself; by education, he was a learned reviver of the ancient past; through will and necessity a level-headed, foresighted politician; and yet through temperament a vivacious writer of popular poems. But for Warburg this was not indicative of weakness. On the contrary, it demonstrated Lorenzo's power to unite the dissimilar characters "of the idealist—whether medievally Christian, or romantically chivalrous, or classically Neoplatonic—and the worldly, practical, pagan Etruscan merchant" in a way that expanded the mental range of humanity.[234] In the essay published in 1907 as "Francesco Sassetti's Last Injunctions to His Sons," Warburg demonstrated a similar capacity to harmonize opposites in the psychology of one of the great Florentine bankers. Examining Sassetti's will and the iconography of his tomb in Santa Trinità, he found an eminent figure of the Italian Renaissance able to reconcile pagan and Christian elements in his thought; a man who believed in the power of fortune and who decorated his tomb with antique figures and yet submitted to the teachings of Christian doctrine.

But if Lorenzo de' Medici and Francesco Sassetti lived in a period of transition between the Middle Ages and the Renaissance, their ability to reconcile seemingly opposite world views was more than just a manifestation of this age of transition; in a manner similar to Albrecht Dürer, these men represented the timeless, "retrospective self-consciousness" recognizing, and exploiting for creative purposes, the forces of its own evolution. In a passage that seems to bear the stamp of the social and political exigencies of his own era, Warburg writes that "when conflicting world views kindle partisan emotions, setting the members of society at each other's throats, the social fabric inexorably crumbles; but when those views hold a balance within a single individual—when, instead of destroying each other, they fertilize each other and expand the whole range of the personality—then they are powers that lead to the noblest achievements of civilization."[235] The eminent citizens of Medicean Florence successfully balanced the Apollonian and Dionysian energies of antiquity's psychological legacy in their lives, just as Lederer did in his art. The result was the blossoming of the merchant republic into one of the most culturally creative and influential cities in the history of Western civilization, something that Warburg, and those who oversaw the Bismarck memorial's construction, could only dream of seeing repeated in Hamburg.

In addition to his ruminations on the monument as a symbol, Warburg also thought about it as a portrait. In contrast to the abstract theorizing of many of his working papers, Warburg's essays on Renaissance Florence reveal his personal and human fascination with portraiture and the personalities of the sitters. In relation to the Bismarck memorial he wrote that "through the unity of architecture and sculpture a portrait will be revealed."[236] The symbolic form that resulted, "despite its one-sidedness," would be filled "with strong personal life, so even out of this restriction the finest aura speaks."[237] If Warburg was suspicious of the mimetic-empathetic urges that he believed characterized artistic naturalism, he never suggested that artists abandon nature as a model.

In *The Art of Portraiture and the Florentine Bourgeoisie*, Warburg emphasized the way in which portraiture bore witness to a religious concept of existence. But it was also suggested in chapter two that he experienced the likenesses of Florentine patrons as profane, that he saw in them "the will to power" of a new class of merchants and materialist entrepreneurs.[238] In this essay, and in "Flemish Art and the Florentine Early Renaissance," (1902) Warburg also argued for the positive role of artistic naturalism in the development of Italian Renaissance art. The attraction for Florentines of the works of painters like Hugo van der Goes (d. 1482) or Hans Memling (d. 1494) and their close observation of detail, was the result of Flemish naturalism's ability to represent the psychological life of individuals. In the essay, Warburg describes the attraction of northern European art as follows: "The Flemish style, with its deft blend of inner spirituality and outer truth to life, was the ideal vehicle for the donor portrait. The individuals portrayed were beginning to detach themselves, as individuals, from their ecclesiastical background." In these portraits, he writes, "there are overtones, as it were, of the worldly personality; and the lineaments of the self-assured observer emerge, spontaneously, from the posture of the worshipper at prayer."[239] He sensed that, as Gombrich writes, "the germ of secularized mentality has penetrated the forms of devotional art and destroys it from within."[240] In these artworks, Warburg discovered a bridge between medieval devotion and secular individualism; if he recognized a persistent desire to come closer to the divine through a painted simulacrum, he also perceived a transition from the piety of the Middle Ages to the humanism of the Renaissance.

In *The Art of Portraiture and the Florentine Bourgeoisie*, Warburg praised Ghirlandaio's ability to mirror the real world in his fresco in the Sassetti Chapel of Santa Trinità. He referred to the artist's naturalistic representation of his subjects' facial features and expressions as of "wonderful power" and admired the "concentrated assurance of these figures, so filled with individual life."[241] Of special importance for Warburg was Ghirlandaio's likeness of Lorenzo de' Medici and he wrote that "Lorenzo's appearance is a matter of profound and universal human interest. Our just desire to have an accurate image of his outward self derives not only from a natural historical curiosity but from the mysterious nature of the phenomenon that he represents: that a man of such exceptional ugliness should have become the spiritual focus of a supreme artistic civilization."[242]

Warburg complained that most portraits of Lorenzo portray a "pinched, unprepossessing, criminal-looking face, or else the shrunken features of a man in pain; of the enchantment that emanated from Lorenzo—the nobility, the dignity, and the humanity—nothing is to be seen." But Ghirlandaio "allows us to sense the spiritual quality that could make such demonic, distorted features so irresistibly attractive." He was the artist who portrayed Lorenzo's "whole personality" breathing "a sense of supreme assurance."[243]

It is not surprising, then, that Warburg should have sought something of the same life in Hamburg's memorial to another great historical figure. Perhaps this is why, in his unpublished papers, he posited a "conflict" between a "statue of remembrance" and a "symbol."[244] In a note that he later crossed out, he suggested that sculpture should express itself in two manners: as "a reverent image of remembrance and a powerful symbol."[245] At one point he writes that the Bismarck memorial should be the former, an "image of remembrance of a dead hero," but that it should also symbolize his "powerful, far-reaching vitality."[246] It was the latter that Lederer sought to memorialize and that members of the Pan-German and Navy Leagues celebrated in patriotic ceremony.

VIII

The contract between the artists and Hamburg's committee for the erection of a Bismarck memorial was signed on 23 September 1902. Excavation began at the end of the next month and the laying of the foundation stone was celebrated on 24 April 1903. The committee had intended the monument to be completed by 1 April 1905 to correspond with Bismarck's ninetieth birthday. But as of this date, Lederer had not supplied the plaster model he was to have delivered in September of 1903. These delays prompted Building Inspector Sperber to accuse Lederer of working without any regard for "the task of the committee, public opinion, and the money of the sponsors."[247] Nonetheless, the plaster model was finally delivered in May 1905 and topping-out was celebrated with the erection of the head stone on 23 August of that year. Hamburg's press followed the construction with interest, giving regular reports on progress and, as of March 1906, speculating as to the date of the unveiling. This occurred on 2 June 1906 despite the fact that the eight allegorical figures intended to adorn the plinth were not completed until April 1908. The Germania relief and the steps ascending to the monument were never undertaken.

Despite the rain, the unveiling ceremony on Saturday, 2 June 1906 was a grand affair.[248] Every official building in Hamburg and all ships lying in the harbor flew the Imperial and the Hamburg flag. In the Helgoländerallee at the base of the Elbhöhe, at least 1,600 guests assembled in a sea of uniforms and civilian formal dress. The senate, citizens' assembly, several guests of honor, financial supporters of the project, four grandchildren of Bismarck (children of the deceased Count Herbert), delegates from the Central Committee of Hamburg's

Citizens' Associations, various male choirs, and children from all of Hamburg's schools were in attendance. At three o'clock, Mayor Burchard ascended the podium and gave the signal for the ceremony to begin. Following an introduction of choral music accompanied by the band of Hamburg's Seventy-sixth Regiment of Infantry, Mayor Mönckeberg rose to present the monument to the city. He outlined the history of its construction, and reiterated the sentiments it was intended to embody and the function it was designed to fulfill. As Mönckeberg concluded, the shroud fell and the monument was greeted by a cheer from the crowd. Mayor Burchard accepted the monument in the name of the city of Hamburg and raised a cheer to the Kaiser. *Deutschland, Deutschland über Alles* was begun by the choir and was taken up by all participants. The music continued while the senate, citizens' assembly, and honored guests viewed the monument. The ceremony ended with the departure of the senate.

The debates that accompanied the exhibition of monument designs in 1902 did not repeat themselves at the unveiling in 1906. By this point, Hamburg's Bismarck memorial was not unique in its conception of the Iron Chancellor as Roland. Arnold Hartmann produced designs for an architectonic, almost completely non-figural representation of Bismarck as Roland for Cologne in 1903.[249] But perhaps more importantly, the memorial met with widespread acclamation and must have been a tremendous boost to Hamburgers' already strong civic pride. When plans to construct a national Bismarck memorial in Bingerbrück were publicized a few years later, the *Hamburgischer Correspondent* asked why this was necessary as such a monument already stood in Hamburg.[250] Anton Lindner described the memorial as "the most important monument in the world."[251]

IX

Did the Bismarck memorial achieve what this chapter has suggested the committee intended? The answer to this question must be no. Firstly, as with any work of art, the memorial's meaning was only completed in the attitude of its viewers, and among Hamburg's working classes it met with widespread rejection. Reports by Hamburg's political police on pub conversations make interesting reading and are themselves an indicator of the insecurity of the political leadership.[252] Some workers complained about the large amount of money spent by the "conspicuously wealthy."[253] Shortly after the unveiling, a coachman is reported as saying that the memorial stood in a proper location because from the hill Bismarck could at least look down upon his disgraceful deeds. "Bismarck," he said, "has inflicted enough political and material hardship on us small people. He did not deserve a memorial."[254] One worker said that the committee had erected a monument to a "high-quality executioner" and warned that Bismarck was so despised in Hamburg that there would be those who would attempt to demolish the memorial.[255] Indeed, the monument did nothing to quell the dissatisfaction of Hamburg's workers. With fifty different strikes and lockouts in the years

1905 to 1907, Hamburg's harbor experienced a heretofore unmatched level of industrial dispute.[256] As Niall Ferguson has noted, of 799 wage disputes recorded between 1910 and 1913, no fewer than 212 led to strikes involving over 50,000 employees.[257]

On 2 June 1906, the *Hamburger Echo*, the daily newspaper of the Social Democrats, reported that "Germany represents in the eyes of Europe today that Bismarckian caesarism which is the greatest enemy of democracy." This had particular significance for Hamburg, it claimed, where "today the gigantic idol of embodied *Borussian* reaction, as it lies today like a demon over all Germany, was unveiled."[258] But neither the Bismarck memorial nor the suffrage robbery could halt the SPD's advance: by 1913, of 160 deputies sitting in the citizens' assembly, twenty were Social Democrats.[259] Instead, the monument stood as a gigantic symbol of the unwillingness of Hamburg's patricians, including Aby Warburg, to deal with the exigencies of social change through political processes offering practical political solutions.

"Hamburg has erected a Bismarck memorial," wrote Georg Muschner in 1906, "and has thereby made good the sins that it, for years and decades through indolence, may have sinned against art."[260] As previously noted, a relatively large number of monuments were erected in Hamburg between 1890 and 1914, most of which were conventional in design. But in respect to monumental or innovative public artworks, indolent ways were not easily eschewed in Hamburg. The only monument of comparable significance to the Bismarck memorial that also consciously broke with convention was the Brahms memorial by Max Klinger. It was unveiled in the foyer of Hamburg's concert hall in 1909. Heavily influenced by Rodin's *Balzac*, it is considered to be the most important contemporary monument dedicated to a musician. Financed by Sophie Laeisz, the contract was awarded to Klinger by Lichtwark.[261] But again, the Brahms memorial was an exception; despite Lichtwark's pleas for a new form of memorial art, and despite the building of the Bismarck memorial and the critique of artistic conventions that it embodied, Hamburg's citizens continued to build small, conventional monuments to senior politicians or to poets of local significance, monuments that Volker Plagemann has described as "without artistic merit."[262] In any case, the city fathers were not prepared to finance any other large art projects in the first two decades of this century. In addition to financing the Kaiser Wilhelm memorial, completed in 1903, the government was engaged in a project to decorate the city hall with frescos by Hugo Vogel. A gigantic undertaking lasting eleven years and costing over 1,000,000 marks, this is explored in the following chapter. Just five years later, the First World War would destroy any enthusiasm that existed for the execution of government-sponsored art projects.[263] Thus the Bismarck memorial's construction must be counted as one of the relatively few occasions when, as Lindner described it, "the giant" shook itself out of its "patriarchal slumber" to exercise "unusual powers" in the pursuit of a "surprisingly great success."[264]

The transformation of the Art Association in March of 1896 was discussed in chapter two as a demonstration of the fact that much patronage of the arts in

Hamburg was dependent upon individuals or private associations whose enthusiasm did not embrace modernism and its products. The fate of *Der Lotse* might be presented as another example; it disappeared long before the Bismarck memorial's unveiling. The critical tone of the journal had occasionally met with strong disapproval, while the publication of poems considered to be offensive and indecent met with increasing indignation. Lichtwark finally withdrew his support and subscribers their money, and the journal was forced out of business in April 1902.[265] The Bismarck memorial was in no way an avant-garde work of art and, from as early as the 1920s, would seem the product of an obsolete tradition of figural sculpture. But at the time of its construction, those who oversaw the project committed themselves to progress and reform of the sculptural arts. It is this enthusiasm for and experimentation with new artistic trends that corroborates the more positive judgment of Hamburg's cultural life that has recently appeared in Anglo-American scholarship.

But at the beginning of this chapter, it was also suggested that the function of the monument as a memorial, its symbolism, and even its semi-abstracted forms were shaped by a tradition of commemorative artworks and monumental sculpture. With its interpenetration of modern and traditional characteristics and functions, the Bismarck memorial mirrored the nature of Hamburg itself. On the one hand, it was a city with a history of republican self-rule and liberal politics that was permeated by bourgeois values and animated by the cosmopolitan spirit of a center of international trade. In this respect, it might be seen as one of the more progressive entities within the German Empire. On the other hand, its political elite mobilized the coercive powers of the state in response to social and political change, making Hamburg as authoritarian as any political entity within the Empire. In fact, by restricting access to the municipal ballot box in 1906, Hamburg earned "the dubious distinction of being more conservative than Prussia."[266] Clearly, an authoritarian—if not imperial—approach to politics was not incompatible with the interests and values of the German bourgeoisie. These trends are reflected in Warburg's political opinions and challenge the usefulness of a binary model of tradition and modernity—in which liberalism is understood as modernizing and authoritarianism as backward—for analyzing the complexities of historical phenomena.

Notes

1. Warburg Institute Archive, London (hereafter WIA) III.10.3: Tagebuch III (1903– 1914), 2 June 1906; also quoted and translated in Ernst Gombrich, *Aby Warburg: An Intellectual Biography*, 2nd ed. (Chicago, 1986), p. 155.
2. After-dinner speech of Mayor Mönckeberg from 5 January 1902 transcribed in "Hamburger Bismarck-Denkmal," *Der Lotse* 2, no. 15 (11 January 1902), p. 1ff.
3. For a linguistic analysis of the inaugural addresses made by Mönckeberg and Burchard see Ilonka Jochum-Bohrmann, *Hugo Lederer: ein deutschnationaler Bildhauer des 20. Jahrhunderts* (Frankfurt a.M., Bern, New York and Paris, 1990), p. 62ff.
4. Inaugural address by Mayor Mönckeberg transcribed in *Hamburger Nachrichten*, 2 June 1906.
5. Karl Scheffler, *Moderne Baukunst* (Berlin, 1907), p. 136.
6. Wilhelm Fagus, "Der Roland von Hamburg," *Deutsche Welt*, 10 June 1906.
7. Staatsarchiv, Hamburg (hereafter St.A.H.) 614–3/8. Bismarck-Denkmal-Comité, A3, Bd. 1: Aufruf zur Errichtung eines Bismarck-Denkmals in Hamburg.
8. For discussions of the memorial see amongst others Jörgen Bracker, "Michel kontra Bismarck," in Werner Hofmann et. al., *Züruck in die Zukunft: Kunst und Gesellschaft, 1900 bis 1914* (Hamburg, 1981), pp. 10–17; Volker Plagemann, *"Vaterstadt, Vaterland, schütz Dich Gott mit starker Hand": Denkmäler in Hamburg* (Hamburg, 1986), pp. 102–106; Harald Olbrich, ed., *Geschichte der deutschen Kunst, 1890–1918* (Leipzig, 1988), p. 237ff.; Jochum-Bohrmann, *Hugo Lederer*, pp. 48–71; Rainer Hering, "Kutscher und Kanzler: Der Bau des Hamburger Bismarck-Denkmals im Spiegel der Vigilanzberichte der Politischen Polizei," *Hamburgische Geschichts- und Heimatblätter* 13 (1993), pp. 38–48; Reinhard Alings, *Monument und Nation: das Bild vom Nationalstaat im Medium Denkmal—zum Verhältnis von Nation und Staat im deutschen Kaiserreich, 1871-1918* (Berlin and New York, 1996), pp. 246–254; Karen Lang, "Monumental Unease: Monuments and the Making of National Identity in Germany," in *Imagining Modern German Culture, 1889–1910*, ed. Françoise Forster-Hahn (Washington, 1996), pp. 275–299.
9. Felix Gilbert, "From Art History to the History of Civilization: Gombrich's Biography of Aby Warburg," *Journal of Modern European History* 44 (1972), p. 390; Christiane Brosius, *Kunst als Denkraum: zum Bildungsbegriff von Aby Warburg* (Pfaffenweiler, 1997), p. 99.
10. WIA. III.27.2.2: Hugo Lederer's Bismarck Monument, fol. 2.
11. For first-hand descriptions of Warburg see Fritz Schumacher, *Selbstgespäche. Erinnerungen und Betrachtungen* (Hamburg, 1949), pp. 299–303; Gustav Hillard, *Herren und Narren Der Welt* (Munich, 1954), p. 285f.; René Drommert, "Aby Warburg und die Kulturwissenschaftliche Bibiliothek in der Heilwigstraße," in *Aby Warburg. "Ekstatische Nymphe … trauernder Flußgott": Portrait eines Gelehrten*, eds. Robert Galitz and Brita Reimers (Hamburg, 1995), pp. 14–18.
12. WIA. III.27.2.2, fol. 6.
13. Lang, "Monumental Unease," p. 290.
14. Gombrich, *Aby Warburg*, p.154.
15. Edgar Wind, "On a Recent Biography of Warburg," in idem, *The Eloquence of Symbols: Studies in Humanist Art* (Oxford, 1993), p. 107.
16. Percy Ernst Schramm, *Neun Generationen: dreihundert Jahre deutscher "Kulturgeschichte" im Lichte der Schicksale einer Hamburger Bürgerfamilie (1648– 1948)*, 2 vols. (Göttingen, 1964), vol. 2, p. 382.
17. Kirchenpauer represented Hamburg in the Bundesrat between 1867 and 1880; see Johann Georg Mönckeberg's description of Kirchenpauer in Renate Hauschild- Thiessen, *Bürgermeister Johann Georg Mönckeberg* (Hamburg, 1989), p. 89ff.
18. See Renate Hauschild-Thiessen, *Bürgerstolz und Kaisertreue: Hamburg und das Deutsche Reich von 1871* (Hamburg, 1979), pp. 79–97.

19. Friedrich Jerchow, "Politik und Parteien," in *Industriekultur in Hamburg: Des Deutschen Reiches Tor zur Welt,* ed. Volker Plagemann (Munich, 1984), p. 363.
20. See Richard J. Evans, *Death in Hamburg: Society and Politics in the Cholera Years, 1830–1910* (Oxford, 1987).
21. For a survey of Hamburg's history see Werner Jochmann and Hans-Dieter Loose, eds., *Hamburg: Geschichte der Stadt und ihrer Bewohner,* 2 vols. (Hamburg, 1986); less useful is Eckart Klessmann, *Geschichte der Stadt Hamburg* (Hamburg, 1981).
22. See Friedrich Jerchow, "Handel, Schiffahrt und Gewerbe," in *Industriekultur in Hamburg,* pp. 46–56.
23. Niall Ferguson, *Paper and Iron: Hamburg Business and German Politics in the Era of Inflation, 1897–1927* (Cambridge, 1995), p. 83f.
24. Evans, *Death in Hamburg,* p. 561.
25. Quoted from the Bürgerbrief of 15 December 1871 in Heinrich von Poschinger, *Fürst Bismarck und seine Hamburger Freunde* (Hamburg, 1903), p. 4f.
26. Schramm, *Neun Generationen,* p. 383; for the relationship between Bismarck and Hamburg's leading citizens—Versmann, Petersen, Burchard, and Mönckeberg—see Poschinger, *Fürst Bismarck und seine Hamburger Freunde.*
27. See St.A.H. 614–3/8. Bimarck-Denkmal-Comité, A3, Bd 1; Hamburg's Bismarck memorial project was one of 500 such projects conceived between 1898 and 1914, at least half of which came to fruition; see Lothar Machtan, *Bismarck und der deutsche National-Mythos* (Bremen, 1994), p. 22.
28. Werner Jochmann, "Handelsmetropole des Deutschen Reiches," in Jochmann and Loose, eds., *Hamburg,* vol. 2, p. 27.
29. Ferguson, *Paper and Iron,* p. 50f.
30. See Evans, *Death in Hamburg.*
31. Walther Classen quoted and translated in Jennifer Jenkins, "Provincial Modernity: Culture, Politics and Local Identity in Hamburg, 1885–1914" (Ph.D. diss., University of Michigan, 1997), p. 62.
32. Geert Seelig, "Von der hamburgischen Regierung," *Der Lotse* 1, no. 27 (6 April 1901), p. 18f.
33. Hans Wilhelm Eckardt, *Privilegien und Parlament: die Auseinandersetzung um das allgemeine und gleiche Wahlrecht in Hamburg* (Hamburg, 1980), p. 46.
34. Werner von Melle, *Das Hamburgische Staatsrecht* (Hamburg and Leipzig, 1891), pp. 134–143.
35. Richard J. Evans, "'Red Wednesday' in Hamburg: Social Democrats, Police and Lumpenproletariat in the Suffrage Disturbances of 17 January 1906," in idem, *Rethinking German History: Nineteenth-Century Germany and the Origins of the Third Reich* (London, 1987), p. 253.
36. Schramm, *Neun Generationen,* vol. 2, p. 438.
37. Eckardt, *Privilegien und Parlament,* p. 37.
38. Evans, "'Red Wednesday,'" p. 253.
39. Ferguson, *Paper and Iron,* p. 68.
40. See Michael Grüttner, *Arbeitswelt an der Wasserkante: Sozialgeschichte der Hamburger Hafenarbeiter, 1886–1914* (Göttingen, 1984), pp. 165–183.
41. Jochmann, "Handelsmetropole," pp. 69 and 25; Jochmann's account of Wilhelmine Hamburg focuses almost exclusively on political and social pressures from below: the development of unions, working-class political participation, and the formation and growth of the SPD.
42. Eckardt, *Privilegien und Parlament,* p. 38.
43. Evans, "'Red Wednesday,'" p. 253; this attitude is reflected in Scrhamm, *Neun Generationen,* where the growth of working-class organization and agitation is portrayed not as a just battle for political representation, but as the destruction of old ways.
44. See Evans, "'Red Wednesday.'"
45. Jürgen Bolland, *Die Hamburgische Bürgerschaft in Alter und Neuer Zeit* (Hamburg, 1959), p. 67.
46. Schramm, *Neun Generationen,* p. 433.

47. Evans, *Death in Hamburg*, pp. 95–99.
48. Julius von Eckardt quoted and translated in Ibid., p. 98.
49. Ibid., p.98.
50. For a history of the costume see Hauschild-Thiessen, *Bürgerstolz und Kaisertreue*, pp. 33–45.
51. Evans, *Death in Hamburg*, p. 99.
52. Alfred Lichtwark, *Hamburg: Niedersachsen* (Dresden, 1897), p. 52.
53. WIA. III.27.2.2, fol. 3.
54. On this point see Evans, *Death in Hamburg*, pp. 87–95.
55. Niall Ferguson, *Paper and Iron*, pp. 68–78; Ferguson speaks of the "fissiparity of the *bourgeoisie*"; Evans writes of "fractions of capital" in *Death in Hamburg*, pp. 28–49.
56. For a recent discussion of this movement see Jennifer Jenkins, *Provincial Modernity: Local Culture and Liberal Politics in Fin-De-Siècle Hamburg* (Ithaca and London, 2003).
57. Bracker, "Michel kontra Bismarck," p. 11.
58. For discussions of the Bismarck memorial type, see amongst others Thomas Nipperdey, "Nationalidee und Nationaldenkmal in Deutschland im 19. Jahrhundert," *Historische Zeitschrift* 206 (1968), pp. 529–585; Volker Plagemann, "Bismarck- Denkmäler," in *Denkmäler im 19. Jahrhundert: Deutung und Kritik*, eds. idem and Hans Ernst Mittig (Munich, 1972), pp. 217–252; Hans-Walter Hedinger, "Bismarck- Denkmäler und Bismarck-Verehrung," in *Kunstverwaltung, Bau- und Denkmal- Politik im Kaiserreich*, eds. Ekkehard Mai and Stephan Waetzoldt (Berlin, 1981), pp. 277–314; Lutz Tittel, "Monumentaldenkmäler von 1871 bis 1918 in Deutschland: ein Beitrag zum Thema Denkmal und Landschaft," in ibid., pp. 215–276; Machtan, *Bismarck und der deutsche National-Mythos*; Lang, "Monumental Unease."
59. For the disparate nature of the Bismarck cult see Hedinger, "Bismarck-Denkmäler," p. 294ff.
60. After-dinner speech transcribed in "Hamburger Bismarck-Denkmal," *Der Lotse* 2, no. 15 (11 January 1902), pp. 1–4.
61. For the design competition see Mark Russell, "The Building of Hamburg's Bismarck Memorial," *The Historical Journal* 43 (2000), pp. 133–156.
62. Friedrich Nietzsche quoted in Machtan, *Bismarck und der deutsche National-Mythos*, p. 17.
63. Max Warburg quoted in Bolland, *Die Hamburgische Bürgerschaft*, p. 73.
64. Johann Georg Mönckeberg quoted in ibid., p. 66.
65. WIA. Kopierbuch I, 158f.: Aby Warburg to Max Warburg, 11 January 1906; also quoted in Michael Diers, *Warburg aus Briefen: Kommentare zu den Kopierbüchern der Jahre 1905–1918* (Weinheim, 1991), p. 163.
66. Eckardt, *Privilegien und Parlament*, p. 44.
67. Warburg quoted in Diers, *Warburg aus Briefen*, p. 164.
68. Max Warburg quoted in Bolland, *Die Hamburgische Bürgerschaft*, p. 73.
69. Max Warburg quoted in ibid.
70. WIA. Kopierbuch I, 158f.: Aby to Max Warburg, 11 January 1906; also quoted in Diers, *Warburg aus Briefen*, p. 163.
71. This and the following quotes in Diers, *Warburg aus Briefen*, p. 163f.
72. Kevin Repp, *Reformers, Critics, and the Paths of German Modernity: Anti-Politics and the Search for Alternatives, 1890–1914* (Cambridge, Mass, 2000), p. 282.
73. Bolland, *Die Hamburgische Bürgerschaft*, p. 73.
74. For other studies that question the liberal nature of Hamburg's government see Hans Wilhelm Eckardt, *Privilegien und Parlament*; Madeleine Hurd, *Public Spheres, Public Mores and Democracy: Hamburg and Stockholm, 1870–1914* (Ann Arbor, 2000).
75. Jenkins, *Provincial Modernity*, p. 8.
76. WIA. Kopierbuch III, 136: Warburg to Dwelshauers, 27 July 1909.
77. Olbrich, *Geschichte der deutschen Kunst*, p. 219.
78. Matthew Rampley, *The Remembrance of Things Past: On Aby M. Warburg and Walter Benjamin*, (Wiesbaden, 2000), p. 90.

79. Aby Warburg, "Pagan-Antique Prophecy in Words and Images in the Age of Luther," in idem, *The Renewal of Pagan Antiquity: Contributions to the Cultural History of the European Renaissance*, trans. David Britt (Los Angeles, 1999), pp. 597–697; see also Carl Hollis Landauer, *The Survival of Antiquity: The German Years of the Warburg Institute* (Ph.D. diss., Yale University, 1984), p. 47.

80. Landauer, *Survival of Antiquity*, p. 45f.

81. WIA. Kopierbuch VI, 353 and 354: Warburg to Marietta Warburg, 8 January 1918.

82. WIA. III. 27.2.1, fol. 1.

83. Warburg quoted in Bernd Roeck, *Der junge Aby Warburg* (Munich, 1997), p. 87

84. Warburg quoted in ibid. p. 86.

85. See especially Ferguson, *Paper and Iron*, p. 63ff.; Evans, *Death in Hamburg*, p. 36f.

86. Alfred Lichtwark, "Wünsche," *Der Lotse* 1, no. 1 (6 October 1900), p. 5.

87. WIA. III.2.1: Zettelkasten 57 (Hamburg), 057 032742.

88. Georg Muschner, "Das Hamburger Bismarck-Denkmal," *Deutsche Kunst und Dekoration* 10 (1906), p. 113.

89. A positive assessment of the city's music life is given in Gustav Schiefler, *Eine Hamburgische Kulturgeschichte, 1890–1920: Beobachtungen eines Zeitgenossen*, eds. Gerhard Ahrens, Hans Wilhelm Eckardt and Renate Hauschild-Thiessen (Hamburg, 1985), pp. 159–167; Johannes Brahms, born in Hamburg in 1833, had to leave the city for Vienna in 1862 because he was unable to find employment; see Evans, *Death in Hamburg*, p. 36.

90. Schiefler, *Hamburgische Kulturgeschichte*, p. 91.

91. Gustav Schiefler quoted and translated in Klessmann, *Geschichte Der Stadt Hamburg*, p. 202.

92. Julius Langbehn, *Rembrandt als Erzieher: von einem Deutschen* (Leipzig, 1890), p. 207.

93. Wilhelm Uhde quoted in Otto Grautoff, "Deutsche Kultur," *Der Lotse* 1, no. 20 (16 February 1901), p. 653.

94. Ibid.

95. Carl Mönckeberg, "Ankundigung," *Der Lotse* 1, no. 1 (6 October 1900), p. 2.

96. For a discussion of *Der Lotse* see Mathias Mainholz, "Hamburger Kulturpolitik vor der Weimarer Republik," in *Bohemiens und Biedermänner: die Hamburger Gruppe 1925 bis 1931*, ed. Rüdiger Schütt (Hamburg, 1996), esp. pp. 143–147; see also Schiefler, *Hamburgische Kulturgeschichte*, pp. 259–263.

97. Mainholz, "Hamburger Kulturpolitik vor der Weimarer Republik, p. 143.

98. Lichtwark, "Wünsche," p.4.

99. WIA. GC: Warburg to Max Warburg, 13 November 1900.

100. WIA. GC: Warburg to Max Warburg, 14 July 1900.

101. Olbrich, *Geschichte der deutschen Kunst*, p. 235.

102. Plagemann, "Bismarck-Denkmäler," p. 235.

103. Karl Scheffler, "Begas und Bismarck," *Der Lotse* 1, no. 39 (29 June 1901), pp. 411–415.

104. Karl Scheffler, *Berlin: Ein Stadtschicksal* (Berlin, 1910); for a summary of Scheffler's criticisms see John H. Zammito, "Der Streit um die Berliner Kultur 1871 bis 1930," *Jahrbuch für die Geschichte Mittel-und Ostdeutschlands* 35 (1986), pp. 234–268.

105. Karl Scheffler, "Berlin als Kunststadt," *Der Lotse* 2, no. 9 (30 November 1901), pp. 257–262.

106. Heinrich Pudor, "Wie baut man volkstümlich in Berlin?," *Der Lotse* 2, no. 16 (18 January 1902), pp. 483–486.

107. Otto Brandis, "Kaiserliche Kunst," *Der Lotse* 2, no. 14 (4 January 1902), pp. 420–423.

108. See amongst others Peter Paret, *The Berlin Secession: Modernism and Its Enemies in Imperial Germany* (Cambridge, Mass. and London, 1980); Marion F. Deshmukh, "Art and Politics in Turn-of-the-century Berlin: The Berlin Secession and Kaiser Wilhelm II," in *The Turn of the Century: German Literature and Art, 1890–1915*, eds. Gerald Chapple and Hans H. Schulte (Bonn, 1981), pp. 463–473; Christopher B. With, *The Prussian Landeskunstkommission, 1862–1911: A Study in State Subvention of the Arts* (Berlin, 1986); Sebastian Müller, "Official Support and Bourgeois Opposition in Wilhelminian Culture," in *The Divided Heritage: Themes and Problems in German Modernism*, ed. Irit Rogoff, (Cambridge, 1991), pp. 163–190.

109. Wilhelm II quoted and translated in Paret, *Berlin Secession*, p. 26f.
110. WIA. III.27.1.2, fol. 1.
111. Cornelius Gurlitt, "Bismarcks Denkmal in Hamburg," *Der Lotse* 2, no. 16 (18 January 1902), p. 481ff.
112. Cornelius Gurlitt, "Über Denkmalskunst," *Der Lotse* 2, no. 17 (25 January 1902), p. 519f.
113. WIA. III.49–50: Leonardo Lectures I and II, 1899–1901; for a summary of these lectures see Gombrich, *Aby Warburg*, pp. 96–105.
114. Warburg quoted and translated in Gombrich, *Aby Warburg*, p. 101.
115. WIA. III.27.2.2, fol. 6.
116. WIA. III.27.2.3, fol. 1.
117. WIA. III.27.2.2, fol. 6.
118. Ibid.; also quoted and translated in Gombrich, *Aby Warburg*, p. 154.
119. WIA. III.27.2.2, fol. 6.
120. Ibid., fol. 4.
121. Rampley, *The Remembrance of Things Past*, p. 63.
122. Warburg quoted and translated in ibid., p. 120, nte. 171; see Aby Warburg, "The Theatrical Costumes for the Intermedi of 1589," in idem, *The Renewal of Pagan Antiquity*, pp. 349–401.
123. Rampley, *The Remembrance of Things Past*, p. 63
124. *Die preisgekrönten Entwürfe zum Bismarck-Denkmal für Hamburg* (Hamburg, 1902), p. 2.
125. For the Bismarck cult see Nipperdey, "Nationalidee und Nationaldenkmal"; Hedinger, "Bismarck-Denkmäler"; Machtan, *Bismarck-Kult.*
126. Quoted in Nipperdey, "Nationalidee und Nationaldenkmal," p. 167.
127. Tittel, "Monumentaldenkmäler," p. 242ff. and 253f.
128. Nipperdey, "Nationalidee und Nationaldenkmal," p. 167.
129. "Hamburger Bismark-Denkmal," p. 2f.
130. Nipperdey, "Nationalidee und Nationaldenkmal," p. 169.
131. Plagemann, *"Vaterstadt, Vaterland,"* p. 103; Jochum-Bohrmann, *Hugo Lederer*, p. 49.
132. St.A.H. 614–3/8. Bismarck-Denkmal-Comité, A3, Bd 1: Erste Sitzung des Ausführungscomités für Errichtung eines Bismarck-Denkmals in Hamburg, Hamburg, den 1. October 1898.
133. The monument was dedicated in 1897; see Tittel, "Monumentaldenkmäler," p. 234f.
134. St.A.H. Senat Cl. VII, Lit. Fc. Nr. 21, Vol. 17, Fasc. 5: An den engeren Ausschuß für die Errichtung eines Bismarck-Denkmals in Hamburg. Bericht des Ausführungs- Comité, erstattet im Januar 1899.
135. Ibid.
136. St.A.H. 614–3/8. Bimarck-Denkmal-Comité, A3, Bd 1: Tagesordnung zur Sitzung des Ausführungs-Comités für die Errichtung eines Bismarck-Denkmals am Dienstag, den 7. März 1899 im Rathhaus.
137. Jochum-Bohrmann, *Hugo Lederer*, p. 50.
138. See Russell, "The Building of Hamburg's Bismarck Memorial."
139. Georg Fuchs, "Zeitgemäße Betrachtungen zum hamburger Wettbewerb," *Deutsche Kunst und Dekoration* 5 (1902), p. 347.
140. Albert Hofmann, "Der Wettbewerb zur Erlangung von Entwürfen für ein Bismarck- Denkmal in Hamburg," *Deutsche Bauzeitung* 36, no. 6 (18 January 1902), p. 34.; the prize jury included the architects Martin Haller, Camillo Sitte, and Paul Wallot plus the sculptors, Robert Diez and Rudolf Maison.
141. Fuchs, "Zeitgemäße Betrachtungen," p. 361f.
142. Speech by Georg Treu quoted in "Hamburger Bismarck-Denkmal," *Der Lotse* 2, no. 15 (11 January 1902), p. 4.
143. *Preisgekrönten Entwürfe*, p. 2.
144. Treu quoted in "Hamburger Bismarck-Denkmal," p. 4.
145. St.A.H. 614–3/8. Bismarck-Denkmal-Comité, A4: Erläuterungen zu einzelnen Wettbewerbsentwürfen: ein Dankesopfer.

146. Waldemar Grzimek, *Deutsche Bildhauer des zwanzigsten Jahrhunderts: Leben, Schulen, Wirkungen* (Wiesbaden, 1969), p. 77.
147. Volker Plagemann, *Kunstgeschichte der Stadt Hamburg* (Hamburg, 1995), p. 270.
148. Jörg Berlin and Rainer Hering, "Vor 85 Jahren: Einweihung des Bismarck- Denkmals 1906," *Hamburg Macht Schule* 3 (1991), p. 26f.
149. Lederer quoted in Grzimek, *Deutsche Bildhauer*, p. 77.
150. St.A.H. 614–3/8. Bismarck-Denkmal-Comité, A3, Bd. 2, Nr. 2: Gutachten des Preisgerichtes über die 11 preisgekrönten und 4 angekauften Entwürfe.
151. WIA. III.10.2: Tagebuch II (1897–1902), 25 January 1902.
152. Olbrich, *Geschichte der deutschen Kunst*, p. 239.
153. See Grzimek, *Deutsche Bildhauer*.
154. Christian Tümpel, ed., *Deutsche Bildhauer, 1900-1945, Entartet* (Königstein im Taunus, 1992), p. 10.
155. *Preisgekrönten Entwürfe*, p. 3.
156. Ibid.
157. See Nikolai Popov, *Das magische Dreieck: Bremen-Riga-Dubrovnik. Rolandfiguren im europäischen Raum* (Oschersleben, 1989); Hans Rempel, *Die Rolandstatuen: Herkunft und geschichtliche Wandlung* (Darmstadt, 1989); Wolfgang Grape, *Roland: die ältesten Standbilder als Wegbereiter der Neuzeit* (Hürtgenwald, 1990).
158. At least newspaper readers were made aware of these monuments and their relation to Lederer's design; see, for example, "Neue Rolands Forschungen," *Hamburger Fremdenblatt*, 22 January 1902.
159. Lang "Monumental Unease," p. 289.
160. Lang has translated this passage to read "complete apotheosis of the figure of Bismarck in the consciousness of the *Volk*"; see ibid.
161. WIA. III.27.2.1, fol. 1.
162. Hofmann, "Der Wettbewerb," p. 59.
163. Karl Scheffler, "Bismarcks Denkmal," *Der Lotse* 2, no. 17 (25 January 1902), pp. 513–519.
164. Fuchs, "Zeitgemäße Betrachtungen."
165. See Plagemann, *"Vaterstadt, Vaterland,"* pp. 98–101; Reinhard Alings, "Handel und Wandel: das Kaiser-Wilhelm-Denkmal in Hamburg (1888–1903)," in idem, *Monument und Nation*, pp. 224–234.
166. Brigitte Meißner, *Bürgherliche Representation im Politischen Denkmal. Bürgermeisterdenkmäler in Stadtrepubliken und Residenzstädten* (Ph.D. diss., University of Hamburg, 1987), pp. 68–73.
167. Petersen quoted in ibid., p. 32.
168. Warburg quoted in Schumacher, *Selbstgespräche*, p. 300.
169. Meißner, *Bürgherliche Representation*, p. 32ff.
170. Heinrich E. Wallsee, "Schlußbemerkungen zum Bismarck-Denkmals-Wettbewerb in Hamburg," *Hamburger Nachrichten*, 22 January 1902.
171. Alfred Lichtwark quoted in Dirk Reinartz and Christian Graf von Krockow, *Bismarck: vom Verrat der Denkmäler* (Göttingen, 1991), p. 42; see Lichtwark, "Denkmaeler," *Pan* 3, no. 2 (1897), p. 105ff.
172. Quoted in Jörg Schilling, "Wahrzeichen der Stadt—Monumente der Reform?: der Wettbewerb zur architektonischen Ausgestaltung von drei Wassertürmen in Hamburg von 1906" (M.A. diss., University of Hamburg, 1992), p. 76; see also Jörgen Bracker, *Hamburg von den Anfängen bis zur Gegenwart: Wendemarken einer Stadtgeschichte* (Hamburg, 1987), pp. 215 and 217.
173. For the negative reactions of the SPD and Hamburg's working classes to the monument see Bracker, "Michel kontra Bismarck"; Hering, "Kutscher und Kanzler."
174. I have concentrated here on letters to the *Hamburgischer Correspondent*, but similar letters can be found in the *Hamburger Fremdenblatt*; the *Hamburger Nachrichten*, which provided a forum for Bismarck, seems not to have admitted dissenting voices.
175. "Sprechsaal," *Hamburgischer Correspondent*, 19 January 1902.
176. Ibid., 21 January 1902.

177. Ibid.
178. Ibid., 17 January 1902.
179. Ibid.
180. Ibid., 21 January 1902.
181. Ibid., 17 January 1902.
182. Ibid.
183. Ibid., 21 January 1902.
184. Ibid., 19 January 1902.
185. Ibid.
186. Ibid.
187. Ibid., 21 Janaury 1902; 23 January 1902.
188. WIA. GC: Johann Georg Mönckeberg to Warburg, 29 January 1902.
189. WIA. III.2.1: Zettelkasten 57 (Hamburg), 057 031973.
190. WIA. III.27.2.2, fol. 2.
191. WIA. GC: Warburg to Theodor Brodersen, 27 April 1913.
192. Ibid.; Georg Treu asked for the loan of Warburg's "collection of Hamburg nonsense" when preparing the catalogue of prize-winning designs for the committee in order to learn more about the public debate; see WIA. GC: Johann Georg Mönckeberg to Warburg, 29 January 1902 and 31 January 1902.
193. WIA. III.27.2.1, fol. 1f.
194. WIA. III.27.2.2, fol. 2.
195. Ibid., fol. 2f.
196. Ibid., fol. 1.
197. Ibid.; also quoted and translated in Gombrich, *Aby Warburg*, p. 154.
198. WIA. III.43, 44 and 45: "Grundlegende Bruchstücke zu einer pragmatischen Ausdruckskunde" also bore the title "Grundlegende Bruchstücke zu einer (monistischen) Kunstpsychologie" (Basic Fragments of a [monistic] Psychology of Art).
199. Rampley, *The Remembrance of Things Past*, p. 78.
200. WIA. III.43.1.2; TS of 43.2, pp. 122–175: "Grundlegende Bruchstücke zu einer pragmatischen Ausdruckskunde," Bd. 2, 1896–1903, no. 439, p. 175 and no. 339, p. 138.
201. WIA. III.45.2; TS of 45.1: Symbolismus als Umfangsbestimmung, 1896–1901, p. 39.
202. WIA. III.43.1.2, no. 328, p. 134.
203. Philippe-Alain Michaud, *Aby Warburg and the Image in Motion* (New York, 2004), p. 178.
204. Ibid., p. 192.
205. Aby Warburg, "A Lecture on Serpent Ritual," *Journal of the Warburg Institute* 2 (1938–39), pp. 277-92.
206. WIA. III.43.1.2, no. 328, p. 133.
207. WIA. III.45.2, p. 11.
208. WIA. III.43.1.2, no. 355, p. 145.
209. Ibid., no. 304, p. 125.
210. WIA. III.45.2, p. 35. and WIA. III.43.1.2, no. 338, p. 138 and no. 341, p. 139.
211. Ibid., no. 341, p. 139.
212. Ibid., no. 321a, p. 131; see also no. 305, p. 125.
213. WIA. III.45.2, p. 23; see also pp. 39 and 41; WIA. 43.1.2, no. 421, p. 169.
214. Rampley, *The Remembrance of Things Past*, p. 78.
215. Ibid., p. 80.
216. WIA. III.27.1.1, fol. 4.
217. Ibid., fol. 5.
218. Ibid., fol. 3.
219. Ibid., fol. 4.
220. Ibid.
221. WIA. III.27.2.3, fol. 1.
222. WIA. III.10.2: Tagebuch II (1897–1902), 25 January 1902.

223. Warburg quoted and translated in Michael Podro, *The Critical Historians of Art* (New Haven and London, 1982), p. 175.
224. WIA. III.43.1.2, no. 439, p. 175 and no. 413, p. 165.
225. Ibid., no. 428, p. 172 and no. 406, p. 164.
226. Warburg quoted and translated in Gombrich, *Aby Warburg*, p. 184.
227. Gombrich, *Aby Warburg*, p. 97.
228. WIA. III.27.1.1, fol. 8 and Warburg quoted and translated in Gombrich, *Aby Warburg*, p. 153.
229. WIA. III.27.1.1, fol. 8.
230. Warburg quoted and translated in Arnaldo Momigliano, "How Roman Emperors Became Gods," *The American Scholar* 55 (1986), p. 181.
231. Aby Warburg, "The Art of Portraiture and the Florentine Bourgeoisie," in idem, *The Renewal of Pagan Antiquity*, p. 189.
232. Warburg quoted and translated in Gombrich, *Aby Warburg*, p. 137.
233. WIA. III.43.1.2, no. 420, p. 168.
234. Aby Warburg, "The Art of Portraiture and the Florentine Bourgeoisie," p. 190.
235. Ibid.
236. WIA. III.27.2.2, fol. 4.
237. WIA. III.27.2.2, fol. 3.
238. Michaud, *Aby Warburg*, p. 106.
239. Aby Warburg, "Flemish Art and the Florentine Early Renaissance," p. 297.
240. Gombrich, *Aby Warburg*, p. 167.
241. Aby Warburg, "The Art of Portraiture and the Florentine Bourgeoisie," p. 204.
242. Ibid., p. 191.
243. Ibid., p. 191ff.
244. WIA. III.27.2.2, fol. 4a.
245. WIA. III.27.2.2, fol. 3.
246. Ibid.
247. Jochum-Bohrmann, *Hugo Lederer*, p. 60.
248. My account is based upon St.A.H. Zeitungsausschnittsammlung, A144, Bismarck- Denkmal: Fest-Zeitung zur Feier der Enthüllung des Bismarck-Denkmals in Hamburg am Sonnabend, den 2. Juni 1906.
249. Plagemann, "Bismarck-Denkmäler," pp. 228 and 425, fig. 28.
250. "Das nationale Bismarck-Denkmal," *Hamburgischer Correspondent*, 22 January 1909.
251. Anton Lindner, "Der Goldene Saal im Hamburger Rathause," *Neue Hamburgische Zeitung*, 14 June 1909.
252. For transcriptions of these see Hering, "Kutscher und Kanzler."
253. Bericht über den 31. Mai 1906, quoted in ibid., p. 45.
254. Bericht über den 11. Juni 1906, quoted in ibid., p. 46.
255. Bericht über den 15. Januar 1902, quoted in ibid., p. 45.
256. Grüttner, *Arbeitswelt*, pp. 196–203.
257. Ferguson, *Paper and Iron*, p. 71.
258. Quoted in Bracker in "Michel kontra Bismarck," p. 10.
259. Eckardt, *Privilegien und Parlament*, p. 47.
260. Muschner, "Das Hamburger Bismarck-Denkmal," p. 114.
261. See Plagemann, *"Vaterstadt, Vaterland,"* pp. 124–128; Plagemann, *Kunstgeschichte der Stadt Hamburg*, p. 270ff.
262. Plagemann, *"Vaterstadt, Vaterland,"* p. 129.
263. Ibid., P. 130.
264. Lindner, "Goldene Saal."
265. Mainholz, "Hamburgerkulturpolitik vor der Weimarer Republik," p. 147.
266. Jenkins, *Provincial Modernity*, p. 8.

Chapter Four

COLLECTIVE MEMORY FAILURE
The Mural Decoration of Hamburg's City Hall, 1898–1909

I

If the Bismarck memorial is an outstanding instance of the employment of public art as public policy in Hamburg, there is none greater than Hamburg's city hall. Built between 1886 and 1897, it was the city's most grandiose and comprehensive public elaboration of governmental authority. Taking its inspiration from the architecture of the German Renaissance, it miraculously survived the intensive bombing of the city in the Second World War and is now regarded as one of the most important examples of historicist architecture in Germany.

The history of the construction and decoration of Hamburg's city hall is long and complex. This chapter focuses on its most controversial episode, the decoration of the building's great hall with the largest murals painted since the Italian Renaissance. (Figure 4.1) Given their gigantic size alone, it is surprising that these monumental artworks have attracted so little scholarly attention.[1] Unlike the Bismarck memorial, they were installed at the very actual and symbolic center of Hamburg's government; they were financed by the city and their execution was overseen by the senate. Yet similar to the one that precedes it, this chapter is the story of a small group of Hamburg politicians, scholars, and cultural administrators who sponsored artistic experimentation at a time of conflict between tradition and innovation in German culture. As with the history of Hugo Lederer's gigantic depiction of the Iron Chancellor, this chapter is also the story of the search for a potent political and cultural symbol that would give imposing expression to Hamburg's independent identity within the Empire. Consequently, the murals

Figure 4.1 Martin Haller et. al. Great Hall in the City Hall, Hamburg, 1886-1897.
Source: The Warburg Institute, London

should be seen within the context of the markedly nationalist bourgeois culture of the German Empire, which sought an art that would proclaim the democratic-republican aspects of its heritage. But ultimately, the following pages are an account of compromise between academic convention and artistic innovation; they provide another example of the interpenetration of traditional and modern characteristics and functions in a monumental public artwork. As such, they tell an intriguing tale of almost ten years of secret negotiations, indecision, political debate, and disappointed hopes that ended with the completion of the murals in 1909 by the Berlin painter and academician Hugo Vogel (1855–1934).

In this instance, however, Aby Warburg is not to be counted among those who promoted monumental art in Hamburg. Instead, he was perhaps the most vehement and vocal opponent of the project, harboring a deep-seated antipathy for Vogel himself. Unlike his views on the Bismarck memorial, Warburg's critical judgment of the city-hall murals was widely circulated in the form of an article published in the influential art journal *Kunst und Künstler* and reprinted in Hamburg's newspapers. This article has received only cursory consideration by Warburg scholars; still less attention has been paid to the unpublished papers and correspondence that provide insight into the ideas which motivated the author.[2] It is, therefore, the intention of this chapter to examine Warburg's writing in some detail and to explain why he found the murals to be both an ineffectual product of misguided artistic compromise and a travesty of his understanding of the role of the artist as an organ of social memory. Because Warburg's criticisms of Vogel and his art were so caustic, this chapter serves, more than any other, to illustrate the degree of seriousness with which Warburg regarded the function of public art in modern Germany. It also emphasizes the extent to which he believed images to be imbued with real power to shape understanding and perception. But while acknowledging the idiosyncratic nature of Warburg's ideas, the chapter demonstrates that some of his criticisms found a wide resonance in Germany's cultural community and shows how he took measures to achieve practical results for his vision. The issue of achieving practical results is also taken up at the end of the chapter by examining an episode that occurred shortly after Warburg's engagement with Vogel's frescoes: his work as an advisor on the pictorial decoration of the first-class public rooms of the steamship *Imperator*, launched by the Hamburg-America Line in May 1912.

In an article decrying the architectural and sculptural decoration of the city hall, an anonymous correspondent to the *Hamburger Echo*, the voice of the Social Democratic Party, once lamented that Hamburg had no art police. In response, this chapter will emphasize several facts that belie the validity of this assertion when applied to the case of Aby Warburg: the extreme gravity with which he regarded the ill effects of Vogel's murals, the detective work he undertook to uncover the artist's previous "misdemeanors", the doggedness with which he pursued his quarry, and the enlistment of his brother, Max Warburg, in an attempt to influence government policy for the sake of protecting Hamburg's public.

II

Hamburg's city hall was just one of about 200 built in Germany between 1850 and 1914.[3] The fire that ravaged much of the city in 1842 also destroyed the government building that had stood since the thirteenth century. For fifty-five years thereafter, Hamburg's government occupied provisional headquarters in the city's former orphanage; from 1860, the citizens' assembly met in the home of Hamburg's Patriotic Society. After two inconclusive architectural competitions, the earliest in 1854/55, satisfactory plans for a new city hall were finally presented to the government by a group of Hamburg architects in 1880. Construction of the massive neo-Renaissance structure, which would accommodate both Hamburg's senate and citizens' assembly, did not begin until 1886 and was finally completed in 1897.

Although many of the government's administrative authorities were still housed in temporary offices that changed location with changing administrations, the period 1890–1914 saw the construction of several imposing official structures that proclaimed governmental authority: the Stadthaus (1890–91), headquarters of Hamburg's police; the headquarters of the ministry of finance on the Rödingsmarkt (1907–10); and the headquarters of the ministry of education (1911–12), designed by Fritz Schumacher. With Hamburg's inclusion in the German Empire came the neo-Renaissance, Ringstraße-like architecture of federal administration, which emphasized the city's ties with the Empire. Apart from the city hall, prominent examples include the criminal justice authority

(1879–82), the post office headquarters (1883–87), the general customs building (1888–91), the national insurance headquarters (1894–95), the civil justice
authority (1897–1903), and the provincial high court (1907–12). As Hermann
Hipp has written, in all of these structures, "the political events of the high point
of industrialization" were given monumental expression.[4]

Situated in the center of Hamburg, southeast of the Inner Alster Lake, the
new city hall was connected by its wings to the city's stock exchange. The union
of the two structures conveyed a symbolic expression of the nexus of socioeconomic and political power in the city.[5] As Niall Ferguson argues, the city hall
was "intended to impress upon the world the vitality and integrity of the old
system; but like so much self-consciously historicist public architecture, it was
at least in part the product of a sense of insecurity."[6] In chapter three, we examined the way in which the senate's turn to the invention or reinvention of pre-
sentational traditions, as well as the Bismarck memorial itself, were responses to
rapid social change and attendant demands for political reform in the 1890s.
The city hall was the most dramatic attempt to engender popular respect for
Hamburg's apparently ancient government and stem working-class support for
the Social Democrats.

Of course, the new structure was also meant to give monumental expression
to the liberal political ideology of Hamburg's merchant families and a government that functioned chiefly to secure the conditions for profitable trade. A
memorandum prepared by Lichtwark for Hamburg's senate gave expression to
these ideas. As it was not the seat of a municipal authority, but home to the government of an independent state, he explained, great demands were made of its
form and decoration. "The strength and standing of our state rests, according to
its unique constitution, on the conscious, self-sacrificing participation of its citizens in public affairs," he wrote. "Therefore the education of the next generation
into Hamburgers," he continued, "as well as that of all the foreign elements flow-
ing into the city from the Empire, must be undertaken with all diligence, the
highest ambition of which is to enable participation in government."[7] The
inscription above the main entrance to the city hall reads: "May posterity strive
worthily to preserve that liberty which our ancestors achieved."[8]

But as noted in the previous chapter, there was clearly a discrepancy between
political ideology and the political practice of liberal governance in Hamburg
that could express itself in almost authoritarian forms of rule.[9] Under the direction of Martin Haller, a team of architects built a monumental structure that
through its massive proportions, its axial and symmetrical forms, and the clarity
inherent in the spatial articulation of its facade gave powerful and articulate
expression to the power vested in Hamburg's government. In appearance, the city
hall took its inspiration from German Renaissance architecture. As early as 1854,
when George Gilbert Scott's plans were awarded first prize in the original design
competition, there was controversy as to the suitability of the Gothic aesthetic for
a secular building. Scott argued that the cultural greatness of German cities was
rooted in the Middle Ages, but critics saw the Gothic aesthetic as an expression

of Catholicism and as a relapse into a past long superseded.[10] In its place, as Jürgen Paul has shown, the neo-Renaissance style acquired widespread appeal as the expression of a "national consciousness that felt itself in cultural, rather than in political, opposition to an image of society shaped by the court and aristocracy in the new Empire."[11] There was a conscious attempt to associate the growing economic and cultural importance of Germany's cities with the blossoming of burgher culture in the sixteenth and early seventeenth centuries. In Hamburg, official comment on the designs for the new city hall read that "no one could deny that it [the neo-Renaissance style] is especially suited to bring to effective expression, for all time, the form and significance of a modern, wealthy commercial city."[12]

"In the city hall," Lichtwark claimed, "the political consciousness of Hamburg's thousand-year polity found visible expression."[13] To this end, the facade prominently displays the statues of emperors—many of whom played no role in Hamburg's history—as a means of elucidating the city's long-standing connection with the German Empire.[14] But we may now question the degree to which the city hall and its decorative program were effective in projecting the intended message. As a correspondent to the *Hamburger Echo* wrote in 1906,

> Poor Hamburg! In the last twenty years we have had the most splendid opportunities to improve the appearance of our city and each time our hopes have been betrayed. I recall the city hall, the great effect of which is certain. But already in the choice and arrangement of the decorative components, the figures and the towers, the great ideas of the design are lost. Instead of uniting the facade in a simple fashion, in order to make its great proportions clear to the eye, it has been constructed with 100 figures that one cannot see.[15]

III

The great hall formed the architectural and symbolic center of Hamburg's city hall; it was situated at the very center of political life. In 1892, the senate decided that the great hall should be decorated with painting and sculpture that celebrated the "glorious thousand-year history" of Hamburg. They insisted that this must be achieved "with the highest means available to art," and should "constitute a monument, which will be an uplifting and agreeable expression of patriotic feeling."[16] Given that so much of Hamburg's past had already disappeared—as the result of various occurrences including French occupation during the Napoleonic Wars, the fire of 1842 that destroyed much of the city, and civic planning that resulted in the destruction of many of its churches—the murals were intended to reconnect Hamburgers to their history. The seriousness of this artistic undertaking is reflected in the enormous sums the government relegated for its execution. The cost of painting the great hall was estimated at 960,000 marks, while the total for decorating all the state rooms was expected to exceed 3,000,000 marks. This was at a time when most Hamburgers could not sustain an annual income of 1,200 marks for five years, the minimum requirement for citizenship and the right to vote. Covering a surface area of 354 square meters, the murals of the great hall would be without equal in the Empire.

After German unification in 1871, the Kaiser, princes, state bureaucracies, and large sections of the middle classes spent huge sums of money on monumental artworks. Between 1889 and 1902 alone, Prussia spent 2.6 million marks on works of art for the public sphere.[17] Most often referred to as academic or official history painting, episodes from German history and legend, allegories, and heroic portraits of German princes and generals came to decorate the walls of the government-controlled public sector throughout the new German nation. They were to be found on the walls of museums, schools, university buildings, government ministries, law courts, and, not least, city halls. These state-sponsored artworks were intended to serve two important functions. Firstly, they were a means by which the *Hohenzollern* kings legitimized their claim to Imperial monarchy. In the restored Imperial Palace at Goslar, for example, where the Reichstag convened in 1871, Hermann Wislicenus painted a mural cycle that celebrated the deeds of the German emperors from Friedrich I in the twelfth century to Wilhelm I in the nineteenth. Painted between 1877 and 1879, the main fresco depicted an apotheosis of Wilhelm I.[18] Here, as elsewhere in the public sphere, German history was presented as a timeless continuum that legitimized unification and emphasized the power and legitimacy of the Imperial monarchy.

Secondly, state-sponsored art was employed in an attempt to transfer feelings of patriotism associated with Germany as a *Kulturnation* (a community bound by a sense of shared language and culture) into sentiment for Germany as a political nation; art was used to foster a sense of national identity and was aimed at the education of the ideal German citizen through the medium of history. The public, pictorial representation of history in the German states was certainly not new to the post-unification period.[19] Prior to 1848, a concept of Germany as a *Kulturnation* had been growing in the German lands.[20] But the conception of Germany as a unified political nation was largely absent among the German populace in the wake of unification. This was largely due to the exclusion of the majority of Germans from a process that had been achieved by the political elite. Anton von Werner gave monumental expression to this reality in his painting *The Proclamation of the German Empire* (first version, 1877), which depicted the Hall of Mirrors in the Palace of Versailles crowded solely with uniformed German princes, generals and soldiers. Thus a political concept of national identity had to be built up, maintained, or at least intensified in the minds of new Germans; "making Germans" became a "project of national pedagogy."[21] As Geoff Eley explains, "the ordering of profound differences within the populations encompassed by the new national state—regional, religious, and ethnic, as well as the social, cultural, and gender differences … and thus the imagining and fashioning of a coherent and integrated national-German culture were a priority of state intervention, associational initiative, and public discourse that extended throughout the imperial period as a whole."[22] Consequently, "more national monuments were erected in Germany than in other European countries whose path to nationhood was paved by the efforts of the middle class."[23] The post-1871 upsurge in the demand for monumental art kept a large number of academically trained mural painters in work. Especially common subjects were the events of recent history: the many battles of the wars of unification as well as the political highlights of the unification period. The first great public art project after unification was the transformation of the Berlin Arsenal into a hall of fame decorated by von Werner, Wilhelm Camphausen, and Peter Johann Janssen with battle scenes and portraits of princes and generals. If unable to view them in the original, many Germans were familiar with these images from popular prints or schoolbook illustrations.

But in many of the murals that decorated Germany's city halls, "legend was at least as popular as history, and the boundary between them fluid."[24] The cycle that Hermann Prell painted for the city hall in Hildesheim between 1889 and 1892, for example, combined Arminian imagery with representations of verifiable events from the city's history.[25] Eric Hobsbawm has argued that after 1870, and in conjunction with the rise of mass politics, the political elite in Europe rediscovered the importance of irrational elements in the maintenance of the social fabric.[26] In the German case, myths, legends, and symbols were employed as an appeal to the German citizen with the hope that he or she would "emotionally vacate the actual contemporary reality of *Gesellschaft*, or society from above, and join the *Gemeinschaft* [community] of common sentiment for a shared Teutonic past."[27]

One of the aims of this book is to illustrate the limits of the influence of Prussia's official art establishment on the German Empire. But it must not be forgotten that it was largely Prussian-trained artists who determined the forms and themes of the official art of Wilhelmine Germany. The Düsseldorf Academy, where Hugo Vogel was trained, was an important center for the education of academic history painters. Furthermore, in Prussia, where Vogel was employed, the fine arts were dependent upon the favor of the government and the Kaiser. The Royal Academy of Fine Arts in Berlin, which "defined the aesthetic standards of society and helped to implement them," was subordinated to the Prussian Ministry of Art and Education, which approved its budget and policies as well as elections to the Academy.[28] Wilhelm II asserted real authority over the affairs of the Academy in that he appointed the minister of art and education, endorsed nominations to the Academy, and personally donated the prizes awarded to artists with his approval and in his name. Presuming to be an expert in all things cultural, his antipathy to modernism in the fine arts is well known. Wilhelm believed that art should take its inspiration from nature and the ancients and proclaimed that its duty was to educate the nation; it was to convey a message of loyalty, pride, and power. These ideas were powerfully furthered by Anton von Werner (1843–1915), artist by appointment to the *Hohenzollern* royal family. Director of the Berlin Academy's art schools from 1875 and three times chairman of the Association of Berlin Artists between 1887 and 1907, von Werner exercised enormous influence on Berlin's cultural politics and was Imperial Germany's premier history painter.[29]

We must also remember that most official art commissions were undertaken outside Berlin. In the last decades of the nineteenth century, many of Germany's new or restored city halls incorporated large-scale historical murals.[30] In 1874, the Prussian Ministry of Art and Education issued a directive regarding the "promotion of monumental painting and sculpture" in the Rhineland with instructions "to create significant works of art also in the provinces."[31] Consequently, with the cooperation of government and private means, an intensified period of monument construction flowered in cities that did not benefit from the patronage of resident princes. To be sure, the depiction of local history and local institutions actually grew in importance in many German cities after 1871, as it did in the cities of Prussia's Rhineland provinces. But, as with the murals painted by Fritz Neuhaus for Bochum's city hall between 1896 and 1901, local history was commonly set within the context of national history.[32] As Robin Lenman explains, emperors and burghers were often depicted as allies who, since the Middle Ages, had worked to achieve Germany's national destiny. Oftentimes, the contribution of cities to this process was conceived of not only in terms of economic and cultural influence; cities sometimes represented themselves as military powers, inasmuch as they resisted antinational feudal princes and Catholic bishops.[33] Ultimately, the creation and transmission of official culture "was very much a two-way process, which reflected middle-class aspirations every bit as much as those of the Kaiser and the 'traditional elites.'"[34]

Much of the didactic mural art of Wilhelmine Germany, especially in its idealizing and allegorical manifestations, can be characterized as melodramatic costume drama. The hyper-realism of military-picture specialists, like von Werner and Camphausen, has been described as "suggestive of both press illustration and waxwork."[35] Unsurprisingly, the entire genre of Wilhelmine history painting has often met with the censure of scholars, if not for being, as Warburg described it, "monumental kitsch," then at least for its conventional or orthodox nature.[36] But the prejudices nurtured by scholars are, at least in part, a consequence of the dearth of research into this aspect of German art history. This dearth is reflected in Peter Feist's assertion that the artistic life of Wilhelmine Germany was shaped more by easel painting than mural painting.[37] Nonetheless, academic history painting should not be seen as constituting a homogeneous stylistic whole. Indeed, a range of styles were employed in the decoration of Germany's public buildings, from the idealizing tendencies of Ferdinand Wagner the Younger through the photographic naturalism of Camphausen to the stylized realism of Arthur Kampf.[38] As Jason Geiger has recently demonstrated in a study of Adolph Menzel, not all nineteenth-century German history painting—be it easel or wall painting—was as conventional as it is often made out to be.[39] Clearly, a certain amount of adaptation to more progressive trends was invoked by an encounter with German, French, and Dutch Realism and Impressionism. Not only was academic art challenged from within its own ranks by the Group of Eleven or the

Berlin Secession, but new influences were introduced into official art by those, like Vogel himself, who stood close to Secessionist movements; without question, this was the major attraction of the artist for the committee entrusted with overseeing the construction of Hamburg's city hall. Some academically trained artists even pioneered an altogether new monumental art, artists like Fritz Erler, Ludwig Dettmann, and Willy von Beckerath, the subject of chapter five.

Robin Lenman takes an understandably cautious approach to gauging the effects of this art. "Whatever effect those large and complex allegorical-symbolical-historical paintings may actually have had on the adult citizens and parties of schoolchildren exposed to them," he argues, "their perceived significance as patriotic and monarchical propaganda can be measured not only by their cost but by the elaborate pageantry and speech-making marking their inauguration."[40] This is certainly the case with the murals in Hamburg's city hall. But it is often contended that this propagandistic art met the aesthetic expectations of Germany's middle classes—the Merckendorffs and Uncle Edwards portrayed in Warburg's play of 1896.[41] More importantly, and more rashly, it is argued that "the pictorial ideology of the scenes of battle and triumph, and the transformation of rulers, politicians, and generals into heroes of the people struck deep into the thought and feelings of the *Bürger* and *Kleinbürger*."[42] But as Heinz-Toni Wappenschmidt has suggested, the invocation of the past in state-sponsored art was less a sign of mastery of the present than an unconscious fear of the future.[43] This assertion is borne out by events in Hamburg enumerated in chapter three: in the face of social change and attendant demands for political reform in the 1890s, the senate turned to the invention of tradition as a means of engendering popular respect for an apparently ancient system of governance. But there was a glaring disjunction between the senate's sixteenth-century costume and the social and economic realities faced by the inhabitants of a city fast becoming a world-class center of trade and commerce. Moreover, there is no evidence to suggest that senatorial costume did anything to stay the support of Hamburg's working classes for the Social Democrats. This disjunction between the forms of state-sponsored art and social reality must also be considered when attempting to gauge the response of the *Bürgertum* to the products of official propaganda.

As Wappenschmidt argues, official history painting "suffered its collapse after it no longer served its purpose as a political and cultural instrument."[44] This was especially so in the Prussian Rhineland provinces, where the depiction of local history had appeared before 1848 in the city halls of those cities that had grown from provincial municipalities into centers of industry and trade.[45] Here official history painting "with its political goals disguised in the form of history and culture" found "no resonance" with the "ambitious, sober industrial *Bürgertum*."[46] As Wappenschmidt explains,

> the belief in the exemplary truth of historical continuity was finally unmasked as a consciously misleading exercise with the development of an industrial economy and attendant social change. The aesthetically mediated image of a past that determines the present with

a single claim to truth could not be transferred to fleeting social reality, nor was it capable of arresting it. The attempt to manipulate consciousness through a culminating fixation on factuality and effective production, failed with a search for authenticity bereft of meaning and the resulting meaningless allegorical projection in history painting.[47]

It could be argued that Wappenschmidt's theory is no less weakened by generalization than the arguments of those who make sweeping claims for the effectiveness of official art. But the attitudes that motivated those who oversaw the painting of the murals in Hamburg's city hall, especially the attitudes of Alfred Lichtwark, lend credence to his claims.

IV

For Lichtwark, Hamburg's neo-Renaissance city hall was an architectural failure. He regarded historicism as the worst consequence of the academic estrangement of art from the real-life circumstances of its existence, a situation that he lamented in numerous publications. Furthermore, Lichtwark believed that, as a republic, Hamburg was called upon to help bring to fruition an art representative of the middle-class nation, an idea that inspired those who oversaw the construction of the Bismarck memorial. It was this idea that motivated Lichtwark's plans for a special collection of paintings of Hamburg to be exhibited in the city's art gallery.[48] The collection was to include a series of portraits by Germany's best contemporary artists, portraits of the city's leading politicians, professional men, and writers. The gallery's director was certain that these would bolster local patriotism, strengthen the city's sense of its own history, reflect Hamburg's republican traditions, and emphasize the city's distinctive character within the new Empire.[49]

Lichtwark championed a modern, republican style of political iconography and state symbolism in Hamburg. He attempted to affect the artistic reform of the government's self-representation, and insisted that the necessary impetus to this reform could be achieved if the senate agreed to the execution of official portraits by progressively minded artists. Thus, as indicated in chapter two, he commissioned Max Liebermann to paint a full-length portrait of Mayor Petersen in his clothes of office in 1891.[50] As we have seen, the unsentimental portrait met with a storm of protest from Petersen and his supporters in the senate; they complained that Liebermann had slandered the mayor by using an impressionist technique that made him look old and common, instead of dignified. Nonetheless, Lichtwark regarded the Petersen portrait as a step towards inaugurating a new tradition of modern German portraiture. By comparison, Hamburg's city hall appeared to him as nothing but "the empty shell of an extinct way of life."[51] As an anonymous correspondent to the *Hamburger Echo* sympathetically lamented in 1906:

> The citizens' assembly has debated seriously for hours about which emperor should stand beside which kings, but it occurred to no one that we are building a city hall and not a Siegesallee. But we have no art police. Men like Brinckmann and Lichtwark have occupied

leading positions in Hamburg for decades, but they are obviously not consulted at all, neither in the case of government nor private projects. [52]

It is true that the memorandum that Lichtwark prepared for the senate regarding the interior decoration of the city hall was ignored.[53] Recommending that the undertaking be awarded to Hamburg artists and craftsmen, he claimed there was scarcely a better way "to win the minds of the people in the service of the conception of the state."[54] But the anonymous correspondent to the *Hamburger Echo* ignored the fact that Lichtwark was one of the most significant actors in the decade of events leading to the completion of the city hall's murals. Like many observers of the German art scene at the turn of the century, Lichtwark believed that monumental history painting was in a state of transition; Warburg asserted the very same sentiment in the first line of his article on the city hall's murals.[55] The first decade of the twentieth century witnessed dramatic changes in German culture; despite all resistance, modern art was finding its place in the museums and important private collections of Germany. State-funded mural production continued until 1914, but "the day of the historical *grande machine* was over."[56] Indeed, many museums were transferring the patriotic, large-format narrative canvases characteristic of the *Gründerzeit* to specialist establishments like the military museum in the Berlin Arsenal, or shipping them to the provinces. This was often the only alternative to "the oblivion of the depot."[57]

In 1899, much to Lichtwark's surprise, Liebermann participated in the design competition mounted by Altona for the decoration of its city hall.[58] The artist submitted landscapes to the prize jury representing the four seasons. For Lichtwark, the Altona competition, and Liebermann's decorative compositions in particular, were indicative of the fact "that monumental art was in a period of regeneration in which a promising new approach became apparent."[59] It was in this atmosphere that Lichtwark, along with Justus Brinckmann, another advisor to the city hall's building committee, "insistently warned" that old-style history painting in the great hall would only be the object of ridicule in the progressive circles of Germany's cultural establishment.[60]

Appointed as an advisor to the building committee, Lichtwark exercised considerable influence in the matter of the great hall's decoration, not least in the form of his influence over Johann Heinrich Burchard, chairman of the committee from 1900 and four times mayor from 1903. Under Lichtwark's influence, Burchard came to believe that the historicism that had informed the architects of the city hall was out of touch with contemporary developments in the arts. As a member of the government's committee for the administration of the Kunsthalle, Burchard shared Lichtwark's views on contemporary art and the need to build the art gallery into a forum for its exhibition. As Hamburg's chief representative to the Bundesrat from 1899–1902, he also shared Lichtwark's deeply felt patriotism. Burchard was an energetic promoter of Hamburg's independent identity within the Empire and enjoyed a personal relationship with the Kaiser. In the role of chairman of the building committee, he was acutely aware of the political significance of the great hall as a forum for government ceremony and the self-presentation of Hamburg as a unique entity within the German Empire. Therefore, if in the building committee's deliberations, questions regarding the historical and political content of the murals often took a back seat to questions regarding their style, questions of style were never about style per se. As with the building of the Bismarck memorial, the decision to adopt a non-academic artistic vocabulary embodied much more than an aesthetic determination to jettison the constraints of academic art. But in this instance, the drive to promote Hamburg as a self-determining center of culture was officially sanctioned and funded.

V

In 1898, a design competition for the great hall's murals came to naught with the death of the two artists whose designs had been selected as suitable by the building committee, Friedrich Geselschap and Carl Gehrts.[61] Another competition was launched in 1899. Dated 4 March, the building committee's announcement provides an insight into how Hamburg's political elite envisioned the city's history. The call for designs requested artists to provide sketches for five sequential images of historical or allegorical content as follows: the first to depict the early Middle Ages, with special emphasis on the founding of Hamburg; the second to reflect the time of the Hanseatic city, with special emphasis on the birth and development of Hamburg's trade; the third was to treat the Reformation in Hamburg, while the fourth would represent the Wars of Liberation of 1813–14; the final image was to incorporate the female allegorical symbol of the city, Hammonia, into an image that stressed the relationship of Hamburg to the German Empire and its global trade.[62] This competition also came to naught when the committee found itself unable to award a first prize. Nonetheless, the designs were exhibited in the city's art gallery and extensively discussed in the press. This would be the last significant insight into the decoration of the great hall that Hamburg's public would have for the next ten years.

Also in 1899, and again as part of his plan to reform the tradition of state symbolism, Lichtwark convinced Burchard and other senators to commission a large group portrait of Mayor Mönckeberg and the entire senate. Burchard's preferred artist was Hugo Vogel. Lichtwark did not share Burchard's preference, but he knew that the senate would not tolerate another experiment like Liebermann's Petersen portrait. In these circumstances, Vogel appeared suitable as his style was not extreme, nor provocative. But with a stylistic orientation to Liebermann and his membership of the Group of Eleven, Vogel had close contact with progressive art movements of the 1890s. His senate portrait, completed in 1901, is reminiscent of the group portraits of seventeenth-century Holland, but it is more a simple likeness than a penetrating psychological analysis. Meeting with the approbation of Hamburg's press and the Kaiser, the picture was a compromise between the traditional art of the academies and the innovation represented in

Liebermann's portrait of Mayor Petersen.[63] This was the compromise that shaped the decoration of the great hall.

Vogel was born in Magdeburg in 1855, and was schooled in the tradition of monumental history painting at the Düsseldorf Academy by Eduard von Gebhardt and Wilhelm Sohn. His career was marked by success in official circles: from 1888, he lived in Berlin where he was named a member of the Royal Academy of Art in 1889, taught at the Berlin Institute of Fine Arts, and was presented with a gold medal by the Kaiser for murals completed in the provincial assembly buildings in Merseburg in 1899. But he first made his name with murals painted for Berlin's city hall. Executed between 1889 and 1892, these depicted scenes from the city's history.[64] At the same time, he became one of the most sought-after society portraitists in Berlin. But while trained in the academic tradition, Vogel gradually turned to more innovative modes of pictorial representation, especially in his use of light and color and his application of paint. While he was influenced by German Realists and Impressionists like Liebermann and Fritz von Uhde, he also took an interest in contemporary French art. But his adoption of innovative forms was never wholehearted; it was born more of a desire to adapt them to the style in which he was educated. These compromises are reflected in Warburg's remark on the artist's "pleasantly pasteurized Impressionism."[65]

The 1890s were marked by increasing tension between conservative and progressive forces in Berlin's art establishments, and Vogel sided with the latter. In February 1892, he became a founding member of the Berlin Eleven, the first oppositional artists' association to appear in 1890s Berlin, and a precursor of the Berlin Secession. Led by Liebermann and including the likes of Walter Leistikow and Franz Skarbina, the Eleven brought together artists of various persuasions for the purpose of exhibitions independent of the official salons.[66] When an exhibition of the work of Edvard Munch was closed by the Berlin Artists' Association in November 1892, Vogel joined Liebermann, Skarbina, and August von Heyden in publishing a declaration in support of Munch in the *Vossische Zeitung*. It was not that Vogel was an enthusiastic supporter of "the aesthetics expressed in Munch's paintings," but he condemned the closure of the exhibition "as a measure that contravenes common decency."[67] Von Werner saw the behavior of Vogel and others as destructive of the comradeship of the faculty at the Institute of Fine Arts and, as a result, Vogel voluntarily resigned his teaching position.

It was while Vogel was at work on the portrait of Hamburg's senate that Burchard became personally acquainted with the artist and discussed the great hall's decoration. Although Vogel had taken no part in the previous design competitions, Burchard nominated him to the building committee as a suitable candidate in December 1900. In that same month, when Vogel presented designs to the building committee, serious doubts about his nomination were raised by members representing the citizens' assembly.[68] It was the artist's means of breaking with academic dogma that caused the greatest consternation. In contradiction to the depiction of historical events called for in the design competition of 1899,

Vogel presented plans for a cycle of generic representations of Hamburg's cultural development. To avoid narrative depictions of the city's history, he argued, was to avoid the illustration-like quality of traditional history painting. His cycle would not be a celebration of Hamburg's history as such, but a celebration of the republic's citizens. Indeed, the artist insisted that there was a dearth of notable events in Hamburg's history that were worthy of representation. These ideas found important supporters in Brinckmann and Lichtwark. Lichtwark was also particularly instrumental in turning the stylistic preferences of the building committee from an old-style history painting to Vogel's more innovative, Impressionist-influenced rendering.

For Lichtwark, the study of culture had always been a means of emphasizing Hamburg's unique character. His study of the city's art history was colored by a strong sense of its Lower-Saxon ethnicity.[69] Along with other commentators, Lichtwark played up the unique aspects of this ethnic identity, mostly as a means of stimulating further cultural production.[70] In concord with Lichtwark's ideas, Vogel's murals were to be a monumental depiction of the origins of Hamburg's *Volk*; they were to illustrate the continuity of a people's culture in their characteristic surroundings; they were to emphasize the city's role as the leading ethnic and cultural center of northwestern Germany. The artist's emphasis on the landscape setting of the murals, indeed his attempt to bind landscape and human figure into "a single structure" did not go unrecognized by the press as a way of illustrating "that inner natural disposition which first determines and characterizes all the outward expressions of the history of a people."[71] Many commentators on the finished product did not fail to notice that every figure and tree was characteristically Lower Saxon.[72]

But for Lichtwark, the study of cultural history was more than a means of encouraging artistic renewal; it was a means of generating patriotism. The civic pride that the murals were meant to instill took on grandiose proportions in his remarks to the building committee. Referring to "the Saxon race" as "the grandmother of the people of Europe," Lichtwark's explication of the intended message of the murals overstepped local boundaries to take on Pan-Germanic overtones, overtones shared by the Bismarck memorial.[73] "The soil on which Hamburg lies," Lichtwark claimed, "belongs to the region of north Europe whose inhabitants, in days gone by, migrating to the south—with the migration of peoples, to the west—with the conquest of England, to the east—with the colonization of the Slavic lands, have provided all Europe and the world with sovereign races."[74]

Nonetheless, many committee members thought Vogel's intended cycle of generic representations of Hamburg's cultural epochs would be ineffectual as political symbols. They insisted that the murals relate specific events from Hamburg's history in a narrative fashion that would immortalize Hamburg's polity. Martin Haller, for example, argued that the committee was not dealing with "the task of decorating the entrance hall of an ethnological museum."[75] But Lichtwark insisted that he knew of no other artist capable of accomplishing the enormous undertaking in a short time and in such a thoroughgoing manner. With Burchard and Senator Holthusen already convinced, Haller and his fellow architects, Wilhelm Meerwein and Friedrich Stamman finally concurred. On 15 December 1900, Vogel was awarded the commission to decorate the great hall. The decision to appoint him without recourse to yet another design competition was explained by the building committee as a means of speeding up a process in which, in any case, there were only a limited number of artists suitable for the task.[76] The committee considered Vogel to be a suitable modern painter; his style was sufficiently progressive to break with the conventions of traditional history painting, but it avoided being extreme or provocative.

And yet this commitment to artistic innovation was undercut from the very beginning. Despite his positive and extensive influence on the building committee, Lichtwark's support for the project was far from wholehearted. There is no doubt that he promoted the idea of using the great hall's murals to give monumental expression to the development of Hamburg's cultural identity and its unique position within the Empire. But he did not see his ideas born out in Vogel's sketches. It was thus in an attempt to protect his reputation as an authority on contemporary art that Lichtwark insisted the minutes of the committee meeting of 15 December 1900 be altered: the passages in which he praised Vogel's qualities as an artist were struck out leaving only those in which he treated conceptual issues.[77] Only a year before, in a similar state of disappointment, Lichtwark had withdrawn from the committee for the erection of a Bismarck memorial in Hamburg. Certainly, by 1902, he was completely disillusioned with the project. Nonetheless, he continued to exercise his influence on Vogel, Burchard, and the building committee, if only to avoid disaster. In a move that did absolutely nothing to endear himself to the scholar, Lichtwark told Warburg, in June 1909, that he had only interfered in the matter merely "to prevent worse."[78] Ultimately, Lichtwark found his ideas unrealized in the completed murals and was even reluctant to have his name associated with them.

VI

The fact that decisions to decorate Hamburg's greatest public building were taken behind closed doors did not go unnoticed. In 1901, the *Hamburger Nachrichten* reported on a notice in the Munich journal *Die Kunst für Alle* that announced that Vogel had been awarded the commission.[79] The paper argued, wrongly in fact, that the decision had never been made public in Hamburg.[80] Nonetheless, it struck a sensitive nerve when it persisted that "Hamburg's public must be thankful to the Munich journal that, as the result of its kindness, it is made aware of what is happening within its own walls." Although it had nothing against Vogel, the paper deplored the unilateral appointment of any artist as detrimental to the quality of the final product. It called, "as in the case of the Bismarck memorial, for the announcement of an unrestricted artistic competition!"

It was in this atmosphere of the suspected and actual secrecy of the building committee that, in May 1902, the citizens' assembly refused to approve the funds necessary to prepare the great hall for painting. They complained of having been shut out of the process by the senate and of having no idea of Vogel's plans. The architect Georg Hauers reported to the building committee that Vogel had "a mass of veiled enemies" in the citizens' assembly. "It is certain," he explained, "that they are looking for an opportunity to attack the artist."[81] The committee was well aware of the fact that there was an influential body of critical opinion against Vogel, not only in the citizens' assembly, but among Hamburg's public. Some of the criticism of Vogel's appointment was attributed by the committee to disappointment with his portrait of the senate.[82] But it was also due to a mural entitled *Victorious Germania*, which Vogel completed as part of a cycle depicting images of Saxon history for the great hall of the newly-constructed provincial assembly buildings in Merseburg between 1897 and 1899.

In an article on the mural written for *Der Kunstwart* in 1902, the journal's editor and Warburg's friend, Ferdinand Avenarius, accused Vogel of artistic plagiarism. Following the lead taken by the Munich journal *Die Werkstatt der Kunst*, he revealed that, for *Victorious Germania*, Vogel had carefully copied a statue of Joan of Arc by the French sculptor Paul Dubois, thus transforming a French national hero into an embodiment of German identity.[83] The seriousness of this "very evil matter" was not simply born of the fact that Vogel was a member of the Royal Academy of Art, decorated with a gold medal by the Kaiser; it was not just that this was a major government commission. The episode was symptomatic of the "frivolity" of official German art, an art that "only decorates ... only trivializes" and lacked content of any import. Referring to France as the land of the "archenemy," Avenarius insisted that Vogel's appropriation of Joan of Arc for the representation of Germania on the wall of a government building demonstrated "a stunning shallowness of feeling." "Here is a plagiarist," Avenarius concluded, "who makes a mockery of our patriotism in front of the world, especially in front of France." As a result of persistent criticism, Vogel was compelled to transform his Germania into a German Michael and eventually into Martin Luther.

Burchard shrugged off the Merseburg affair and the criticism it aroused. "These people, in their anonymous denunciations," he wrote, "pose as the representatives of a specially exalted artistic morality, and make therewith a certain undeniable impression upon imperfectly educated readers and listeners. Now, I think, that Professor Vogel will brilliantly vanquish the existing prejudices against him by means of the work he is undertaking in the city hall."[84] Nonetheless, in this critical atmosphere, the senate reserved its right to keep the project secret and, as the senators conceived it, avoid the judgments of nonexpert opinion.[85] They were anxious to protect the reputation of the artist and avoid endangering it by presenting Vogel's designs to the citizens' assembly for debate.[86] Public criticism of the project, they believed, would only have deleterious effects on the productive capacity of the artist. Although it produced reports for the citizens' assembly, many of the building committee's protocols were marked as "strictly confidential." Looking back from 1909, Denis Hofmann described the events leading to the completion of the murals as follows: "the doors were protected by guards like the gates of a harem … only a little news seeped onto the street, only unverifiable facts reached the ear of the uninitiated. Of the hard artistic battle that played itself out within the four huge walls on the city-hall square, only a small circle of direct or indirect participants were apprised."[87]

On 14 December 1902, the building committee viewed new sketches by Vogel in his atelier in Berlin. It was hoped that here, the event would not attract the attention of his detractors in Hamburg.[88] Lichtwark emphasized the originality of Vogel's compositions in comparison to what was to be found in other city halls. The committee agreed that the sketches "guaranteed a superb solution to the task incumbent upon the artist." A series of historical episodes was conclusively ruled out and the committee opted for a nonallegorical image of Hamburg's modern harbor above the senatorial podium.[89]

VII

What followed was over six years of debates and crises that threatened, on occasion, to result in disaster. Much of the great hall's architecture, including the pediment of the main portal with all its sculptural decoration, had to be removed to accommodate Vogel's ideas. His demands for these alterations resulted in serious conflicts with Martin Haller.[90] Disappointed and embittered, Haller finally quit his post on the building committee. Debates also arose with the citizens' assembly, which was repeatedly called upon to allot funding for the project. Given the various delays, it is hardly surprising that this body voiced impatience with the undertaking.[91] Indeed, Wilhelm Meerwein reported to the building committee in 1906, that if the citizens' assembly saw the unfinished state of the murals, they would undoubtedly cease to vote more money for the project and an "unpleasant controversy" would ensue in the press.[92]

The frescoes themselves underwent continual transformation until, in 1908, Vogel decided to begin anew. It was at this late date that Lichtwark intervened to encourage the artist and to speed the process along. But by this point, as Rainer Donandt points out, there was scarcely any talk of pictorial content from Lichtwark. Instead, in the interest of completion, he urged "a harmonious result in terms of decoration, the convincing formal disposition of mass, and gradations of color on the gigantic image areas."[93] After several years of work, the murals that survive today were completed in only fourteen months. As the building committee's reports to the citizens' assembly were discussed in the press, the public was not entirely unaware of these developments. Vogel's decision to repaint the images was public knowledge, as were the changes to the great hall's architectural decoration. Both developments fueled speculation as to the success of his working relationship with the building committee.[94] Unsurprisingly, the press not only expressed frustration at the length of time taken to bring the great hall to completion, but voiced doubts about the quality of the final product. In January 1908, the *Hamburger Nachrichten* wrote that "hopefully the result, which is supposed to present representations of the local countryside and local history, will be worth so much care and effort."[95]

Vogel was assisted in his task by two Hamburg painters, Heinrich Kugelberg and Wilhelm Eberhardt. The frescoes diverged from the conventional, aesthetically conservative images of official history painting in two important respects: in the use of an Impressionist-influenced style and in the representation of history not as a succession of specific events with specific personages, but as an anonymous process; all of Vogel's figures are types, not historical personalities or allegorical figures. Interestingly, the images contrasted dramatically with the painted decoration of the other state rooms of the city hall, especially with the neo-Baroque allegories of Venice, Amsterdam, Rome, and Athens painted by Alexander von Wagner in the of Hall of the Republics (1898–99).[96] A panoramic landscape was the artist's priority.[97] Characterized by a cloudy sky and shimmering water, the mural cycle was executed in pale, cool, silvery tones calculated to contrast with the warm, golden hues of the great hall. With a single horizon broken by few vertical lines, the cycle extends to almost seventy meters in a practically unbroken panorama around the room. The continual motif of the Elbe River, as well as the dramatic contrast between the tone of the murals and the hall, helped create a sense that the interior space expanded into a realm behind the pilasters of the wall. The Elbe was also an important formal means of connecting all five images. It was in this Lower-Saxon landscape, along the waterway on which Hamburg had grown and which provided its lifeblood, that Vogel set his cultural epochs.

In a statement to the citizens' assembly composed in December 1908, Vogel described the content of the murals.[98] Starting with the first image, *Primeval Landscape*, situated above the music gallery, the viewer finds a depiction of the Lower-Saxon landscape as it may have appeared before human settlement. (Figure 4.2) From behind a low rise of land, the vista extends to the watery valley of the Alster Lake that empties into the River Elbe. Vogel chose a late-autumn atmosphere in order to emphasize the bleakness of Hamburg's prehistory. The adjoining long wall is decorated with three images. The first of these, *The Prehistoric Age*, depicts the primitive manifestations of human settlement in the pre-Christian era. (Figure 4.3) The occupations and habits of these Iron-Age Lower Saxons are shown to be born of the land that they inhabit: fishing in the Elbe and animal husbandry on its banks. The central image of the long wall represents the "most important turning point" in Hamburg's history; *The Beginning of the Christian Era* illustrates the arrival of "civilization" in the time of Charlemagne. (Figure 4.4) Under the protection of the "conquerors," who are "smoothing the way" for Christianity, a procession of Christian clerics dominates the center of the image. They bear a reliquary and are led by bishops. On the right, a docile crowd of locals seemingly await baptism as they listen to the bishop's oration. They bow humbly before the cross of Christ, "and therewith recognize the transformation of their existence."

Figure 4.2. Hugo Vogel, *Primeval Landscape,* fresco, 1909, Hamburg, City Hall.
Source: The Warburg Institute, London

Figure 4.3. Hugo Vogel, *The Prehistoric Age,* fresco, 1909, Hamburg, City Hall.
Source: The Warburg Institute, London

Figure 4.4. Hugo Vogel, *The Beginning of the Christian Era,* fresco, 1909, Hamburg, City Hall.
Source: The Warburg Institute, London

The beginning of Hamburg's modern history was represented in the following image, *The Hanseatic Port.* (Figure 4.5) Here the viewer finds that "primitive fishing boats have become proud sailing ships." The left foreground is dominated by figures intended to be types from contemporary trade: a merchant confers with a sea captain while stevedores load a cargo vessel. In the right background can be seen the gray outlines of the port and medieval city. The last image is entitled *The Modern Harbor.* (Figure 4.6) Situated over the senatorial podium and consciously brought into symbolic relationship with it, the cycle reaches its culmination in this image, which "gives expression to the high standing that Hamburg has achieved through its world-dominating harbor." "The greatness of Hamburg as a product of its harbor," Vogel explained, "is given better expression here than through any apotheosis. This representation is not intended as a photographic illustration, but, as it were, an extract of that which characterizes this world harbor—built of a cosmopolitan spirit—with its multifarious enterprise."

Figure 4.5. Hugo Vogel, *The Hanseatic Port,* fresco, 1909, Hamburg, City Hall.
Source: The Warburg Institute, London

Figure 4.6. Hugo Vogel, *The Modern Harbor,* fresco, 1909, Hamburg, City Hall.
Source: The Warburg Institute, London

VIII

The dedication ceremony took place on 13 June 1909, a Sunday being chosen to emphasize the solemn nature of this major state occasion. Numerous politicians, officials, and guests assembled in the Emperor's Hall to hear Burchard give the dedication address. Besides Vogel and his family, the assemblage included the senate and citizens' assembly, including Max Warburg; architects Eggert and Schwechten of the building committee; representatives of business, education, and the arts; Count Götzen, Berlin's representative in Hamburg; Professors Hans Hermann and Franz Skarbina of the Royal Academy of Art; and editors from all of the Hamburg newspapers.[99] Aby Warburg received an invitation to the ceremony from Vogel himself, but it is unclear whether he attended.[100]

Besides thanking Vogel in the name of the government and Hamburg's citizens, Burchard emphasized the difficulties Vogel had faced in the process of integrating the gigantic mural cycle into the city hall's architectural fabric, difficulties he had successfully overcome.[101] He gave two reasons why the building committee had agreed to murals depicting "great phases of development, as were experienced by Hamburg's lands along the Elbe in the course of the millennia." Firstly, he reiterated the argument that Vogel had made to the building committee, but made it palatable for popular consumption by setting it into the tradition of Hamburg's representation in art: it was not that Hamburg lacked an interesting past, he explained, "but in earlier centuries this past had not stood in the foreground to the extent that what we consider the most significant historical events, while acknowledging their painterly usefulness, would have earned the right to be recorded and glorified in large scale on the wall." Secondly, the committee did not want to bind the artist to historical episodes "as the history painter—insomuch as historical accuracy, portrait accuracy, the correctness of costume, local atmosphere, the specifications of figural details, probably also great gestures, are significant for his images—occasionally runs the risk of hindering the free unfolding of his artistic personality and being restricted in his creative energies." According to Burchard, Vogel had utilized this freedom successfully. He praised the "novelty" of Vogel's work and, in so doing, he proclaimed that "Professor Vogel has opened a new page in the history of German monumental painting." "No allegories present the viewer with puzzles to solve, no celebration of individual personalities restricts the artist's ideas or detracts from the grandness of the artistic conception." He thanked Lichtwark and Brinckmann for their expert advice as well as the senate and citizens' assembly for their patience, trust, and munificence. Finally, Vogel was presented with the State Medal in gold. The guests then entered the great hall to view the murals for which Vogel provided an interpretation.

The dedication made front-page news in Hamburg. Representatives of the press were admitted to the hall from the beginning of 1909 and some wrote genuinely laudatory reviews. Denis Hofmann, for example, described the murals as "a good step forwards on the dark road to modern *Raumkunst*" (the art of interior design).[102] But although the tone of press reports in Hamburg was generally one of admiration, it was not one of rapture; it is incorrect to speak of a unanimous "cannonade of fame," as Warburg did. Instead, many reviews simply commended Vogel for overcoming difficulties with the hall's architecture and for establishing the unity of the five images in both color and composition.[103] The dedication was also reported throughout Germany and reviews in many of the Berlin newspapers were laudatory, seeing in Vogel's murals a step towards a new monumental art.[104] But a cooler reception is evident in many other German newspapers, which simply related the events of the ceremony without passing judgment on the artworks.[105]

The most highly placed admirer of the murals was the Kaiser himself. During a visit to Hamburg on 21 June 1909, Wilhelm II was greeted at the city hall by Burchard, Mayor O'Swald, Senators Holthusen and Westphal, the chief architect, Meerwein, and Vogel. He spent an hour touring the building. When he entered the great hall, it was reported that he remarked, "Splendid! Splendid! My word, this reminds one of the most beautiful Italian rooms in the Quirinal!"[106] He was most impressed by the manner in which the images were linked by the motif of the Elbe River and had "words of high praise" for the representation of Hamburg's modern harbor. Viewing some of Vogel's preparatory studies for the murals, he found them "solid and thorough," commenting on the figures that "there one sees immediately that they are humans!" (Warburg noted in the margin of his newspaper cutting, "That's logical!???") Given his well-known antipathy to innovation in the arts, the enthusiasm of the Kaiser is itself a damning indictment of the conventional nature of Vogel's achievement.

Helmut Leppien has argued that Hamburg's public never warmed to Vogel's murals; the romantic landscapes by Valentin Ruths in the entrance hall of the Kunsthalle were much more to their taste.[107] Vogel's renunciation of episodes drawn from Hamburg's history was certainly the source of some public criticism.[108] But there are doubts as to how many people, at least from the lower end of the social scale, actually saw the murals in situ. An anonymous writer to the *Hamburger Fremdenblatt*, for instance, asked whether it would be possible, on two days during the week, to allow free entry to the public for the purposes of viewing the murals.[109] As they had been financed by the state, this was the right of every citizen of Hamburg, he claimed. Most men "of simple means," the author complained, could not afford the entry fee of fifty pfennig per person. For this author, not only were the frescoes a means of instilling patriotic feeling, they were a form of art education for the public, even a means of "awakening ideals for life in our children."

Criticism came again from the *Hamburger Echo*, which had previously decried the architectural and sculptural decoration of the city hall.[110] Anticipating Warburg's criticisms, the paper stated that in his construction of form, use of light and color, as well as the gestures and facial expressions of his figures, Vogel had failed to break the bonds of a "delicate aesthetic" that lacked vitality. "Clever moderation," it pointed out, "becomes weakness—an elegant, civilized aesthetic culture that ventures nothing." How much more full of "meaningful energy" and "intelligent passion," it mused, would have been murals by Lovis Corinth. It was to head off just such criticism that the senate commissioned and financed a publication of its own: a richly illustrated book entitled *The Wall Paintings of the Great Hall in Hamburg's City Hall*, which appeared in 1909.[111] The author was Richard Graul, a colleague whom Lichtwark had secured for the job. Lichtwark thoroughly instructed Graul in the manner of the book's execution, while insisting that his name not be mentioned in its pages.[112] As director of the Museum of Art and Industry in Leipzig, Graul was a champion of German Impressionism, but also a supporter of Carl Vinnen's manifesto of 1911, *A Protest of German Artists*, which criticized the ill effects of foreign art on German national characteristics.

Graul's book was a work of propaganda that glossed over the acrimonious nature of a process that had resulted in compromises from both the artist and building committee and had bordered on disaster. In a reflection of their frustration with the artist, the senate instructed the author that the book was not to be about Vogel per se and he was not to be quoted in its pages; it was to be, strictly speaking, a history of the murals. Nonetheless, Vogel was described by Graul as an artist who had exercised "a rare energy" in overcoming all difficulties in "the final victory of his individual artistic vision."[113] This vision was a modern one and the author described Vogel as "an artist of fresh, progressive spirit," saying that,

> in spite of widely held prejudices and rigid conventions, and resolving himself to stand in opposition to his own early history painting, he had stood himself on the side of our progressive art. In his conception of the essence of monumental landscape painting, in his colorist vision and in his technical performance, he is at one with the moderns. That gives his works the freshness and the invigoration of a new painterly beauty, as we find it in no other similar great work of monumental painting in Germany.[114]

According to Graul, Vogel's paintings constituted "a milestone in the history of contemporary German decorative art."[115]

IX

It is hardly surprising that Warburg showed great interest in the painting of Vogel's frescoes. This interest was generated, on the one hand, by his study of monumental fresco painting at several locations in Italy including Florence, Rome, Ferrara, and Padua. Indeed, Warburg considered his concern for modern German art as the duty of "a diligent, cerebral animal" and one of the principal tasks of an art historian who had learned in Italy to respect "really great art."[116] On the other hand, as we have noted, he was a proud citizen of Hamburg who applauded efforts to dispel the city's reputation for cultural philistinism. But for Warburg, Vogel was a typical representative of the academic history painting that he disliked, an art that produced only "worthless products of eclectic compromise" and "monumental kitsch."[117]

Warburg paid close attention to events in the city hall. His thoughts also turned to Vogel's *Victorious Germania* fresco in Merseburg and he referred to the affair as "intellectual thievery in the fine arts."[118] He was amazed that "the foreign feathers" that adorned Vogel's Germania had been so quickly forgotten.[119] (The seemingly odd use of the word feathers here is born of the fact that Warburg sometimes characterized Vogel as a bird, the German meaning of his name.) He was indignant that the career of an artist whom he knew to be an unrepentant plagiarist had been rehabilitated so quickly and that this had happened in Hamburg "where the genuine native conscientiousness is supposed to waken art to a new life!"[120]

Warburg read Graul's book extremely closely and made substantial notes.[121] His marginal comments illustrate how his criticism could take on a mocking and humorous tone in private. For example, he added a subtitle to the title page which reads "or Hugo's development of the great hall into a sampling room." Under an illustration of Vogel, Warburg wrote "Hugo, I'm frightened of you," (*Hugo, mir grault vor Dir*) a pun based on the similarity between the German verb *graulen* and the name of the book's author. Beside a quotation from Burchard's dedicatory speech to the effect that Vogel had "opened a new page" in the history of German monumental painting, Warburg scrawled that Vogel had only opened "an index of errors." In a facetious mood, someone close to Warburg pasted together a small, gold-painted cardboard medallion on which a photograph of Warburg appears alongside one of Vogel. The medallion bears the inscription *viribus unitis* (with united forces).[122]

Warburg paid particularly close attention to the illustrations in Graul's book, many of which reproduced the artist's studies or ideas that were abandoned.[123] They allowed him to reconstruct the course of Vogel's changing approaches to the project and his working methods. He ordered photographs of other works by Vogel from the Berlin firm Amsler and Ruthardt.[124] He also assiduously collected reviews of Vogel's murals from newspapers published throughout Germany, recording quotations that he considered of particular importance.[125] All this work was in preparation for a critical article that he intended to publish. Although his correspondence on these matters was often marked "personal" or even "strictly confidential," Warburg's intentions became known to many of his friends and acquaintances before the article's appearance in May 1910. In March of that year, Wilhelm Bode, General Director of the Royal Museums in Berlin and a senatorial member of the Royal Academy of Art, wrote to Warburg that the news in the capital was that "from henceforth, you want to devote all your time and energy to a death struggle against the old 'history' painting of Prell, Werner, Vogel, etc. and to propagandize for the 'great new art' of Hodler and Co."[126] Knowing Warburg as a student of the Italian Renaissance, Bode was surprised. "What a young enthusiast you still are," he wrote, "that you believe you can abandon our decadent art with sharp criticism or that you can even alter the taste of the 'educated!'"[127] "But as a young, sprightly warrior," Bode quipped, Warburg would undoubtedly regard his comments as mere "senile chattering."

For his part, Warburg had great respect for Bode. It is perhaps for this reason, and because he was uncertain of Bode's opinion of Vogel, that he attempted to portray his interest in the artist's murals as secondary to his ongoing research on the iconography of the frescoes in the Palazzo della Ragione in Padua.[128] But in response to being challenged as a herald of modernism, Warburg claimed, in his own right, to be holding to a long-established ideal of art's purposes. He replied to Bode that his efforts were not a matter "of some flag waving for the benefit of the most modern."[129]

Warburg's ruminations on the subject of Hamburg's Bismarck memorial have illustrated his low opinion of the official art of Wilhelmine Germany. In a letter to his brother Max, he complained about Lichtwark's role in facilitating the expression of this type of art in Hamburg: "He [Lichtwark] has—what is also unforgivable—not only not objected on principle, but influenced Vogel to make corrections 'in order to prevent worse'—the greatest expression of contemporary opportunism."[130] It was such artistic opportunism, Warburg told Ferdinand Avenarius, that "is now the highest wisdom." In contrast, he complained, "whoever is attracted to the categorical imperative is an obsolete ideologue."[131] Nonetheless, he assured Avenarius that he was doing his utmost to ensure that Vogel would have no further opportunity to practice his art in Hamburg. In another letter to his brother, he emphasized that Hamburg's citizens' assembly needed to put up resistance to court circles and expressed his dismay that the assembly had not had the courage to send Vogel packing.[132]

Vogel also became apprised of Warburg's intentions and, on 1 March 1910, paid a visit to his home.[133] The artist wanted to dissuade Warburg from writing an article that was critical of the murals. Warburg told Vogel that he had nothing against him; he simply wanted to write a review of Graul's book.[134] But Warburg subsequently wrote to Karl Scheffler that "the necessity of a rather critical treatment of Vogel's monumental art is made clear by the incompetent behavior of the artist himself, who tries to influence every criticism with all the means of his graces (arts?)."[135] In letters addressed but never sent to Bode, Warburg expressed his anger at Vogel's intentions.[136] It was certainly not his aim, he argued, to sling mud or conduct a witch hunt; he intended to remain true to his "science." It was for "purely objective reasons" that he was "morally compelled to speak out in questions of modern art," and he demanded nothing but respect for his "impersonally motivated scholarly character." Warburg's interest in contemporary art was indeed founded upon his "science," but as a patriotic citizen of Hamburg, it was not always easy for him to remain objective.

Unable to stay Warburg in his course, Vogel was nonetheless sure that the scholar's publication would find no resonance in the popular press.[137] It is true that the artist found favor with several art critics. Heinrich E. Wallsee, critic for the *Hamburger Nachrichten*, and Max Osborn, editor of the *National Zeitung* and author of numerous books on nineteenth-century art, praised Vogel for taking a significant step towards a modern style of wall painting.[138] And yet Warburg's low opinion of the artist was shared by many cultural commentators. When, for example, he approached the editors of *Der Cicerone* about the possibility of publishing an article on the murals, they communicated their intention to completely ignore Vogel's "most hideous soggy mass." Only, they stipulated, if the author had something negative to say about the frescoes would they be interested in publishing his essay.[139] Ultimately, Warburg found a publisher in *Kunst und Künstler*. Founded by Bruno Cassirer in 1903, the journal was a better-edited and better-designed successor to *Pan* and became Germany's leading art periodical and organ of contemporary art, especially Impressionism.[140] From 1907, its editor was the Hamburg-born Scheffler who, apart from Julius Meier-Graefe, was the most influential critic writing about contemporary developments in the arts.

Warburg's article, full of irony and astute critical analysis, was ostensibly a review of Graul's book.[141] "The perhaps unduly emollient tones that he coaxes from the trumpet of Fame," he wrote, "leave the art historian with the answering duty of making a dispassionate analysis of a deeply problematic enterprise." Warburg began his essay by noting that Vogel's murals were painted "at a critical moment of transition in the evolution of monumental history painting." Developments in this genre of art, he explained, mirrored transformations that were changing the shape of history writing itself: "in both, the tendency now is to move away from the confines of a single antiquarian and political narrative and toward a typological approach, spanning whole cultural epochs." Rainer Donandt has pointed to the similarity between Vogel's murals and the purview of Warburg's scholarly research.[142] While Vogel painted cultural epochs, Warburg pursued the study of culture and sought to establish an institutional basis for cultural history in Hamburg. But the mostly microhistorical focus of Warburg's essays are a testament to his awareness of the dangers posed to German historical scholarship by the inclination to hasty synthesis; his research led him to question the notion of a *Zeitgeist* and to feel the inadequacy of its generalizations, to abandon the generalities of *Geistesgeschichte* (the history of ideas) in his published work and concentrate on individual images and people. Yet Donandt speculates, correctly it seems, that Warburg drew parallels between Vogel's murals and a sweeping approach to the study of culture of which he was skeptical. He did this, Donandt claims, not on the basis of Vogel's choice of subject matter, but on the way in which the artist structured the formal relationship of figures to their settings.[143]

Vogel's primary concern had been the creation of a suggestive atmosphere through landscape; he wanted to paint a Lower-Saxon air that would dominate the murals and the room. As Warburg understood it, the "skillful handling of both techniques"—the old art of "close narrative" for figures and the "impressionistic art of distant effects" for the landscape background—gave the murals "the captivating impression of symphonic cooperation between man and landscape." Warburg believed the pictorial effect mirrored images of the past created by certain contemporary historians, like Kurt Breysig and Karl Lamprecht, who conceptualized broad cultural phenomena as the background to political change invoked by individual historical actors.[144] Warburg was also aware of similar approaches to the study of society taking place outside the historical discipline. Scholars like Max Weber, Werner Sombart, Ernst Troeltsch, and Eberhard Gothein, who took a multidisciplinary approach to their studies, conceived of their research into the cultural significance of capitalism, the formative power of the religious content of consciousness on lifestyle, or the ambivalence of contemporary urban-industrial ways of life, as *Kulturgeschichte* (the history of civilization).[145] Warburg did not fully elaborate upon these parallels in his article. But a single piece of marginalia in Warburg's copy of Graul's book lends credence to Donandt's speculation. In the margin beside the passage reading "he [Vogel] wants to illustrate culture, not history," Warburg wrote the name "Lamprecht," immediately identifying Vogel's approach to history with that of Karl Lamprecht, whose lectures Warburg attended in Bonn in 1887.[146] As noted in chapter one, Gombrich referred to Lamprecht as "Warburg's real teacher."[147]

Engendering acrimonious debate among German historians, Lamprecht abandoned the Rankean vision of history with its emphasis on the free will of the historical individual and its belief that political events and institutions alone were worthy of historical investigation. Instead, Lamprecht emphasized the socioeconomic foundations of politics. He believed that changes in individual consciousness were caused by changes in the structure of society and posited five stages of consciousness in the rise of human civilization, each representing a dominant psychological attitude. These ideas structured his twelve-volume *German History*, which attempted to arrive at the characterization of his stages of consciousness on a purely inductive basis. His work amounted to a statistical analysis of countless manifestations of life, demonstrating the domination of an identical form of mentality behind the forms of economic production, legal contracts, political institutions, philosophic reasoning, and artistic creation. But as Warburg was undoubtedly aware, Lamprecht's attempts at sweeping generalizations were seriously flawed by haste and carelessness; in the so-called *Methodenstreit* (methodological controversy) of the 1890s, Lamprecht's critics in the German historical community castigated him for methodological faults, his casual appropriation of the work of other scholars, and his many errors of historical fact.

In his article, Warburg explained that Vogel, Burchard, and the building committee were aware of these developments in historical scholarship and that they sought an artistic style commensurate with them: "a stylistic compromise between the old and the new" that "rendered historical actors in a clearly delineated fashion and evoked the landscape background by means of an atmospheric impressionism."[148] According to Warburg, progress was to have been achieved by ridding the murals of all the "theatrical vices" in gesture, accessories, and background common to academic history painting. These were to have been replaced by the representation of "calm and collected humanity." But this effort "to jettison the formal niceties customary in the higher monumental echelons" had resulted in a compromise full of inadequacies. The grandiose scale of the artworks entitled the viewer to expect both "artistic energy and coherent meaning." But what Warburg found was the "avoidance of psychological tension" in the murals to the extent that he excoriated "the superficial nature of the whole creative process."

Warburg considered Vogel's panoramic landscape background as "an undoubted artistic achievement," suited to the decorative requirements of large-scale mural art. It accurately captured the misty Lower-Saxon atmosphere and even, at least in the first image, held out the promise "of a stylistic transformation and spiritualization of the decorative aspects of landscape." But turning to *The Prehistoric Age*, Warburg complained of the "psychological neutrality" of the figures. He acknowledged Vogel's debt to the French artist Pierre Puvis de Chavannes (1824–98), evident in the abandonment of lively gesticulation for the sake of "still, calm, self-contained humanity."[149] This serenity had also characterized Vogel's work in Merseburg and was much praised by critics.[150] "But, whereas the outward tranquility of the French artist's figures conveys the disciplined self-possession of sentient fellow beings," Warburg asserted that "the fisherfolk in *The Prehistoric Age* are tranquilized by the apathetic passivity of the artist's model"; the figures "infuse no active energy whatever into the still life of their conventionally drawn musculature."

The ill effects of "stillness and vacancy" were transferred to an entire composition in the succeeding image, *The Beginning of the Christian Era*. Here Warburg focused on the "baptismal gesture" of the bishop. It was not that Vogel had chosen a hackneyed subject. Indeed, Warburg insisted that "a creative artist" had no need to shy away from such subjects, "provided always that he takes the refashioning of a traditional theme as a spur to his own instinctive desire for intensity of expression." But changes to the composition, as the result of the removal of the upper half of the great hall's main portal to accommodate the artist's desire for an unbroken expanse of wall, had separated the bishop from the congregation of pagans. This "process of dilution" had reduced the bishop's gesture to "a meaningless rhetorical flourish."[151] Again Warburg recognized Puvis de Chavannes as a source, in particular his mural in the Panthéon in Paris depicting the encounter between Saint Geneviève and Saint Germain. But while the stillness that enfolded Puvis's figures was "the outward sign of a concrete religious experience," in Vogel's case it marked a shrinking "from the vivid embodiment of emotion, for sheer lack of retrospective sympathy"; it amounted to the reduction of a profound collective experience to "the empty proprieties of a dutiful art."

In *The Hanseatic Port*, "the stylistic crisis took a decisive turn." Warburg postulated that Vogel had been faced with an important decision: "the types must either be costume figures or representatives of the popular soul." As Warburg wrote, "the popular soul emerged victorious." The figures did not look like "an organic selection of those fittest for monumental survival"; they were common and possessed no "inner grandeur." While critical of errors of historical accuracy with regard to the figures' accouterments, Warburg insisted that nothing of substance was concealed behind their historical costume. Here he seems to have grasped the essential message of the murals. They were to be a celebration of the constancy of a people deeply rooted in their native soil. As noted above, this afforded Vogel some respect in the press. Graul also wrote admiringly of how Vogel had traveled in the Lower-Saxon countryside to make sketches of the physiognomy of the local population. But from Warburg's point of view, shaped as it was by the idealizing tendencies of Italian Renaissance art, this expression of the "popular soul" amounted to nothing more than *Heimatkunst* (a product of local arts and crafts). This seems yet another criticism of the artistic results of Lichtwark's stimulation of local patriotism, results which Warburg derided as dilettantism. "This artist has felt no urgent, ingrained compulsion to simplify," he explained. "No agonizing profusion of inner experience has ever compelled him to respond with the synthesis—the true mark of genius—in which imaginative creations take on the intuitive symbolism of ideal humanity." In his role as art critic for the *Hamburgischer Correspondent*, Warburg's academic assistant, Wilhelm Waetzoldt, gave particular emphasis to these criticisms.[152] Instead of using his models as "a more or less dispensable control" on his artistic imagination, Waetzoldt insisted that Vogel remained too closely tied to their appearances. The result was the absence of a "powerful transformation of natural models," no "infusion of potency, still less an entirely great effect." Warburg was outraged that, in the depiction of Hamburg's Hanseatic port, Vogel had dared to inflate a banal genre scene to the scale of monumental art. The result was "a kind of life-size folk realism that would have been more at home on the modest scale of an illustrated book." In this respect, Vogel fell far short of the achievements, not only of old masters like Albrecht Dürer, but of modern masters like Hugo Lederer and Warburg's friend, Willy von Beckerath. While Warburg was writing his article, Beckerath was at work on murals for Hamburg's Volksheim. Discussed in chapter five, these depicted idealized figures disporting themselves in idyllic landscapes.

Warburg criticized the final image of the cycle, *The Modern Harbor*, for its "lack of content." "Its function," Warburg insisted, "is to draw a veil over his [Vogel's] failure to reforge the components of artistic experience in the crucible of style to create a higher unity." Warburg's criticism of the murals' vacuous nature culminates in the indictment that the artist, and those who oversaw his work, had evaded their duty to act as a proper organ of social memory:

> An artist who undertakes to make a public historical statement is binding himself to operate as an organ of social memory, bringing the retrospective self-consciousness face to face with the essential forces of its own evolution. But if this gigantic triptych of a seashore idyll, a religious ceremony, and a landing-stage is to stand as adequate symbolic expression for the quintessence of Hamburg and its contribution to civilization—then it would seem that Hamburg people, by straining their historical memory to the utmost, could find in their heads not a single great or even basic human idea deserving of monumental utterance.

Warburg was amazed that Vogel and Hamburg's senate could conceive of no events in Hamburg's history that were of sufficient import to merit monumental expression. This reflected poorly on Hamburg and was an embarrassing sign of the intellectual poverty of the undertaking. But Warburg's denunciation of the "apathetic passivity" of Vogel's figures cuts much deeper to touch upon issues fundamental to his scholarship.

What occupied Warburg in the years 1908–1914 was the study of astrological imagery, in particular the ways in which the ancient gods were preserved and transformed in the collective memory of the Italian and northern European Renaissance. This meant that while studying Vogel's frescoes in Hamburg, Warburg's scholarly eye was attracted to several other cycles of wall painting: Raphael's depiction of the seven planets in Olympian form on the ceiling of the Chigi Chapel in Rome, which Warburg first saw in October 1908; the astrological fresco cycle painted by Francesco del Cossa, Ercole de' Roberti, and others in the Palazzo Schifanoia in Ferrara in 1469–70, upon which Warburg did substantial work from 1909; the cosmological fresco cycle of the Palazzo della Ragione in Padua, on which Warburg was working in 1910; and Baldassare Peruzzi's depictions of planet-gods and zodiacal signs painted on the ceiling of the Sala di Galatea of the Villa Farnesina in Rome around 1511, of which Warburg read in 1912. Just as with his ruminations on the Bismarck memorial, Warburg's interest in Vogel's work was bound up with his scholarly work on the Italian Renaissance; the "really great art" of Italy was one lens through which he regarded the city hall murals.[153]

To fully understand Warburg's response to Vogel's art, we must elaborate upon aspects of his ideas that have been previously discussed. Once again we find him viewing the artworks from the predominantly nonevolutionary perspective of his scholarly enterprise and evaluating them within the framework of psychic time, detached from any simple dismissal of what was considered traditional at the time. Warburg believed that artworks must portray emotion and psychological tension if they were to bring "the retrospective self-consciousness face to face with the essential forces of its own evolution." The pictorial and hence psychic gestures that bore anxieties and passions long stored in the collective subconscious were to be sublimated by the artist. Warburg understood the history of art not as a succession of changing styles, but as a history of individual artists who, when faced with the legacy of archaic passion, were forced to make a moral choice. "For every artist intending to assert his individuality," Warburg wrote, "the compulsion to enter into critical engagement with the world of preestablished forms and expressive values presents a crisis of decisive significance."[154] An ancient gesture born of fear, for example, could be transformed into an expression of triumph through a process of symbolic idealization; pathos could become superior formal poise. It was individual artists who carried out the task of cultural advancement by creatively reworking their cultural tradition. As Matthew Rampley explains, "Warburg clearly valued those artists that rose above the simple repetition of history."[155] In "Dürer and Italian Antiquity" (1905), Warburg drew a picture of an artist who, through the free act of choice, employed the heritage of serene Apollonian beauty to counter Dionysiac passion.[156] He thought the same way about masters like Raphael and Rembrandt who employed energies from the primitive strata of humanity's experience in the service of enlightenment and humanization.[157] This is one of the reasons why Warburg was interested in the frescoes in the Sala di Galatea in Rome.[158] In his famous lecture on the astrological fresco cycle in the Palazzo Schifanoia, Warburg explained that

> our enthusiastic wonderment at the inconceivable achievement of artistic genius can only be strengthened by the recognition that genius is both a blessing and conscious transformatory energy. The great new style that the artistic genius of Italy bequeathed to us was rooted in the social will to recover Greek humanism from the shell of medieval, Oriental-Latin "practice." With this will toward the restitution of antiquity, the "good European" began his struggle for enlightenment.[159]

In Warburg's eyes, Vogel was no genius and his work possessed no "transformatory energy."

Because Vogel's choice of artistic form had been based upon a sense of fashion instead of creative engagement with a tradition, he was guilty of creating an art of "apathetic passivity," of empty rhetoric. As discussed in chapter one, the concept of bipolarity was fundamental to Warburg's thought. While his theories of artistic creation are built around dynamic contrasts of logic and magic, reason and unreason, Warburg conceived of these energies in terms of polarity, not contradiction. Consciousness oscillated between these opposites in a process of compensation; there was never a resolution or neutralizing synthesis. Thus if he saw passion as a potential threat to the values of civilized humanity and looked for its sublimation in art, he also saw it as an essential component of artistic expression; along with rational deliberation, it gave shape to *Denkraum*, the space of calm reflection. But there was no emotive power in Vogel's work; there was nothing of the passion of Arnold Böcklin, or what he would later find in the painting of his friend Willy von Beckerath and the German Expressionists. Vogel's art did nothing to facilitate a contemplative bond between humanity and the world in which it sought to orientate itself. For Warburg, the artist's choice was justified and aesthetically successful if it "sprang from a real urge to use the maximum of expressive power that a human figure can yield."[160] But if the choice of form was only based on a sense of fashion or sensationalism, the artist would be guilty of employing superlatives that rendered pathos hollow and movement theatrical. Warburg believed the disjunction between form and meaning was typical of the inflated allegorical imagery of the Baroque era. Baroque allegories had "lost their grounding in the emotive states at their origin"; the pathos formulae had become empty formulae. Heightened rhetoric was employed "to compensate for the fact that the actual image is no longer connected to its original expressive 'mint.'"[161] This heightened rhetoric also characterized the neo-Baroque art of the nineteenth century. Warburg had seen this art supplanted in Hamburg's Bismarck memorial, but Vogel's art was a case in which cultural enlightenment undermined itself.

In his article, Warburg did not provide his criticisms of Vogel with the theoretical foundation elaborated here. Nonetheless, his indictment of the artist was expressed in grave terms that the educated nonspecialist reader could understand. In keeping with his conception of the recovery of Greek humanism in the Renaissance as "rooted in the social will," the murals were presented as a symptom of the ills of Wilhelmine society; the age of Goethe, when "works of art were still expected 'to stimulate and to be useful'" had given way to an age in which "the influence of work-weary humanity on the culture of art" exercised a deleterious influence. As he had in the 1890s and during the debates over the Bismarck memorial, Warburg directed his displeasure at the German bourgeoisie. Repeating Lichtwark's words, he suggested that Vogel's murals could stand as "an object lesson in the social psychology of an age that was content to 'avoid something worse' when it ought to have demanded the very highest." Furthermore, Hamburg's elevation of "pseudomonumental surrogates for a genuinely large-minded understanding of the past" was a grievous disservice to the historical understanding of future generations.

Warburg's article was widely read. One correspondent responded to its publication with the words "your comment has been awaited by a wide circle for a long time with impatience and excitement."[162] Warburg sent copies of the article to many of his highly placed friends and acquaintances in Hamburg's cultural life. Offprints also went to friends in many other German cities, as well as Vienna and Florence: Ferdinand Avenarius, Wilhelm Bode, Max Dvořák, Adolph Goldschmidt, and Max Liebermann among many others.[163] Judging by the responses Warburg received, many of the recipients agreed with his assessment of the murals, especially on the point that they did not depict "the most concise moments of Hamburg's historical development."[164] But Warburg's criticisms were not confined to a circle of cultural adepts; they were known to a wider audience than the readers of *Kunst und Künstler*. Because of "the importance of the Hamburg art historian," the *Hamburgischer Correspondent* thought it best to reprint Warburg's article in full.[165]

X

The article in *Kunst und Künstler* by no means marked an end to Warburg's campaign against Vogel. Soon his attention turned to Hanover, where the government was considering the artist for the decoration of their city hall. In the summer of 1909, on Helgoland, Warburg spoke personally of Vogel to Senator Fritz Beindorff who subsequently argued the case against Vogel to Hanover's government. It is not clear what role Warburg's views played, but the artist was dropped from consideration. In December 1909, Beindorff reported to Warburg that Hanover had "a modern artist" in mind for the interior decoration of their city hall.[166] The commission was finally awarded to Ferdinand Hodler who completed a mural for the joint-assembly chamber entitled *Unanimity* in 1913.[167]

But there were more pressing issues developing at home. In December 1909, the publisher Otto Meissner, having obtained the exclusive rights from Vogel, announced that he was offering high quality photogravure reproductions of the frescoes for sale. A brochure described the murals as follows: "Immediate intelligibility is a chief characteristic of these paintings. Academic education is not required in order to comprehend their meaning. No allegory presents the viewer with a riddle to solve, no glorification of individual personalities circumscribes the artistic ideas."[168] But long before Meissner brought reproductions onto the market, and before Warburg expressed fears that such developments would occur, Hamburg's education ministry planned to purchase a set of reproductions for each of Hamburg's 164 elementary schools. This serves as an important reminder that even if large segments of the population could not view them directly, the murals that decorated Germany's public buildings often reached a wide public through photographs and other graphic techniques, and especially through the medium of newspapers and journals.

The initiative came from the school inspector Hans Heinrich August Fricke in May 1909. Although he did not regard them strictly as teaching aids, Fricke told a meeting of his fellow inspectors that "these engravings are superbly suited to foster a sense, in the up-and-coming youth, for the development of their hometown, to fill them with pride for Hamburg and promote love for their homeland."[169] Hung in school corridors, Fricke also suggested that "the parents who frequented the schoolhouses would find pleasure in the pictures."[170] He even recommended that the education ministry arrange for teachers to view the frescoes in the city hall so that they could become acquainted with the originals.[171] Meissner offered the series to the ministry for the reduced price of 100 marks each; with the price of framing and glazing, the cost of 164 series would amount to 21,935 marks.[172] The ministry agreed with Fricke's plans and approached the senate for official authorization.

However, on 19 August, 1910, the senate informed the director of the education ministry, Senator Johann Refardt, of its decision not to authorize Fricke's scheme. Requests to provide reproductions for half the number of schools or to allow all schools to purchase only the image of the modern harbor were also rejected.[173] The senate provided no explanation for its decision, although it seems as if the ostensible reason was insufficient funds. But what is interesting, if hardly surprising, is that inserted in the file of education ministry and senate documents preserved in Hamburg's government archive—letters, memoranda, and minutes that record the considerations of both bodies regarding the purchase of the engravings—is a copy of Warburg's article.[174] It is almost certain that most, if not all, of the senators considering the recommendations of the education ministry had read it.

In contrast to his promotion of the art of Albrecht Dürer to the working-class patrons of the Volksheim in 1905, Warburg was vehemently opposed to the use of Vogel's "monumental kitsch" to decorate Hamburg's halls of learning. In January 1910, he wrote an excited letter to his friend Friedrich von Borstel in which he described Hamburg's elementary schools as being under threat from Vogel's work; he promised to speak out publicly on the matter. He hoped that the "elementary schools are still to be saved" by virtue of Hamburg's "miserable financial position."[175] He also suspected that Fricke was behind the scheme, having clashed with him in 1905 over the Art Education Day when the school inspector had attempted to bar Warburg and other members of Hamburg's social elite from taking part in the conference. Gustav Schiefler described Fricke as having connections with the Social Democrats and of viewing questions regarding education through the lens of class struggle.[176] But Warburg's opposition to the installation of Vogel's images in Hamburg's elementary schools was not motivated by political considerations nor was it a function of the fact that he derided art education in the schools as "inconsequential stimulation."[177] It was based on the power and importance he ascribed to images.

It is difficult to evaluate the degree to which Warburg's article played a role in dissuading the senate from authorizing Fricke's scheme. But even if many senators did not share Warburg's particular criticisms, their own misgivings were almost certainly compounded by the resonance that Warburg's article found among members of the cultural establishment. What can be determined is that Warburg was able to exercise some influence on the government through his brother Max, who shared his dislike of the murals. In January 1910, Max Warburg wrote to a colleague on the budget committee of the citizens' assembly that the idea of hanging reproductions of Vogel's frescoes in Hamburg's elementary schools was "highly unnecessary." Addressing artistic matters first, he wrote that "these pictures do not possess any artistic merit at all." "That may, however, be a matter of taste. But most certainly," he added as a secondary consideration, "our current financial situation does not justify such an undertaking."[178]

XI

Warburg's invectives did not put an end to Vogel's career. On the contrary, the artist was chosen to represent Germany to the world in 1910: he was commissioned to paint a giant canvas for the German Hall of Industry at the World's Fair in Brussels. The work, entitled *Prometheus Brings Fire to Man*, represented a Prometheus that Vogel had "reminted as an Aryan genius."[179] Although Vogel's selection for this commission prompted Avenarius to renew his attacks on the artist as a plagiarist, his career progressed uninhibited and he continued to be awarded official commissions.[180] In June 1914, for example, he completed a mural entitled *The Art of Engineering* for the headquarters of the Association of German Engineers in Berlin; during the First World War he was commissioned to paint portraits of Generals Hindenburg and Ludendorff. In 1924, he was also back in Hamburg. In November of that year, the *Hamburger Nachrichten* reported that the artist was busy retouching his city-hall murals. The work was necessitated by the premature darkening of the colors. Nonetheless, Vogel again received the thanks of the senate and Mayor Petersen.[181]

If Warburg was powerless to influence the mural decoration of Hamburg's city hall or to affect Vogel's continued success as an officially sponsored artist, his efforts to combat the popular propagation of the images had met with success. But his forays into the public sphere were not always successful. Shortly after the Vogel affair, Warburg was engaged in a different undertaking involving art in the public realm, but here his efforts met with failure. Nonetheless, the events explored below clearly attest to his affiliation with a climate of cultural and social renewal among the *Bürgertum*; they demonstrate his sympathies with the ambitions of those who sought a form of aesthetic expression that would more accurately reflect the rapidly changing social, economic, and cultural dimensions of their world, and who believed that a society based on industry and commerce could no longer rely on means of expression developed by the aristocracy. They are another example of the way in which Warburg combined ardent nationalism with opposition to Germany's imperial leadership. In this case, however, the intended audience was not only, nor even principally other Germans; it was the ocean-going public of Europe and North America.

Almost every afternoon in the early 1900s, Max Warburg took a turn around Hamburg's Inner Alster Lake with a close friend and business associate, Albert Ballin (1857–1918), general director of the Hamburg-America Line (hereafter referred to as the HAL). Under the directorship of Ballin, the HAL developed into the world's foremost shipping concern; presiding over an armada of 194 ships in 1914, its fleet surpassed the size of the merchant marine of every continental power save Germany itself.[182] In 1908, Ballin decided to build a trio of passenger vessels larger and more luxurious than anything its competitors— North German Lloyd, Cunard, and White Star—had produced; these would be christened *Imperator, Vaterland*, and *Bismarck* and were intended to serve the passenger trade between Hamburg and New York. They quickly became symbols of German aspirations to maritime and world power. The company signed a contract for the *Imperator's* construction with the shipbuilder, Vulcan Werke, in March 1910 and the keel was laid in June of that year.[183] Probably prompted by Max Warburg during one of their constitutionals, Ballin hired Aby Warburg in 1912 as an advisor on the pictorial decoration of the first-class public rooms of the *Imperator*.[184] Launched in May of that same year, the *Imperator* was, at the time, the largest passenger ship in the world.[185] When Warburg went aboard the ship in August 1912, he was enthralled. Describing it as "an awesome Cyclops' mill," he was disappointed that no artists were painting the ship while it was under construction.[186]

The building and decorating of the *Imperator's* interiors was contracted to several firms; most were German, but French and English concerns were also employed. The entire project was supervised by the architect Charles Mewès of the Cologne firm, Mewès and Bischoff. A major concern of the Hamburg-America Line was to secure the patronage of America's nouveau riche by providing them with floating versions of belle époque hotels. Consequently, the technical modernity of the ship was hidden behind a host of historical styles: the main staircase, the first-class dining room, and the winter garden were to be decorated in the style of Louis XVI; the ballroom in the style of Louis XIV; the Ritz-Carlton restaurant in the French Empire style; the smoking room in English Tudor style; and the swimming pool in "Pompeian" style.[187] Comparatively speaking, the cost of the paintings commissioned to decorate these interiors was insignificant.

Warburg had been aboard six of the company's largest steamers in the summer of 1912 and said he found pictures that had the effect of "a succession of servile compliments to bad taste." "The HAL," he wrote, "symbolizes German boldness and respectability, and that is why I wanted to contribute to the elimination of that laughable, incongruous style … which pastes these proud, gigantic fish with mawkish postcards."[188] The interior of the HAL's new passenger liners—expressly intended to showcase Germany to the world—were ideal sites for a markedly nationalist, middle-class culture to install artworks that would proclaim its liberal and democratic contribution to the modern German nation. Consequently, Warburg's voice was one among many calling for the company to outfit its ships with the products of contemporary German art and design.

For the *Imperator,* and in consultation with Warburg, the HAL hired Paul Kayser, Hermann Bruck, Friedrich Lissmann, and Hugo Schnars-Alquist to paint seascapes, landscapes, and still-life pictures for the first-class dining room.[189] These were Hamburg artists who, to varying degrees, worked in a late-Impressionist style. Warburg was consulted regarding the sums to be spent on the artworks; he visited the artists to view sketches and made reports to Chief Superintendent Sachse and to Ballin himself.[190] Despite his interest in avantgarde art forms, Warburg made it clear to the HAL that he did not think it should use its ships as a means of educating the public in the most modern styles. He wanted to find a middle ground between the conventional and the modern.[191] Thus after viewing sketches by Hermann Bruck, he reported to Sachse that the artist would produce a "really delightful still life" for the first-class dining room that would be neither too traditional, nor too modern.[192] His responsibilities also included one of the ship's most important pieces of traditional symbolism: the main staircase was to be dominated by a full-length portrait of the Kaiser in his admiral's uniform. Warburg said he preferred a strong characterization of Wilhelm II, but one without pathos, and recommended Hans Olde, then director of the Royal Art Academy in Kassel.[193] He was pleased with the final product, finding it full of life and dignity and without bombastic rhetoric.[194]

Yet the conviction that Warburg expressed to the HAL was that, if there was to be a reform of German art, "then obviously the doors must be opened to competent modern artists."[195] For Warburg, the *Imperator* was an important means of exhibiting contemporary German art and design to the world. Other figures prominent in German cultural life, like Fritz Schumacher, shared this conviction. Responding to recent criticism of the state of German design, Schumacher penned an article for the *Hamburgischer Correspondent* that praised the ability of German artists to achieve superior results "without deliberate borrowing from other periods and foreign peoples." He also stated his belief that the HAL's construction of new passenger ships provided Hamburg with the opportunity of "sending swimming symbols of German artistic skill as pioneers to foreign lands."[196] In early 1913, Schumacher wrote to Warburg recommending various artists and architects who would be suitable for work on the new ships, including Peter Behrens and Hermann Muthesius.[197] Like Warburg, both were members of the *Deutsche Werkbund.*

Ultimately, however, Warburg's hopes were not to be realized aboard the *Imperator.* As indicated above, Ballin and the HAL were concerned to secure the patronage of an international public, especially Americans, and it was assumed that luxury, historicist interiors aboard its vessels was the best means of doing so. Warburg had said that he wanted nothing to do with the decoration of the public rooms per se. Yet from early on he expressed his dismay that the HAL's directorship saw the paintings as nothing more than accompaniment to the interior's decorative schemes.[198] The architect, Charles Mewès feared inconsistency between the ship's interior design and its pictures; he protested that the paintings recommended by Warburg upset the architectonic form of his rooms.[199] In July 1913, Ballin wrote to Warburg stating that the paintings had to conform to the ship's interior decoration and not vice versa. Even if the company's directorship were not experts, he explained, they had the right to judge whether an artwork was beautiful or not. More to the point, most of the ship's passengers would not be schooled in matters of art and thus it was necessary either to hang paintings that were merely decorative and aroused no criticism, or to purchase works by Rembrandt.[200] For his part, Ballin favored the work of Ascan Lutteroth and Fritz Scwhinge, and commissioned the latter to paint two large landscapes for the first-class dining room and at least nine landscapes and rural scenes for the second-class public rooms. These appear quite sentimental in contemporary reproductions.[201] The work of these artists, Warburg wrote, was exactly the type which the HAL should avoid.[202] But Ballin would not be moved and when the pictures commissioned from Kayser and others were removed without consulting him, Warburg was outraged. On the one hand, he felt humiliated in the eyes of the artists he had engaged; "to myself and in the eyes of the artists I am now only a disavowed art agent of the HAL," he wrote to Ballin.[203] On the other, he was distressed by what he regarded as the philistinism of the company's directorship, saying that art was a matter of "irresponsible play" for Ballin.[204] When he pleaded for a chance to contest the director's decision, Ballin consented and invited Warburg aboard the *Imperator*'s test run.[205] But when Warburg refused to go, his services were terminated.

The building, launching, and outfitting of the *Imperator* was closely followed by the press in Hamburg and across Germany. Much of what appeared in print amounted to little more than an enumeration of technical details accompanied by expressions of astonishment at the size and luxury of the vessel. Some commentary, however, directly addressed the issue of the ship's interior decoration and the paintings intended to adorn its walls. There were critics who concurred with

Warburg's opinion that an opportunity to showcase the best in modern German art and design had been lost.[206] It was with this in mind that Warburg criticized Felix von Eckardt, editor of the *Hamburgischer Correspondent*, for not mounting a criticism of the French-style interiors. The HAL, Warburg complained, could get away with anything and protect itself from every criticism.[207] Other commentators struck a strident note of political and cultural nationalism, often complaining about the foreign feel of the ship's interiors and the fact that they had been built, in part, by foreign firms employing foreign labor. The *Hamburger Nachrichten*, for example, mounted its criticism within the context of a greater problem that it identified as the regrettable German weakness for foreign art. Germans, the author believed, should protest against the derision of their "Germanness." What would the Kaiser say if he discovered that the ship was, in part, the product of French and English labor?[208] An anonymous article in *Der Kunstwart* also complained about the French aesthetic of the interiors. This may have been penned by the journal's editor, Ferdinand Avenarius. It claimed that "Louis XVI appears to be the real emperor" aboard the *Imperator*. The ship, it continued, should have promoted German industry and served as an exhibition to the world of modern German art and design. Why had the HAL employed French and English firms? Were German talents not sufficient? Striking a note of mystic nationalism, the author added that only contemporary artistic styles resonated with "our inner life in its greatest profundity."[209]

Max Warburg shared his brother's disappointment with the *Imperator*'s interiors.[210] In September 1913, however, he was able to report that he had convinced Ballin to outfit a vessel as a showcase for contemporary German design; the general director, he told his brother, had already been in contact with Fritz Schumacher in this respect.[211] However, the First World War would put an end to these plans. A year before the outbreak of war, in August 1913, Warburg posted a letter to Richard Meyer, director of Hamburg's School of Art and Industry, in which he renounced any further ideas of art sponsorship that demanded his personal commitment: "I firmly intend, by the way, to concern myself with nothing that does not directly concern my research; above all, I want no responsibility for emerging talents."[212] Established as professor for monumental painting at Hamburg's School of Art and Industry, the painter Willy von Beckerath was certainly not a new talent. Perhaps it was for this reason, then, that several months before he announced his withdrawal into scholarly work, Warburg had initiated an undertaking with Beckerath, Hamburg's senate, and the School of Art and Industry that would see him embroiled once more in a debate over art in Hamburg's public realm.

Notes

1. The murals are discussed in Heinz-Jürgen Brandt, *Das Hamburger Rathaus: eine Darstellung seiner Baugeschichte und eine Beschreibung seiner Architektur und künstlerischen Ausschmückung* (Hamburg, 1957), pp. 94–103; more recently see Rainer Donandt, "'Ein anschwellendes Gedicht von der Kultur': Hugo Vogels Wandgemälde im großen Festsaal," in *Das Rathaus der Freien und Hansestadt Hamburg*, ed. Joist Grolle (Hamburg, 1997), pp. 53–60; this article grew out of an M.A. dissertation: see idem, "Auf der Suche nach 'modernem' staatlichem Repräsentationsstil: Hugo Vogels Monumentalgemälde im Hamburger Rathaus" (M.A. diss., University of Hamburg, 1996); I have relied heavily on both of the latter works.
2. Warburg's article receives only fleeting mention in Ernst Gombrich, *Aby Warburg: An Intellectual Biography*, 2nd ed. (Chicago, 1986), p. 241f; cursory, but more substantial treatment is to be found in Michael Diers, *Warburg aus Briefen: Kommentare zu den Kopierbüchern der Jahre 1905–1918* (Weinheim, 1991), pp. 74–85; Donandt, "'Ein anschwellendes Gedicht von der Kultur,'" p. 59f.
3. Jürgen Paul, "Das 'Neue Rathaus'—eine Bauaufgabe des 19. Jahrhunderts," in *Das Rathaus im Kaiserreich: Kunstpolitische Aspekte einer Bauaufgabe des 19. Jahrhunderts*, eds. Ekkehard Mai, Jürgen Paul and Stephan Waetzoldt (Berlin, 1982), p. 30.
4. See Hermann Hipp, "Herrschaftsarchitektur in Hamburg?," in *Industriekultur in Hamburg: Des Deutschen Reiches Tor zur Welt*, ed. Volker Plagemann (Munich, 1984), p. 174ff.
5. See Richard Evans, *Death in Hamburg: Society and Politics in the Cholera Years, 1830–1910* (Harmondsworth, 1987), p. 105.
6. Niall Ferguson, *Paper and Iron: Hamburg Business and German Politics in the Era of Inflation, 1897–1927* (Cambridge, 1995), p. 77.
7. Alfred Lichtwark, "Denkscrhift über die innere Ausstattung des Hamburger Rathauses," in idem, *Drei Programme* (Berlin, 1902), p. 67.
8. Evans, *Death in Hamburg*, p. 88.
9. On this point see ibid.
10. Paul, "Das 'Neue Rathaus,'" p. 38.
11. Ibid., p. 48.
12. "Erläuterungs-Bericht zum Entwurf für das Hamburger Rathaus," quoted in Hermann Hipp, "Das Rathaus der Freien und Hansestadt Hamburg," in *Das Rathaus im Kaiserreich*, p. 201.
13. Lichtwark, "Denkschrift über die innere Ausstattung des Hamburger Rathauses," p. 67.
14. Brandt, *Das Hamburger Rathaus*, p. 60.
15. "Neuere Bauten in Hamburg," *Hamburger Echo*, 1 June 1906.
16. Staatsarchiv, Hamburg (St.A.H.) 111–1. Senat Cl. VII, Lit. Fc. Nr. 11, Vol. 12 c, Fasc. 20. Rathaus: ein vollständige Sammlung sämtlicher gedrückter Verhandlungen zwischen Senat und Bürgerschaft betr. den Rathausbau, 1868–1902: Mittheilung des Senats an die Bürgerschaft, no. 214, Hamburg, den 23. November 1892, p. 631; see also Anlage A to ibid; ibid., Vierter Bericht, betr. Ausstattung der Innenräume des Rathauses, p. 642f.
17. Robin Lenman, *Artists and Society in Germany, 1850–1914* (Manchester and New York, 1997), p. 36.
18. Peter H. Feist, *Geschichte der deutschen Kunst, 1848–1890* (Leipzig, 1987), p. 338.
19. See Frank Büttner, "Bildung des Volkes durch Geschichte: zu den Anfängen öffentlicher Geschichtsmalerei in Deutschland," in *Historienmalerei in Europa: Paradigmen in Form, Funktion und Ideologie*, ed. Ekkehard Mai (Mainz am Rhein, 1990), pp. 77–94.
20. Literature on the concept of the Kulturnation includes Erhard Hexelschneider, *Kultur als einigendes Band? Eine Auseinandersetzung mit der These von der "einheitlichen deutschen Kulturnation"* (Berlin, 1984); Mattias von Hellfeld, *Die Nation erwacht: zur Trendwende der deutschen politischen Kultur* (Cologne, 1993).
21. Geoff Eley, "Introduction 1: Is There A History of the Kaiserreich?," in idem ed., *Society, Culture, and the State in Germany, 1870–1930* (Ann Arbor, 1996), p. 40.

22. Ibid.
23. Karen Lang, "Monumental Unease: Monuments and the Making of National Identity in Germany," in *Imagining Modern German Culture, 1889–1910*, ed. Françoise Forster-Hahn (Washington, 1996), p. 276.
24. Lenman, *Artists and Society in Germany*, p. 39.
25. Gerd Unverfehrt, "Bistum, Stadt und Reich: das Programm der Fresken Hermann Prells im Rathaus zu Hildesheim," in *Das Rathaus im Kaiserreich*, pp. 231–259.
26. Eric Hobsbawm, "Mass-Producing Traditions: Europe, 1870–1914," in *The Invention of Tradition*, eds. idem and Terence Ranger (Cambridge, 1999), pp. 263– 307.
27. Lang, "Monumental Unease," p. 281.
28. Peter Paret, *The Berlin Secession: Modernism and Its Enemies in Imperial Germany* (Cambridge, Mass., 1980), p. 10f.
29. See Dominik Bartmann, *Anton von Werner: zur Kunst und Kunstpolitik im deutschen Kaiserreich* (Berlin, 1986).
30. See Heinz-Toni Wappenschmidt, *Studien zur Ausstattung des deutschen Rathaussaales in der 2. Hälfte des 19. Jahrhunderts bis 1918* (Bonn, 1981).
31. Quoted in Monika Wagner, *Allegorie und Geschichte: Ausstattungsprogramme öffentlicher Gebäude des 19 Jahrhunderts in Deutschland: von der Cornelius Schule zur Malerei der Wilhelminischen Ära* (Tübingen, 1989), p. 252.
32. See Heinz-Toni Wappenschmidt, "Rathäuser im rheinisch-westfälischen Industriegebiet: die Bildprogramme in Krefeld, Bochum und in Elberfeld," in *Das Rathaus im Kaiserreich*, pp. 261–299.
33. Lenman, *Artists and Society in Germany*, p. 38f.
34. Matthew Jeffries, *Imperial Culture in Germany, 1871–1918* (Houndmills, 2003), p. 44.
35. Ibid., p. 37.
36. WIA. General Correspondence (hereafter GC): Warburg to Wilhelm Bode, 6 March 1910 (two letters).
37. Feist, *Geschichte der deutschen Kunst*, p. 337.
38. Amongst other commissions, Wagner decorated the city hall in Passau (1886–1893) and the Turmsaal in Hamburg's city hall (1899), Camphausen decorated the Berlin Arsenal, and Kampf decorated the Kaiser-Friedrich-Museum in Magdeburg (1906) and the great hall of the Humboldt University in Berlin (1913–14); see Harald Olbrich, ed., *Geschichte der deutschen Kunst, 1890–1918* (Leipzig, 1988), p. 52.
39. Jason Geiger, "Modernity in Germany: The Many Sides of Adolph Menzel," in *The Challenge of the Avant-Garde*, ed. Paul Wood (New Haven and London, 1999), pp. 91–111.
40. Lenman, *Artists and Society in Germany*, p. 4.
41. See Paret, *The Berlin Secession*, p. 28 where the author asserts that the Kaiser and the art establishment upheld not only their own aesthetic concerns, but the tastes and values of the majority.
42. Feist, *Geschichte der deutschen Kunst*, p. 336.
43. Heinz-Toni Wappenschmidt, "Historienmalerei im späten 19. Jahrhundert: Verfügbarkeit und Auflösung eines Bildungspolitischen Konzepts am Beispiel des Zweiten Deutschen Kaiserreichs," in *Historienmalerei in Europa*, p. 340.
44. Ibid.
45. Wagner, *Allegorie und Geschichte*, p. 250.
46. Wappenschmidt, "Historienmalerei im späten 19. Jahrhundert," p. 340.
47. Ibid., p. 343; these issues are dealt with at greater length in Heinz-Toni Wappenschmidt, *Allegorie, Symbol und Historienbild im späten 19. Jahrhundert* (Munich, 1984), esp. pp. 40–75.
48. See Carsten Meyer-Tönnesmann, "Bilder aus Hamburg," in *Kunst ins Leben: Alfred Lichtwarks Wirken für die Kunsthalle und Hamburg von 1886 bis 1914*, exh. cat. (Hamburger Kunsthalle, 9 December 1986—1 February 1987), pp. 69–78.
49. These aims are stressed in Alfred Lichtwark, *Das Bildnis in Hamburg*, 2 vols. (Hamburg, 1898).

50. See Carolyn Kay, *Art and the German Bourgeoisie: Alfred Lichtwark and Modern Painting in Hamburg, 1886–1914* (Toronto, 2002), pp. 41–69.

51. Lichtwark quoted in Donandt, "Auf der Suche nach 'modernem' staatlichem Repräsentationsstil," p. 53.

52. "Neuere Bauten in Hamburg," *Hamburger Echo*, 1 June 1906.

53. Lichtwark, "Denkschrift über die innere Ausstattung des Hamburger Rathauses," pp. 67–91.

54. Ibid., p. 67f.

55. Aby Warburg, "The Mural Paintings in Hamburg City Hall," in idem, *The Renewal of Pagan Antiquity*, trans. David Britt (Los Angeles, 1999), pp. 711–716.

56. Lenman, *Artists and Society in Germany*, p. 61.

57. Ibid.

58. See Donandt, "Auf der Suche nach 'modernem' staatlichem Repräsentationsstil," pp. 59–64.

59. Ibid., p. 62.

60. Donandt, "'Ein anschwellendes Gedicht von der Kultur,'" p. 57.

61. For an analysis of their designs see ibid., p. 54ff.

62. St.A.H. 322–1. Rathausbaukommission, 165: Die Ausmalung des großen Festsaales 1894–1899, no. 19.

63. Max Jordan, "Hugo Vogel," *Die Weite Welt* (4 March 1904), p. 947.

64. Christa Schreiber, "Das Berlinische Rathaus—Versuch einer Entstehungs—und Ideengeschichte," in *Das Rathaus im Kaiserreich*, p. 126f.

65. Warburg, "The Mural Paintings in Hamburg City Hall," p. 712.

66. Active until 1899, the Eleven exercised little influence on official prejudices; see Nicolaas Teeuwisse, *Vom Salon zur Secession: Berliner Kunstleben zwischen Tradition und Aufbruch zur Moderne, 1871–1900* (Berlin, 1986), pp. 155–183.

67. Quoted in Paret, *The Berlin Secession*, p. 51f.; for the "Munch Affair" see Teeuwisse, *Vom Salon zur Secession*, pp. 183–197.

68. St.A.H. 111–1. Senat Cl. VIII, Lit. Fc. Nr. 11, Vol. 12d, Fasc. 6c. Acta des Herrn Bürgermeister Dr. Burchard, betr. die künstlerische Ausstattung des großen Rathaussaales, mit einigen Senatsaktenstücken 1897–1902: Protokoll des Sitzung der Rathausbaukommission von 13/15 Dezember 1900 betrf. Ausschmuckung des großen Saales.

69. See for example Alfred Lichtwark, *Hamburg: Niedersachsen* (Dresden, 1897).

70. Donandt, "Auf der Suche nach 'modernem' staatlichem Repräsentationsstil," p. 81.

71. Curt Bauer, "Die Wandgemälde Hugo Vogels im Hamburgischen Rathaus," *Der Türmer* (December 1909), p. 473ff.

72. Donandt, "'Ein anschwellendes Gedicht von der Kultur,'" p. 59.

73. Donandt, "Auf der Suche nach 'modernem' staatlichem Repräsentationsstil," p. 76.

74. St.A.H. 111–1. Senat Cl. VIII, Lit. Fc. Nr. 11, Vol. 12d, Fasc. 6c.

75. Haller quoted in Donandt, "'Ein anschwellendes Gedicht von der Kultur,'" p. 60.

76. See the senate's statement preserved in St.A.H. 111–1. Senat Cl. VIII, Lit. Fc. Nr. 11, Vol. 12d, Fasc. 6c.; this was published in Hamburg's major newspapers on 1 and 2 February 1901; see also WIA. IV.10: Mitteilungen des Senats über den Rathausbau, 1–13, 1872–1909: Dreizehnter Bericht, 2 January 1909.

77. Donandt, "Auf der Suche nach 'modernem' staatlichem Repräsentationsstil," p. 76.

78. WIA. Kopierbuch III, 73–76: Warburg to Max Warburg, 2 June 1909.

79. *Hamburger Nachrichten*, 3 March 1901.

80. In fact, the decision had been made public in Hamburg's major newspapers on 1 and 2 February 1901; see "Die Wandgemälde im grossen Saale des Hamburger Rathauses," *Hamburger Nachrichten* and *Hamburgischer Correspondent*, 1 February 1901 and *Hamburger Fremdenblatt*, 2 February 1901.

81. St.A.H. 322–1. Rathausbaukommission, 172a, Bd. 1: Malerische Ausschmückung des großen Festsaales durch Prof. Hugo Vogel 1900–02, No. 51, Sitzung der Rathausbau- Commission vom 1. Juli 1902.

82. Ibid., No. 39: Sitzung der Rathausbau-Commission vom 2. Juni 1902.

83. Ferdinand Avenarius, "Wie's gemacht wird," *Der Kunstwart* 16, no. 3 (1902), p. 143f.

84. St.A.H. 322–1. Rathausbaukommission, 172a, Bd. 1, No.70: Burchard to Wilhelm Bode, 25 August 1902.

85. Ibid., No. 100: Sitzung der Rathausbau-Commission vom 11. December 1902.

86. Ibid., No. 51: Sitzung der Rathausbau-Commission vom 1. Juli 1902.

87. Denis Hofmann, "Bei Professor Hugo Vogel: eine Impression von Rathaussaal," *Hamburger Fremdenblatt,* 24 January 1909.

88. St.A.H. 322–1. Rathausbaukommission, 172a, Bd. 1, No. 100: Sitzung der Rathausbau-Commission vom 11 December 1902.

89. Ibid., No. 104: Sitzung der Rathausbau-Commission vom 14 December 1902.

90. See St.A.H. 322–1. Rathausbaukommission 172c, Bd.1: Protokoll der Sitzung der Rathausbaukommission am 6. Januar 1906; 29. September 1906; 15. Dezember 1906; 12. Oktober 1907; 30. November 1907.

91. Ibid., Bürgerschafts—Sitzung vom 11. Marz 1908.

92. Ibid., Protokoll der Sitzung der Rathausbaukommission am 15. Dezember 1906.

93. Donandt, "'Ein anschwellendes Gedicht von der Kultur,'" p. 58.

94. See for example *Hamburgischer Correspondent,* 29 September 1907 and 13 January 1909; *Hamburger Nachrichten,* 14 January 1909.

95. "Rathausmalereien," *Hamburger Nachrichten,* 5 January 1908.

96. For a detailed discussion of the decoration of the state rooms see Brandt, *Das Hamburger Rathaus,* pp. 84–103.

97. Rainer Donandt, "'Ein anschwellendes Gedicht von der Kultur,'" p. 54.

98. WIA. IV.10: Anlage zu dem Bericht der Rathausbaukommission von 2. Januar 1909; this statement was published in the local press; see *Hamburgischer Correspondent,* 13 January 1909; *Hamburger Nachrichten,* 14 January 1909.

99. See "Hugo Vogels Wandgemälde im großen Rathaussaal," *Hamburgischer Correspondent,* 14 June 1909; Heinrich E. Wallsee, "Zur Enthüllung der Wandgemälde im großen Saal des Rathauses," *Hamburger Nachrichten,* 13 and 14 June 1909.

100. WIA. III.2.1: Zettelkasten 50 (Mod. Kst.), 050 027945.

101. Burchard's dedication address was reprinted in local newspapers and in Richard Graul, *Die Wandgemälde des Grossen Saales im Hamburger Rathaus* (Leipzig, 1909), p. 59ff.

102. Denis Hofmann, "Die Wandgemälde Professor Hugo Vogels," *Hamburger Fremdenblatt,* 15 June 1909; but Hofmann was not an unreserved supporter of Vogel; see Wilhelm Waetzoldt's synopsis of Hofmann's lecture on the murals in Wilhelm Waetzoldt, "Vortrag in der Galerie Commeter," *Hamburgischer Correspondent,* 7 March 1910; also laudatory is Anton Lindner, "Der Goldene Saal im Hamburger Rathause," *Neue Hamburgischer Zeitung,* 14 June 1909.

103. See, for example, Heinrich E. Wallsee, "Zur Enthüllung der Wandgemälde im großen Saal des Rathauses," *Hamburger Nachrichten,* 13 June 1909; "Prof. Hugo Vogels neue Wandgemälde im Hamburger Rathaus," *Die Hamburger Woche,* 17 June 1909.

104. Hofmann, "Die Wandgemälde Professor Hugo Vogels" was reprinted in *Berliner Tageblatt,* 15 June 1909; see also "Die neuen Wandgemälde im großen Rathaussaal zu Hamburg," *Vossische Zeitung,* 14 June 1909; "Hugo Vogel's Hamburger Rathausbilder," *National Zeitung,* 16 June 1909.

105. Most of the newspaper articles in Warburg's collection were not critical of the murals, but most were simply factual accounts of the history of their execution that did not praise them in glowing terms; see WIA. IV.30. Art: Press-Cuttings.

106. "Die Besichtigung der neuen Rathausgemälde durch den Kaiser," *Neue Hamburger Zeitung,* 21 June 1909; Warburg's copy with underlinings and marginalia is preserved in WIA. IV.30. Art: Press-Cuttings.

107. Helmut R. Leppien, "Der Hamburger Künstlerverein," in *Industriekultur in Hamburg,* p. 342.

108. "Hugo Vogels Gemälde im Rathause," *Hamburger Fremdenblatt,* 25 July 1909.

109. "Freier Eintritt zu den Wandgemälden im Rathaus, *Hamburger Fremdenblatt,* 13 July 1909.
110. "Hugo Vogel's Wandgemälde im Rathaussaal," *Hamburger Echo,* 4 July 1909.
111. Graul, *Die Wandgemälde des Grossen Saales im Hamburger Rathaus.*
112. Donandt, "'Ein anschwellendes Gedicht von der Kultur,'" p. 58; see also St.A.H. 322–1. Rathausbaukommission, 172c, Bd.1: Lichtwark to Ruts Schmitz, 25 May 1909.
113. Graul, *Die Wandgemälde des Grossen Saales im Hamburger Rathaus,* p. 54.
114. Ibid.
115. Ibid., p. 55.
116. WIA. GC: Warburg to Wilhelm von Bode, 6 March 1910.
117. Warburg quoted in Diers, *Warburg aus Briefen,* p. 80.
118. WIA. III.2.1: Zettelkasten 50 (Mod. Kst.), 050 027951.
119. WIA. Kopierbuch III, 68: Warburg to Ferdinand Avenarius, 29 May 1909.
120. WIA. Kopierbuch III, 86f.: Warburg to Wilhelm Heyden, 20 June 1909.
121. WIA. III.28.1.2: zu Vogel Entw.
122. WIA. III.2.1: Zettelkasten 50 (Mod. Kst.), between 050 027961 and 050 027962.
123. WIA. III.28.1.3: Hugo Vogel Abbildungsmaterial.
124. Diers, *Warburg aus Briefen,* p. 75.
125. WIA. III.28.1.1: Hugo Vogel, "Laudatorisches Quellenkritik."
126. WIA. III.2.1: Zettelkasten 50 (Mod. Kst.), 050 027 971: Wilhelm Bode to Warburg, 4 March 1910.
127. Ibid., 050 027969: Wilhelm Bode to Warburg, 13 February 1910.
128. Diers, *Warburg aus Briefen,* p. 84f; it seems that Bode admired Vogel's decorative talent, but was also aware of his limitations; see Donandt, "'Ein anschwellendes Gedicht von der Kultur,'" p. 60.
129. WIA. GC: Warburg to Wilhelm Bode, 6 March 1910 (two letters).
130. WIA. Kopierbuch III, 73–76: Warburg to Max Warburg, 2 June 1909.
131. WIA. Kopierbuch III, 85: Warburg to Ferdinand Avenarius, 15 June 1909.
132. WIA. Kopierbuch III, 73–76: Warburg to Max Warburg, 2 June 1909.
133. WIA. III.2.1: Zettelkasten 50 (Mod. Kst.), 050 027946: diary entry for 1 March 1910.
134. See WIA. Kopierbuch III, 86f.: Warburg to Wilhelm Heyden, 20 June 1909, where he tells Heyden that "I am completely indifferent to Vogel as a person, but not as a pseudo-monumental painter."
135. WIA. Kopierbuch III, 324: Warburg to Karl Scheffler, 6 March 1910.
136. WIA. GC: Warburg to Wilhelm Bode, 6 March 1910 (2 letters) and Warburg to Wilhelm Bode, 7 March 1910.
137. WIA. III.2.1: Zettelkasten 50 (Mod. Kst.), 050 027946: diary entry for 7 March 1910.
138. Heinrich E. Wallsee, "Die Wandmalereien Hugo Vogels im Hamburger Rathaus," *Die Kunst für Alle* 24 (August 1909), p. 496; Max Osborn, "Hugo Vogels Wandgemälde im Hamburger Rathaus," *Illustrierte Zeitung,* 24 June 1909.
139. WIA. III.2.1: Zettelkasten 50 (Mod. Kst.), 050 027988: *Der Cicerone* to Warburg, 22 June 1909.
140. Paret, *The Berlin Secession,* p. 72.
141. The following quotations are taken from the recent English translation of Warburg's article: Aby Warburg, "The Mural Paintings in Hamburg City Hall."
142. Donandt, "'Ein anschwellendes Gedicht von der Kultur,'" p. 59.
143. Ibid.
144. In the years before 1900, issues of the *Historische Zeitschrift* began to reflect a shift from a predominant occupation with political history to a consideration of culture; see Georg Iggers, *The German Conception of History: The National Tradition of Historical Thought from Herder to the Present* (Middletown, Conn., 1983), p. 200; for the development of the study of cultural history at this time see Stefan Haas, *Historische Kulturforschung in Deutschland, 1880–1930: Geschichtswissenschaft zwischen Synthese und Pluralität* (Cologne, Weimar, and Berlin, 1994), esp. pp. 69–185.

145. See Gangholf Hübinger, *Kultur und Kulturwissenschaften um 1900: Krise der Moderne und Glaube an die Wissenschaft*, eds. Rüdiger vom Bruch, Friedrich Wilhelm Graf and Gangolf Hübinger (Stuttgart, 1989), pp. 25–43.

146. For Lamprecht see Roger Chickering, *Karl Lamprecht: A German Academic Life (1856–1915)* (Atlantic Highlands, NJ, 1993); see also Luise Schorn-Schütte, *Karl Lamprecht: Kulturgeschichtsschreibung zwischen Wissenschaft und Politik* (Göttingen, 1984).

147. Gombrich, *Aby Warburg*, p. 37.

148. Lichtwark, for example, was well informed of developments in the historical profession; he was a personal friend of the historian Ernst Bernheim and conducted a sporadic correspondence with Karl Lamprecht; see Donandt, "Auf der Suche nach 'modernem' staatlichem Repräsentationsstil," p.77f.

149. For Puvis de Chavanne's powerful influence on artists from Manet to Picasso, see Richard J. Wattenmaker, *Puvis de Chavannes and the Modern Tradition*, exh. cat. (Toronto, Art Gallery of Ontario, 24 October–30 November, 1975).

150. See Jordan, "Hugo Vogel," p. 945.

151. In his working papers, Warburg also described this as "a banal atelier gesture"; see WIA. III.2.1: Zettelkasten 50 (Mod. Kst.), 050 027948.

152. Waetzoldt made these comments in a review of an exhibition of Vogel's preparatory studies for the murals in Hamburg's Commeter Art Galleries in early 1910; Wilhelm Waetzoldt, "Hugo Vogel-Ausstellung bei Commeter," *Hamburgischer Correspondent*, 6 March 1910.

153. WIA. GC: Warburg to Wilhelm Bode, 6 March 1910 (two letters).

154. Warburg quoted and translated in Matthew Rampley, *The Remembrance of Things Past: On Aby Warburg and Walter Benjamin* (Wiesbaden, 2000), p. 127, nte. 246.

155. Ibid., p. 99.

156. Aby Warburg, "Dürer and Italian Antiquity," in idem, *The Renewal of Pagan Antiquity*, pp. 553–558.

157. Gombrich, *Aby Warburg*, p. 187.

158. Kristen Lippincott, "Aby Warburg, Fritz Saxl and the Astrological Ceiling of the Sala di Galatea," in *Aby Warburg: Akten des internationalen Symposions, Hamburg, 1990*, eds. Horst Bredekamp, Michael Diers, and Charlotte Schoell-Glass (Weinheim, 1991), p. 228.

159. Aby Warburg, "Italian Art and International Astrology in the Palazzo Schifanoia in Ferrara," in *German Essays on Art History*, ed. Gert Schiff (New York, 1988), p. 252f.

160. Gombrich, *Aby Warburg*, p. 179.

161. Rampley, *The Remembrance of Things Past*, p. 63.

162. WIA. III.2.1: Zettelkasten 50 (Mod. Kst.), 050 028029: C.H. Becker to Warburg, 10 May 1910.

163. WIA. III.28.1.6: Offprint distribution list.

164. WIA. III.2.1: Zettelkasten 50 (Mod. Kst.), 050 028066: E. Michahelles to Warburg, 11 January 1911; similar judgments are found in the many letters to Warburg preserved in this Zettelkasten.

165. *Hamburgischer Correspondent*, 15 May 1910.

166. WIA. III.2.1: Zettelkasten 50 (Mod. Kst.), 050 027980: Fritz Beindorff to Warburg, 20 December 1909.

167. See Charlotte Kranz-Michaelis, "Das Neue Rathaus Hannovers—ein Zeugnis der 'Ära Tramm,'" in *Das Rathaus im Kaiserreich*, p. 403ff.

168. St.A.H. 361–2. Oberschulbehörde V, 434 b, Bd. I, no. 13: brochure from Otto Meißners Verlag, Dezember 1909.

169. Ibid., no. 16: Fricke to the Oberschulbehörde, 17 December 1909.

170. Ibid., nos. 23–24: Oberschulbehörde, Sektion für das Volksschulwesen: Protokollauszug, 24 February 1910.

171. Ibid., nos. 4–6: memorandum signed by Schulinspektor Fricke, 1 September 1909.

172. Ibid., no. 16: Fricke to the Oberschulbehörde, 17 December 1909.

173. Ibid., no. 27: Auszug aus dem Protokolle des Senats, 19 August 1910.

174. Ibid., nos. 25–26.

175. WIA. Kopierbuch III, 301: Warburg to Friedrich von Borstel, 22 January 1910.

176. See Christiane Brosius, *Kunst als Denkraum: zum Bildungsbegriff von Aby Warburg* (Pfaffenweiler, 1997), p. 131f; Gustav Schiefler, *Eine hamburgische Kulturgeschichte, 1890–1920: Beobachtungen eines Zeitgenossen,* eds. Gerhard Ahrens, Hans Wilhelm Eckardt, and Renate Hauschild-Thiessen (Hamburg, 1985), pp. 304 and 306.

177. WIA. Kopierbuch II, 171f.: Warburg to Wilhelm Bode, 17 October 1907.

178. WIA. III.2.1: Zettelkasten 50 (Mod. Kst.), 050 027990: Max Warburg to Ehlers, 11 January 1910.

179. Wagner, *Allegorie und Geschichte,* p. 240.

180. Ferdinand Avenarius, "Hugo Vogel und die Weltaustellung," *Kunstwart* 22, no. 23 (1909), p. 279f.

181. *Hamburger Nachrichten,* 25 November 1924.

182. For Ballin see Lamar Cecil, *Albert Ballin: Business and Politics in Imperial Germany, 1888–1918* (Princeton, 1967); for the HAL see amongst others Susanne and Klaus Wiborg, *1847–1997: unser Feld ist die Welt: 150 Jahre Hapag-Lloyd* (Hamburg, 1997); Otto J. Seiler, *Nordamerikafahrt: Linienschiffahrt der Hapag- Lloyd AG im Wandel der Zeiten* (Herford, 1988); Hans-Jürgen Witthoft, *HAPAG: Hamburg-Amerika Linie* (Herford, 1973).

183. St.A.H. 621–1 HAPAG—Reederei 2656 Band 3: Verträge und Vereinbarungen zu Schiffsneubauten Band 3: D "Imperator" 1910–1914, MUG 128A 04 05, A—Bau– Offerte und Bauvertrag.

184. For a brief discussion of Warburg's work for the HAL see Diers, *Warburg aus Briefen,* pp. 85–91.

185. For the *Imperator* and ships of its class see Arnold Kludas, *Die Geschichte der deutschen Passagierschiffahrt,* 5 vols. (Augsburg, 1994), vol. 4, pp. 11–32.

186. WIA. Family Correspondence (hereafter FC): Warburg to Mary Warburg, 9 or 10 July 1912.

187. St.A.H. 621–1 HAPAG—Reederei 2656 Band 3.

188. WIA. GC: Warburg to the HAL, 2 July 1913.

189. WIA. IV.36: Hamburg-Amerika Linie [HAPAG] (Imperator and Vaterland); WIA. III.2.1: Zettelkasten 57 (Hamburg) HAL; St.A.H. 621–1. HAPAG—Reederei. 2656 Band. 3.

190. See, for example, WIA. Kopierbuch V, 128–30: Warburg to Albert Ballin, 30 March 1913.

191. WIA. GC: Warburg to the HAL (Schiffbautechnische Abteilung), 30 June, 1913.

192. WIA. GC: Warburg to Sachse, 6 November 1912.

193. WIA. GC: Warburg to Sachse, 7 June 1912.

194. WIA. Kopierbuch V, 128–130: Warburg to Albert Ballin, 30 March 1913.

195. WIA. GC: Warburg to the HAL (Schiffbautechnische Abteilung), 30 June 1913.

196. Fritz Schumacher, "'Aesthetische Kultur,'" *Hamburgischer Correspondent,* 28 January 1913.

197. WIA. GC: Fritz Schumacher to Warburg, 9 February 1913.

198. WIA. GC: Warburg to Sachse, 6 September and 6 November 1912.

199. WIA. Kopierbuch V, 141: Warburg to Hans Olde, 9 April 1913; WIA. GC: Albert Ballin to Warburg, 9 April 1913.

200. WIA. GC: Albert Ballin to Warburg, 6 July 1913.

201. Dr. W., "Gemälde für den Imperator, im Auftrag der Hamburg-Amerika-Linie gemalt von Fritz Schwinge," *Die Hamburger Woche,* undated clipping found in WIA. IV.36.2.

202. WIA. GC: Warburg to the HAL, 2 July 1913.

203. WIA. Kopierbuch V, 136f.: Warburg to Albert Ballin, 7 April, 1913.

204. WIA. FC: Warburg to Mary Warburg, 21 September 1913 and 19 July 1914.

205. WIA. Kopierbuch V, 136f.: Warburg to Albert Ballin, 7 April, 1913.

206. WIA. IV.36.1–2: untitled newspaper clipping, 14 June 1913.

207. WIA, Kopierbuch V, 185: Warburg to Felix von Eckardt, 18 June 1913.

208. "Ausländerei," *Hamburger Nachrichten,* 29 April 1913.

209. "'Imperator' und 'Vaterland,'" *Der Kunstwart* 26, no. 19 (July 1913), p. 67f.
210. WIA. Kopierbuch V, 247–249: Max Warburg to Warburg, 22 September, 1913.
211. WIA. GC: Max Warburg to Warburg, 18 September, 1913.
212. Warburg to Richard Meyer, 18 August 1913, quoted in Diers, *Warburg aus Briefen,* p. 90f.

Chapter Five

A MOMENT OF CALM IN THE CHAOS OF WAR
Willy Von Beckerath's "Eternal Wave," 1913–1918

I

The need for rational, self-reflective calm was never more apparent to Warburg than it was during the First World War. The war definitively proved to him that barbarism and irrationality did not belong to the past. As an interested observer in 1906, he had looked to the Bismarck memorial as a tool for the amelioration of local class conflict. Now, in the years between 1913 and 1918, he became an active participant in a project that he hoped would calm the psychological and social chaos of the war years: the mural decoration of Hamburg's School of Art and Industry by Willy von Beckerath (1868–1938). Beckerath was the School's professor of monumental wall painting from 1907 to 1931 and his murals were seen as a means of enhancing Hamburg's cultural reputation.

Warburg was more than simply an admirer of Beckerath's work: he was an important financial supporter of the artist between 1909 and 1927. His intervention on the Beckerath's behalf was of the utmost importance in the execution of large-scale commissions in Hamburg. He was also interested in purchasing Beckerath's work for his private collection. The same is true of other members of the Warburg family. Warburg's mother, Charlotte, possessed at least one of Beckerath's drawings.[1] On his return from Palestine in 1929, Max Warburg had Beckerath paint an image of Moses on the wall of his office at Kösterberg, a Moses "in his yearning for the beloved land that he never entered." When he finally left Germany for New York in 1938, Max Warburg took a photograph of the mural and placed it on his desk in his new home.[2]

Notes for this section begin on page 213.

On 23 March 1918, Aby Warburg gave an address in the School of Art and Industry to mark the dedication of Beckerath's mural cycle. He spoke of the function and importance of art in Hamburg's public realm to an audience of patrician elite. In private, Warburg wrote to his brother Max that, "looking back, I can stress, to our joy, that I am convinced that with this undertaking we have achieved something, objectively and personally, upon which Hamburg will be able to look back with satisfaction, perhaps even with pride."[3] But the words he spoke in public were even more glowing, and he praised his friend's creation as an important addition to monumental art in Hamburg. This may seem puzzling given that the mostly prosaic and highly sentimental symbolism of Beckerath's work prompted many contemporary viewers to question its effectiveness as art. Subsequently, he has been almost completely forgotten by art-historical scholarship.[4] What was it, in Warburg's eyes, that made the murals so deserving of praise and how did he understand their public function? His dedicatory address is an extremely important source for answering these questions and for understanding the manner in which he judged the art of his era.[5] It is also important as a very public reaction on his part to a period of political and social crisis, both local and national.

II

Warburg first worked with Beckerath in 1909. In that year, the artist and his students painted a mural cycle in the great hall of the Volksheim in Rothenburgsort. Warburg acted as an artistic advisor to the Volksheim and pledged 600 marks toward Beckerath's work.[6] More funding was supplied by Warburg as the work progressed, winning the artist's thanks for his willingness to "jump into the breach" and keep the work on schedule.[7] The paintings were ceremoniously dedicated on 9 October 1910.

Unfortunately, Beckerath's murals were destroyed as early as the mid-1920s and no photographic record seems to exist.[8] But contemporary reports provide a good idea of the work's form and content. The six wall surfaces of the great hall were painted with brightly sunlit, idyllic summer landscapes in which nude or semi-clothed figures pursued a life of pastoral bliss, conversing, strolling, and listening to music.[9] It is likely that the murals were painted in Beckerath's hieratic, static, flat and linear style. At the time of their dedication, Wilhelm Hertz's report for the monthly bulletin of the Volksheim resounded with praise for Beckerath's murals.[10] But many of the working-class patrons of the institution were bewildered by the new decoration of the great hall. Their response echoes that which had greeted Warburg's Dürer exhibition in 1905. Nothing in the murals spoke of, or to, the lives of the people who made use of the establishment. Their style and content were alien; they told no story nor did they relate an episode from history. This problem did not go unrecognized by the board of directors, who instituted lectures to help make the murals comprehensible to patrons. According to

Friedrich von Borstel, these were well attended and even resulted in serious debates about painting and its techniques. They helped, he believed, to instill a serious appreciation of the murals.[11] This was more than what Warburg's Dürer exhibition appears to have achieved.

Beckerath's Volksheim murals were the first examples in Hamburg of the type of monumental wall painting that he practiced. Warburg's response was enthusiastic, if guarded as to the artistic maturity of the students whom Beckerath directed. In an undated notation, he writes that "if, of course, one cannot yet speak of seeing qualified monumental painters in his students, their enthusiastic earnestness earns them, especially in this condition of becoming, moral and practical support."[12] With Warburg's compliance, Wilhelm Waetzoldt published a review of the murals.[13] Here he backed away from describing Beckerath as a new Hans von Marées (1837–87) or Ferdinand Hodler (1853–1918) and from describing the paintings as a "definitive masterpiece." He described them, instead, as a "promising attempt" and praised Beckerath for bringing a unity of form and color to the several wall areas:

> what matters much more in artistic matters, in our opinion, is will instead of ability. And if we compare the two locations of monumental wall painting in Hamburg, the hall of the *Rathaus* [a reference to Vogel's frescoes] and the hall of the Volksheim, there can be no doubt: there—in the most ceremonial location—the routine ability of a man, who demonstrates no great will to overcome the art of the atelier, has displayed itself; here—in the location of simple social work—an artistic movement, with still undeveloped ability, makes itself known; a movement that leads further and therefore demands, if not unreserved approval, then of course, respect.

In Beckerath, Warburg found an artist and teacher who shared his intensely intellectual approach to art. Described as a *Gedankenmaler*—a painter of ideas—Beckerath was a late symbolist who gave expression to religious and Arcadian themes. Abstruse ideas were often matched by a recondite rendering in paint. Born in Krefeld in 1868, Beckerath studied painting under Peter Janssen at the Düsseldorf Academy. The members of the von Beckerath family were long-time friends of the composer Johannes Brahms, and the artist first came to public attention with a portrait of the aged maestro. *Brahms at the Piano* was painted in 1896 and widely distributed as a lithograph in Britain and the United States.[14] It is an obvious example of the life-long influence of music on Beckerath's work.

From 1899–1907, Beckerath lived in Munich and turned his attention to interior and furniture design. He founded the *Werkstätten für Wohnungseinrichtung* (Household Furnishing Studios) with the architects Karl Bertsch (1873–1933) and Adelbert Niemeyer (1867–1932), and also became a member of the *Deutsche Werkstätten für Handwerkskunst* (German Arts and Crafts Studios). Working in a sober, even austere *Jugendstil* aesthetic, he was guided by a desire to reform the applied arts in the spirit of modern developments.[15] As a painter, Beckerath's work belongs to that genre of monumental wall painting denoted by the term *Stilkunst* and practiced by artists such as Fritz Erler

(1868–1940), Ludwig von Hofmann (1861–1945), and Hans Adolph Bühler (1877–1951). Aimed at a cultivated bourgeois audience, this monumental art opposed the sketchiness of Impressionism and the non-objective tendencies of Expressionism. It emphasized large, simple forms and figures, linearity, symmetry, emphatic gesture, and expressive power and its subjects were most often ancient Germanic warriors, medieval knights, Siegfrieds, Armins, and Germanias.

Most of Beckerath's early pictures treated religious themes, common in German art of the 1890s. So too were the Arcadian motifs and celebrations of youth, which came to form the standard subject matter of his painting. His simplified and flattened forms, shallow picture space, emphatic linearity, use of unnatural colors, and the stylized gestures of his figures lend his work an air of cold abstraction. In the forward to a book by the painter and art theorist Rudolph Czapek entitled *The Basic Problems of Art* (1908), Beckerath stated that "nature is the enemy of the artist, who strives to overcome it so that it may serve him as a slave in the construction of his own world."[16] While professor of monumental wall painting in Hamburg, he insisted, in contradiction to the official art academies, that the starting point for a student's work must be ideas, not studies from nature. But ultimately, Beckerath was indebted to nature; his studies of the human form were praised as "capturing the expression of pulsating life."[17] Indeed, the artist admitted that he executed many studies from life for the murals in Hamburg's School of Art and Industry.[18]

The work that gained him popular recognition was the mural painted in the sculpture hall of Bremen's art gallery in 1906. Entitled *The Elysian Fields*, it was his first major commission.[19] Divided into three sections, it represents the ideal life of a highly civilized culture. In the beatific peace of an Arcadian landscape, idealized, partially clothed or nude men and women weave crowns of flowers, pluck fruit from trees, listen to music, or walk upon a sunny meadow. The mural was executed in a pointillist style and earned Beckerath the title of a "modern prophet of beauty" from at least one critic.[20] He was occasionally compared to the French Symbolist painter Pierre Puvis de Chavannes, and may have been influenced by the neoclassical themes and figures of Hans von Marées and the work of Symbolist painters like Max Klinger and Franz von Stuck.[21] But it is the influence of Ferdinand Hodler that is immediately and unmistakably recognizable in Beckerath's art. Hodler was especially esteemed by contemporaries for his large-scale history paintings, and Beckerath considered the Swiss artist's work as an integral part of German art.[22] In Hamburg, Lichtwark praised Hodler for the "power and directness" of his colors that evinced both an ethereal and inwardly penetrating quality. He also admired the boldness and clarity of his line.[23] Warburg was also an admirer, writing to Lichtwark that "Hodler is also wonderfully enchanting: he certainly blows an uncomfortable *fortissimo* into the ears of the bourgeois."[24]

An exhibition mounted by the Art Association in January 1911 constituted Beckerath's popular debut in Hamburg. This consisted of sixteen paintings and 125 drawings.[25] Reviews in Hamburg's major newspapers agreed that the artworks were those of a highly talented and sensitive artist. All recognized the influence of Hodler on Beckerath, as well as the striving after a monumental artistic vocabulary. Wilhelm Waetzoldt commended Beckerath's efforts to supersede Impressionism, a style that he saw as completely unsuitable for an art that was to appeal "to all sides and powers of our spirituality."[26] But despite this critical acclaim, at least one observer expressed doubts about the certainty of Beckerath's continued success in Hamburg. Heinrich Wallsee wrote that "whether Hamburg possesses patrons who have the courage and, we say, also the necessary spiritual verve to assign worthy commissions to Beckerath's talent is, of course, again a question for themselves."[27] But within less than two years, Warburg was busy obtaining financial support for Beckerath's greatest work.

The artist's turn to monumental wall painting, his approach to its artistic form and content, were rooted in firm convictions about the purposes of art and the enormous tasks facing German artists in particular. He shared, with many cultural critics and commentators, a desire for the moral reform of Germany through the power, virtue and knowledge embodied in art. Amongst his papers is a text entitled "Speech to the Germans" that he prepared in August and September 1911.[28] This was delivered on the site intended for the national Bismarck memorial near Bingerbrück. Taking up ideas voiced as early as the 1870s by Friedrich Nietzsche and popularized by cultural critics such as Julius Langbehn and Paul de Lagarde, it is a spirited and damning indictment of the effects of economic modernization, politicization, bureaucratization, and militarization on the German nation.

Beckerath believed that Germany had lost its soul in 1870, at the Battle of Sedan. Since then, it had nurtured a monster that was now consuming it: "economic interest ... whose obesity we call politics ... and whose flatulence we call patriotism!" Germany had become a society of "producers, entrepreneurs, middlemen, consumers ... statistical numbers, economic entities" guided only by economic self-interest and the dictates of Mammon. The commercialization of cultural goods and the creation of a culture industry meant that art was dominated by businessmen and the need to turn a profit. This had disastrous effects on German culture: the "pure love of art" and "selfless devotion" in its pursuit was now a rare phenomenon replaced largely by the sensationalism of the theater, cinema, and circus. Two years earlier, in 1909, Beckerath had published a lament for the state of contemporary German art that also advocated a way out of this predicament. It appeared in the form of an article written for the journal *Deutsche Kunst und Dekoration*, an enthusiastic supporter of modern trends in painting, sculpture, and architecture.[29] According to Beckerath, since the seventeenth century, German painting had become increasingly separated from its Germanic roots. By the late nineteenth century, it was nothing more than the worthless imitation of foreign art. This degeneration, and the predilection of the nouveau riche, intellectuals, and critics for French art, was described by Beckerath as the death of German national consciousness. It was only an expression of national impotence to suggest that German art must conform to a European standard;

"only national culture," Beckerath insisted, "is of value." These ideas were, of course, not uncommon among the German artistic community, even among the Secession movements. Carl Vinnen, a landscape painter associated with the Worpswede School, gave them expression in a polemical tract entitled *A Protest of German Artists*, which he published in 1911 and to which 118 artists appended their names.[30]

But the solutions that Beckerath proposed to this predicament may surprise those who have been too hasty in typecasting the artist as a mouthpiece for German nationalism, militarism, and imperialism, and those who are suspicious of work painted in a style similar to that favored by the Nazi regime. Without question, Beckerath called for a new German art devoid of foreign influences and propounded a notion of the regenerative power of nationalism as a counteractive force to the supposed degeneration of German culture. He seems also to have believed in the dominance of German *Innerlichkeit* (inwardness) and spirituality over the frivolity and shallowness of French culture. Many practitioners of monumental art similar to Beckerath's, like Fritz Erler and Wolfgang Willrich, did not need to change their style nor their convictions to prosper under Nazi patronage. Franz Stassen, for example, was invited by Hitler to decorate the new Reich Chancellery.[31] Beckerath's depiction, in the School of Art and Industry, of what appears to be a Germanic savior who descends to earth to the adulation of a host of idealized Germanic figures was foreign, even offensive, to the generations of students attending Hamburg's renamed College of Fine Art in the years after 1945. The paintings have suffered as a result: they were removed from the walls of the lecture hall from 1952 to 1956 and were once aggressively attacked with tomatoes. A similar fate has befallen Hamburg's Bismarck memorial which has often been defaced by graffiti.

But Beckerath was not a supporter of Nazism or its immediate antecedents. Although he espoused chauvinist ideas, he was no militarist and quickly became disgusted by the horrors of the First World War. Correspondence with Warburg reveals, instead, liberal political sympathies. Indeed, unlike Warburg, he did not regard the revolution of 1918 as a cataclysm. "I have nothing against the introduction of a German republic," he wrote. "I even consider the republican state as the prerequisite for the establishment of a league of nations and an international legal authority."[32] In 1910, he had written to Warburg that "I am for an international republican constitution." In an attack on the Kaiser, he continued, "The old man may choose for himself a retirement home on a star of the third or fourth rank and leave the business of state to the administration itself."[33] But as for the introduction of a republic, there was an important caveat in his thought: "It depends on which republic should be founded: I reject a republic after the French model, in which bankers and lawyers play the leading roles, as much as a Bolshevik republic in which only the propertyless have political rights."[34] Like other members of the nobility and *Großbürgertum*, what Beckerath wanted most of all was to continue pursuing his old way of life, "family, friends, art, an intellectual life."[35] Under the influence of one of his students, Rudolf Führmann, who belonged to a small group of communist artists in Hamburg—the German Association of Revolutionary Artists—Beckerath produced designs for wall paintings that depict oppressed and revolting workers in the late 1920s.[36]

Ultimately, the artist's solutions for the rejuvenation of German art were based upon active engagement with the exigencies of modern life instead of a return to the past. Like Lichtwark, he believed that German artists must look, not to Rembrandt, as Julius Langbehn would have it, but to the present.[37] The way forward, Beckerath explained, was demonstrated by contemporary applied art and design, with its belief that the only foundation for artistic idealization was "the expedient nature of contemporary life." Recalling ideas to which he had been exposed during his time in Munich, he explained that contemporary German designers were guided by "a modern, that is to say, natural feeling for the function of interior space and its decoration." This was the impetus for a "German program" and Beckerath hoped that "with the growing desire for harmony and the organic extension of the relationship of life's purposes to its forms, painting, as the finest sign of this relationship, will again win control of the walls that it lost in barbarous times." "Only on walls can painting be revitalized," he proclaimed. "Only architecture provides the conditions for this revitalization. The return to architecture is the program, the necessity for German artists." According to Beckerath, it was the "essentially German" Hodler who showed the way.

III

Beckerath's ideas on the mutually supportive connection of painting and architecture were widely shared, most importantly by the painter Richard Meyer (1863–1953), director of Hamburg's School of Art and Industry. Beckerath's biography is closely bound up with the School; he came to Hamburg in 1907 with a strong sense of purpose and a determination to reform German painting. This was reflected in the phrase he adopted as the motto of his pedagogic principles: "to the barricades."[38] His artistic energies climaxed at the School between 1913 and 1918, with his highly controversial cycle of murals for the large lecture hall.

The first decade of the twentieth century was a time of dramatic change for German art schools. Especially in Prussia, Hermann Muthesius (1861–1927)—one of the leading architectural reformers of the time—was instrumental in ensuring that "new principals and new teachers were appointed everywhere."[39] Hamburg's School of Art and Industry was formed as an institution separate from the city's trade school in 1896 and Meyer was appointed as its director in 1905. The new institution's mandate was to offer practical education for artists and craftsmen. At the same time, it was invested with the high hopes of its supporters. Many of these believed that the School would enhance Hamburg's artistic reputation and that it would promote a uniquely German art. This would be showcased to the world, especially in the interior decoration of the many ships built in Hamburg's shipyards.[40] Gustav Schiefler hoped the School would be a model for the "longed-for substitute for the unfruitful overproduction of the pseudoartistic forces of the dilapidated academies."[41] The range of instruction, combining fine and applied arts, gave the School a special position among the mostly trade- and craft-oriented schools of its kind in Germany.[42]

Richard Meyer explained the aims of the School in a memorandum of 1906. In so doing, he echoed the ideals of the international Art Nouveau movement, known in Germany as *Jugendstil*. "The students," he wrote, "should conceive and feel the great unity that is common to all works of art." The School would "bring together what has been separated, will restore harmony among the sister arts of architecture, sculpture, and painting and thereby help to fulfill the great yearning for a German art that will give a transfigured expression to our time."[43] This vision was promoted by Wilhelm Niemeyer (1874–1960), the school's art historian. "We live today," he explained in 1913, "with a unitary concept of all arts … as in the best epochs of ancient art."[44] The form this "German art" would take in Hamburg would be born of various, turn-of-the-century reactions to the eclectic historicism of the nineteenth century: the *Sezessionstil* of Vienna; the *Jugendstil* aesthetic of Munich; the reform movements in the applied arts occurring especially in Munich, Berlin, Weimar, and Darmstadt; and the monumental style of wall painting practiced, most famously, by Hodler. It is true that Hamburg's architecture remained little influenced by impulses like *Jugendstil*, which, in other German cities, was replacing the neo-Renaissance style of the *Gründerzeit* after 1900.[45] But this was not so in painting, sculpture, and design. An important champion of *Jugendstil* artists was the director of Hamburg's Museum of Art and Industry, Justus Brinckmann. Especially through his collection of Japanese prints, Brinckmann influenced Peter Behrens, Hans Christiansen, and Otto Eckmann, artists who made important contributions to the development of a *Jugendstil* aesthetic. In 1900, Brinckmann received 100,000 marks from Hamburg's senate to purchase 400 objects of *Jugendstil* art and design at the World's Fair in Paris. Even now, this collection of fine and decorative *Jugendstil* art is considered to be one of the best in the world.[46]

But Hamburg did not become the "*Jugendstil* center of the German northwest" until, in 1907, Meyer called eleven artists from Vienna, Munich, Leipzig, Darmstadt, Mainz, Friedenau, and Warnsdorf to professorships at the School of Art and Industry.[47] The director turned his particular attention to Vienna, as the city played a prominent role in the avant-garde art movement around 1900. Four of the Viennese Secession's talents answered Meyer's call: in 1907, the sculptor Richard Luksch and the graphic artist Carl Otto Czeschka, both of whom were designers for the *Wiener Werkstätte*; in 1908 the painter Anton Kling; and in 1909, the painter and textile designer Franz Karl Delavilla.[48] Beckerath and the architect and sculptor Friedrich Adler formed the smaller contingent from Munich.

Most of the new faculty members were soon at work decorating the School's new home, a building that Meyer saw as essential to the achievement of its goals.[49] In 1910, Hamburg's senate and citizens' assembly gave almost 2,000,000 marks for the new structure, an indication of the serious and optimistic attitude with which the School's mission was regarded.[50] Erected in the Hamburg suburb of Lerchenfeld, the new building was one of the first designed for the city by the architect Fritz Schumacher, the city's building director from 1909. Conservative by comparison to new trends in German and international architecture, the bulky, cuboid, red-brick structure was a new expression of the style that became known in Hamburg as *Heimatstil.*[51] Construction began in March 1911 and was completed in September 1913.[52] The lecture hall was designed especially for a cycle of decorative wall paintings by Beckerath; to lend preeminence to the paintings, the interior was styled in a neutral fashion and painted in bright gray tones with some of the architectural lines emphasized in black.[53] (Figure 5.1)

Figure 5.1. Fritz Schumacher, Lecture Hall in the School of Art and Industry, Hamburg, 1911-1913. *Source:* The Warburg Institute, London

However, as the School's new home neared completion in 1913, insufficient funds were available to finance the paintings. Beckerath estimated they would cost 20,000 marks.[54] Warburg convinced Schumacher that he was best able to deal with the issues pertaining to the painting of the lecture hall and, consequently, took it upon himself to approach Hamburg's senate and gain its support for the project.[55] In November of 1912, Warburg sent preparatory drawings by Beckerath to Senator Johannes August Lattmann. The senator was immediately won over and pledged 3,000 marks in support of the project.[56] In cooperation with Lattmann and Toni O'Swald, the wife of a prominent merchant, Warburg then set about raising more funds for Beckerath. At his request, M.M. Warburg & Co. established an account to handle personal donations in support of the artist's work.[57] Contributions came both from within and without Hamburg; the Warburgs pledged 1,750 marks for each of three years.[58] Aby Warburg took heart that there were so many willing patrons; "it is quite good that here one can allow 'fair play' to one's artistic talent: otherwise one would have to concur with the lament regarding Hamburg philistinism."[59]

It was decided, with the artist's agreement, to donate the completed murals to the city. A statement to Hamburg's senate dated April 1913 and signed by Warburg, O'Swald, and Lattmann in the name of all the patrons, argued that the decoration of the lecture hall was an opportunity to show off the accomplishments of Hamburg's artistic community. "It would be a valuable artistic gain for Hamburg," they claimed, "to possess a great, unified work by this man."[60] The senate agreed, saying that the members greeted the initiative "with great satisfaction that you have thereby placed the artist in a position to bring his art to full maturity and at the same time produce a distinguished place of noble art for the state."[61] Beckerath chose Warburg to deliver the dedicatory address.

The artist began making preparatory studies for the murals in 1911. The execution on canvas was labor intensive; the elaborate border decoration, for example, with its ever-changing ornament and occasional symbolic content, was not stenciled, but painted by hand. Nonetheless, most of the work was completed by 1 September 1914 when Beckerath was forced to vacate the lecture hall and his atelier upon the School's conversion into a hospital.[62] He would return to complete the paintings early in 1918.[63] But it seems that the work did not go ahead without difficulties, especially between Beckerath and Schumacher.[64] "I will be happy," he wrote in February of that year, "to have this matter behind me. In the end, I have had to summon the utmost of my energy, in order to succeed. The help of my student Danneboorn was, in these circumstances, of great worth. Alone, I would have scarcely completed it. It is less a decreasing interest in the matter as an evident, general consumption of strength that has made completion so difficult for me.'[65]

The murals take their title from a poem which Beckerath's friend, the medical doctor, author, and poet Hans Much (1880–1932), penned to accompany them: "The Eternal Wave."[66] In 1913, Beckerath wrote to Warburg that "all great art is grounded on extra- artistic elements—and that the artist is a fool, if he works in order to produce 'art.' Art has nothing at all to do with art. At its best, art is a result not a motivating force."[67] But Beckerath insisted that "the paintings gave rise to Much's poem—not the other way around."[68] Long before 1918, Much pleaded publicly for private and official support for the artist, believing that the walls of Hamburg's public buildings offered a wonderful opportunity for the city to refute its image as a city hostile to art.[69] Warburg once referred to Much as Beckerath's "shield bearer."[70] Much of what is known of Much today is the result of his involvement with the Hamburg Group, a collection of writers and artists founded in 1925.[71] Much published books on the Gothic art and architecture of north Germany, volumes of poems, accounts of his travels to the Middle East, and descriptions of his encounter with Buddhism. He retained a strong interest in all things spiritual and mystical. Warburg corresponded with Much on art-historical, astrological, and cultural questions. He collected Much's books for his library and a manuscript version of "The Eternal Wave" is preserved among Warburg's papers.[72] Distributed at the dedication ceremony, the poem was to set the mood for the paintings, not to be a literal interpretation thereof. As a result, Beckerath was often at pains to explain the giant figures that he painted on the walls of the lecture hall. Fortunately, the artist recorded the ideas upon which the murals are based and elucidated their content in a letter to Gustav Ophüls of 1918 and a memorandum of 1920.[73]

The paintings gave expression to a conception of history as a process that "does not peak in a pyramid of great perfection, but moves always in horizontal wavelengths with high and low points." Beckerath believed that the history of humanity expressed itself in cultural epochs, great expressions of the human spirit, that rose and fell like waves in an eternally recurring process. Although these overlapped each other, they were also distinct entities in their rise, climax, and decline. In his murals, Beckerath wanted to show the typical course of these cultural waves "reduced to one wave as a prototype." He admitted that his conception of history "stands very much in opposition to modern conceptions of the world based upon historical development, just as, formally, they [the murals] stand in contradiction, indeed even in outspoken opposition, to the leading direction [in art]."

The murals are arranged in a cycle of eight images, deliberately reminiscent of a well-established genre in European art that recounted the times of the day, the seasons of the year, and the ages of man. A celebrated example of this genre was already to be seen in Hamburg in the main staircase of the Kunsthalle, painted by Valentin Ruths and Arthur Fitger in the 1880s. Beckerath's first image depicts the figure of a woman gazing from a height onto a stylized, mystical landscape lit by the first light of dawn. (Figure 5.2) This represents "the first presentiment of the coming evolution to an epoch of spiritual blossoming." But this is only a presentiment; the bound and hooded female of the second image emphasizes the slowness with which "spiritual forces" break their shackles. (Figure 5.3)

Freedom is slowly attained in the third, and larger image which is situated directly above the hall's dais and is divided into two halves. On the left

Figure 5.2. Willy von Beckerath, *Ascent*, oil on canvas, 1918, Hamburg, College of Fine Art. *Source:* Photo by author.

Figure 5.3. Willy von Beckerath, *Bound,* oil on canvas, 1918, Hamburg, College of Fine Art. *Source:* Photo by author.

we see a female figure driving off armed men, or warriors. (Figure 5.4) This illustrates that "reactionary spiritual elements," or "the enemies of culture," "must be overcome before a new growth can establish itself." On the right, a man calls, with "prophetic gestures," to a group of sleeping or slowly waking figures who represent the "arousal of new life forces." (Figure 5.5) "The consciousness of a new epoch has awoken" in the fourth image, where we find a female figure "with the gestures of a person who, after a long period of darkness, sees light again for the first time." (Figure 5.6) This flowering of the human spirit takes the form of a child blossoming from a flower in the fifth image. (Figure 5.7) Two female figures stand and "wonder at this process of the new unfolding of life" in an image strongly reminiscent of the mystical canvases of the Romantic painter, Philipp Otto Runge (1777–1810).

Figure 5.4. Willy von Beckerath, *Annunciation,* oil on canvas, 1918, Hamburg, College of Fine Art, left side. *Source:* Photo by author.

Figure 5.5. Willy von Beckerath, *Annunciation,* oil on canvas, 1918, Hamburg, College of Fine Art, right side.
Source: Photo by author.

Figure 5.6. Willy von Beckerath, *Enlightenment,* oil on canvas, 1918, Hamburg, College of Fine Art.
Source: Photo by author.

Figure 5.7. Willy von Beckerath, *Blossoming,* oil on canvas, 1918, Hamburg, College of Fine Art. *Source:* Photo by author.

The long wall opposite the hall's windows is dominated by the sixth and largest painting in the cycle. Representing "the culmination point—the height of the wave," which is reached with "the appearance of the hero," it is divided into three figural groups. The middle group shows the arrival on earth of "the bearer of light, the genius, the great personality." (Figure 5.8) Suspended as a mediator between the heavenly and earthly realm, this god-like male figure steps from a cloud onto the earth. The halo around the hero's head points to his "mission of reconciliation in the eternal conflict between heavenly and earthly powers." He is flanked by six draped and veiled females who, oblivious to the events around them, "represent the idea—in the Platonic sense—that the genius imparts anew to earthly beings." The group to the left of center depicts male and female figures "in a great crescendo from waking to full consciousness"; they greet the heavenly messenger with joy and jubilation. (Figure 5.9) "The new life—inspired by the sight of the hero—breaks forth with all power"; "the released forces gather around their leader." The group to the right of center illustrates the excitement with which the hero's ideas are received and the way in which they are played out in the world. (Figure 5.10) At the right of this group, an exultant woman on a blue horse represents enthusiasm, passion, and power, without which a significant cultural product cannot be created. But this enthusiasm is held in check by a male figure, representing moderation, who strides before the horse with a restraining gesture that prevents passion from degenerating into unruliness. The trumpeting, herald-like female that flies above hints at the "way to the transcendental—symbolized by the floating on a mantle of stars and the making of music."

Figure 5.8. Willy von Beckerath, *Fulfillment,* oil on canvas, 1918, Hamburg, College of Fine Art, central portion.
Source: Photo by author.

Figure 5.9. Willy von Beckerath, *Fulfillment,* oil on canvas, 1918, Hamburg, College of Fine Art, left side.
Source: Photo by author.

Figure 5.10. Willy von Beckerath, *Fulfillment,* oil on canvas, 1918, Hamburg, College of Fine Art, right side. *Source:* Photo by author.

The creative genius of the human spirit given full expression, the high-point of the cultural epoch attained, the wave begins to sink again. Three dancers bearing golden balls or fruit are seen in the seventh image. (Figure 5.11) They reveal that "the great inspiration, the spiritual movement, already turns to play"; it degenerates into "virtuosic superficiality." The last image depicts two female figures immersing themselves in the sea. (Figure 5.12) "They withdraw themselves from the great disc of the sun that has already half disappeared behind the horizon of the sea." "The trough of the wave has been reached, the cultural movement is over." But as Beckerath explained, "the trough of the wave begins again—and whoever desires, can now begin once more with the first image, sunrise—because it is logically connected to the final image."

Despite Beckerath's qualifications about its usefulness as an interpretation of his murals, Warburg was grateful to Much for his explanations of the ideas that informed Beckerath's work and counted on his support at the dedica-

Figure 5.11. Willy von Beckerath, *Play,* oil on canvas, 1918, Hamburg, College of Fine Art. *Source:* Photo by author.

Figure 5.12. Willy von Beckerath, *Setting,* oil on canvas, 1918, Hamburg, College of Fine Art. *Source:* Photo by author.

tion ceremony.[74] As abstruse and symbolic as the paintings, Much's poem is divided into eight titled sections, each corresponding to an image: "Ascent," "Bound," "Annunciation," "Enlightenment," "Blossoming," "Fulfillment," "Play," and "Setting." Written in the first person, the poem's symbolism relates a cycle of emotions matched to events: yearning, despair, anticipation, and hope for the coming of a "hero" who will dispel darkness and violence; joy, intoxication, and wonder at the descent to earth of one whose "word is direction and instruction." But whereas Beckerath's description of the murals focused more on the workings of impersonal, spiritual forces in the flowering of human creativity, Much's poem stressed an aspect that strikes any observer: that the high point of human creativity is reached only with the coming of a man, "the hero in splendor."

Throughout his career, Beckerath was plagued by self-doubts about his artistic abilities. Shortly after completing the murals, in March 1918, he wrote that "my art is not an essential part of contemporary cultural life—and will also never be an essential part in the future."[75] But in May of that same year he wrote to Ophüls that

I don't imagine that I produced a work of genius and epoch-making significance, because I know well where the limits of my abilities lie. However, I believe I am able to say that the value of this work can, at this time, not yet be appreciated. A contribution to the foundations of future painting has, in any case, been achieved here, and in the future, one will not be able to overlook this foundation stone if one can grasp the particular future development of painting. In my cycle, I play, as it were, the role of the prophet, a task that talent fulfills while genius, upon which it finally depends, must complete the deed. With the completion of this work, I believe I have said the essential things that I was capable of saying. What, for me, still may remain to be done will add nothing important to what is completed. I have, therefore, reached the peaceful endpoint. It is entirely enough to have once summarized all to which the powers extend. I think that whoever was granted the ability to do this has done enough, has fulfilled his duty to mankind.[76]

Beckerath realized that observers could not fail to connect his conception of human history with that espoused by Oswald Spengler (1880–1936) in his book *The Decline of the West*, the first volume of which appeared in 1918. Spengler argued that cultures are moved by an inherent destiny and succeed one another by a process of rise and decline, eventually dying away like individuals.[77] But Beckerath insisted that he could not be accused of plagiarism, as the idea for his murals had arisen ten years previously. Any similarities, he argued, were due to the fact that similar ideas had much currency among contemporaries.[78] Furthermore, he emphasized that his work was not meant to be prophetic in anything but the realm of painting. "It is always a difficult venture," he wrote, "to forecast future world events. The way of fate is not to be calculated, like the course of a star, and in this venture Spengler finally fails—must fail." Moreover, Beckerath did not agree with Spengler's extreme pessimism and his conclusions. Instead, he insisted that he "wanted to paint hope on the walls, which is emphasized to me by my activities as a teacher and the daily contact with promising youth."[79]

IV

The murals were dedicated at an urbane and self-consciously artistic ceremony held in the lecture hall on 23 March 1918. On this occasion, Warburg's audience could not have been more different from the one he had addressed in the Volksheim in 1905. Now he spoke to the city's patrician elite and his guest list illustrates the eminent nature of the those in attendance: Mayor Werner von Melle, Senators Johannes Lattmann and Gottfried Holthusen, the future Mayor Carl Wilhelm Petersen, the judge and author Carl Mönckeberg, the poet Richard Dehmel, the art historian Adolph Goldschmidt, M.M. Warburg & Co.'s legal advisor Carl Melchior, his brother Max Warburg, and many other artists, scholars, and friends of Beckerath.[80] An orchestra opened the ceremony with a performance of the overture and first movement of Bach's Suite in D Major.[81] As the music died, Warburg rose to formally present the paintings to Hamburg's senate.

The majority of his address focused not on Beckerath's subject matter, but on his style.[82] As he had done in his work on Albrecht Dürer, Warburg depicted his friend's art as a response to an age of cultural change. Dürer had been exposed to Italian interpretations of antique art, but had set his own artistic course; "no artistic vanity" had deterred him "from taking the heritage of the past and making it his own."[83] Warburg was enthusiastic about artistic developments in the years before the First World War. These had long been turning from the imitation of visible reality towards the expression of human emotion by means of abstracted line and color. He was aware of and approved of the modern and progressive status to which Expressionist art laid claim or to which it was exalted. But on this occasion he praised Beckerath's symbolism as a courageously independent approach to art and as a demonstration of the "purity of an artistic conscience." "Willy von Beckerath," he said, "has dared to follow his artistic conscience and to swim against the current in the choice of allegorical subject matter and in his formal vocabulary, which strives for clear harmony in outline and color. Without doubt, to use common parlance, that is not 'modern.'" As with his response to the work of Lederer and Vogel, Warburg's assessment of Beckerath's murals was not guided by a concern for the extent to which they were embedded in tradition or the degree to which they participated in a modern spirit. Once again, his judgment was informed by his interest in exploring the oscillations of human consciousness in psychic time.

Warburg spoke to his nonspecialist audience in terms of his scholarly interests. He made it clear that the success or failure of artistic expression was not bound up with a particular style. As previously noted, Warburg did not envision artistic styles evolving according to predetermined laws. "The psychology of style," he writes, "is not the kind of issue that can be forcibly brought to a head by imposing the categories of military and political history."[84] Instead, style was a matter of individual choice and, as such, a symptom of the attitude of the artist. As Gombrich explains, Warburg "saw individuals involved in situations of choice and of conflict. In giving life to a traditional theme, religious or pagan, they had to look for a language, a vocabulary fit to express their vision, and it was this choice that was symptomatic of their personality, its strength or its weakness."[85] We have seen that this was the lens through which Warburg viewed Hugo Vogel's murals in Hamburg's city hall. In 1918, he told his audience that "those who regard the well-ordered, art-historical entry system with its labels for general trends such as 'modern,' 'Gothic,' or 'Impressionistic' only as an auxiliary tool—albeit a justifiable one—will see in such a resistance against the vogue of the day one more reason for striving all the more seriously to enter into the spirit of the artist's work."

Although twenty-first-century viewers may disagree, Warburg did not see Beckerath's art as one of empty rhetoric. "Others may follow another ideal of style," he said of Beckerath. "The essential thing is only that the chosen formal vocabulary brings the spiritual world of figures, in which this artist lives, to exhaustive expression." He told his audience that "apart from the pleasure that his artistry may give us, such an artist who convinces us instinctively that he has found the necessary style for the communication of his visions—be his name Albrecht Dürer or Franz Marc—will help us in our own attempts to grasp the idea of things in their evanescent appearance." Striving to achieve his own style of artistic expression, Beckerath's work bore "the stamp of inner necessity." "When an artist grips us from this side," Warburg said, "we greet him with more than admiration; we greet him with belief!" It was the lack of "inner necessity" and the readiness to submit to artistic fashion that disturbed Warburg when he considered Vogel's frescoes in Hamburg's city hall.

But if Beckerath produced an art of strong emotive power, he also produced work pervaded by rational deliberation; his murals were an art of distance and detachment from the emotive states of their origin. Warburg particularly admired the clarity of Beckerath's forms and figures, these "finely tuned instruments of a symphony." Speaking of the artist's "controlled temperament," he praised his ability to balance imagination and emotion with self-conscious deliberation and abstract thought. Just as he extolled Böcklin's art for standing as a corrective to a materialistic and hyperrationalistic society—a society in which self-conscious contemplation of the world was being threatened by the speed of electro-techni-cal information—Warburg saw Beckerath's murals as an expression of mythical and symbolic thinking that helped sustain *Denkraum*. Like Dürer, Beckerath was a master of that state of consciousness that Warburg hoped would be installed as a permanent social function. This hope motivated his exhibition of Dürer's drawings in the Volksheim in 1905 and informed his positive response to the Bismarck memorial. In a manner similar to these artists, Beckerath's vision was an ethical and human one, and Warburg told Hamburg's patricians that his *Ideenkunst* (art of ideas) would reward the viewer who reflected seriously upon the conceptions to which it gave expression. Referring to a busy thoroughfare, he said that "direct access to the artwork is open to those whose eye lingers, but there is no *Königstrasse* for hurried visitors."

Warburg extolled the murals as an example to be followed by the students and teachers of the School:

> The staff and students of this institution do not need my words to tell them what it means for them that in their hall the purity of an artistic conscience, combined with masterly skill, has created a sphere that demands the effort of leaving humdrum reality behind in order to reach it. But we who are less intimately connected with the school may also be permit-ted to congratulate it and ourselves in the hope of being allowed, at least as spectators, to share in this ascent towards the brighter regions: for the artist and the friend of art meet in the community of the heliotropic, the seekers of light.

Clearly, Beckerath's art was not simply an exercise in escaping "humdrum reali-ty." Nor was it merely a didactic instrument, the product of an enlightened artis-tic conscience to be explained and viewed as a model of self-reflective, rational calm. In 1905, Warburg ascribed the failure of his Volksheim exhibition to the fact that an interpreter was not constantly present to assist the workers' under-standing of the drawings. But to an audience of educated patricians, Warburg did not see the need to act as interpreter. He stated that it was enough for him to indicate the importance of the murals; their essence would become clear to those who contemplated them. In fact, he was afraid of spoiling this contemplation by saying too much.

In his eyes, Beckerath's murals had transformed the lecture hall itself into a calm intellectual space; it was a physical locus of enlightenment and calm reflection in the midst of the passions and chaos of war. The murals were "a monument to peace" that would be "an object of respectful and understanding admiration." In its report on Beckerath's murals, the *Hamburger Fremdenblatt* stated that "we must be thankful that in the midst of wild war, we may continue to bear the properties of culture."[86] But for Warburg, the murals were more than evidence that war-time Germany remained a cultured nation. While he shared Beckerath's understanding of the murals as a message of hope, he also saw them as a way of helping to prepare the ground for German victory. In his address, he stated that Germans should demonstrate their thanks to those who continued to "protect Germany" at the front by dutifully fulfilling their calling "so that those who return will find the ground prepared for the bright future of a strong, victorious Fatherland."

V

The majority of German intellectuals supported their country's cause in the First World War. Much of the enthusiasm for war was founded on a belief that it would be beneficial for a German culture long weakened by the materialist mentality of bourgeois society. Certainly by the fall of 1916, it was clear that this consensus had broken down; the intellectual community split into various factions with pacifist and anti-war views becoming much more evident.[87] But Warburg's diary entries and correspondence reveal that he was not only swept along on a wave of nationalist euphoria in 1914; he remained a stalwart supporter of Germany's cause to the end. His personality was split when it came to the war: he was both a participant in madness and a detached, rational observer thereof.

The entries Warburg made in his diary in August 1914 became more agitated in their script as the month progressed, testifying to his excited state.[88] He believed it was Germany's duty to help Austria in the face of "the unheard-of impudence of the Serbian gang of murderers."[89] He lashed out at the English "hypocrites" for guaranteeing Belgian neutrality and excoriated the Russian "vandals" who had secretly planned to attack Germany. Warburg believed that Germany was waging "a war of independence" for the entire world against Britain. Seeming to set rational contemplation on one side, Warburg quoted the propaganda slogan, "Britannia rules—not the waves—but the slaves."[90] Early in 1915, he wrote to Carl Mönckeberg that "the difference between our war and the war of our enemies is that the Entente powers fight a political war for booty, whilst we fight a people's war to protect the Fatherland." "The stupidity and the disappointed rapacity of our opponents must and will help us to victory in the end."[91]

One of the most disturbing aspects of this patriotic response to the outbreak of hostilities is Warburg's reaction to the German Army's destruction of the Belgian city of Louvain between 25 and 28 August 1914. In a city noted for its High Medieval and Renaissance architecture, two thousand buildings were destroyed including the university library and its 300,000 volumes; most of the city's

42,000 residents were expelled. These events attracted widespread European and American condemnation.[92] But in a letter to Jan Veth dated 2 September 1914, Warburg defended the actions of German soldiers against a civilian population that had shown itself to be hostile. Exclaiming that he was an art historian and "good European," Warburg told Veth that, given the circumstances, he would also have given the order to destroy Louvain. In the same letter he explained that "Germany is fighting a war of desperation for Europe against Asia."[93] We should remember that the actions of the German Army in Belgium were defended by many of the nation's scholars and writers, several with international reputations. Furthermore, it is hard to imagine that Warburg would not have been deeply troubled by the destruction of one of Europe's finest libraries. Thus, while it is disturbing to find a devoted scholar and passionate bibliophile endorsing actions that resulted in such destruction, it is also a measure of the passions that the outbreak of war released on both sides of the conflict.

In September 1914, Warburg met Prince von Bülow and offered to launch a journal to inform Italy of Germany's views on the European situation. The purpose was to prevent Italy's desertion of the Triple Alliance. Edited by Warburg, Georg Thilenius, and Giulio Panconcelli-Calzia, the first of only two issues of *La guerra del 1914–15. Rivista illustrata* appeared in October 1914. The covers of both were designed by Beckerath. Warburg also pressed for the reopening of the German Art-Historical Institute in Florence and presided over its first session in February 1915. Thus when Italy joined the Entente powers in late April 1915, Warburg felt betrayed. On 21 May, he published an anonymous article on the front page of the *Hamburger Echo* entitled "From the Deathbed of the Italian Conscience." Also published by the *Frankfurter Zeitung* and the *Straßburger Post* in the following days, the article gave expression to his disappointment and attacked the author Gabriele D'Annunzio for his support of Italy's entry into the war on the side of the Entente powers.[94] But a letter written to a former assistant, Paul Hübner, expressed his feelings in a vitriolic tone: "Incidentally, I will help to annihilate Italy, however and where I can. This bordello must disappear."[95]

Active in the upper echelons of power, Max Warburg kept a more level head. In 1916, he described the war as follows: "It is not a crusade, not a racial war, not a religious war; it is a war that we fight for the security of our Fatherland, and for the free foreign movement of our labor. We do not want to be dictated to by a state like England in respect of the extent to which we might act in the world."[96] But always critical of government policy and, in particular, unrestricted submarine warfare, he was pessimistic about Germany's chances against the Triple Entente and regarded a war against the United States as hopeless. Instead, he favored a negotiated peace and a shift in the German constitution towards parliamentary government.[97] Yet, like his brother, Max Warburg was also very much influenced by prevailing political and ideological trends. Also in 1916, he argued for the creation of German colonies in the Baltic territories of Latvia and Courland. "The Latvians would be easily evacuated," he suggested. "In Russia, resettlement is not regarded as cruel in itself."[98]

It is interesting to note that the support of Max and Aby Warburg for the German war effort did not diminish in the face of the unequal treatment of Jewish soldiers by the German military and continued anti-Semitism. Before the war, Aby Warburg took an interest in the status of German Jews in the military, especially in relation to their exclusion from the status of reserve officer; newspaper cuttings in his archive attest to this.[99] In the summer of 1916, he had the opportunity to employ this documentation in an act of political intervention. During those months, Max Warburg penned a memorandum entitled "The Jewish Question in the Framework of German Politics"; although Max's name appeared on the completed document, Aby Warburg considered himself to be its co-author.[100] This was distributed by Max Warburg in the official circles of Berlin, including the Foreign Ministry, during November of 1916. Apart from a general dissatisfaction with the government's unequal treatment of German-Jewish soldiers, the Warburg brothers did not document a particular reason for this undertaking. But there can be little doubt that the urgency of such action was heightened by the shock of the Jewish census (*Judenzählung*) of October 1916. This was ordered by senior military officers to demonstrate that Jews were underrepresented in the army and to show that those who were serving their country were avoiding combat duty; it was to provide a pretext for the continued exclusion of Jews from the officer corps after the end of the war. But although it was designed to "reveal the cowardly and disloyal nature of the Jews," the census actually proved that Jews were overrepresented in the army and, in particular, at the front. Consequently, the results of the census were suppressed, but "the knowledge that it had been ordered caused a great deal of anger among German Jews."[101]

Warburg's memorandum begins by stating that the position of Jews in Germany is of extraordinary importance, not simply for Jews, but for the German state. Max Warburg emphasized that he was not speaking out for the purpose of personal gain, nor was he writing as a representative of Jewish interests. Although he emphasized the love of Jews for Germany and stressed their identification with the Empire's war efforts and aims, he made it clear that it was not as a Jew that he was penning the document, but as a "German of the Jewish faith." As a German, and a member of a family who had lived in Germany for at least 300 years—a family "that had honestly and successfully contributed to the development of German business, had given its honest share for art, science, and charity and that had offered its blood sacrifice in the war of 1870/71, as in the present war"—he felt compelled to make Germans aware of the gravity of this issue. His interests were those of the German Empire and his concern was for "a better German realism in domestic affairs and therefore also in foreign ones."

Anti-Semitism was presented by Max Warburg as a matter of religious intolerance, not as an expression of racism; Jews, he explained, were excluded from positions in the military and civil service and prevented from holding high offices of state because of their religious faith. Warburg's idea of the state is that of "a rational agent of mediation standing above interests" and he uses the pronoun "we" to state that Christians and Jews must, out of love for the Fatherland, work together for the benefit of the Empire.[102] In keeping with this belief, Warburg stressed that the *Burgfriede*—the political truce agreed upon in 1914—must be more than simply a war measure; it must become a constant feature of German society; "the *Burgfriede* between Protestants, Catholics, and Jews must not be a superficial truce, but must emerge from the war as a sincere, lasting truce!"

The memorandum argues that equal treatment of Jews by the government and military was of critical importance for Germany in terms of its war effort, the legitimization of this effort, and the Empire's international reputation. Charlotte Schoell-Glass has suggested that the document displays a "blindness for the imperviousness against rational, objective, and moral arguments" displayed by those in the military who supported the census.[103] But it may be more indicative of a stubborn refusal to abandon such arguments than any blindness to their effectiveness. To shut Jews out of positions in the civil service and the military, Warburg claimed, was to deprive the state of talent and resources. "The value of each individual must be assessed and employed according to the interest of the state. That must be the goal." For example, Germany would have had many more competent officers at the outbreak of war if Jews had been awarded commissions. In terms of Germany's war aims, Warburg writes that "we have no right to make Poland independent and to free the oppressed—including millions of Jews—if we do not ourselves demonstrate in our own country that we are also just to Jews who have proved themselves good Germans over generations, because he who is an unjust father to his own children is not suitable as a protector of someone else's." In respect of Germany's international reputation, Warburg states that Germans are falsely denounced as brutal because of their anti-Semitism. Foreign observers maintain that Germany is not a fully developed nation under the rule of law because Jews are not allowed to hold the position of reserve officer. Furthermore, Warburg claimed that the impact that the just treatment of Germany's Jews would have among their co-religionists in other lands would have a positive effect on Germany's image. "One should not undervalue the propaganda," he writes, "that could be made for Germany in this respect." Ultimately, Max Warburg's outlook on the relation of Germans and Jews was positive. In a letter dated 13 June 1916, and again in the memorandum, he makes reference to Zionism and "the international Jewish question," and states that he feels Germany, rather than England or France, was best able to resolve this problem. "Just as anti-Semitism was justified scientifically in Germany," he writes, "the solution of this difficult question, as paradoxical as it sounds, can also be dealt with in Germany."[104]

Unfortunately, there is nothing in the Warburg Institute Archive that provides a sense of the way in which the memorandum was received. Ron Chernow, however, relates that Max Warburg met personally with the War Minister in March 1917 and "pleaded with him to issue a statement that Jews and Christians had fought with equal bravery." The Minister refused to do so.[105] Also unknown are the particulars of Aby Warburg's reaction to the anti-Semitic ideology of the

Fatherland Party. Founded in September 1917 by Grand Admiral Alfred von Tir-
pitz and Wolfgang Kapp with the support of General Erich Ludendorff, this
union of right-wing, nationalist groups blamed Germany's Jews for the loss of the
war.[106] But what is clear is that Warburg suffered horribly under the weight of the
conflict. On one level, he was troubled by the social and economic transformations it brought to Hamburg. The First World War damaged Hamburg's economy more than that of any other German city. An end to trade with Britain, in
particular, meant that shipping lines and merchant houses suffered great capital
losses. As Niall Ferguson has shown, the material demands of war meant that
heavy industry and labor benefited at the expense of the middle classes.[107] But as
Ferguson also suggests, the trauma of deprivation and a decline in living standards
was not confined to the middle classes. The *Burgfriede* of 1914 gave way to the
strikes of 1917 and 1918, which quickened a process of social polarization that
was preparing the way for the revolutionary events of 1918/19.[108] For families of
the *Großbürgertum*, like the Schramms, "dearth was more than just a matter of
physical deprivation; it was a moral and cultural humiliation." "To have to eat
meat-paste made from the Alster swans was symbolic of Hamburg's degradation,"
while buying food on the black market represented a traumatic break with the
principles to which the *Großbürgertum* subscribed before 1914. Although they still
ate with silver spoons, the Schramms took in a lodger during the war years and
closed up the ground floor of their home to save on heating. For Percy Ernst
Schramm, this marked the end of the lifestyle of the *Großbürgertum*.[109]

Yet on a more profound level, the First World War definitively proved to Warburg that barbarism and irrationality did not belong only to the past. Early in the
struggle, he decided to use the weapon he had at hand, his library, in a desperate
effort to understand humanity's descent into unreason.[110] As he wrote to Gustav
Pauli, "we intellectuals must show, at long last, [enough?] Protestant strength in
order to [escape?] from the odium of European foolishness; otherwise, we are
nothing but hangers-on with our fingers on the triggers of bloody frenzy."[111]
These years saw Warburg engaged in the feverish collection and cataloguing of
newspaper articles, pamphlets, brochures, and books—every article of printed
matter that documented the war's major events, worldwide reactions to them,
and the effects of propaganda. In a turmoil of emotion, he sought to combat propaganda and understand the truth. As his sometime student, Carl Georg Heise
relates, "his working space appeared ever more like a battlefield, upon which he
commanded a growing staff of helpers with short, clear orders."[112] He also struck
out once more against Hugo Vogel in respect to a portrait the artist painted of
General Hindenburg.[113] "That the agents of kitsch could have collected themselves from the beginning around H.[indenburg] and L.[udendorff] was to me,
as you know, gravely ominous ... and if H.[indenburg] does not want to be
painted by Liebermann, that is a deep-rooted symptom of the barbarous insensitivity to the value of culture."[114]

When Italy entered the war against Germany, Warburg cut himself loose from
his concern with Italian culture. Henceforth, he sought to apply his knowledge

and experience of political propaganda, acquired during the war years, to another period of crisis in German history, the Reformation. In this undertaking, he shared the view of General Erich Ludendorff who wrote in July 1917 that "the war has demonstrated the paramount power of images and of film as means of enlightenment and influence."[115] The fruits of his investigations were first presented in lectures in the autumn of 1917 and published in 1920 under the title "Pagan-Antique Prophecy in Words and Images in the Age of Luther." As we have noted, in this essay Warburg examined the popular astrological pamphlets and literature of the early sixteenth century. In so doing, he demonstrated how humanists like Melancthon, who aided Germany in its struggle for liberation from the Christian paganism of Rome, were themselves in the grip of superstitious fears with their talk of comets, portents, prophecies, and their belief in astrology. This was yet more proof of the persistence of irrationality in human thought; in demonstrating the polarity of reason and unreason in humanity's psyche, Warburg claimed to be furnishing "new grounds for a more profoundly positive critique of a historiography that rests on a purely chronological theory of development."[116] The hero in modern man's struggle for intellectual emancipation was again presented as Albrecht Dürer, who embodied the contemplation that balances primitive fears and irrational thought processes with rational reflection. Dürer's struggle was the perpetual struggle of humanity; as Warburg phrased it, "Athens must always be conquered afresh from Alexandria."[117] For Warburg, himself descending into the chaos and darkness of mental illness, Beckerath embodied the voice of Athens.

Compared to Warburg, Beckerath was not overly enthusiastic about Germany's participation in the war. Watching the many trains transporting German soldiers through Bad Pyrmont to the front, he noted in a diary entry of 6 August 1914 that "this war will show that war today has become a tool of destruction that shatters the national existence of the victors and the vanquished."[118] He expressed concern at the overindulgence of Germans in the supposed superiority of the German spirit and wrote that it was now a "curse" to have been born a German artist.[119] But when the news of the bombardment of Reims Cathedral reached him on 23 September 1914, concern and criticism turned to bitter disgust with the war and "an unbounded hate for living man." In a dramatic passage, Beckerath expresses his loathing for "dastardly humanity":

> Here dies in me the consciousness of belonging to a nation that is fighting for its existence. Here dies any respect for the living generations—that are ready to crush everything in pursuit of the way of their "civilization" created by the great genius of humanity! No matter who bears the guilt here—according to the assessment of "official" objectivity—the entire living generation cannot be washed clean of the crime, which—whether by accident, whether out of military necessity—was committed here—because it is the spirit of our times, the spirit of our "modern civilization" that no longer cares if it exerts its miserable existence.[120]

Furthermore, Beckerath wanted to propagandize against the Fatherland Party that, in addition to its anti-Semitic ideology, demanded an annexationist peace and was opposed to a negotiated end to the conflict and to all political change. Gaining a large following among the middle classes, and surpassing the Social Democratic Party as a mass movement, the Fatherland Party mobilized support for war aims that were no longer possible in 1918. Beckerath was disturbed by this phenomenon and described the group as "this dangerous organization," noting that "under its influence people seem to take leave of their senses."[121] But he continued to harbor anti-English sentiment and believed that peace could not be achieved if England was not defeated.[122] He wrote to Gustav Ophüls on 1 July 1915 that "it only remains for us to hope that our enemies will thoroughly, and for a long time, learn the meaning of fear. Hopefully our 'organized destruction' will engrave irremovable furrows on the face of this world that speak of fear and horror. With the marks of Cain on its face, the world may then again be proud of its exalted civilization, humanity, and freedom—but at least it will leave us Germans in peace."[123]

But peace was not to be granted to Warburg; the feverish work that he undertook during the war years had a debilitating effect on his body and mind. He suffered from sleeplessness and fear, especially the fear of falling seriously ill; he became increasingly pessimistic, irritable, and bad tempered. The novelist Gustav Hillard describes how, a few months before the end of the war, Warburg came to him in a state of great excitement proclaiming that Hamburg was in imminent danger of an English aerial bombardment. He produced detailed plans for Hamburg's defense including anti-aircraft batteries, bunkers, air raid shelters, observation posts, and signal installations. As Hillard admits, such a massive aerial attack was a technical impossibility in 1918 as were Warburg's elaborate defensive measures.[124] Eerily, Warburg seems to have foreseen the terrible destruction that would be visited on Hamburg by aerial bombardment twenty-five years later, in July 1943. In this state of mind, it is difficult to imagine that he also shouldered the burdens of the conflict that surrounded Beckerath's murals. In September 1918, he wrote to his friend von Eckardt that he was breaking contact with the outside world. He refused to read the newspapers in order "to detach myself and gain some distance from my enemies, contemporary events."[125] Warburg knew he was fighting for his sanity. Finally, in October of that year, he suffered a mental collapse, a fate he long feared would befall him.

It is the chaos of Warburg's mental ailments that has often been suggested as the wellspring of his interest in cultural psychology and, in fact, there can be no doubt that he had a considerable personal investment in his scholarship. But as indicated in chapter one, attempting to draw a definitive causal link between his illness and his theories of art and culture involves much speculation. However, if we remember the turmoil into which Warburg was thrown by the events of the war, it is perhaps not unreasonable to suggest that he had a very personalized vision of Beckerath's art as embodying the voice of reason. In his address, he interpreted "the young hero" descending to earth as the embodiment of "superhuman power taking up the battle against chaos."

VI

Ultimately, Warburg's hopes for the efficacy of Beckerath's murals went unrealized. His dedicatory address assumed unanimous approbation for Beckerath's work among the staff and students of the School of Art and Industry. This, however, was far from the truth: faculty members of the school, especially those giving instruction in painting, boycotted the dedication ceremony in protest. In 1919, Beckerath informed a friend that faculty and students at the school thought his work of little value and made no secret of their opinions.[126] A group of students even called for the removal of the paintings.[127] Depressed, he wrote that he was "completely justified, to preserve my work in folders (and to mount no more exhibitions)."[128]

Of the dedication ceremony, Beckerath wrote that "nature was woven into an exceptionally beautiful spring magic (on the day of the opening), but thoughts of the battle that was simultaneously raging strongly dampened this pleasure."[129] In the summer of 1918, the lecture hall was hired out as an exhibition space. Surrounded by murals that Beckerath and Warburg described in terms of hope and peace, the hall became the venue for a display of propaganda posters by enemy nations entitled "Enemy Propaganda and Warmongering."[130] Beckerath felt slighted and complained that his murals were being neglected. The exhibition and its trappings detracted from the artworks that, as a public monument, he insisted, needed to be properly protected.[131] The murals that Warburg proclaimed would be truly honored as a monument to peace engendered nothing but conflict.

Although information on the issues is incomplete, it seems that much of the strife that surrounded Beckerath's murals had its origins in the power struggles that divided the School's faculty and administration. Those artists who had come to Hamburg from Vienna—Czeschka, Luksch, and Delavilla—soon became known as the "Viennese Clique"; they kept their distance from native Hamburg artists and had no desire to accommodate their art to a uniquely north German style.[132] All continued to work for the *Wiener Werkstätte* while in Hamburg.[133] For their part, members of the Hamburg Artists' Club felt robbed by the newcomers of their leading positions in Hamburg's art establishment; Julius Wohlers and Arthur Illies were never reconciled with the Viennese artists.[134] Furthermore, the native Hamburgers and other faculty members, including Beckerath, complained that Meyer was dominated by the Viennese. The latter faction held the pragmatic Meyer in contempt as less an artist than an administrator. Meyer always felt the "Viennese Clique" sought to depose him for this very reason and he clashed with Wilhelm Niemeyer over the nature of instruction at the school. In 1919, tension boiled over when Meyer's effectiveness as director was called into question because he failed to enlist the painter Ahlers-Hestermann and the architects Walter Gropius and Heinrich Tessenow to the faculty.[135] Exasperated, Meyer explained that he was unable to direct the various artists and their disparate styles in a coordinated effort for the benefit of the School and its students.

He tendered his resignation, believing that the opposition of much of the faculty to Beckerath's murals was opposition to his directorship.[136]

Much to his misfortune, Beckerath seems to have made enemies on both sides. He quarreled bitterly with Niemeyer over the aesthetic value of the brick Gothic architecture of northern Germany.[137] On one occasion, he wrote of Meyer that "this man would be happy if he found men that silently killed me. I am only in the way of the ambition of serving the School of Art and Industry to the world as a perfect Wiener Schnitzel."[138] Beckerath thought the climate at the School so unhealthy that, when he came upon an exceptionally talented young student by the name of Streckenbach, he advised him to escape the School's influence by pursuing his studies in another city. As he was afraid of clashing with Meyer over the issue, he solicited Warburg's assistance as his colleague.[139] Warburg stood firmly on the side of Beckerath against the decorative tendencies of the "Viennese Clique" when he argued that the greatest danger for the School was to concentrate on the purely formal aspects of art. Beckerath's murals, he insisted, "are not enlarged picture postcards; they have grown large in content and form and, therefore, demand respect from the students for their substance and intellectual content, which would not be achieved by the other group of teachers (the Austrians)."[140]

Faced with attacks from within the School, Beckerath and Warburg often confronted an uninterested or hostile press without. The murals attracted little attention at the time of their dedication. Shortly thereafter, Beckerath wrote "I have here a small, but really devoted public—there is no doubt of that. The press appears not to know how they should begin with painting. And so they have kept unanimous silence."[141] This was not entirely true, but nor was the neglect due solely to the preponderance of war news. The short but favorable notice of the murals' dedication that appeared in the *Hamburgischer Correspondent* on 26 March 1918, for example, was preceded by a review of Verdi's "Rigoletto" at the Stadttheatre and two reviews of violin recitals.[142] Warburg had anticipated a critical response on the part of the press, which he labeled "today's mob"; he knew that "today's critical pack of hounds will certainly fall upon him [Beckerath]" and realized the necessity of mustering "art historical specialists" to the artist's support.[143] He readily agreed that Beckerath's murals could be criticized for being overly intellectual in nature.[144] But he was anxious to get favorable press reviews and was not helped by Beckerath's lack of self-promotional skills. Indeed, this deficiency caused Warburg much frustration.[145] Also lamenting the lack of press interest, the architect Martin Haller suggested that "perhaps here the admirers of symbolist art in the manner of Puvis de Chavannes are less numerous than elsewhere, perhaps the inclination for perfect drawing and the most sensitive use of colors is less developed in the local population."[146] But in words penned in 1913, Warburg took a dimmer and typically caustic view of the current state of art appreciation in Hamburg: "The philistines are conducting the successful work of moles; feudal and proletarian incredulity have joined forces against those who seek and those who hope. But we want to fight them."[147]

It is worth noting that the criticism leveled against the murals, both from inside and outside the School, was not informed by an express preference for an art more in tune with German Expressionism. As Beckerath completed his mural cycle, or shortly thereafter, Expressionist murals by Otto Fischer-Trachau, Alfred Ehrhardt, and Karl Kluth were painted in Hamburg.[148] Nonetheless, reviewers analyzed Beckerath's work in terms of its own genre; they compared them to the work of Ferdinand Hodler and found them wanting. In the *Hamburger Nachrichten*, Carl Anton Piper described the murals as "Hodler seen through the temperament of an academic." He could find nothing of great art in them.[149] The *General Anzeiger für Hamburg-Altona* derided the murals as "decorative Symbolism," as an "arts and crafts *Weltanschauung* art."[150] The *Hamburgischer Zeitschrift für Heimatkultur* accused Beckerath of stylistic disunity, of the unsuccessful combination of a decorative and naturalistic approach. Unlike Hodler, it claimed that the figures displayed empty poses that were "laughable." "In his paintings, there is nothing of greatness, nothing of joy or powerful tragedy." "We north Germans," the journal insisted, "demand painterly forms which are full of life, not southern linearity and model-like forms."[151]

Of course, there were several influential figures, in addition to Gustav Pauli, who promoted Expressionist art in Hamburg. These included the art enthusiast and author Gustav Schiefler, who published the first catalogue of Emil Nolde's graphic works, and the independent art historian, author, and lecturer Rosa Schapire (1874–1954) who actively and successfully promoted *Die Brücke* artists.[152] Berlin's Expressionist art movement, *Sturm*, had its most important branch in Hamburg in 1917 and 1918 where Lothar Schreyer was the editor of the Berlin-based journal *Der Sturm*. He organized *Sturm* exhibitions in the galleries of Louis Bock & Son and, in 1917, in the city's art gallery where the works of Lionel Feininger, Wassily Kandinsky, and Paul Klee were exhibited.[153] Founded in 1919, the Hamburg Secession was clearly influenced by Expressionist tendencies.[154]

Warburg's unpublished papers and correspondence reveal little about his engagement with these artistic currents, which, at any rate, was relatively negligible. But what they do suggest quite clearly is that his predilection for Beckerath's art did not result in a negative judgment of German Expressionism as its corollary. Just as he had embraced exponents of Impressionism and Symbolism in the 1890s, Warburg admired the products of Expressionist artists seemingly as much as he did the *Stilkunst*, or late Symbolism of Beckerath. In his opinion, Expressionism was an artistic current to be welcomed as a creative reworking of a cultural tradition and a broadening of humanity's mental range in the service of enlightenment; it was a sophisticated facet of modern German culture. Warburg admired Emil Nolde and met him personally on at least one occasion. When Carl Georg Heise wrote his former mentor about two Nolde paintings he had selected for an exhibition in Hamburg—*Red Clouds* and *Flower Painting with White Lilies*—he asked Warburg not to buy them, as he felt they belonged in a museum.[155] Erwin Panofsky relates that the painting by Franz Marc that Warburg bought around 1916, *"pour épater le bourgeois,"* was entitled *The Blue*

Horses. "It was hanging in the big hall of his private house," he wrote to William Heckscher, "and looked quite harmless according to present-day standards—except that the horses were indeed blue."[156] When the *Hamburger Fremdenblatt* published an article denouncing Futurism, Cubism, and Expressionism, Warburg wrote an angry letter to the paper's editor, Felix von Eckardt.[157] The article lacked respect, he wrote, for those artists "who strove after the distant, invisible goal. No large German newspaper in the Empire would dare to close its mind so shamelessly to the new." "Only here in the provinces," he insisted, could "a thick-nosed and uneducated public still thankfully accept … that empty kitsch (Vogel) is praised."[158] In 1912, an exhibition of Italian Futurist art in Hamburg elicited a letter of censure from Warburg. "As an art historian who is very interested in the problems of the Futurists," he wrote to the organizers,

> I would like to bring it to your attention that the outward furnishing of the local exhibi-
> tion does not satisfy the simplest standards and thus makes it very difficult for the public
> to view the paintings favorably. No effort was made to hang the larger pictures appropri-
> ately: they simply stand on the floor and, what is the worst, a horrible, dirty-yellow wall-
> paper, which clashes strongly with the green-papered baseboard, does not give the artworks
> a neutral background. It is to be very much regretted that the necessary consideration for
> Hamburg's public in these matters has not been taken.[159]

Although we know almost nothing about the particular reasons for his inter-est in Expressionist art, it is possible to speculate about this based on what we have already learned. It hardly needs to be restated that Warburg would not have been attracted by the novelty of a new style, nor would he have been motivated by purely aesthetic considerations. As always, the psychology of artistic expres-sion and a concern for the moral choices made by individual artists as they engaged with the world of preestablished forms and expressive values would have been the principal lenses through which Warburg viewed Expressionist art. As with the art of Böcklin, it is likely that he valued the emotive power and sym-bolic content of Expressionism as an antidote to hyperrationalism and materi-alism. He probably shared the opinion of his sometime academic assistant, Wilhelm Waetzoldt who, as indicated in chapter two, admired the emotive strength of Nolde's color and the way in which his religious images portrayed "passionate ardor." Unlike the work of Hugo Vogel, the art of a painter like Nolde was not an art of apathetic passivity or empty rhetoric; instead, it embod-ied the passion which Warburg believed was an essential component of artistic expression and which, along with rational deliberation, gave shape to *Denkraum.* Waetzoldt also valued the powerful expression wrought by the "con-traction" and "abbreviation of reality" in Nolde's graphic work. This is some-thing that Warburg must have also admired about Expressionist art, and we recall that he approved of the way in which Impressionist painters regarded the real appearance of the world with sharpened vision. The art of Marc and Nolde was not governed by a mimetic impulse that, for Warburg, indicated a lack of self-consciousness and the absence of conceptual abstraction. On the contrary, it was a sophisticated form of symbolic mediation that opened a mental space pervaded by discursive thought.

Warburg's most important commitment to German Expressionism came in his support of Gustav Pauli, who succeeded Lichtwark as director of the Kunsthalle on 1 April 1914.[160] While Warburg insisted that Pauli be nominated to succeed Lichtwark, Wilhelm Bode was shocked by Pauli's appointment, describing him as a "fanatical modernist and Cassirer-trainbearer."[161] Warburg counted Pauli among his close friends and the success of their relationship was due, in large part, to the fact that Pauli was an academic. Unlike Lichtwark, Pauli had acquired a rigorous art-historical education under Anton Springer and Jacob Burckhardt. He had close connections to the art historian Erwin Panofsky and the philosopher Ernst Cassirer, and was committed to building Hamburg's art gallery into "the foremost place for the study of art in Hamburg."[162] As Panofsky once explained it, "for Lichtwark, the creation and understanding of art was the means of getting hold of a culture, for Pauli the possession and knowledge of culture was the self-evident prerequisite for the creation and understanding of art."[163] Amidst the stresses and strains of the war years, Warburg was grateful to have Pauli as a colleague.[164] For his part, Pauli found reading Warburg's work to be a great inspiration and even considered it "a favor of destiny to have met him."[165]

Pauli's directorship was marked by the academic reappraisal of the Kunsthalle's holdings and its conversion into a modern museum. This included the opening of a large new wing in 1919—more properly described as a new building—planned mostly by Lichtwark before his death in 1914. Another important development was the establishment of a department for modern art in which Pauli shifted the gallery's focus to the collection of non-Hamburg artists. This shift was important, as the legacy of Lichtwark's "collection and commission policies, as well as the teaching activity of Hamburg's Artists' Club, ensured that painting in Hamburg remained moderate, figurative, and realistically orientated."[166] The majority of those artists who constituted the Hamburg Secession, for example, formed themselves around the painter Friedrich Ahlers-Hestermann whose work was still very much influenced by the traditions of the Artists' Club.

In 1917, Pauli wrote to Warburg that "some powers must be harnessed for the hall of Expressionist painting with which I would like to conclude (and, in the opinion of Rosa Schapire, certainly also crown) the modern gallery."[167] In 1918, he acquired *The Mandrill* by Franz Marc. This painting was the source of much public controversy and, according to Pauli, daily attracted groups of visitors who debated the picture's legitimacy as a work of art.[168] By the middle of 1919, Pauli had acquired paintings by Max Beckmann, Ernst Ludwig Kirchner, Paula Modersohn-Becker, Edvard Munch, Emil Nolde, and Karl Schmidt-Rottluff.[169] As Oktavia Christ explains, "with the opening of the new building, Hamburg's art gallery could present itself as one of the most modern German museums of its time."[170] Warburg was enthusiastic about these developments. But ultimately, the two men disagreed on the question of Beckerath. In a letter inviting Pauli to the dedication of the murals, Warburg writes, "I know that you do not really like Beckerath's art. All the same, as he embodies the honesty of the artwork in completely exceptional and welcome purity, he appears to me to have a claim on the presence of all decent friends of art."[171]

VII

Warburg's mental collapse would soon remove him from the debates surrounding Beckerath's murals and from Hamburg itself for several years. Despite having reached a low point in self-confidence, Beckerath mounted an exhibition of landscape drawings in Hamburg's Art Association in June 1918. This met with critical success. Carl Müller-Rastatt described Beckerath's abstracted landscapes as the product of a "sensitive personality that, in its artistic visions and the means by which to achieve them, is completely clear-sighted."[172] The reviewer for the *Neue Hamburger Zeitung* even counted Beckerath as part of "the latest tendency in art" that sought to give personal expression to nature.[173] In an earlier review of the exhibition, the same newspaper added that Beckerath's mural cycle in the School of Art and Industry was "the greatest occurrence in Hamburg's art world since the unveiling of the Bismarck memorial."[174] But after 1918, Beckerath devoted most of his time to teaching. He did not begin to work intensively again on his own projects until the late 1920s. In 1928, he founded an artists' association called *Der Block: Neue Hamburger Sezession*, which exhibited for the first time in the Kunsthalle in April 1930. Their program remained in the tradition of the *Deutsche Werkbund*: it advocated the unification of all arts in comprehensive projects and emphasized the functionality of form and the development of art from craftsmanship. In 1928, on the occasion of his sixtieth birthday, Beckerath was celebrated in the *Hamburger Fremdenblatt* as a monumental painter of the first rank and *The Eternal Wave* heralded as the high point of his oeuvre.[175] He retired in 1931 and died in 1938.

As for the School of Art and Industry, it disappointed the hopes of its early supporters. Writing in the early 1920s, Gustav Schiefler's estimation was that the School failed to keep pace with modern developments and had failed to foster a uniquely Hamburg style.[176] If the Viennese artists brought fresh ideas and stimuli to Hamburg in 1907, they remained excessively committed to these to the detriment of the introduction of new styles, indeed, to the point of stagnation. Czeschka, for example, remained true to the style in which he was educated for all of his thirty-six years at the School.[177] In the 1920s, the School boasted modern, but not avant-garde artists. As Christian Weller has shown, despite the fact that Beckerath proved open to stylistic innovation, painting remained firmly in the grip of the Hamburg version of Impressionism and its teachers Arthur Illies, Julius Wohlers, and Eduard Steinbach. The plans articulated by Wilhelm Niemeyer in these years for making the School into a leading force for artistic innovation came to naught.[178]

For his part, Warburg remained a stalwart supporter of Beckerath and what he had achieved in the School of Art and Industry. In 1927, just two years before his death, he wrote his friend and complained about the way in which his paintings had been "so contemptibly treated." He promised Beckerath that he would not hesitate to leap, with all vigor, back into the public eye if private initiative, "from which our republic draws its inner life" was again threatened by "clumsy philistinism."[179]

Notes

1. Warburg Institute Archive, London (hereafter WIA): General Correspondence (hereafter GC): Beckerath to Warburg, 24 December 1910; WIA. GC: Eduard (?) Sack to Warburg, 16 January 1911.
2. Max Warburg, *Aus meinen Aufzeichnungen* (New York, 1952), p. x.
3. WIA. GC: Warburg to Max Warburg, 24 March 1918.
4. See *Willy von Beckerath*, exh. cat. (Munich, Galleria del Levante, September – October 1973); he received very limited attention in Richard Hamann and Jost Hermand, *Stilkunst um 1900* (Berlin, 1967), p. 433f; Susanne Harth, "Werkstättenunterricht und Gesamtkunstwerk," in *Nordlicht: die Hamburger Hochschule für bildende Künste am Lerchenfeld und ihre Vorgeschichte* (Hamburg, 1989), pp. 50, 52, and 54; Christian Weller, "Moderne Zeiten: Reformbestrebungen unter Max Sauerlandt," in ibid, pp. 178 and 186ff.; Hermann Hipp, *Freie und Hansestadt Hamburg: Geschichte, Kultur und Stadtbaukunst an Elbe und Alster* (Köln, 1989), p. 431; Volker Plagemann, ed., *Kunst im öffentlichen Raum: ein Führer durch die Stadt Hamburg* (Hamburg, 1997), p. 84; interestingly, no mention of the artist is to be found in Detlef Heydorn, *Maler in Hamburg, 1886–1945* (Hamburg, 1974) nor in Volker Plagemann, *Kunstgeschichte der Stadt Hamburg* (Hamburg, 1995).
5. A portion of this has been published and translated in Ernst Gombrich, *Aby Warburg: An Intellectual Biography*, 2nd ed. (Chicago, 1986), p. 318f.
6. WIA. Kopierbuch III, 127–129: Warburg to Beckerath, 15 July 1909.
7. WIA. GC: Beckerath to Warburg, 16 July 1910; WIA. GC: Beckerath to Warburg, 26 October 1910.
8. WIA. GC: Beckerath to Warburg, 18 September 1927.
9. A description of the murals is given in Wilhelm Waetzoldt, "Die Wandbilder in Volksheim," *Hamburgischer Correspondent*, 13 October 1910.
10. St.A.H. Bibliothek Z760/1: Wilhelm Hertz, "Neue Kunst im Volksheim," *Monatliche Mitteilungen des Volksheims* 10 (October 1910), u.p.
11. Ibid. Friedrich von Borstel, "Mitteilungen," *Monatliche Mitteilungen des Volksheims* 10 (November 1910), u.p.
12. WIA. III.28.2: Beckerath Frescoes; other notes made by Warburg do not give a clear idea of his attitude toward the murals; see WIA. III.2.1: Zettelkasten 57 (Hamburg), 057 032581–85.
13. Wilhelm Waetzoldt, "Aus Hamburg's Kunstsälen," *Hamburgischer Correspondent*, 8 January 1911.
14. Kurt Stephenson, *Johannes Brahms und die Familie von Beckerath* (Hamburg, 1979); a reproduction of this painting can be found on the frontispiece to Gustav Ophüls, *Erinnerungen an Johannes Brahms* (Berlin, 1921).

15. Georg Habich, "Neue Münchener Interieurs: Willy von Beckerath, Adalbert Niemeyer und Peter Birkenholz," *Die Kunst: Monatshefte für Freie und Angewandte Kunst* 10 (1904), pp. 444 and 446.

16. Beckerath quoted in Otto Kellner, "Willy von Beckerath," in *Willy von Beckerath*, u.p.

17. A. Tscherkoff, "Moderne Schönheit-Propheten," *Beiblatt zur Schönheit* 6, no. 7 (October 1908), p. 37.

18. Archiv für verfolgte Künstler in Hamburg (hereafter AVK). Abschriften aus dem schriftlichen Nachlass von Willy von Beckerath (hereafter Abschriften), p. 6: Beckerath to his mother, 21 January 1915.

19. A detail is illustrated in E.W. Bredt, "Tradition oder Fortschritt?," *Deutsche Kunst und Dekoration*, 22 (1908), p. 35.

20. Tscherkoff, "Moderne Schönheit-Propheten," pp. 306–310; "Von Austellungen und Sammlungen," *Die Kunst: Monatshefte für Freie und Angewandte Kunst* 13 (1906), p. 110.

21. For comparisons to Puvis see Karl Schaefer, "Willy von Beckerath's Wandgemälde in der Bremer Kunsthalle," *Deutsche Kunst und Dekoration* 10 (1906), p. 3; "Von Austellungen und Sammlungen," *Die Kunst* 13 (1906), p. 110.

22. WIA. GC: Beckerath to Warburg, 22 October 1914; see Sharon L. Hirsh, *Ferdinand Hodler* (New York, 1982), pp. 7–54.

23. Alfred Lichtwark, *Briefe an die Kommission für die Verwaltung der Kunsthalle*, 20 vols. (Hamburg, 1917), vol. 17, p. 229.

24. WIA. Kopierbuch V, 261f.: Warburg to Alfred Lichtwark, 18 October 1913.

25. *Jahres-Bericht des Kunstvereins in Hamburg für 1911* (Hamburg, 1911), u.p.

26. Waetzoldt, "Aus Hamburgs Kunstsälen"; a favorable review was also published by Denis Hofmann, "Willy von Beckerath," *Hamburger Fremdenblatt*, 17 January 1911.

27. Heinrich Wallsee, "Willy von Beckerath (Kunstverein)," *Hamburger Nachrichten*, 10 January 1911.

28. AVK. Beckerath file: "Rede an die Deutschen."

29. Willy von Beckerath, "Schüler-arbeiten der Klasse für Wand-malerei an der Kunstgewerbeschule zu Hamburg," *Deutsche Kunst und Dekoration* 24 (1909), pp. 275– 280.

30. See Peter Paret, *The Berlin Secession: Modernism and Its Enemies in Imperial Germany* (Cambridge, Mass., 1980), pp. 182–199.

31. Hamann and Hermand, *Stilkunst um 1900*, p. 368.

32. Beckerath to Gustav Ophüls, 7 November 1918 quoted in Willy von Beckerath and Gustav Ophüls, *Briefwechsel, 1896–1926: Zeugnisse einer geistigen Freundschaft*, ed. Erika Ophüls (Merseburg, 1992), p. 196.

33. WIA. GC: Beckerath to Warburg, n.d; kept with correspondence of 1910.

34. Beckerath to Gustav Ophüls, 7 November 1918 quoted in *Briefwechsel, 1896– 1926*, p. 196.

35. Beckerath to Gustav Ophüls, 26 December 1918 quoted in ibid.

36. See Heydorn, *Maler in Hamburg*, p. 134ff.; an example of Beckerath's designs is illustrated in Weller, "Moderne Zeiten," p. 187.

37. See Beckerath, "Schüler-arbeiten der Klasse für Wand-malerei an der Kunst- gewerbeschule zu Hamburg."

38. AVK. Beckerath file: Beckerath to Hellwag, 7 May 1908.

39. Nikolaus Pevsner, *Pioneers of Modern Design: From William Morris to Walter Gropius* (Harmondsworth, 1991), p. 36.

40. Heinrich E. Wallsee, "Die Kunstgewerbe-Schule zu Hamburg und ihre neuen Lehrer," *Deutsche Kunst und Dekoration* 22 (1908), pp. 1–11.

41. Gustav Schiefler, *Eine Hamburgische Kulturgeschichte*, eds. Gerhard Ahrens, Hans Wilhelm Eckardt, and Renate Hauschild-Thiessen (Hamburg, 1985), p. 153.

42. Harth, "Werkstättenunterricht und Gesamtkunstwerk," p. 52.

43. Meyer quoted in Verena Passarge and Manuela Reiche, "Sehnsucht nach einer deutschen Kunst: Fritz Schumachers Hoschule für bildende Kunst am Lerchenfeld in Hamburg," in

Werner Hofmann et. al. *Zurück in die Zukunft: Kunst und Gesellschaft, 1900 bis 1914* (Hamburg, 1981), p. 123.

44. *Die staatliche Kunstgewerbeschule zu Hamburg* (Hamburg, 1913), p. 13f.
45. Hipp, *Freie und Hansestadt Hamburg*, p. 72.
46. For a list of works purchased see Heinz Spielmann, ed., *Der Jugendstil in Hamburg* (Hamburg, 1965), p. 16; Justus Brinckmann, "Die Ankäufe auf der Weltausstellung Paris 1900," *Der Lotse* 1, no. 35 (1 June 1901), p. 303ff.
47. Heydorn, *Maler in Hamburg*, p. 36.
48. See Susanne Harth, "Wiener Jugendstil an der Hamburger Kunstgewerbeschule," in *Nordlicht*, p. 90f.
49. For the contributions of various artists see Plagemann, ed., *Kunst im öffentlichen Raum*, p. 84f.
50. Passarge and Reiche, "Sehnsucht nach einer deutschen Kunst," p. 124.
51. See Goerd Peschken, "Fritz Schumachers Neubau am Lerchenfeld," in *Nordlicht*, p. 76; Hipp, *Freie und Hansestadt Hamburg*, p. 72.
52. For a discussion of its architecture and interior decoration see Peschken, "Fritz Schumachers Neubau am Lerchenfeld," pp. 73–88.
53. *Die Staatliche Kunstgewerbeschule zu Hamburg*, p. 7.
54. WIA.GC: Beckerath to Warburg, 2 April 1912; ideally, Warburg and O'Swald hoped to be able to provide Beckerath with 10,000 marks for each of three to four years; see WIA. Kopierbuch IV, 301: Warburg to Beckerath, 18 April 1912.
55. WIA. GC: Warburg to Fritz Schumacher, 15 April 1913.
56. WIA. GC: Johannes August Lattmann to Warburg, 17 November 1912; by that point, Warburg, O'Swald, and Much had raised 25,000 marks; see WIA. Kopierbuch IV, 391: Warburg to Johannes August Lattmann, 16 November 1912.
57. WIA. GC: Warburg to Max Warburg, 3 December 1912; WIA. GC: Fritz Warburg to Warburg, 4 December 1912.
58. WIA. GC: Max Warburg to Warburg, 11 December 1912 and 19 December 1912; WIA. GC: Warburg to Max Warburg, 21 December 1912; Warburg's mother and his brother Max donated 500 marks each, while Aby and his brother Fritz both donated 250 marks; see WIA. Kopierbuch IV, 407: Warburg to Fritz Warburg, 6 December 1912.
59. WIA. Kopierbuch IV, 398: Warburg to Henry Budge, 19 November 1912.
60. St.A.H. 111–1 Senat Cl. VII, Lit. He, Nr. 7, Vol. 72, Fasc. 2e, no. 1 and Anlage.
61. Ibid., no. 4: Carl August Schröder to Toni O'Swald, 13 June 1913; see also ibid., no. 3: Carl August Schröder to Beckerath, 13 June 1913.
62. AVK. Abschriften, p. 3: diary entries of 19–20 August 1914.
63. Ibid., p. 6: Beckerath to his mother, 25 February 1918.
64. WIA. GC: Warburg to Fritz Schumacher, 14 March 1918.
65. AVK. Abschriften, p. 6: Beckerath to his mother, 25 February 1918.
66. Hans Much, *Die Ewige Welle* (Hamburg, 1918).
67. WIA. GC: Beckerath to Warburg, 6 March 1913.
68. Beckerath to Gustav Ophüls, 7 May 1918, quoted in *Briefwechsel, 1896– 1926*, p. 175.
69. AVK. Beckerath file: article from an unidentified newspaper, 3 May 1911.
70. WIA. GC: Warburg to Wilhelm Waetzoldt, 19 January 1916.
71. See Rüdiger Schütt, *Bohemiens und Biedermänner. Die Hamburger Gruppe 1925 bis 1931* (Hamburg, 1996), p. 246ff.
72. WIA. III.28.2.10.2: Hans Much, "Die Ewige Welle"; the date of April 17 suggests that this is not Much's original manuscript, but a later copy with two extra stanzas and three altered section titles.
73. AVK. Beckerath file: Beckerath to Gustav Ophüls, 7 May 1918; memorandum dated December 1920. I have drawn heavily upon these in the description that follows.
74. WIA. GC: Warburg to Hans Much, 20 February 1918.
75. AVK. Abschriften, p. 6f: Beckerath to his mother, March 1918.

76. Beckerath to Gustav Ophüls, 7 May 1918 quoted in *Briefwechsel, 1896– 1926,* p. 175.
77. Oswald Spengler, *The Decline of the West,* trans. Charles Francis Atkinson, 2 vols. (New York, 1926).
78. AVK. Abschriften, p. 5: Beckerath to Ferdinand Proehl, 5 December 1920.
79. Ibid.
80. WIA. III.28.2.12: Guest list.
81. The musical contribution to the ceremony was financed, in part, by M.M. Warburg & Co.; see WIA. GC: Warburg to Max Warburg, 16 March 1918; WIA. GC: Max Warburg to Warburg, 18 March 1918.
82. WIA. III.28.2.5: Address on the Occasion of the Unveiling of Murals by W. von Beckerath, Hamburg, Kunstgewerbeschule, 23 March 1918; unless otherwise indicated, the following quotations are taken from this and from the portion translated in Gombrich, *Aby Warburg,* p. 318f.
83. Aby Warburg, "Dürer and Italian Antiquity," in idem, *The Renewal of Pagan Antiquity,* p. 556.
84. Ibid., p. 558.
85. Gombrich, *Aby Warburg,* p. 314f.
86. "Bildereinweihung im Hörsaal der Kunstgewerbeschule," *Hamburger Fremdenblatt,* 24 March 1918.
87. See Wolfgang Mommsen, *Bürgerliche Kultur und Künstlerische Avantgarde, 1870– 1918: Kultur und Politik im deutschen Kaiserreich* (Frankfurt a.M and Berlin, 1995), pp. 117–128.
88. WIA. III.10.3: Tagebuch III (1903–1914): entries for August 1914.
89. WIA. Kopierbuch V, 411ff.: Warburg to Paul Warburg, 28 August 1914.
90. WIA. Kopierbuch VI, 244: Warburg to Miss von Schmidt Pauli, 21 August 1916.
91. WIA. Kopierbuch VI, 62f.: Warburg to Carl Mönckeberg, 20 April 1915.
92. See John Horne and Alan Kramer, *German Atrocities, 1914: A History of Denial* (New Haven and London, 2001), pp. 38–42; John Keegan, *The First World War* (Toronto, 2000), p. 82ff.
93. WIA. Kopierbuch V, 417–18, 421: Warburg to Jan Veth, 2 September 1914.
94. Björn Biester, "Ernst Troeltschs Artikel 'Der Völkerhaß'" (Mai 1915) und die Reaktion von Werner Weisbach, Aby M. Warburg und Wilhelm Dibelius," *Mitteilungen der Ernst-Troeltsch-Gesellschaft* 15 (2002), p. 30.
95. WIA. Kopierbuch VI, 82: Warburg to Paul Hübner, 21 May 1915; also quoted in Ron Chernow, *The Warburgs: The Twentieth-Century Odyssey of a Remarkable Jewish Family* (New York, 1993), p. 176.
96. Max Warburg quoted in Charlotte Schoell-Glass, *Aby Warburg und der Antisemitismus: Kulturwissenshcaft als Geistespolitik* (Frankfurt a.M., 1998), p. 257.
97. Niall Ferguson, *Paper and Iron: Hamburg Business and German Politics in the Era of Inflation, 1897–1927* (Cambridge, 1995), esp. pp. 135–143; see also Warburg, *Aus meinen Aufzeichnungen,* pp. 34–60.
98. Max Warburg quoted in Ferguson, *Paper and Iron,* p. 137.
99. See WIA. IV.68: Jewish Question I, 1900–1914; WIA. IV.69: Jewish Question II, 1916–1927; WIA. IV.70: Antisemitism, Fascism, and National Socialism, 1915–1929.
100. The memo is reprinted in Schoell-Glass, *Aby Warburg und der Antisemitismus,* pp. 256–269; the following quotations from the document are taken from this source.
101. Richard J. Evans, *The Coming of the Third Reich* (New York, 2004), p. 150.
102. Schoell-Glass, *Aby Warburg und der Antisemitismus,* p. 141.
103. Ibid., p. 140.
104. Max Warburg quoted in Schoell-Glass, *Aby Warburg und der Antisemitismus,* p. 135.
105. Ron Chernow, *The Warburgs,* p. 172.
106. See Heinz Hagenlücke, *Deutsche Vaterlandspartei: Die nationale Rechte am Ende des Kaiserreiches* (Düsseldorf, 2001).
107. Ferguson, *Paper and Iron,* p. 141.

108. See Werner Jochmann, "Handelsmetropole des Deutschen Reiches," in *Hamburg: Geschichte der Stadt und ihrer Bewohner*, eds. Werner Jochmann and Hans-Dieter Loose, 2 vols. (Hamburg, 1986), vol. 2, p. 114ff.
109. Ferguson, *Paper and Iron*, p. 135.
110. For a concise account of Warburg's activities during the war see Karl Königsreder, "Aby Warburg im 'Bellevue,'" in *Aby M. Warburg. "Ekstatische Nymphe … trauernder Flußgott": Portrait eines Gelehrten*, eds. Robert Galitz and Brita Reimers (Hamburg, 1995), pp. 74–98.
111. WIA. Kopierbuch VI, 104: Warburg to Gustav Pauli, 11 July 1915.
112. Carl Georg Heise, *Persönliche Erinnerungen an Aby Warburg*, eds. Björn Biester and Hans-Michael Schäfer (Wiesbaden, 2005), p. 57.
113. WIA. Kopierbuch VI, 275: Warburg to Carl Georg Heise, 23 December 1916.
114. WIA. GC: Warburg to Gustav Pauli, 10 October 1918.
115. Erich Ludendorff quoted in Peter Jelavich "German Culture in the Great War," in *European Culture in the Great War: The Arts, Entertainment, and Propaganda, 1914–1918*, eds. Aviel Roshwald and Richard Sites (Cambridge, 1999), p. 42.
116. Aby Warburg, "Pagan-Antique Prophecy in Words and Images in the Age of Luther," in idem, *The Renewal of Pagan Antiquity*, p. 599.
117. Aby Warburg, "Heidnisch-antike Weissagung in Wort und Bild zu Luthers Zeiten," in idem *Gesammelte Schriften. Die Erneuerung der heidnischen Antike: Kulturwissenschaftliche Beiträge zur Geschichte der europäischen Renaissance*, eds. Horst Bredekamp and Michael Diers, 2 vols. (Berlin, 1998), vol. 2, p. 534.
118. AVK. Abschriften, p. 3: diary entry for 6 August 1914.
119. Ibid., p. 4: diary entries for 14 and 21 September 1914.
120. Ibid., diary entry for 23 September 1914.
121. WIA. GC: Beckerath to Warburg, 15 February 1918.
122. Beckerath to Gustav Ophüls, 5 January 1917 quoted in *Briefwechsel, 1896–1926*, p. 156.
123. Beckerath to Gustav Ophüls, 1 July 1915 quoted in ibid., p. 128.
124. Gustav Hillard, *Herren und Narren der Welt* (Munich, 1954), p. 286.
125. WIA. III.2.1: Zettelkasten 50 (Mod. Kst.), 050 027937.
126. Maike Bruhns, "Willy von Beckeraths 'Die Ewige Welle': Voraussetzungen, Rezeption und Spurensuche", unpublished typescript (Hamburg, n.d.), p. 3.
127. St.A.H. Bestand Berufsschulbehörde 1, Akte D 315: Antrag des Direktors um Entlassung aus seinem Amte (Richard Meyer) Hamburg, den 17. Juni 1919; the paintings were removed from the lecture hall between 1952–56, but are now to be seen in their original location.
128. AVK. Abschriften, p. 6f: Beckerath to his mother, March 1918.
129. Ibid.
130. "Hamburger Chronik," *Die Literarische Gesellschaft* 4, no. 6 (1918), p. 213f.
131. WIA. GC: Beckerath to Fritz Schumacher, 5 June 1918.
132. Schiefler, *Hamburgische Kulturgeschichte*, p. 152.
133. Harth, "Wiener Jugendstil an der Hamburger Kunstgewerbeschule," p. 92.
134. Ibid., p. 105.
135. Harth, "Werkstättenunterricht," p. 69.
136. St.A.H. Bestand Berufsschulbehörde 1, Akte D 315.
137. Ibid.; see also WIA. GC: Warburg to Wilhelm Waetzoldt, 19 January 1916.
138. WIA. GC: Beckerath to Warburg, 16 July 1910.
139. WIA. GC: Beckerath to Warburg, 15 February 1914.
140. WIA. Kopierbuch VI, 363: Warburg to Eugen Petersen, 29 March 1918.
141. Beckerath to Gustav Ophüls, 14 April 1918 quoted in *Briefwechsel, 1896–1926*, p. 173.
142. "Die Wandbilder der Kunstgewerbeschule," *Hamburgischer Correspondent*, 26 March 1918; favorable reviews also appeared in "Hamburg," *Die Literarische Gesellschaft* 4, no. 6 (1918), p. 215f; "Bildereinweihung im Hörsaal der Kunstgewerbeschule," *Hamburger Fremdenblatt*, 28

March 1918; Wolfgang von Oettingen, "Monumentale Gemälde in Hamburg," *Der Tag*, 10 July 1918.

143. WIA. GC: Warburg to Gustav Pauli, 14 February 1918.

144. WIA. GC: Warburg to Fritz Schumacher, 14 February 1918; some reviews highlighted the difficulty of understanding the murals; see Heinrich E. Wallsee "Hamburg," *Kunstchronik* 29 (3 May 1918), p. 311f.

145. WIA. GC: Warburg to Dr. H. Merck, 28 June 1918 and 2 July 1918.

146. WIA. IV.86: Public Activities, 1912–1918: Martin Haller to Walter Dammann, 15 May 1918.

147. WIA. Kopierbuch V, 261f.: Warburg to Alfred Lichtwark, 18 October 1913.

148. Bruhns, "Willy von Beckeraths 'Die Ewige Welle.'"

149. Carl Anton Piper, "Willy von Beckerath," *Hamburger Nachrichten*, 20 June 1918.

150. "Willy v. Beckeraths Wandgemälde in der Hamburger Kunstgewerbeschule," *General Anzeiger für Hamburg-Altona*, 26 March 1918.

151. W. Spanier, "Professor von Beckeraths Wandgemälde in der Aula der hiesigen Kunstgewerbeschule," *Hamburgische Zeitschrift für Heimatkultur* 9, no. 1/2 (1919), p. 3f.

152. For Rosa Schapire see Schiefler, *Eine Hamburgische Kulturgeschichte*, p. 302; Edith Oppens, *Der Mandrill: Hamburgs zwanziger Jahre* (Hamburg, 1969), p. 97ff.

153. Roland Jaeger and Cornelius Steckner, *Zinnober: Kunstszene Hamburg, 1919–1933* (Hamburg, 1983), pp. 10 and 13.

154. See the *Katalog der ersten Ausstellung der Hamburgischen Sezession*, exh. cat. Hamburg, January 1920.

155. WIA. GC: Carl Georg Heise to Warburg, 16 June 1916; see also WIA. GC: Warburg to Felix von Eckardt, 19 July 1916 where Warburg refers to "Nolde's genius."

156. Erwin Panofsky quoted in William S. Heckscher, "The Genesis of Iconology," in idem, *Art and Literature: Studies in Relationship* (Baden-Baden, 1985), p. 271, nt. 43; Heckscher illustrates the painting, p. 279, fig. 3 and writes that it passed into the collection of Peter Braden, Warburg's son-in-law, before being sold on the Swiss art market.

157. The article which raised Warburg's ire is "Dülberg-Ausstellung in Kunsthaus Bock," *Hamburger Fremdenblatt*, 10 January 1907.

158. WIA. GC: Warburg to Felix von Eckardt, 11 January 1917; see also WIA. GC: Warburg to Felix von Eckardt, 19 July 1916 in which Warburg complains about another article pandering to the "brutal ignorance of the Philistine."

159. Aby Warburg quoted and translated in Heckscher, "The Genesis of Iconology," p. 271, nt. 43; see WIA. GC: Gesellschaft zur Förderung moderner Kunst to Warburg, 6 July 1912 where the exhibition's organizers explain that the artists insisted that their large paintings stand on the floor.

160. See Oktavia Christ, "Vom Erbe Lichtwarks zum 'Museum einer Weltstadt': die Hamburger Kunsthalle unter Gustav Pauli," in *Hamburger Kunsthalle: Bauten und Bilder*, eds. Uwe M. Schneede and Helmut R. Leppien (Leipzig, 1997), pp. 78–92; Siegfried Salzmann, "Gustav Pauli und das moderne Kunstmuseum," in *Avantgarde und Publikum: zum Rezeption avantgardistischer Kunst in Deutschland, 1905–1933*, ed. Henrike Junge (Cologne, Weimar, and Vienna, 1992), pp. 235–242.

161. WIA. Kopierbuch V, 341: Warburg to Newman, 5 February 1914; WIA. GC: Wilhelm Bode to Warburg, 15 February 1914; Warburg also thought that Wilhelm Reinhold Valentiner (1880–1958) should not go unconsidered for the post; making his name as a Rembrandt scholar, the German-born Valentiner was a curator at the Metropolitan Museum of Art in New York from 1908 and was responsible for promoting German Expressionist painters to two generations of American collectors; see WIA. Kopierbuch V, 339: Warburg to Wilhelm Bode, 4 January 1914.

162. *Jahresbericht der Kunsthalle zu Hamburg für 1914*, quoted in Christ, "Vom Erbe Lichtwarks," p. 79; the art gallery was first declared an academic institution by Hamburg's government in 1921, when its administration was assumed by the Hochschulbehörde.

163. Panofsky quoted in Oppens, *Der Mandrill*, p. 86.
164. Kopierbuch VI, 210f.: Warburg to Kautzsch, 31 March 1916.
165. WIA. GC: Gustav Pauli to Warburg, 31 May 1915 and 19 November 1915.
166. Plagemann, *Kunstgeschichte der Stadt Hamburg*, p. 329; see also *Katalog der ersten Ausstellung der Hamburgischen Secession*.
167. WIA. GC: Gustav Pauli to Warburg, 12 December 1917.
168. See Oppens, *Der Mandrill*, p. 90f.
169. A comprehensive list is to be found in "Die 'Kunst der Lebenden' in Deutschen Museen," *Das Kunstblatt* 8 (August 1919), pp. 235–239.
170. Christ, "Vom Erbe Lichtwarks," p. 82.
171. WIA. GC: Warburg to Gustav Pauli, 14 February 1918.
172. Carl Müller-Rastatt, "Kunstverein in Hamburg: Willy von Beckerath," *Hamburgischer Correspondent*, 31 May 1918.
173. Hans Leip, "Zeichnungen Willy von Beckeraths im Kunstverein," *Neue Hamburger Zeitung*, 5 June 1918.
174. "Von der Ausstellung des Künstlervereins im Kunstverein, Kunsthalle," *Neue Hamburger Zeitung*, 12 April 1918.
175. Heinrich Ehl., "Willy von Beckerath, ein Monumentalmaler in Hamburg: zu seinem 60. Geburtstage am 28. September," *Hamburger Fremdenblatt*, 27 September 1928.
176. Schiefler, *Hamburgische Kulturgeschichte*, pp. 147 and 152.
177. See Weller, "Die zwanziger Jahre am Lerchenfeld. Vom expressionistischen Aufbruch zur Zigarettenreklame," in *Nordlicht*, pp. 155–160.
178. Ibid., p. 141.
179. WIA. GC: Warburg to Beckerath, 22 September 1927.

CONCLUSION

After an extended period of mental illness, Aby Warburg returned to Hamburg in 1924 to find the city transformed by war and revolution. The Social Democrats, who denounced the construction of the city's Bismarck memorial in 1906, now governed in conjunction with a portion of the traditional elites.[1] With much of the Wilhelmine order swept away, the arts flourished as never before; the shock of war and revolution, and the introduction of a democratic constitution, fostered a spirit of hope and renewal that encouraged artistic experimentation, especially among the younger generation.[2] This is not to say that Hamburg's cultural life was dominated by avant-garde artists during the 1920s: despite the successes of Expressionist theater, much of what appeared on Hamburg's stages was drawn from a conventional repertoire; the artists' association founded in 1919 as the Hamburg Secession was criticized for being too tame; and the city's musical life was little influenced by contemporary trends. Furthermore, monetary inflation meant that private patronage of the arts actually decreased. And yet the level of state sponsorship increased dramatically, as Hamburg's government established a centralized cultural authority for the first time in its history. A special commission was established by the senate that, from 1920, offered prizes and grants and commissioned works of art from Hamburg's writers, composers, painters, and sculptors. The state also helped pay the salaries of the philharmonic orchestra, rebuilt the Stadttheater into one of the most technologically advanced opera houses in Europe, and enabled the Art Association to mount exhibitions in its own facilities. As a result, Hamburg became "the scene of a stirring cultural life."[3]

This image of transformation in the 1920s is in keeping with a perspective in historical scholarship that sees the Weimar Republic, not the German Empire, as synonymous with the flowering of modern German culture. Such thinking emphasizes the profound impact of the First World War and the establishment of a republican government on Germany's creative imagination. But increasingly, historians are challenging the extent to which the events of 1918/19 marked a

Notes for this section begin on page 223.

point of rupture and new beginning for German arts and letters; it is becoming more common to emphasize the personal, institutional, and stylistic continuities within German culture between the 1890s and early 1930s.[4] This book is intended as a contribution to an ever-growing body of research demonstrating that, contrary to previous prejudices, Hamburg was the site of cultural activity, cultural change, and new developments in the two decades before 1914. Of course, scholars may question the extent to which any of this was avant-garde and the degree to which a taste for innovation in the arts was disseminated among Hamburg's middle classes. But while acknowledging the enormous impact of the First World War on German culture, it would be misleading to construe the events of 1918/19 as an unqualified point of cultural rupture and new beginning for Hamburg and Germany.[5] As Matthew Jeffries contends, the 1920s witnessed a transformation in "the context of cultural production and consumption," but not a change "in personnel, or in style."[6] Shaped by industrialization, urbanization, and the rise of mass politics, the German Empire also spawned revolutions in painting, architecture, literature, and music that had an impact far beyond its national borders.

Much of the vitality of this cultural life was the result of middle-class initiatives. In chapter five, we noted that Warburg once characterized Hamburg's cultural climate in the following terms: "feudal and proletarian incredulity have joined forces against those who seek and those who hope. But we want to fight them."[7] It is not known if the expression "feudal and proletarian" is to be read literally and, consequently, if Warburg was referring to the German middle classes with the phrase "those who seek and those who hope" and with the pronoun "we." Yet it is entirely possible that this remark was intended as a succinct expression of a mindset prevalent among the *Bürgertum*: that they, and not the aristocracy or proletariat, were the purveyors of a modern German culture. Despite his constant criticism of the German bourgeoisie and its lack of cultural sophistication, Warburg clearly believed in its potential and necessary role as the cultural arbiter of the German Empire. So did influential elements of Hamburg's patrician elite who, motivated by politico-cultural opposition to the Imperial aesthetic fostered in Berlin, were prepared to experiment with artistic form and iconography in the building of public artworks.

Yet it would be an exaggeration to suggest that these artworks are proof that Hamburg's elite was coming to terms with the entire spectrum of artistic modernity in the early years of the last century. Instead, their histories support the more modest, but nonetheless significant claim made by Thomas Nipperdey that even when it proceeded haltingly, "modern art prevailed not despite the middle class, but in conjunction with it."[8] The cultural policies of Hamburg's *Bürgertum* through the seventeenth to the twentieth centuries may sometimes have resulted in stagnation, decline, or even destruction, but they also repeatedly stimulated reform and renewal. Of course, just as they did not form a unitary front in opposition to working-class politicization, the members of Hamburg's middle classes responded in various and conflicting manners to artistic modernism. The cultural landscape revealed by the history of the monuments examined in this book points to the way in which this encounter with cultural innovation brought Hamburg's middle classes into conflict with themselves. But what the preceding chapters have attempted to capture is the spirit—both cultural and political—behind the creation of some of the most important monuments constructed in the German Empire. No matter their failings in the eyes of historians or twenty-first century observers, the building of these public artworks illustrates that Hamburg's cultural life was no stranger to innovation and debate during the Wilhelmine age.

Aby Warburg took an active role in much of this activity and was in no way a hermetic scholar. This book has often emphasized the complexity of his thinking on the nature of artistic expression, and has examined the particulars of the scholarly perspective from which he engaged with the issues of his day. In addition to their idiosyncratic nature, Warburg's ideas are highly contestable and this book has attempted to describe his thinking without endorsing it. Yet while emphasizing the sophisticated and nuanced nature of Warburg's thought, we might direct our attention to one particular passage as expressing an essential aspect of the disposition that underlay his engagement with art in Hamburg's public realm. In the address he gave to mark the dedication of Willy von Beckerath's murals in the School of Art and Industry in 1918, Warburg spoke of the artist as a seeker of light. This idea is found in much of his thinking on art, from notations on the psychology of artistic expression penned in the 1880s and 1890s to opinions expressed in "Images From the Region of the Pueblo Indians of North America," the lecture he prepared early in 1923. In the latter, Warburg emphasized that

> we, however, do not want our imagination to fall under the spell of the serpent image, which leads to the primitive beings of the underworld. We want to ascend to the roof of the worldhouse, our heads perched upwards in recollection of the words of Goethe: "If the eye were not of the sun / It could not behold the sun." All humanity stands in devotion to the sun. To claim it as the symbol that guides us upward from nocturnal depths is the right of the savage and the cultivated person alike.[9]

In the broadest sense, this was the spirit that animated his response to the topical issues of materialism, hyper-rationalism, cultural transformation, political displacement, and social strife, which exercised many of the members of his generation in Hamburg and the German Empire.

Seen in broad perspective, Warburg's life and work open a window onto the world in which he lived. His attitude to the multiple and varied processes of modernization roughly approximates a cultural stance among Germany's middle classes which has been labeled "ambivalent modernism." Marion Deshmukh describes the concept as follows: "a type of turn of the century modernism echoed by many cultural and intellectual figures, such as Julius Meier-Graefe, Friedrich Naumann, and Walter Rathenau. It can be described as a generally positive outlook toward the rapidly changing social, economic, and scientific

German landscape, but tempered by an occasional nostalgic regard for features of a preindustrial community."[10] And yet, in Warburg's case, the politically, socially, and culturally conservative aspects of his thinking amounted to more than a mere "nostalgic regard" for the past.

Such a mixed response to political, social, and cultural modernization was not uncommon and Aby Warburg's biography serves to emphasize the complexity of the society in which he lived. In its exploration of this complexity, recent scholarship on Imperial Germany has even challenged the usefulness of a binary model of "tradition" and "modernity" for analyzing historical change in the *Kaiserreich*. Of course, the very nature of modernization has long been disputed by scholars, and one influential argument has stated that it did not simply consist of "the substitution of one set of attributes for another … but rather in their mutual interpenetration and transformation."[11] This perspective has evoked a productive response among historians of modern Germany and has been identified as continuing to shape an avenue of advance for future research. Kevin Repp, for example, has demonstrated that those middle-class reform movements that sought to stamp the German Empire with their own values and aesthetic sense were just as comfortable with the discourse of cultural despair—which denounced the destruction of *Kultur* by mechanistic *Zivilisation*—as they were with the discourse of progressive optimism.[12] A recent collection of essays on the legacies of Wilhelminism has described the deconstruction of "the long-established dichotomous framework of 'modernizing economy' and 'backward political culture'" as "one of the pressing needs of Wilhelmine historiography"; the editors advocate the unpacking of "the heterogeneous meanings of 'the modern.'"[13] With these perspectives in mind, Aby Warburg's life and work does more than simply enrich the scholarly image of the *Kaiserreich*; it also highlights the problems of conceiving of "tradition" and "modernity" in Imperial Germany—and in any society— in terms of mutual exclusivity.

Notes

1. See Ursula Büttner, *Politische Gerechtigkeit und sozialer Geist: Hamburg zur Zeit der Weimarer Republik* (Hamburg, 1985).
2. See Roland Jaeger and Cornelius Steckner, *Zinnober: Kunstszene Hamburg, 1919–1933* (Hamburg, 1983), p. 7; Edith Oppens, *Der Mandrill: Hamburgs zwanziger Jahre* (Hamburg, 1969).
3. Jaeger and Steckner, *Zinnober*, p. 7.
4. See Matthew Jeffries, *Imperial Culture in Germany, 1871–1918* (Houndmills, 2003).
5. For a similar argument see Birgit-Katharine Seemann, *Stadt, Bürgertum und Kultur: Kulturelle Entwicklung und Kulturpolitik in Hamburg von 1839 bis 1933 am Beispiel des Museumswesen* (Husum, 1998), p. 209f.
6. Jeffries, *Imperial Culture in Germany*, p. 264.

7. WIA. Kopierbuch V, 261f.: Warburg to Alfred Lichtwark, 18 October 1913.
8. Thomas Nipperdey, *Wie das Bürgertum die Moderne fand* (Berlin, 1988), p. 63.
9. Aby Warburg, *Images From the Region of the Pueblo Indians of North America*, trans. Michael P. Steinberg (Ithaca and London, 1995), p. 51f.
10. Marion F. Deshmukh, "'Politics is an art': The Cultural Politics of Max Liebermann in Wilhelmine Germany," in *Imagining Modern German Culture, 1889–1910*, ed. Françoise Forster-Hahn (Washington, 1996), p. 167.
11. Dean Tipps quoted in Matthew Jefferies, *Politics and Culture in Wilhelmine Germany: The Case of Industrial Architecture* (Oxford and Washington, 1995), p. 4; see also Dean Tipps "Modernization Theory and the Comparative Study of Societies: A Critical Perspective," *Comparative Studies in Society and History* 15 (1973), pp. 199–266; Anthony Smith, *The Concept of Social Change: A Critique of the Functionalist Theory of Social Change* (London, 1973).
12. Kevin Repp, *Reformers, Critics and the Paths to German Modernity: Anti-Politics and the Search for Alternatives, 1890–1914* (Cambridge, Mass. and London, 2000).
13. Geoff Eley and James Retallack eds., *Wilhelminism and Its Legacies: German Modernities, Imperialism, and the Meanings of Reform, 1890–1930* (New York and Oxford, 2003), p. 6.

BIBLIOGRAPHY

Archival Sources

I. Hamburg: Staatsarchiv der Freien und Hansestadt Hamburg.

St.A.H. 111–1. Senat Cl. VIII Lit. Fc. Nr. 11, Vol. 12d, Fasc. 6c. Acta des Herrn Bürgermeister Dr. Burchard, betr. die künstlerische Ausstattung des großen Rathaussaales, mit einigen Senatsaktenstücken, 1897–1902.

St.A.H. 111–1. Senat Cl. VII Lit. Fc. Nr. 11, Vol. 12c, Fasc. 20. Rathaus: Ein vollständige Sammlung sämtlicher gedrückter Verhandlungen zwischen Senat und Bürgerschaft betr. den Rathausbau, 1868–1902.

St.A.H. 111–1. Senat Cl. VII Lit. Fc. Nr. 21, Vol. 17, Fasc. 5. An den engeren Ausschuß für die Errichtung eines Bismarck-Denkmals in Hamburg: Bericht des Ausführungs-Comités, erstattet im Januar 1899.

St.A.H. 111–1. Senat Cl. VII Lit. He. Nr. 7, Vol. 72, Fasc. 2e, nos. 1 and Anlage, 3 and 4.

St.A.H. 322–1. Rathausbaukommission 165: Die Ausmalung des großen Festsaales, 1894–1899, No. 19.

St.A.H. 322–1. Rathausbaukommission 172a Bd. 1: Malerische Ausschmückung des großen Festsaales durch Prof. Hugo Vogel, 1900–02.

St.A.H. 322–1. Rathausbaukommission 172c Bd. 1: Malerische Ausschmückung des großen Festsaales durch Prof. Hugo Vogel, 1906–10.

St.A.H. 361–6. Hochschulwesen – Dozenten – und Personalakten, II, 474: Aby Warburg.

St.A.H. 361–2. Oberschulbehörde V 434b Bd. I nos. 2, 4, 5, 6, 13, 16, 17, 20, 21, 23, 24, 27, 28.

St.A.H. 368–1. Berufschulbehörde I B 505 No. 14.

St.A.H. 614–3/8. Bismarck-Denkmal-Comité A3 Bd. 1: Schriftwechsel und Aufzeichnungen des beratenden Beamten der Ball – Deputation; darin Preisausschreiben, 1898–1900.

St.A.H. 614–3/8. Bismarck-Denkmal-Comité A3 Bd. 2: Schriftwechsel und
Aufzeichnungen des beratenden Bauten der Baudeputation; darin
Preisausschreiben, 1902–1906, No. 2.

St.A.H. 614–3/8. Bismarck-Denkmal-Comité A4: Erläuterungen zu einzelnen
Wettbewerbsentwürfen.

St.A.H. 621–1. HAPAG – Reederei. 2656: Verträge und Vereinbarungen zu
Schiffsneubauten. Bd. 3 D: Imperator.

St.A.H. Bestand Berufsschulbehörde 1, Akte D 315.

St.A.H. Bibliothek A507/32: "Das Volksheim in Hamburg: Jahresberichte
1901–1911."

St.A.H. Bibliothek Z760/1: Monatliche Mitteilungen des Volksheims.

St.A.H. Zeitungsausschnittsammlung A143: Rathaus, Hamburg bis 1945.

St.A.H. Zeitungsausschnittsammlung A144: Bismarck-Denkmal.

St.A.H. Zeitungsausschnittsammlung A752: v. Beckerath, Willy.

St.A.H. Zeitungsausschnittsammlung 517: Kunstverein.

II. Hamburg: Hamburgisches Welt-Wirtschafts-Archiv.

HWWA. Abteilung Bibliothek. A9n2/2. *Jahresbericht der Detaillistenkammer zu
Hamburg für 1905–1913.*

III. Hamburg: Warburg Haus: Archiv für Verfolgte Künstler in Hamburg.

AVK. Willy von Beckerath file.

IV. London: Warburg Institute Archive.

WIA. FC (Family Correspondence)

WIA. GC (General Correspondence)

WIA. III.2.1. Zettelkästen

WIA. III.10. Notebooks-Diaries, 1894–1918.

WIA. III.17.2. "Warburgismen," collected by Max Adolph Warburg.

WIA. III.26. Poems and Dramatic Sketches, 1893–1900.

WIA. III.27. Contemporary Art I, 1900–1901.

WIA. III.28. Contemporary Art II.

WIA. III.43. Grundlegende Bruchstücke zu einer pragmatischen Ausdruckskunde
(monistischen Kunstpsychologie).

WIA. III.44. Grundlegende Bruchstücke zur Psychologie der Kunst, 1888–1901.

WIA. III.45. Symbolismus als Umfangsbestimmung, 1896–1901.

WIA. III.49. Leonardo Lectures, I. Hamburg, 1899.

WIA. III.50. Leonardo Lectures, II. Hamburg, 1899–1901.

WIA. III.60. Dürer and Antiquity, 1905.

WIA. IV.10. Mitteilungen des Senats über den Rathausbau, 1–13, 1872–1909.

WIA. IV.30. Art: Press-Cuttings.

WIA. IV.32. The Bismarck Monument in Hamburg by H. Lederer.

WIA. IV.36. Hamburg-Amerika Linie, HAPAG (Imperator and Vaterland).

WIA. IV.47. Volksheim, Hamburg.

WIA. IV.68. Jewish Question I, 1900–1914.

WIA. IV.69. Jewish Question II, 1916–1927.

WIA. IV.70. Antisemitism, Fascism, and National Socialism, 1915–1929.

WIA. IV.86. Public Activities, 1912–1918.

Published Primary Sources

I. Books, Catalogs, Journal Articles.

Avenarius, Ferdinand. "Hugo Vogel und die Weltausstellung." *Kunstwart* 22, no. 23 (September 1909), pp. 279–280.

_____."Wie's gemacht wird." *Der Kunstwart* 16, no. 3 (November 1902), pp. 143–144.

Bauer, Curt. "Die Wandgemälde Hugo Vogels im Hamburgischen Rathaus." *Der Türmer* (December 1909), p. 473–475.

Beckerath, Willy von. "Schüler-arbeiten der Klasse für Wand-malerei an der Kunst- gewerbeschule zu Hamburg." *Deutsche Kunst und Dekoration* 24 (April-September, 1909), pp. 275–280.

Beckerath, Willy von, and Gustav Ophüls. *Briefwechsel, 1896–1926: Zeugnisse einer Geistigen Freundschaft.* Ed. Erika Ophüls. Beiträge zur Rheinischen Musikgeschichte, vol. 146. Merseburger, 1992.

Brandis, Otto. "Kaiserliche Kunst." *Der Lotse* 2, no. 14 (4 January 1902), pp. 420–423.

Bredt, E.W. "Tradition oder Fortschritt?" *Deutsche Kunst und Dekoration* 22 (1908), pp. 35–38.

Brinckmann, Justus. "Die Ankäufe auf der Weltausstellung Paris 1900." *Der Lotse* 1, no. 35 (1 June 1901), pp. 303–306.

Fuchs, Georg. "Zeitgemäße Betrachtungen zum hamburger Wettbewerb." *Deutsche Kunst und Dekoration* 5 (April 902), pp. 347–362.

Graul, Richard. *Die Wandgemälde des großen Saales im Hamburger Rathaus: die Entwürfe von Gehrts und Geselschap: das Ergebnis des allgemeinen deutschen Wettbewerbs: Umgestaltung des Saales: die Ausführung von Hugo Vogel.* Leipzig, 1909.

Grautoff, Otto. "Deutsche Kultur." *Der Lotse* 1, no. 20 (16 February 1901), pp. 650–653.

Gurlitt, Cornelius. "Bismarcks Denkmal in Hamburg." *Der Lotse* 2, no. 16 (18 January 1902), pp. 481–483.

_____. "Über Denkmalskunst." *Der Lotse* 2, no. 17 (25 January 1902), pp. 519–520.

Habich, Georg. "Ein letzter Besuch bei Böcklin." *Der Lotse* 2, 28 (12 April 1902), pp. 31–37.

_____. "Neue Münchener Interieurs: Willy von Beckerath, Adalbert Niemeyer und Peter Birkenholz." *Die Kunst: Monatshefte für Freie und Angewandte Kunst* 10 (1904), pp. 443–448.

"Hamburg." *Die Literarische Gesellschaft* 4, no. 6 (1918), pp. 215–216.

"Hamburger Bismarck-Denkmal." *Der Lotse* 2, no. 15 (11 January 1902), pp. 1–4.

"Hamburger Chronik." *Die Literarische Gesellschaft* 4, no. 6 (1918), pp. 213–214.

Hofmann, Albert. "Der Wettbewerb zur Erlangung von Entwürfen für ein Bismarck- Denkmal in Hamburg." *Deutsche Bauzeitung* 36, nos. 6–8 and 10 (18 January – 1 February 1902), pp. 33–37; 41–43; 45–50; 57–59.

Illies, Arthur. *Aus Tagebuch und Werk, 1870 bis 1952.* Ed. Kurt Illies. Hamburg, 1981.

"Imperator und Vaterland." *Der Kunstwart* 26, no. 19 (1 July 1913), pp. 67–68.

Jahres-Bericht des Kunst-Vereins in Hamburg für 1911. Hamburg, 1911.

Jahresbericht der Kunsthalle zu Hamburg für 1914. Hamburg, 1914.

Jessen, Peter. "J. Liberty Tadd's Neue Wege zur Kunsterziehung." *Der Lotse* 1, no. 22 (2 March 1901), pp. 737–741.

Katalog der ersten Ausstellung der Hamburgischen Sezession. Hamburg, 1920.

"Die 'Kunst der Lebenden' in Deutschen Museen," *Das Kunstblatt* 8 (August 1919), pp. 235–239.

Langbehn, Julius. *Rembrandt als Erzieher: von einem Deutschen.* Leipzig, 1890.

Lichtwark, Alfred. *Das Bildnis in Hamburg.* 2 vols. Hamburg, 1898.

_____. *Briefe an die Kommission für die Verwaltung der Kunsthalle.* 20 vols. Hamburg, 1920.

_____. *Briefe an Max Liebermann.* Hamburg, 1947.

_____. "Denkmaeler." *Pan* 3, no. 2 (1897), pp. 105– 107.

_____. *Drei Programme.* Berlin, 1902.

_____. *Hamburg: Niedersachsen.* Dresden, 1897.

_____. *Julius Oldach.* Hamburg, 1899.

_____. *Makartbouquet und Blumenstrauß.* Munich, 1894.

_____. *Palastfenster und Flügelthür.* Berlin, 1899.

_____. "Wünsche." *Der Lotse* 1, no. 1 (6 October 1900), pp. 3–7.

Melle, Werner von. *Das Hamburgische Staatsrecht.* Hamburg and Leipzig, 1891.

Mönckeberg, Carl. "Ankundigung." *Der Lotse* 1, no. 1 (6 October 1900), pp. 1–3.

Much, Hans. *Die Ewige Welle.* Hamburg, 1918.

Muschner, Georg. "Das Hamburger Bismarck-Denkmal." *Deutsche Kunst und Dekoration* 10 (1906), pp. 113–121.

Naumann, Friedrich. *Form und Farbe.* Berlin-Schöneberg, 1909.

Ophüls, Gustav. *Erinnerungen an Johannes Brahms.* Berlin, 1921.

Poschinger, Heinrich von, *Fürst Bismarck und seine Hamburger Freunde.* Hamburg, 1903.

Die Preisgekrönten Entwürfe zum Bismarck-Denkmal für Hamburg. Hamburg, 1902.

Pudor, Heinrich. "Wie baut man volkstümlich in Berlin?" *Der Lotse* 2, no. 16 (18 January 1902), pp. 483–486.

Schaefer, Karl. "Willy von Beckerath's Wandgemälde in der Bremer Kunsthalle." *Deutsche Kunst und Dekoration* 10 (1906), pp. 1–10.

Scheffler, Karl. Berlin: *Ein Stadtschicksal*. Berlin 1910.

_____. "Begas und Bismarck." *Der Lotse* 1, no. 39 (29 June 1901), pp. 411–415.

_____. "Berlin als Kunststadt." *Der Lotse* 2, no. 9 (30 November 1901), pp. 257–263.

_____. "Bismarcks Denkmal." *Der Lotse* 2, no. 17 (25 January 1902), pp. 513–519.

_____. "Max Klinger." *Der Lotse* 2, no. 38 (21 June 1902), pp. 329–335.

_____. *Moderne Baukunst*. Berlin, 1907.

Schiefler, Gustav. "Arnold Böcklins künstlerischer Nachlaß." *Der Lotse* 2 (1902), pp. 204–208.

_____. *Eine hamburgische Kulturgeschichte, 1890–1920: Beobachtungen eines Zeitgenossen*. Eds. Gerhard Ahrens, Hans Wilhelm Eckardt, and Renate Hauschild-Thiessen. Veröffentlichungen des Vereins für Hamburgische Geschichte, vol. 27. Hamburg, 1985.

Seelig, Geert. "Von der hamburgischen Regierung." *Der Lotse* 1, no. 27 (6 April 1901), pp. 14–19.

Spanier, W. "Professor von Beckeraths Wandgemälde in der Aula der hiesigen Kunstgewerbeschule." *Hamburgische Zeitschrift für Heimatkultur* 9, no. 1/2 (1919), pp. 3–4.

Spengler, Oswald. *The Decline of the West*. Trans. Charles Francis Atkinson. 2 vols. New York, 1926.

Die staatliche Kunstgewerbeschule zu Hamburg. Hamburg, 1913.

Tscherkoff, A. "Moderne Schönheit-Propheten." *Beiblatt zur Schönheit* 6, no. 7 (October 1908), pp. 306–310.

"Von Austellungen und Sammlungen." *Die Kunst: Monatshefte für Freie und Angewandte Kunst* 13 (1906), pp. 105–118.

Wallsee, Heinrich E. "Hamburg." *Kunstchronik* 29, no. 29 (3 May 1918), pp. 311–312.

_____. "Die Kunstgewerbe-Schule zu Hamburg und ihre neuen Lehrer." *Deutsche Kunst und Dekoration* 22 (April-September 1908), pp. 1–11.

_____. "Die Wandmalereien Hugo Vogels im Hamburger Rathaus." *Die Kunst für Alle* 24, no. 21 (1 August 1909), pp. 489–496.

Warburg, Aby M. *Ausgewählte Schriften und Würdigungen*. Ed. Dieter Wuttke. Saecula Spiritalia, vol. 1. Baden-Baden, 1979.

_____. *Gesammelte Schriften: Die Erneuerung der heidnischen Antike. Kulturwissenschaftliche Beiträge zur Geschichte der europäischen Renaissance*. Eds. Horst Bredekamp and Michael Diers. Berlin, 1998.

_____. *Images from the Region of the Pueblo Indians of North America*. Ed. Michael P. Steinberg. Ithaca and London, 1995.

_____. "Italian Art and International Astrology in the Palazzo Schifanoia in Ferrara." *German Essays On Art History*. Ed. Gert Schiff. Trans. Peter Wortsman. New York, 1988, pp. 234–254.

_____. "A Lecture On Serpent Ritual." Trans. W.F. Mainland. *Journal of the Warburg and Courtauld Institutes* 2 (1939), pp. 277–292.
_____. *The Renewal of Pagan Antiquity: Contributions to the Cultural History of the European Renaissance.* Trans. David Britt. Los Angeles, 1999.

II. Newspapers.

Berliner Tageblatt. 15 June 1909.
Deutsche Welt. 10 June 1906.
General Anzeiger für Hamburg-Altona. 26 March 1918.
Hamburgischer Correspondent. 1 February 1901; 17, 19 and 21 January 1902; 22 January 1909; 14 June 1909; 6–7 March 1910; 17 February 1910; 13 October 1910; 6 December 1910; 8 January 1911; 28 January 1913; 26 March 1918; 31 May 1918.
Hamburger Echo. 1 June 1906; 4 July 1909.
Hamburger Fremdenblatt. 2 February 1901; 22 January 1902; 10 January 1907; 24 January 1909; 15 June 1909; 13 July 1909; 25 July 1909; 17 January 1911; 24 March 1918; 28 March 1918; 27 September 1928.
Hamburger Nachrichten. 1 February 1901; 22 January 1902; 5 January 1908; 13–14 June 1909; 10 January 1911; 20 June 1918.
Die Hamburger Woche. 17 June 1909.
Illustrierte Zeitung. 24 June 1909.
National Zeitung. 16 June 1909.
Neue Hamburger Zeitung. 14 June 1909; 21 June 1909; 5 June 1918; 12 April 1918.
Der Tag. 10 July 1918.
Vossische Zeitung. 14 June 1909.

SECONDARY SOURCES

Alings, Reinhard. *Monument und Nation: das Bild vom Nationalstaat im Medium Denkmal – zum Verhältnis von Nation und Staat im deutschen Kaiserreich, 1871–1918.* Berlin and New York, 1996.
Andree, Rolf. *Arnold Böcklin: die Gemälde.* Basel and Munich, 1977.
Applegate, Celia. *A Nation of Provincials: The German Idea of Heimat.* Berkeley, 1990.
Bartmann, Dominik. *Anton von Werner: zur Kunst und Kunstpolitik im deutschen Kaiserreich.* Berlin, 1986.
Bauer, Franz J. *Bürgerwege und Bürgerwelten: familienbiographische Untersuchungen zum deutschen Bürgertum im 19. Jahrhundert.* Göttingen, 1991.
Bauerle, Dorothee. *Gespenstergeschichten für Ganz Erwachsene: ein Kommentar zu Aby Warburgs Bilderatlas, Mnemosyne.* Münster, 1988.
Berlin, Jörg and Rainer Hering. "Vor 85 Jahren: Einweihung des Bismarck-Denkmals 1906." *Hamburg Macht Schule* 3, no. 6 (1991), pp. 26–27.
Biester, Björn. "Ernst Troeltschs Artikel 'Der Völkerhaß' (Mai 1915) und die Reaktion von Werner Weisbach, Aby M. Warburg und Wilhelm Dibelius." *Mitteilungen der Ernst-Troeltsch-Gesellschaft* 15 (2002), pp. 21–34.

Bing, Gertrude. "A.M. Warburg." *Journal of the Warburg and Courtauld Institutes* 28 (1965), pp. 299–313.

_____. "The Warburg Institute." *The Library Association Record* 1, no. 1 (August 1934), pp. 262–266.

Blackbourn, David, and Richard J. Evans, eds. *The German Bourgeoisie: Essays on the Social History of the German Middle Class from the Late Eighteenth to the Early Twentieth Century*. London and New York, 1991.

Blackbourn, David, and Geoff Eley. *The Peculiarities of German History*. Oxford and New York, 1984.

Bolland, Jürgen. *Die Hamburgische Bürgerschaft in Alter und Neuer Zeit*. Hamburg, 1959.

Bracker, Jörgen. *Hamburg von den Anfängen bis zur Gegenwart: Wendemarken einer Stadtgeschichte*. Hamburg, 1987.

Brandt, Heinz-Jürgen. *Das Hamburger Rathaus: eine Darstellung seiner Baugeschichte und eine Beschreibung seiner Architektur und künstlerischen Ausschmückung*. Hamburg, 1957.

Bredekamp, Horst, Michael Diers, and Charlotte Schoell-Glass, eds. *Aby Warburg: Akten des internationalen Symposions, Hamburg, 1990*. Weinheim, 1991.

Brosius, Christiane. *Kunst als Denkraum: zum Bildungsbegriff von Aby Warburg*. Pfaffenweiler, 1997.

Bruch, Rüdiger vom, Friedrich Wilhelm Graf, and Gangolf Hübinger, eds. *Kultur und Kulturwissenschaften um 1900: Krise der Moderne und Glaube an die Wissenschaft*. Stuttgart, 1989.

Bruhns, Maike. "Willy von Beckeraths 'Die Ewige Welle': Voraussetzungen, Rezeption und Spurensuche." Unpublished typescript, Hamburg, n.d.

Burckhardt, Lucius, ed. *The Werkbund: History and Ideology*. Woodbury, N.Y., 1980.

Burleigh, Michael and Wolfgang Wippermann. *The Racial State: Germany, 1933–1945*. Cambridge, 1991.

Büttner, Ursula. *Politische Gerechtigkeit und sozialer Geist: Hamburg zur Zeit der Weimarer Republik*. Hamburg, 1985.

Campbell, Joan. *The German Werkbund: The Politics of Reform in the Applied Arts*. Princeton, 1978.

Carey, Frances, and Anthony Griffiths. *The Print in Germany, 1880–1933: The Age of Expressionism*. London, 1984.

Cecil, Lamar. *Albert Ballin: Business and Politics in Imperial Germany, 1888–1918*. Princeton, 1967.

Chapple, Gerald and Hans H. Schulte, eds. *The Turn of the Century: German Literature and Art, 1890–1915*. Bonn, 1981.

Chernow, Ron. *The Warburgs: The Twentieth-Century Odyssey of a Remarkable Jewish Family*. New York, 1993.

Chickering, Roger. *Karl Lamprecht: A German Academic Life, (1856–1915)*. Atlantic Highlands, N.J., 1993.

Crew, David F., ed. *Nazism and German Society, 1933–1945*. London and New York, 1994.

Didi-Huberman, Georges. *L'image survivante: Histoire de l'art et temps des fantômes selon Aby Warburg*. Paris, 2002.

Diers, Michael, ed. *Porträt aus Buchern: Bibliothek Warburg und Warburg Institute, Hamburg, 1933, London*. Hamburg, 1993.

_____. *Warburg aus Briefen: Kommentare zu den Kopierbüchern der Jahre 1905–1918*. Schriften des Warburg-Archivs im kunstgeschichtlichen Seminar der Universität Hamburg, vol. 2. Weinheim, 1991.

_____. "Warburg and the Warburgian Tradition of Cultural History." *New German Critique* 22 (1995), pp. 59–73.

Donandt, Rainer. "Auf der Suche nach "modernem" staatlichem Repräsentationsstil: Hugo Vogels Monumentalgemälde im Hamburger Rathaus." M.A. diss., University of Hamburg, 1996.

Doren, Alfred. "Aby Warburg und sein Werk." *Archiv für Kulturgeschichte* 1 (1931), pp. 1–25.

Eckardt, Hans Wilhelm. "Bücher und Geschichte: zur Entwicklung der Gesellschaft der Bücherfreunde zu Hamburg." *Zeitschrift des Vereins für Hamburgische Geschichte* 74/75 (1989), pp. 177–188.

_____. *Privilegien und Parlament: die Auseinandersetzung um das allgemeine und gleiche Wahlrecht in Hamburg*. Hamburg, 1980.

Eley, Geoff. *From Unification to Nazism: Reinterpreting the German Past*. Boston, 1986.

_____, ed. *Society, Culture, and the State in Germany, 1870–1930*. Ann Arbor, 1996.

_____, and James Retallack, eds. *Wilhelminism and Its Legacies: German Modernities, Imperialism, and the Meanings of Reform, 1890–1930*. New York and Oxford, 2003.

Ettlinger, Leopold D. "Kunstgeschichte als Geschichte," *Jahrbuch der Hamburger Kunstsammlungen* 16 (1971), pp. 7–19.

Evans, Richard J. *The Coming of the Third Reich*. New York, 2004.

_____. *Death in Hamburg: Society and Politics in the Cholera Years, 1830–1910*. Oxford, 1987.

_____. *Rethinking German History: Nineteenth-Century Germany and the Origins of the Third Reich*. London, 1987.

_____ ed. *Society and Politics in Wilhelmine Germany*. London, 1978.

Farrer, David. *The Warburgs: The Story of a Family*. New York, 1974.

Feist, Peter H. *Geschichte der deutschen Kunst, 1848–1890*. Leipzig, 1987.

Ferguson, Niall. *Paper and Iron: Hamburg Business and German Politics in the Era of Inflation, 1897–1927*. Cambridge, 1995.

Ferretti, Silvia. *Cassirer, Panofsky and Warburg: Symbol, Art and History*. Trans. Richard Pierce. New Haven and London, 1989.

Ferris, David, ed. *The Cambridge Companion to Walter Benjamin*. Cambridge, 2004.

Flach, Sabine, Inge Münz-Koene, and Marianne Streisand, eds. *Der Bilderatlas im Wechsel der Künste und Medien*. Munich, 2005.

Forster, Kurt W. "Aby Warburg's History of Art: Collective Memory and the Social Mediation of Images." *Daedalus* 105 (1976), pp. 169–176.

Forster-Hahn, Françoise, ed. *Imagining Modern German Culture, 1889–1910.* Studies in the History of Art 53. Washington, 1996.

Gaethgens, Thomas W., ed. *Künstlerischer Austausch / Artistic Exchange: Akten des XXVIII. Internationalen Kongresses für Kunstgeschichte, Berlin, 1992.* Berlin, 1993.

Galitz, Robert, and Brita Reimers, eds. *Aby M. Warburg.: "Ekstatische Nymphe . . . . trauernder Flußgott": Portrait eines Gelehrten.* Schriftenreihe der Hamburgischen Kulturstiftung 2. Hamburg, 1995.

Gall, Lothar. *Bürgertum in Deutschland.* Berlin, 1989.

_____. *Stadt und Bürgertum im 19. Jahrhundert.* Munich, 1990.

Gall, Lothar, and Dieter Langewiesche, eds. *Liberalismus und Region: zur Geschichte des deutschen Liberalismus im 19. Jahrhundert.* Munich, 1995.

Gay, Peter. *Freud, Jews and Other Germans: Masters and Victims in Modernist Culture.* New York, 1978.

_____. *Pleasure Wars.* New York and London, 1998.

_____. *Weimar Culture: The Outsider as Insider.* New York and Evanston, 1968.

Ghandchi, Sabina. "Die Hamburger Künstlerin Mary Warburg, geb. Hertz: Werkliste." M.A. diss., University of Hamburg, 1986.

Gilbert, Felix. "From Art History to the History of Civilization: Gombrich's Biography of Aby Warburg." *Journal of Modern History* 44 (1972), pp. 381–391.

Gombrich, Ernst H. *Aby Warburg: An Intellectual Biography.* 2nd ed. Chicago, 1986.

Grape, Wolfgang. *Roland: die ältesten Standbilder als Wegbereiter der Neuzeit.* Hürtgenwald, 1990.

Grolle, Joist, ed. *Das Rathaus der Freien und Hansestadt Hamburg.* Hamburg, 1997.

Grüttner, Michael. *Arbeitswelt an der Wasserkante: Sozialgeschichte der Hamburger Hafenarbeiter, 1886–1914.* Göttingen, 1984.

Grzimek, Waldemar. *Deutsche Bildhauer des zwanzigsten Jahrhunderts: Leben, Schulen, Wirkungen.* Wiesbaden, 1969.

Guidi, Benedetta Cestelli, and Nicholas Mann, eds. *Photographs at the Frontier: Warburg in America, 1895–1896.* London, 1998.

Habermas, Jürgen, ed. *Observations on the Spiritual Situation of the Age.* Cambridge, Mass., 1984.

Hagenlücke, Heinz. *Deutsche Vaterlandspartei: Die nationale Rechte am Ende des Kaiserreiches.* Düsseldorf, 2001.

Hamann, Richard and Jost Hermand. *Impressionismus.* Munich, 1973.

_____. *Naturalismus.* Munich, 1973.

_____. *Stilkunst um 1900.* Berlin, 1967.

Hardtwig, Wolfgang. *Nationalismus und Bürgerkultur in Deutschland, 1500–1914.* Göttingen, 1994.

Hardtwig, Wolfgang, and Harm-Hinrich Brandt, eds. *Deutschlands Weg in die Moderne: Politik, Gesellschaft und Kultur im 19. Jahrhundert.* Munich, 1993.

Hardtwig, Wolfgang, and Hans-Ulrich Wehler, eds. *Kulturgeschichte Heute.* Göttingen, 1996.

Haas, Stefan. *Historische Kulturforschung in Deutschland, 1880–1930: Geschichtswissenschaft zwischen Synthese und Pluralität.* Cologne, Weimar, and Berlin, 1994.

Hauschild-Thiessen, Renate. *Bürgermeister Johann Georg Mönckeberg.* Hamburgische Lebensbilder in Darstellungen und Selbstzeugnissen 1. Hamburg, 1989.

——. *Bürgerstolz und Kaisertreue: Hamburg und das Deutsche Reich von 1871.* Hamburg, 1979.

Heckscher, William S. *Art and Literature: Studies in Relationship.* Ed. Egon Verheyen. Baden-Baden, 1985.

Heise, Carl Georg. *Persönliche Erinnerungen an Aby Warburg.* Eds. Björn Biester and Hans-Michael Schäfer. Wiesbaden, 2005.

Hellfeld, Mattias von. *Die Nation erwacht: zur Trendwende der deutschen politischen Kultur.* Cologne, 1993.

Hering, Rainer. "Kutscher und Kanzler: der Bau des Hamburger Bismarck-Denkmals im Spiegel der Vigilanzberichte der Politischen Polizei." *Hamburgische Geschichts- und Heimatblätter* 13 (1993), pp. 38– 48.

Heydorn, Volker Detlef. *Maler in Hamburg, 1886– 1945.* Hamburg, 1974.

Hexelschneider, Erhard. *Kultur als einigendes Band? Eine Auseinandersetzung mit der These von der "einheitlichen deutschen Kulturnation."* Berlin, 1984.

Hillard, Gustav. *Herren und Narren der Welt.* Munich, 1954.

Hipp, Hermann. *Freie und Hansestadt Hamburg: Geschichte, Kultur und Stadtbaukunst und Elbe und Alster.* Cologne, 1989.

Hirsch, Erika. *Jüdisches Vereinsleben in Hamburg bis zum Ersten Weltkrieg: jüdisches Selbstverständnis zwischen Antisemitismus und Assimilation.* Frankfurt a.M., Berlin, Bern, New York, Paris, and Vienna, 1996.

Hobsbawm, Eric, and Terence Ranger, eds. *The Invention of Tradition.* Cambridge, 1999.

Höhns, Ulrich, ed. *Das ungebaute Hamburg: Visionen einer anderen Stadt in architektonischen Entwürfen der letzten hundertfünfzig Jahre,* Hamburg, 1991.

Hofmann, Werner, Georg Syamken, and Martin Warnke. *Die Menschenrechte des Auges: über Aby Warburg.* Frankfurt a.M., 1980.

Hofmann, Werner, Manfred Sack, Hermann Hipp, and Armin Sandig. *Zurück in die Zukunft: Kunst und Gesellschaft, 1900 bis 1914.* Hamburg, 1981.

Hohendahl, Peter, ed. *Patriotism, Cosmopolitanism, and National Culture: Public Culture in Hamburg, 1700–1933.* Amsterdam and New York, 2003.

Horne, John and Alan Kramer. *German Atrocities, 1914: A History of Denial.* New Haven and London, 2001.

Hurd, Madeleine. *Public Spheres, Public Mores and Democracy: Hamburg and Stockholm, 1870–1914.* Ann Arbor, 2000.

Iggers, Georg. *The German Conception of History: The National Tradition of Historical Thought from Herder to the Present.* Middletown, Conn., 1983.

In Pursuit of Beauty: Americans and the Aesthetic Movement. Exh. cat. New York, The Metropolitan Museum of Art, 23 October 1986 – 11 January 1987.

Iversen, Margaret. "Retrieving Warburg's Tradition." *Art History* 16 (1993), pp. 541–553.

Jaeger, Roland and Cornelius Steckner. *Zinnober: Kunstszene Hamburg, 1919–1933*. Hamburg, 1983.

Jeffries, Matthew. *Imperial Culture in Germany, 1871–1918*. Houndmills, 2003.

———. *Politics and Culture in Wilhelmine Germany: The Case of Industrial Architecture*. Oxford and Washington, 1995.

Jelavich, Peter. *Munich and Theatrical Modernism: Politics, Playwriting, and Performance, 1890–1914*. Cambridge, Mass., 1985.

Jenkins, Jennifer. "The Kitsch Collections and *The Spirit in the Furniture*: Cultural Reform and National Culture in Germany." *Social History* 21, no. 2 (May 1996), pp. 123–141.

———. "Provincial Modernity: Culture, Politics and Local Identity in Hamburg, 1885–1914." Ph.D. diss., University of Michigan, 1997.

———. *Provincial Modernity: Local Culture and Liberal Politics in Fin-De-Siècle Hamburg*. Ithaca and London, 2003.

Jensen, Robert. *Marketing Modernism in Fin-de-Siècle Europe*. Princeton, 1994.

Jesinghausen-Lauster, Martin. *Die Suche nach der symbolischen Form: der Kreis um die Kulturwissenschaftliche Bibliothek Warburg*. Saecula Spiritalia 13. Baden-Baden, 1985.

Jochmann, Werner, and Hans-Dieter Loose, eds. *Hamburg: Geschichte der Stadt Hamburg und ihrer Bewohner*. 2 vols. Hamburg, 1982–1988.

Jochum-Bohrmann, Ilonka. *Hugo Lederer: ein deutschnationaler Bildhauer des 20. Jahrhunderts*. Frankfurt a.M., Bern, New York, and Paris, 1990.

Junge, Henrike, ed. *Avantgarde und Publikum: zum Rezeption avantgardistischer Kunst in Deutschland, 1905–1933*. Cologne, Weimar, and Vienna, 1992.

Kany, Roland. *Mnemosyne als Programm: Geschichte, Erinnerung und die Andacht zum Unbedeutenden im Werk von Usener, Warburg und Benjamin*. Studien zur deutschen Literatur 93. Tübingen, 1987.

———. *Die religionsgeschichtliche Forschung an der Kulturwissenschaftlichen Bibliothek Warburg*. Bamberg, 1989.

———. "Schon die Mitwelt versetzte Aby Warburg unter die Wandelsterne." *Frankfurter Allgemeine Zeitung*, 11 March 1999.

Kay, Carolyn. *Art and the German Bourgeoisie: Alfred Lichtwark and Modern Painting in Hamburg, 1886–1914*. Toronto, 2002.

Kayser, Werner. *Alfred Lichtwark*. Hamburger Bibliographien, vol. 19. Hamburg, 1977.

Keegan, John, *The First World War*. Toronto, 2000.

Kerbs, Diethart, and Jürgen Reulecke, eds. *Handbuch der deutschen Reformbewegungen, 1880–1933*. Wuppertal, 1998.

Kern, Josef. *Impressionismus im Wilhelminischen Deutschland: Studien zur Kunst- und Kulturgeschichte des Kaiserreichs*. Würzburg, 1989.

Klessmann, Eckart. *Geschichte der Stadt Hamburg*. Hamburg, 1988.

Kludas, Arnold. *Die Geschichte der deutschen Passagierschiffahrt*. 5 vols. Augsburg, 1994.

Kocka, Jürgen, ed. *Bürger und Bürgerlichkeit im 19. Jahrhundert*. Göttingen, 1987.

———, ed. *Bürgertum im 19. Jahrhundert: Deutschland im europäischen Vergleich*. 3 vols. Munich, 1988.

Kocka, Jürgen, and Allen Mitchell, eds. *Bourgeois Society in Nineteenth-Century Europe*. Oxford and Providence, 1993.

Köster, Herm L. *Aus Hamburgs Kulturgeschichte, 1871–1950*. Hamburg, 1953.

Krohn, Helga. *Die Juden in Hamburg: die politische, soziale und kulturelle Entwicklung einer jüdischen Grossstadt-gemeinde nach der Emanzipation, 1848–1918*. Hamburger Beiträge zur Geschichte der Deutschen Juden 4. Hamburg, 1974.

Kunst ins Leben: Alfred Lichtwarks Wirken für die Kunsthalle und Hamburg von 1886 bis 1914. Exh. cat. Hamburg, Kunsthalle, 9 December 1986 – 1 February 1987.

Landauer, Carl Hollis. "The Survival of Antiquity: The German Years of the Warburg Institute." Ph.D. diss., Yale University, 1984.

Laqueur, Walter. *Weimar: A Cultural History 1918–1933*. New York, 1974.

Lengefeld, Cecilia. *Anders Zorn: Eine Künstlerkarriere in Deutschland*. Berlin, 2004.

_____. "Ich kann leichter Kunstfreunde gewinnen als du Was?" *Frankfurter Allgemeine Zeitung*, 31 December 2002.

Lenman, Robin. *Artists and Society in Germany, 1850–1914*. Manchester and New York, 1997.

_____. *Die Kunst, die Macht und das Geld: zur Kulturgeschichte des kaiserlichen Deutschland, 1871–1918*. Frankfurt a.M., 1994.

Lerm, Christa-Maria. "Das jüdische Erbe bei Aby Warburg." *Menora: Jahrbuch für deutsch-jüdische Geschichte* (1994), pp. 143–171.

Lewis, Beth Irwin. *Art for All? The Collision of Modern Art and the Public in Late-Nineteenth-Century Germany*. Princeton and Oxford, 2003.

Liebeschütz, Hans. "Aby Warburg as Interpreter of Civilization." *Leo Baeck Institute Yearbook* 16 (1971), pp. 225–236.

Lucie-Smyth, Edward. *Symbolist Art*. London, 1972.

Machtan, Lothar. *Bismarck und der deutsche National-Mythos*. Bremen, 1994.

Mai, Ekkehard, ed. *Historienmalerei in Europa: Paradigmen in Form, Funktion und Ideologie*. Mainz a.R., 1990.

Mai, Ekkehard, and Peter Paret, eds. *Sammler, Stifter und Museen: Kunstforderung in Deutschland im 19. und 20. Jahrhundert*. Cologne, 1993.

Mai, Ekkehard, and Stephan Waetzoldt, eds. *Kunstverwaltung, Bau- und Denkmal-Politik im Kaiserreich*. Berlin, 1981.

Mai, Ekkehard, Jürgen Paul and Stephan Waetzoldt, eds. *Das Rathaus im Kaiserreich: kunstpolitische Aspekte einer Bauaufgabe des 19. Jahrhunderts*. Berlin, 1982.

Maikuma, Yoshihiko. *Der Begriff der Kultur bei Warburg, Nietzsche und Burckhardt*. Königstein/Ts., 1985.

Makela, Maria. *The Munich Secession: Art and Artists in Turn-of-the-Century Munich*. Princeton, 1990.

Mann, Thomas. *Buddenbrooks*. Frankfurt a.M., 1901.

Max Klinger: Zeichnungen, Zustandsdrucke, Zyklen. Exh. cat. Munich, Museum Villa Stuck, 24 October 1996 –12 January 1997.

McEwan, Dorothea. "Aby Warburg's (1866–1929) Dots and Lines. Mapping the Diffusion of Astrological Motifs in Art History." *German Studies Review* 29, no. 2 (2006), pp. 243–268.

_____. "Gegen die 'Pionere der Diesseitigkeit.'" *Zeitschrift des Zentrums für Literaturforschung Berlin* 4, no. 8 (2004), pp. 4–11.

Meissner, Brigitte. "Bürgherliche Representation im Politischen Denkmal. Bürgermeisterdenkmäler in Stadtrepubliken und Residenzstädten." Ph.D. diss., University of Hamburg, 1987.

Melle, Werner von. *Dreißig Jahre Hamburger Wissenschaft 1891–1921: Rückblicke und persönliche Erinnerungen.* 2 vols. Hamburg, 1923.

Meyer, Anne Marie. "Aby Warburg in His Early Correspondence." *The American Scholar* 57 (1988), pp. 445–452.

Meyer-Tönnesmann, Carsten. *Der Hamburgische Künstlerclub von 1897.* Frankfurt a. M., 1985.

Michaud, Philippe-Alain. *Aby Warburg and the Image in Motion.* New York, 2004.

Mittig, Hans Ernst, and Volker Plagemann, eds. *Denkmäler im 19. Jahrhundert: Deutung und Kritik.* Munich, 1972.

Momigliano, Arnaldo. "How Roman Emperors Became Gods." *American Scholar* 55 (1986), pp. 181–193.

Mommsen, Wolfgang J. *Bürgerliche Kultur und künstlerische Avantgarde 1870–1918: Kultur und Politik im deutschen Kaiserreich.* Frankfurt a.M. and Berlin, 1995.

_____. "Die Herausforderung der bürgerlichen Kultur durch die künstlerische Avantgarde: zum Verhältnis von Kultur und Politik im Wilhelminischen Deutschland." *Geschichte und Gesellschaft* 20 (1994), pp. 424–444.

_____. *Imperial Germany, 1867–1918: Politics, Culture and Society in an Authoritarian State.* London, 1995.

Mosse, George L. *The Crisis of German Ideology.* London, 1966.

_____. *German Jews Beyond Judaism.* Bloomington and Cincinnati, 1985.

Mosse, Werner. *The German-Jewish Economic Elite, 1820–1935: A Socio-Cultural Profile.* Oxford, 1989.

Niethammer Lutz, et. al. *Bürgerliche Gesellschaft in Deutschland: historische Einblicke, Fragen, Perspektiven.* Frankfurt a.M., 1990.

Nipperdey, Thomas. *Deutsche Geschichte, 1866–1918.* 2 vols. Munich, 1990.

_____. *Gesellschaft, Kultur, Theorie. Gesammelte Aufsätze zur neueren Geschichte.* Göttingen, 1976.

_____. "Nationalidee und Nationaldenkmal in Deutschland im 19. Jahrhundert." *Historische Zeitschrift* 206 (1968), pp. 529–585.

_____. *Wie das Bürgertum die Moderne fand.* Berlin, 1988.

Nordlicht: die Hamburger Hochschule für bildende Künste am Lerchenfeld und ihre Vorgeschichte. Hamburg, 1989.

Olbrich, Harald, ed. *Geschichte der deutschen Kunst, 1890–1918.* Leipzig, 1988.

Oppens, Edith. *Der Mandrill: Hamburgs Zwanziger Jahre.* Hamburg, 1969.

Paret, Peter. "The Artist as 'Staatsbürger': Aspects of the Fine Arts and the Prussian State Before and During the First World War." *German Studies Review* 6 (1983), pp. 421–437.

_____. *The Berlin Secession: Modernism and Its Enemies in Imperial Germany.* Cambridge, Mass. and London, 1980.

_____. "Literary Censorship as a Source of Historical Understanding: A Comment." *Central European History* 18 (1985), pp. 360–364.

Paret, Peter, and Beth Irwin Lewis. "Art, Society and Politics in Wilhelmine Germany." *Journal of Modern History* 57 (1985), pp. 696–710.

Peukert, Detlev. *The Weimar Republic.* Harmondsworth, 1991.

Pevsner, Nikolaus. *Pioneers of Modern Design: From William Morris to Walter Gropius.* Harmondsworth, 1991.

Pfotenhauer, Helmut. "Das Nachleben der Antike: Aby Warburg's Auseinandersetzung mit Nietzsche." *Nietzsche-Studien* 14 (1985) pp. 298–313.

Plagemann, Volker. *Kunstgeschichte der Stadt Hamburg.* Hamburg, 1995.

_____. *"Vaterstadt, Vaterland, schütz Dich Gott mit starker Hand": Denkmäler in Hamburg.* Hamburg, 1986.

_____, ed. *Industriekultur in Hamburg: des Deutschen Reiches Tor zur Welt.* Munich, 1984.

_____, ed. *Kunst im öffentlichen Raum: ein Führer durch die Stadt Hamburg.* Hamburg, 1997.

Platte, Hans. *150 Jahre Kunstverein in Hamburg, 1817–1967.* Hamburg, 1967.

Podro, Michael. *The Critical Historians of Art.* New Haven and London, 1982.

Pommeranz-Liedtke, Gerhard. *Moritz von Schwind: Maler und Poet.* Dresden, 1984.

Popov, Nikolai. *Das magische Dreieck: Bremen-Riga-Dubrovnik: Rolandfiguren im europäischen Raum.* Oschersleben, 1989.

Präffcke, Hans. *Der Kunstbegriff Alfred Lichtwarks.* Hildesheim, 1986.

Pulzer, Peter. *Jews and the German State: The Political History of a Minority, 1848–1933.* Oxford, 1992.

Rampley, Matthew. "From Symbol to Allegory: Aby Warburg's Theory of Art." *Art Bulletin* 79 (1997), pp. 41–55.

_____. *The Remembrance of Things Past: On Aby Warburg and Walter Benjamin.* Wiesbaden, 2000.

Raulff, Ulrich. "Von der Privatbibliothek des Gelehrten zum Forschungsinstitut: Aby Warburg, Ernst Cassirer und die neue Kulturwissenschaft." *Geschichte und Gesellschaft* 23 (1997), pp. 28–43.

Reinartz, Dirk, and Christian Graf von Krockow. *Bismarck: vom Verrat der Denkmäler.* Göttingen, 1991.

Reinharz, Jehuda, and Walter Schatzberg, eds. *The Jewish Response to German Culture.* Hanover, N.H. and London, 1985.

Rempel, Hans. *Die Rolandstatuen: Herkunft und geschichtliche Wandlung.* Darmstadt, 1989.

Rennhofer, Maria. *Kunstzeitschriften der Jahrhundertwende in Deutschland und Österreich, 1895–1914.* Vienna and Munich, 1987.

Repp, Kevin. *Reformers, Critics and the Paths to German Modernity: Anti-Politics and the Search for Alternatives, 1890–1914.* Cambridge, Mass. and London, 2000.

Retallack, James. *Germany in the Age of Kaiser Wilhelm II*. London and New York, 1996.

Roeck, Bernd. "A. Warburgs Seminarübung über J. Burckhardt im Sommersemester 1927." *IDEA: Werke-Theorien-Dokumente: Jahrbuch der Hamburger Kunsthalle* 10 (1991), pp. 65–89.

———. *Florenz, 1900: Die Suche Nach Arkadien*. Munich, 2001.

———. *Der junge Aby Warburg*. Munich, 1997.

Rogoff, Irit, ed. *The Divided Heritage: Themes and Problems in German Modernism*. Cambridge, 1991.

Romdahl, Axel. *Anders Zorn als Radierer*. Dresden, 1924.

Rosenbaum, Eduard and Ari J. Sherman. *M.M. Warburg & Co., 1798–1938: Merchant Bankers of Hamburg*. London, 1979.

Roshwald, Aviel, and Richard Sites, eds. *European Culture in the Great War: The Arts, Entertainment, and Propaganda, 1914–1918*. Cambridge, 1999.

Russell, Mark. "The Building of Hamburg's Bismarck Memorial." *The Historical Journal* 43, no. 1 (2000), pp. 133–156.

Schäfer, Hans-Michael. *Die Kulturwissenschaftliche Bibliothek Warburg: Geschichte und Persönlichkeiten der Bibliothek Warburg mit Berücksichtigung der Bibliothekslandschaft und der Stadtsituation der Freien und Hansestadt Hamburg zu Beginn des 20. Jahrhunderts*. Berliner Arbeiten zur Bibliothekswissenschaft 11. Berlin, 2003.

Schilling, Jörg. "Wahrzeichen der Stadt – Monumente der Reform?: der Wettbewerb zur architektonischen Ausgestaltung von drei Wassertürmen in Hamburg von 1906." M.A. diss., University of Hamburg, 1992.

Schmidt, Peter. *Aby M. Warburg und die Ikonologie*. Bamberg, 1989.

Schneede, Uwe M, and Helmut R. Leppien, eds. *Hamburger Kunsthalle: Bauten und Bilder*. Leipzig, 1997.

Schoell-Glass, Charlotte. *Aby Warburg und der Antisemitismus: Kulturwissenschaft als Geistespolitik*. Frankfurt a.M., 1998.

Schorn-Schütte, Luise. *Karl Lamprecht: Kulturgeschichtsschreibung zwischen Wissenschaft und Politik*. Göttingen, 1984.

Schramm, Percy Ernst. *Neun Generationen: dreihundert Jahre deutscher "Kulturgeschichte" im Lichte der Schicksale einer Hamburger Bürgerfamilie (1648–1948)*. 2 vols. Göttingen, 1964.

Schult, Johannes. *Geschichte der Hamburger Arbeiter*. Hannover, 1967.

Schulz, Andreas. "Weltbürger und Geldaristokraten: hanseatisches Bürgertum im 19. Jahrhundert." *Historische Zeitschrift* 259 (1994), pp. 637–670.

Schütt, Rüdiger. *Bohemiens und Biedermänner: die Hamburger Gruppe, 1925 bis 1931*. Hamburg, 1996.

Schumacher, Fritz. *Selbstgespräche: Erinnerungen und Betrachtungen*. Hamburg, 1949.

Schwartz, Frederic. *The Werkbund: Design Theory and Mass Culture Before the First World War*. New Haven and London, 1996.

Seemann, Birgit-Katharine. *Stadt, Bürgertum und Kultur: Kulturelle Entwicklung und Kulturpolitik in Hamburg von 1839 bis 1933 am Beispiel des Museumswesen*. Husum, 1998.

Seibt, Ferdinand et. al. *Deutsche Brüder: zwölf Doppelporträts*. Berlin, 1994.

Seiler, Otto J. *Nordamerikafahrt: Linienschiffahrt der Hapag-Lloyd AG im Wandel der Zeiten*. Herford, 1988.

Sheehan, James J. *German Liberalism in the Nineteenth Century*. Chicago and London, 1978.

Smith, Anthony. *The Concept of Social Change: A Critique of the Functionalist Theory of Social Change*. London, 1973.

Spielmann, Heinz, ed. *Der Jugendstil in Hamburg*. Hamburg, 1965.

Stephan, Inge and Hans-Gerd Winter, eds. *"Heil über dir, Hammonia": Hamburg im 19. Jahrhundert: Kultur, Geschichte, Politik*. Hamburg, 1992.

Stephenson, Kurt. *Johannes Brahms und die Familie von Beckerath*. Hamburg, 1979.

Stern, Fritz. *The Politics of Cultural Despair: A Study of the Rise of the Germanic Ideology*. Berkeley, 1974.

Stockhausen, Tilmann von. *Die Kulturwissenschaftliche Bibliothek Warburg: Architektur, Einrichtung und Organisation*. Hamburg, 1992.

Syamken, Georg. "Warburgs Umwege als Hermeneutik 'More Majorum.'" *Jahrbuch der Hamburger Kunstsammlungen* 25 (1980), pp. 15–26.

Teeuwisse, Nicolaas. *Vom Salon zur Secession: Berliner Kunstleben zwischen Tradition und Aufbruch zur Moderne 1871–1900*. Berlin, 1986.

Ther, Anne-Gabriele. "Ernst Eitner: Leben und Werk." Ph.D. diss., University of Hamburg, 1985.

Thornton, R.K.R. *The Decadent Dilemma*. London, 1983.

Tipps, Dean. "Modernization Theory and the Comparative Study of Societies: A Critical Perspective." *Comparative Studies in Society and History* 15 (1973), pp. 199–266.

Tumasonis, Elizabeth. "Böcklin's Reputation: Its Rise and Fall." *Art Criticism* 6, no. 2 (1990), pp. 48–71.

Tümpel, Christian, ed. *Deutsche Bildhauer, 1900–1945, Entartet*. Königstein im Taunus, 1992.

Vagts, A. "M.M. Warburg & Co.: ein Bankhaus in der deutschen Weltpolitik, 1905– 1933." *Vierteljahrsschrift für Sozial- und Wirtschaftsgeschichte* 45 (1958), pp. 289– 398.

Vaughan, William. *German Romantic Painting*. New Haven and London, 1994.

Villhauer, Bernd. *Aby Warburgs Theorie der Kultur: Detail und Sinnhorizont*. Berlin, 2002.

Volkov, Shulamit. *The Rise of Popular Antimodernism in Germany: The Urban Master Artisans, 1873–1896*. Princeton, 1978.

Voss, Heinrich. *Franz von Stuck, 1863–1928: Werkkatalog der Gemälde mit einer Einführung in seinen Symbolismus*. Munich, 1973.

Wagner, Monika. *Allegorie und Geschichte: Ausstattungsprogramme öffentlicher Gebäude des 19. Jahrhunderts in Deutschland: von der Cornelius Schule zur Malerei der Wilhelminischen Ära*. Tübingen, 1989.

Wappenschmidt, Heinz-Toni. *Allegorie, Symbol und Historienbild im späten 19. Jahrhundert*. Munich, 1984.

_____. *Studien zur Ausstattung des deutschen Rathaussaales in der 2. Hälfte des 19. Jahrhunderts bis 1918*. Bonn, 1981.

Warburg, Max M. *Aus meine Aufzeichnungen*. New York, 1952.

_____. "Rede gehalten bei der Gedächtnis-Feier für Professor Warburg am 5. Dezember 1929." Unpublished typescript. Hamburg, 1929.

Wattenmaker, Richard J. *Puvis de Chavannes and the Modern Tradition*. Exh. cat. Toronto, Art Gallery of Ontario, 24 October – 30 November 1975.

Wehler, Hans-Ulrich. *Das Deutsche Kaiserreich, 1871–1918*. Göttingen, 1973.

_____ ed. *Sozialgeschichte Heute*. Göttingen, 1970.

West, Shearer. *The Visual Arts in Germany, 1890–1937: Utopia and Despair*. New Brunswick, N.J., 2001.

Wiborg, Susanne and Klaus Wiborg. *1847–1997: Unser Feld ist die Welt: 150 Jahre Hapag-Lloyd*. Hamburg, 1997.

Willy von Beckerath. Exh. cat. Munich, Galleria del Levante, September – October 1973.

Wind, Edgar. *The Eloquence of Symbols: Studies in Humanist Art*. Oxford, 1993.

With, Christopher. *The Prussian Landeskunstkommission, 1862–1911: A Study in State Subvention of the Arts*. Berlin, 1986.

Witthoft, Hans-Jürgen. *HAPAG: Hamburg-Amerika Linie*. Herford, 1973.

Woesthoff, Indina. *"Der glückliche Mensch": Gustav Schiefler (1857–1935): Sammler, Dilettant und Kunstfreund*. Hamburg, 1996.

Wood, Paul, ed. *The Challenge of the Avant-Garde*. New Haven and London, 1999.

Woodfield, Richard, ed. *Art History as Cultural History: Warburg's Projects*. Amsterdam, 2001.

Wuttke, Dieter. "Die Emigration der Kulturwissenschaftlichen Bibliothek Warburg und die Anfänge des Universitätsfaches Kunstgeschichte in Grossbritannien." *Artibus et Historiae* 10 (1984), pp. 133–146.

Zammito, John H. "Der Streit um die Berliner Kultur 1871 bis 1930." *Jahrbuch für die Geschichte Mittel-und Ostdeutschlands* 35 (1986), pp. 234–268.

INDEX

Roberti, Ercole de', 32, 163. *See also* Palazzo
  Schifanoia
Rodin, Auguste
  Balzac, 124
Roeck, Bernd, 41
Roland and Roland columns, 109, 111, 123
Rome, 34, 102, 156, 163-64, 205
  Aby Warburg in, 119
  allegory in Hamburg's city hall, 151
  Art Historical Congress in (1912), 32
Roon, Albrecht von, 101
Rothschild family, 21
Rucellai, Giovanni, 28
Runge, Philipp Otto, 62, 191
Ruskin, John, 74
  Aby Warburg compared to, 44
Ruths, Johann Georg Valentin, 61, 71-72
  and Hamburg's Bismarck memorial,
    105-6
  murals in Hamburg's Kunsthalle, 72,
    155, 190

S

Sack, Eduard, 67
Sala di Galatea, Villa Farnesina (Rome)
  Aby Warburg's research on frescoes in,
    163-64
Santa Maria Novella, Florence. *See*
  Tornabuoni Chapel
Sassetti, Francesco and Sassetti Chapel,
  Santa Trinità (Florence)
  Aby Warburg's alleged affinity with, 41
  Aby Warburg's research on, 28-29, 119-
    21
Sargent, John Singer, 77
Saxl, Fritz, 31, 35-36, 48, 59
  on Aby Warburg's library, 31
Schaper, Alfred Friedrich, 65
Schapire, Rosa, 209, 211
Schaudt, Johann Emil, 9, 107-9, 111, 118
  Alfred Lichtwark's criticism of, 111
Scheffler, Karl, 4, 100, 104, 158-59
  as critic of Berlin, 101
  on Hamburg's Bismarck memorial, 88,
    109
  on Max Klinger, 70
Schiefler, Gustav, 62, 67, 99, 167
  "The Campaign Against the New
    Direction in Art", 67
  on Carl Mönckeberg's *Illusions,* 73

catalogues Emil Nolde's graphic works,
    209
  on Hamburg's Art Association, 68
  and *Der Lotse,* 100
  on Hamburg's School of Art and
    Industry, 186-87, 212
Schiller, Friedrich von
  Hamburg's monument to, 110
Schilling, Johannes
  Hamburg's monument to Kaiser
    Wilhelm I, 110
Schmarsow, August, 24
Schmidt-Rottluff, Karl, 211
Schmitz, Bruno, 108
  designs for Bismarck monuments, 95
  memorial to Kaiser Wilhelm I in
    Koblenz, 106
Schnars-Alquist, Carl Wilhelm Hugo, 1
  and the S.S. *Imperator,* 169
Schoell-Glass, Charlotte, 37, 203
Schramm, Percy Ernst, 37, 91, 93-94, 99,
    204
Schreyer, Lothar
  and *Der Sturm,* 209
Schumacher, Fritz, 136
  on Aby Warburg, 1
  architect of the School of Art and
    Industry, 188-89
  on the S.S. *Imperator,* 169-71
Schwind, Mortiz Ludwig von, 1, 61, 71
Schwinge, Fritz, 170
Scott, George Gilbert, 137
Second World War, 134
Seelig, Geert, 92
Shaw, Bernard, 56
Siebelist, Arthur, 73
Sieveking family, 92
Sieveking, Hermann Georg, 1
Skarbina, Franz, 146, 154
Slevogt, Max, 64
Smithsonian Institution (Washington), 26
Social Democracy, Social Democratic Party
  (SPD), 9, 57, 94, 127n41, 136-37, 142,
    167, 206, 220
  Aby Warburg's criticism of, 96, 98
  electoral success in Hamburg, 44-45, 93,
    124
  and Hamburg's Volksheim, 45
Sohn, Wilhelm, 146
Sombart, Werner, 57, 160
Sonderweg, 12
Speckter, Otto, 71

Der Cicerone and, 159
correspondence with Aby Warburg, 158
critics of, 146-49, 155
describes his murals in Hamburg's city
hall, 151, 153
and the Düsseldorf Academy, 140
early career, 146
and Ferdinand Avenarius, 149
and the Group of Eleven, 145-46
and Hanover's city hall, 165
honored by the City of Hamburg, 154
and Johann Heinrich Burchard, 145-46,
149, 154
and Justus Brinckmann, 147
the Kaiser's opinion of, 155
mural for the Association of German
Engineers, 167
mural designs for Hamburg's city hall,
146-47, 150
painting for the World's Fair in Brussels
(1910), 167
portrait of Hamburg's senate, 145-46
portraits of Paul von Hindenburg and
Erich Ludendorff, 167, 204
reproductions of his murals in
Hamburg's city hall, 166-67
restores murals in Hamburg's city hall,
167
Richard Graul on, 156
and secessionist movements, 142, 146
Victorious Germania fresco in Merseburg,
149, 157
Wilhelm Waetzoldt on, 162, 182
Volkmann, Arthur, 108
Vossische Zeitung, 146
Vuillard, Eduard, 64
Vulcan Werke (Hamburg), 168

W

Waetzoldt, Wilhelm, 1
"Conversation on Art at Christmas", 63
on Emil Nolde, 63, 210
on Hugo Vogel, 162
on Willy von Beckerath, 182, 184
Wallsee, Heinrich E., 184
on Hugo Vogel, 158-59
Wagner, Alexander von
allegories in Hamburg's city hall, 151
Wagner, Ferdinand the Younger, 141,
173n38
Wappenschmidt, Heinz-Toni, 142-43

Warburg, Aby
American travels, 26, 73, 78, 116
on astrological imagery, 32-33. *See also*
Lectures and Publications
on Baroque and neo-Baroque aesthetics,
6, 30, 81, 90, 103-4, 164
Bildung and, 40, 46-47, 115
on the concept of the Apollonian, 22,
24, 26, 29, 118, 120, 163
on the concept of *Nachleben*, 22
on the concept of the *Denkmensch*, 115-
17
on the concept of *Denkraum*, 30, 44,
46-47, 50n62, 80-81, 114, 116, 118,
164, 199, 210
on the concept of the Dionysian, 24, 29-
30, 79, 103, 120
on the concept of the *Greifmensch*, 115-
17
on the concept of *Pathosformeln*, 22
as Dionysian figure, 25-26
and Enlightenment thought, 22, 24, 26,
40-41, 46, 103
Habilitationsschrift, 30
illness of, 16, 34-35, 40-41, 205-6, 212,
220
"The Jewish Question in the Framework
of German Politics", 202-3
Jewish identity of, 4, 21, 25, 36-40, 58,
69-70, 72, 99
La guerra del 1914-15. Rivista illustrata,
201
Lectures and Publications
"American Chapbooks", 73
*The Art of Portraiture and the
Florentine Bourgeoisie*, 27, 117,
120-22
"Dürer as Human Being and Artist",
46
"Dürer and Italian Antiquity", 28-
29, 163
"Flemish Art and the Florentine
Early Renaissance", 27, 121
"Flemish and Florentine Art in
Lorenzo de' Medici's Circle around
1480", 119
"Francesco Sassetti's Last Injunctions
to His Sons", 28, 120
"From the Deathbed of the Italian
Conscience", 201